D1591090

Obedient Autonomy

WITHDRAWN

MONTGOMERY COLLEGE
GERMANTOWN CAMPUS LIBRARY
GERMANTOWN MARYLAND

Erika E.S. Evasdottir

Obedient Autonomy:
Chinese Intellectuals and the
Achievement of Orderly Life

UNIVERSITY OF HAWAI'I PRESS
HONOLULU

313973

APR 2 6 2006

© UBC Press 2004
All rights reserved

Published in paperback 2005 in the United States by
University of Hawai'i Press
2840 Kolowalu Street
Honolulu, HI 96822

First published in Canada by
UBC Press
The University of British Columbia
2029 West Mall
Vancouver, BC V6T 1Z2

Printed in Canada by Friesens

Library of Congress Cataloging-in-Publication Data

Evasdottir, Erika E. S., 1968-
  Obedient autonomy : Chinese intellectuals and the achievement of orderly life /
Erika E.S. Evasdottir.
    p. cm.
Includes bibliographical references and index.
    ISBN 0-8248-2860-7 (alk. paper)
    1. Interpersonal relations—China. 2. China—Social conditions—1976- I. Title.
HM1106.E93 2004
306'.0951—dc22
                                       2003023787

Most of life is so dull there is nothing to be said about it, and the books and talk that would describe it as interesting are obliged to exaggerate, in the hope of justifying their own existence. Inside its cocoon of work or social obligation, the human spirit slumbers for the most part, registering the distinction between pleasure and pain, but not nearly so alert as we pretend. There are periods in the most thrilling day during which nothing happens, and though we continue to exclaim: 'I do enjoy myself,' or, 'I am horrified,' we are insincere. 'As far as I feel anything, it is enjoyment, horror' – it's no more than that really, and a perfectly adjusted organism would be silent.

– E.M. Forster, *A Passage to India*

Contents

Acknowledgments

Thanks are in order first to the Pacific Cultural Foundation and Harvard Yenching Foundation for their support of the fieldwork component. Thanks also to the Izaak Walton Killam Foundation for a generous postdoctoral fellowship at the University of British Columbia as well as to the Davies Charitable Foundation and Green College for their kind support. James L. Watson, Michael Herzfeld, and Carl Lamberg-Karlovsky have provided invaluable advice and intense browbeating. Professors Fumiko Ikawa-Smith and the late K.C. Chang have been truly inspirational role models, and I cannot thank them enough. Aubrey Cannon probably does not even remember, but long ago he started the whole thing off by introducing me to a world of new ideas. Robert Preucel only made the situation worse by refusing to allow me to be lazy and by debating everything that I said even while encouraging me to say it. Among the many teachers whom I met along the way, Shui Tao, Tu Cheng-Sheng, Tsang Cheng-hwa, Wu Chunmin, and Wu Jianmin have been especially helpful, insightful, and graciously patient. Thanks are also due to the many friends and colleagues who have been critically supportive: Tracy Hoffman, Cao Yin, Tseng Lan-ying, Janice Graham, Emily Patterson-Kane, Tsai Li-ling, Sarah Salter, Kim Gutschow, Alex Barnett, Luis Campos, Joseph Thywissen, He Donghui, Catherine Wearing, Li Hui, Joshua Wright, and Amy Farber. All mistakes and misinterpretations are most definitely my own.

And, finally, special thanks to Sandra Henriksen.

Introduction

When a man comes forward with an idea and others approve, that's
enough to encourage him to go on; if they disapprove, that's enough
to goad him into keeping up the struggle. But a *real* tragedy occurs
when he cries out in the realm of the living and there's no response
at all – no approval, and no opposition either. It was like finding
myself in the midst of a boundless and desolate plain where there
were no reference points, nothing to lay one's hand to – an agoniz-
ing plight.

> – Lu Xun, *Cheering from the Sidelines*

Lu Xun was an intellectual, in the full Chinese sense of the term, and it is
therefore fitting that his words begin this ethnographic case study of Chinese intellectuals. It is even more fitting that Lu here describes a situation
that most intellectuals, Chinese or not, surely wish to avoid: a tragic vision
of intellectual loneliness in which thoughts not subject to discussion and
criticism shrivel and wither away. Strangely, there are those who would
describe the same situation as a form of 'freedom': the freedom to be left
alone. Some might even insist that a person thrives and becomes creative,
individual, and autonomous only by being self-governing, self-directed, and
self-interested – in short, by being free from any kind of state, familial, or
religious 'interference.' I refer to this type of autonomy as 'uncompromising autonomy' to recall that underlying sense of obdurate self-interest.

In this case study, it is not uncompromising autonomy but Lu Xun's
vision that must guide our understanding of the core terms 'individual,'
'autonomy,' and 'freedom.' These terms take their meaning from a context in which it is taken as a given that a person cannot be (and would not
desire to be) subjected to a separation from society but is instead always
immersed in a web of social rules, hierarchies, structures, stereotypes, and
norms. This conceptual reorientation of the relationship between self and

society is combined with two fundamental assumptions. The first is that, as social restrictions increase, so do the practical opportunities to combine and reinterpret such restrictions. This assumption thus presents a vision of pragmatic fluidity, individuality, and change. Such fluidity appears sharply curtailed, however, by a second basic assumption: that the systems and hierarchies subject to recombination are (or ought to be) fixed and unchanging. It is this combination of pragmatic fluidity and abstract immutability that gives rise to what I will call 'obedient autonomy': a self-directed control over change that takes effect only through the concerted effort to achieve and maintain a discourse of order and immutability.

The quest for an understanding of obedient autonomy is difficult not simply because translating alterity is an intricate dance of exaggeration and simplification but also because the word *obedient* itself constantly trips up the argument. The word often seems to evoke a frightening vision of collusion, oppression, and coerced submission. What is called to the Euro-American (by which I mainly mean the Anglo-North American and Anglo-European) mind by a book that seeks to present the words *obedient, credentials,* and *state bureaucracy* in a positive light? What kind of book attempts to cast people who obey others in the role of autonomous individuals? At first glance, such a book is not simply revisionist but also, and worse, an apologetic justification of 'oppressive' rules and structures.

I hope that a second, more patient glance will forestall any charges of revisionism and conservatism. Let me be clear: the system that I describe unquestionably maintains certain people in positions of privilege and reduces the choices and quality of life of others. And what system does not? Inequality is endemic to all systems, past or present, capitalist or communist. It is too crude to criticize the Chinese system for being unjust (which it is) without asking the more interesting question of why this particular system *persists*. We must ask why Chinese intellectuals – who are, after all, highly educated and have a Marxist predilection to be painfully aware of systemic oppression – do not join together to change or destroy the system.

The answer to this question is both simple and complex. The simple answer acknowledges that there are benefits and incentives encouraging participants to preserve their way of doing things. The Chinese context is (perhaps) different from many others in that these benefits are rarely restricted to crass perquisites such as buckets of money, great privilege, or naked hierarchical superiority. Indeed, we will soon discover that those in hierarchically junior positions have the most compelling reasons to maintain the system and will do so at the expense of their seniors. Self-interest is also involved, but self-interested benefits are derived from cooperative behaviours of mutual benefit rather than acts of 'dog eat dog' competition. The high status of the intellectual class is certainly a factor, but it is a status that can limit intellectuals as often as it can enable them. In short, there are enough incentives and enough redistributive checks and balances in the system that the vast majority of people benefit sufficiently to be satisfied with it.

The complex answer begins by noting that the very concept of obedient autonomy causes the question of why the oppressed do not overthrow their oppressors to lose meaning. That question is predicated on an image of a world divided a priori into oppressors and oppressed. That diametric opposition lends itself too easily to a conception of society as a place where those in power react harshly to any threat of revolution, where those in disadvantaged positions are either mystified by false consciousness or are like the *bricoleur* who tosses a wrench into the workings of the system, and where a 'hero' is the autonomous individual who defines himself in the struggle against the machine of power.

When the dichotomy of oppressor and oppressed is merged instead into an image of mutual interdependence, the very definitions of concepts such as hierarchy, authority, power, and autonomy must change. Under mutual interdependence, a person's identity and reputation are constituted by the assessments made of him by the people among whom he lives and works. Identity is no longer an individual matter but is located in the eyes of an actual or imagined audience. Any hero of this story cannot want to create individual identity through struggle because his identity arises directly out of the maintenance and strengthening of social relationships. The hero becomes more involved in society, not less; becomes more connected, not separated; becomes someone who acts and effects change by participation, not destruction.

At first glance, such a hero will seem to be conservative, but the task of this book, and of the reader, is to understand how participation in and obedience to the rules can be used for change, redistribution of resources, or enhancement of individual lives. A person forges responses to the demands of society in this system as people must do in any system. That such plans are made according to certain rules does not logically require that the plans be conservative. As we will see, 'rules' may appear to be fixed but in practice are so open to interpretation, manipulation, and juxtaposition that they may limit but rarely control any one person's plan. The other half of the title of this book, 'the achievement of orderly life,' is concerned with exactly these strategies of rule manipulation and juxtaposition available to the obediently autonomous individual.

The term 'obedient autonomy' is used because it appears irreconcilably paradoxical to those steeped in a culture of 'uncompromising autonomy.' It is intended as an irritant, as a reminder to the reader that there are many possible kinds of autonomy that arise out of (and in turn create) substantially different practices and expectations. I do not claim that obedient autonomy is the only type of autonomy available in the Chinese context any more than uncompromising autonomy is the only kind available in Euro-American thought.

Nevertheless, obedient autonomy is emphasized here simply because it is the favoured mode among the people who allowed me to learn from their lives and experiences. As will be explored further in Chapter 1, Chinese archeologists are a subset of the intellectual class, fascinating by virtue of their positioning relative to discourses of history, science, and communism. To understand archeologists, one must first understand archeology as a discipline and the roles and responsibilities of Chinese intellectuals. Chapter 1 therefore presents the necessary social, political, and historical background to understand why archeologists tend to use strategies of obedient autonomy more often than other intellectuals. In addition, since the notion of obedient autonomy *appears* to violate most if not all tenets of Euro-American theories of morality and agency, an intervention in the form of vocabulary definition is required to set the stage for understanding the values and incentives that drive Chinese archeologists to achieve their orderly and obedient lives. Much of Chapter 1 is therefore caught up in the illustration of words and the traps that they represent for the unwary.

Chapter 2 moves on to what makes archeologists most interesting to the anthropologist: the fact that archeology is an apprenticeship-type discipline in which older archeologists teach newly arrived youngsters the 'tricks' of the trade. Those tricks tend, once again simply because of the requirements of archeology, to be overt expressions of the same strategies of rule and relationship manipulation that make up obedient autonomy. The understanding of obedient autonomy, then, is best begun as if we too were young students learning how to become proper archeologists. Chapter 2 examines the process by which a young person learns to play the role of 'student' in relation to teachers and fellow students and, at the same time, learns to view these roles, and their attendant rules of interaction, as resources useful in the planning of his own career. The chapter thereby examines the logic underlying two issues: why juniors consent to the control of their seniors and why juniors police each other to enforce conformity.

Chapter 3, 'The Rule of Law,' examines the rule of reciprocity and its effects on gift-giving practices and on the choice of gifts to be given. The effects of class on both gift choice and gift giving are examined. This chapter concentrates, on the analysis of two key concepts, 'trustworthiness' and 'compatibility,' and on the description of the relationship between these concepts and two kinds of gifts, 'self-positioning' and 'being positioned.' Data are drawn from both the experiences of students as they continue to learn to be archeologists and the interactions between full archeologists and technical and peasant workers during excavations.

The title of Chapter 4, 'The Separation of Powers,' is a particularly apt description of the three separate command structures that affect archeologists. Non-Chinese observers of Chinese archeology appear to have missed both the sheer multitude of controls that affect archeology and the fact that there are several different categories of archeologist. Each type tends to engage with the separation between hierarchy and authority differently, but all use it to secure significant benefits. Strategies of obedient autonomy flourish in a context of strict yet multitudinous rules and are useful both in campaigns of competitive aggression and in operations of mutual cooperation.

'Credentials' are a form of stereotype useful in strategies of obedient autonomy. Credentials do not carry the negative reputation held by stereotypes in other social systems, and are enormously useful tools in the maintenance of order in the social world – that is, as long as everyone, or at least the majority, agrees to preserve them. Chapter 5, 'Majority Rule,' uses the credentials of class, schooling, and regional background to illustrate the enormity of the effort required to achieve and preserve order. These examples also allow us to glimpse the many benefits conferred by social order and that impel participants to continue in its preservation.

Despite the best efforts of everyone concerned, the achievement of order can be disrupted by the misapplication or mismanagement of credentials. That orderly life is an achievement requiring vast effort even as it is ever on the verge of failure is nowhere more apparent than in the struggles of archeologists to cross the urban-rural divide and create mutually beneficial relations with the peasants. Chapter 6 examines how the urban-rural divide is perpetuated in traditions of scholarship and everyday life alike to create two 'interest groups,' the composition and goals of which are presumed to be utterly different. The somewhat desperate attempts of urban archeologists to create ties with rural peasants are described in detail. Strategies become dances that attempt to claim similarity where no similarity is expected to exist, to separate hierarchy from authority as a show of respect rather than aggression, or to claim the junior position in hierarchical role relations in an effort to mollify class resentment.

Most strategies of obedient autonomy depend on convincing the audience to accept the claim being made: that the actor has the right to play a particular role and to take certain actions in the capacity of that role. Roles can combine social characteristics to create positions of almost unimaginable power. Chapter 7 examines how age, gender, and the discourses of experience and empiricism combine to support a minority of males, called oligarchs, in their control over publication opportunities, research topics, permits to excavate, or relations with foreign archeologists. The 'minority rights' of oligarchs bestow on them significant control over all aspects of archeology. In direct contrast, women's social characteristics combine to devalue women in the eyes of their teachers and thereby diminish their chances of success in archeology. Interestingly, women have relatively fewer rules and restrictions applied to them and are concomitantly less obediently autonomous. The relative abilities of oligarchs and women to engage in strategies of obedient autonomy are compared in order to tease out further the beneficial effects of rules and restrictions on agency.

Many a non-Chinese archeologist has read these pages and hastened to tell me how the same things happen in North American and British academic contexts. Teacher-student relations, institutional hierarchies (oh, those deans!), personal animosities, barriers against women, regionalist proclivities, and authoritarian oligarchs are structures and institutions that, one way or another, affect archeologists and their fellow academics all over the world. May it be understood, then, that I make no claims about the 'Chineseness' of the strategies of obedient autonomy. I do claim, however, that the implications, meanings, and goals of such strategies are unique to the Chinese context. As any archeologist knows, two artifacts can appear similar at first glance, but the meanings and implications of each are only understood when each is placed in its sequence, assemblage, site, and settlement contexts. Social and cultural practices cannot be termed analogous merely because of functional or other superficial similarities. It would be a grave misunderstanding to imagine that Chinese strategies of obedient autonomy are experienced in the same way as submission might be experienced in the Euro-American context, are undertaken for similar goals, or are similarly valued.

Obedient Autonomy

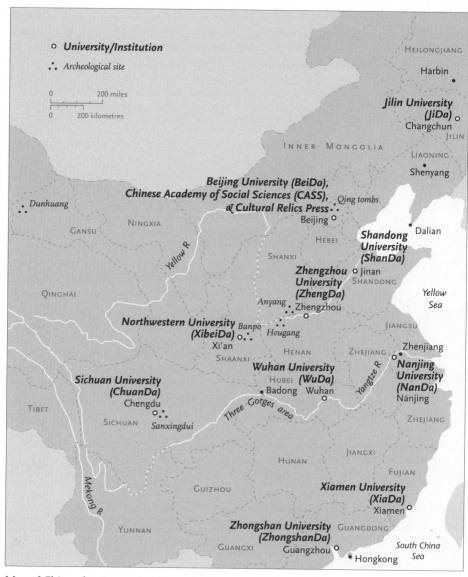

Map of China, showing major sites and cities mentioned in the text.

Autonomy and Autonomies

Between people of distant climes there is always the possibility of romance, but the various branches of Indians know too much about each other to surmount the unknowable easily. The approach is prosaic. 'Excellent,' said Aziz, patting a stout shoulder and thinking: 'I wish they did not remind me of cow-dung'; Das thought: 'Some Moslems are very violent.' They smiled wistfully, each spying the thought in the other's heart, and Das, the more articulate, said: 'Excuse my mistakes, realize my limitations. Life is not easy as we know it on earth.'

– E.M. Forster, *A Passage to India*

The group of archeologists, young and old, sat resting in the courtyard. The director of the excavation, responding to my presence, began to lecture his students and younger colleagues on the always fascinating topic of how to deal with foreigners:[1] 'Remember, when asked to compromise on issues of method, money, or time, most foreigners act crazy: they shout and will accuse you of all sorts of things. Not her, of course [politely waving a hand at me]. The best thing is just not to tell them what's going on. Oh, and above all, do not let them talk to the peasants.'[2]

Laughing, a senior archeologist then told the story of the foreigner who, having met a Chinese farmer for the first time, went on at length about his own experiences on a farm and even tried to tell the farmer how to plant his oranges more efficiently. 'And then this guy got angry when the farmer asked for more money!' He shook his head in amazement.

The director nodded in appreciation of this story but went on gently: 'Well, it's not just that they insult the peasants. It gets worse. They are always talking about archeology and what tools and workers they need to excavate, and they do not seem to care if the peasants hear or not.' The students present looked faintly horrified.

'It's true,' the senior archeologist agreed, 'and then the foreigners will turn around and blame you when the peasants make demands for more money, even though it's their own fault.'

Another senior archeologist shook his head. 'No, it is when they drink at banquets that they are really a problem. They are always drinking, even when no one has proposed a toast. Well, they know they also have to drink during the toasts. So then they get drunk and feel sick. And then they complain that there are too many banquets. So when we reduce the number of banquets and the peasants complain and raise their prices, the foreigners say it is all our fault and yell about money again. You can't win with foreigners.'

By this point, I was confounded by a sort of double vision. I have heard these stories from the other side since every foreigner has a story to tell of something incomprehensible occurring while in China. Those who do not have the resources to understand what is going on, or no incentive to find out, sometimes articulate their frustrations in paranoid and racial terms. They speak of how 'sly' and 'clever' those Chinese archeologists are at cheating the foreigner, obstructing excavations, and keeping the results for themselves. Or they blame everything on 'the Communist Party' and how it 'oppresses' the locals. To avoid falling into the trap of reinscribing old and orientalist stories, we need to unpack the social, bureaucratic, cultural, and economic structures that underlie the fundamental Chinese assumption that the 'good' or 'proper' archeologist is humble with the peasants, keeps quiet about any plans he has for the excavation, can banquet every night, and drinks only when toasted. A warning at the outset: as Forster's character Das tells us, life is not easy as we know it here on Earth, and what is particularly difficult is the bridging of cultural, moral, and social divides.

Archeology and Archeologists

Although there is a long tradition of interest in material artifacts and their social meanings dating back at least to the time of the Han Dynasty, archeology in disciplinary form is usually considered to have begun in 1927 with Li Chi's excavations at Anyang. Li Chi, who received his PhD at Harvard, was the first Chinese scholar to lead an excavation; earlier excavations had all been run by foreigners. Archeology nearly immediately went on hiatus from the beginnings of the Japanese invasion in 1932 until the end of the Civil War in 1949. Archeology then had eight 'bright years of progress' from 1950 to 1958, during which time approximately 300 archeologists were produced to complement the 20 or so that already existed. After 1957, archeology was severely impacted by political events beginning with the Great Leap Forward. Although the Great Leap lasted only about three years, its impact continued to affect archeology for the next three years during the period called *san nian zai hai* or 'three years of natural disasters' (a combination of human and natural causes that created a massive three-year famine).

The policy of sending intellectuals to the countryside to help the peasants *(xia xiang)* began in 1964. At this time, it was mostly middle-aged and older archeologists who were sent to the farms; younger archeologists would join them in increasing numbers throughout the 1960s. Very little analysis or publishing was accomplished during this time. The Cultural Revolution that began in 1966 is, of course, well known for the chaos that it brought to most people's lives. While the archeologists were relatively better off than most intellectuals since they could escape the city by 'excavating' in the countryside, they did not actually engage in any excavations during this time. Some archeologists did return to work in 1972 with the discovery of the Han tomb of Mawangdui and, in 1974, of the Qin Terra Cotta Warriors. Unfortunately, most *danwei* (work units) remained paralyzed by the events of the Cultural Revolution and did not really begin work again – neither analysis nor excavation – until the 1980s or, in places such as the northwest, even until the early 1990s. In short, Chinese archeology has seen only about twenty years in which work could be done.[3]

Whatever the age or background of an individual archeologist – and intergenerational conflicts are common – archeologists tend to be some of the most welcoming and entertaining men anywhere in China. I say this not simply because they were kind to me but also because they take great pride in their ability to accept strangers and create relationships across seemingly impossible gulfs of age, gender, and class. Other Chinese intellectuals, and Chinese people more generally, often become uncertain and nervous when presented with someone, like me, who is a foreigner (Canadian), of a different 'race' (white), and of a problematic gender (female).[4] Such social distinctions engender preconceived notions that shape social relationships.

Archeologists, in contrast, are rarely troubled by the social distinctions that can so discombobulate their compatriots. Instead of being a disturbance, my arrival at any site is treated as yet another opportunity for archeological elders to illustrate techniques of relationship cultivation to their students or younger colleagues. It is exactly this artistry and intensity that archeologists apply to their relationships with peasants, local officials, high officials, women, foreigners, or anyone else different from them that gives rise to my appreciation of the practices of 'obedient autonomy.'

Before approaching the topic of obedient autonomy itself, we must understand how certain aspects of archeological life and disciplinary practice combine to set archeologists apart from other intellectuals. Archeology as a career and a lifestyle has three vital characteristics: access to material remains (artifacts and sites), participation in excavation, and an unusual number of bureaucratic systems administering the archeological profession.

First, archeologists' access to material remains has a reinforcing effect on their relations with teachers and fellow students. Among Chinese intellectuals generally, the relationships between teacher and student and among students are highly valued. Ideally, these are relationships that should last forever and be a source of friendship and mutual aid. For the most part, intellectuals live up to these ideals as often as can be expected – spottily. Archeologists, in contrast, are more hard-nosed about living up to these ideals. Their determination to maintain academic relationships is reinforced by the fact that each relationship is a potential conduit to *data*. Data are indubitably the most important of all resources for the archeological career, and 'hard' data – artifacts *(wenwu)* and sites *(yizhi)* – are thus the most coveted of gifts. These gifts are used to create both careers and, most importantly, opportunities for collegial collaboration.

Second, excavation *(fajue)* is not merely the core of archeology and the source of data; from the archeological perspective, excavation represents an opportunity to meet people. Other intellectuals will occasionally leave their comfortable urban homes to visit family or attend a conference, but it is rare indeed to find an intellectual who spends long periods of time in the countryside, who lives among the peasants in the peasants' own homes, and who digs (disruptively) in the peasants' backyards and fields. These disruptions of local lives necessitate negotiations among a large number of people. To excavate successfully, the archeologist must get to know officials in the agricultural, construction, railway, and hydroelectric industries; officials who manage counties, towns, and villages; the peasant workers; and the peasants with whom he lives. The result is an intellectual unusual not only for his experience in the countryside but also for the size of his 'Rolodex.' In the Chinese economic and political system, a large and varied Rolodex is in itself a valuable source of gifts, in the form of names and contacts, that can be bartered.

The size and utility of archeological Rolodexes were demonstrated to me many times. Given the archeological proclivity to disappear into rural areas for long periods, I had to go to significant lengths to find the 332 archeologists and students whom I observed and interviewed. Over a period of fifteen months, I managed to travel to Beijing, each provincial capital and 'special economic zone' (save for the provinces of Tibet, Hainan, and Heilongjiang), eleven universities, and several small, out-of-the-way towns, villages, and farms. My travel was made immeasurably more pleasant because of the networks commanded by archeologists. No matter where I wanted to go, an archeologist knew someone in my destination who ran a good (cheap) hotel, a great restaurant, or even a good place to buy a winter coat. To help me get there cheaply, archeologists always knew someone who could secure hard-sleeper tickets; if I needed a haircut, an archeologist knew a hairdresser who would be undeterred by foreign hair; if I needed a bath, an archeologist's sister would take me to the local bathhouse. All of China is said to run on *guanxi* (social networks), but it is rare to find people who control networks that cross all of China and include people from such diverse backgrounds that I could travel, shop, eat, or sleep anywhere from Beijing to Kunming and still be assured of personalized, contact-based amenities. As one archeologist put it, 'If you are an archeologist, then nothing is forbidden you *(baiwu jinji)*.'

Third, the diversity of archeological networks is enhanced by the fact that archeology is managed by no fewer than three different bureaucratic institutions or *xitong*. These are hierarchies controlled by the central government in Beijing. *Xitong* do not link horizontally to each other at any one level in the hierarchy. The division of 'archeology' into three *xitong* makes excavation a complex matter of dispute over jurisdiction and authority. Nevertheless, incentives encourage archeologists to make the extreme efforts required to cooperate across *xitong* boundaries. Data, of course, are among the most important of incentives, but archeological career goals of promotion, publishing, and fame also provide ample reasons to cooperate. Such is the importance of these boundaries that four chapters of this book are devoted to the description of both the myriad incentives for the crossing of *xitong* boundaries and how that crossing is accomplished.

Given this peculiar complex of characteristics, the attention paid by archeologists to their personal relationships is intense. Most interestingly, teachers of archeology explicitly endeavour to teach strategies of relationship creation and maintenance to young archeologists, with an attention to detail that makes the heads of both anthropologist and student archeologist spin. The extreme nature of the situation in which archeologists find themselves is nevertheless useful for the clarity that it bestows on the strategies of obedient autonomy used among (male) Chinese intellectuals. I cannot vouch for the transferability of these strategies to the members of other classes.[5] My observations suggest that peasants find it useful to engage in similar strategies at least in their interactions with intellectuals. But whether these strategies have the same meaning for peasants is another matter entirely and not dealt with here.

Throughout this book, the pronoun *he* will be used to refer to archeologists. I use this pronoun not in its universal use but because archeologists tend overwhelmingly to be men. The comparison of female and male forms of obedient autonomy can shed light on the reasons for the disparity in the position of women relative to men, but the focus of this book remains firmly on men. Thus, when women are discussed, their experiences are meant only as a comparison useful in the explication of *male* agency. Similarly, most Chinese archeologists are of Han ethnicity; when non-Han archeologists are discussed, their experience is also meant to shed light on Han Chinese practices. This study is therefore to be conceived narrowly as one of middle-class masculinity and strategies of obedient autonomy among male Han Chinese and should not be extended further.

'Trailing Clouds of Epistemology'

J.L. Austin's expression 'trailing clouds of epistemology'[6] refers to the linguistic, contextual, and intellectual baggage that intimately affects the meanings of words. Every anthropological description of a social system, using a language not of that system, must encounter the difficulties of linguistic translation. The remainder of this chapter endeavours to supply to English words different implications from those that usually trail after them. To accomplish this feat, we must begin by examining the baggage encumbering certain words in the English-speaking context and then proceed to show how those meanings change as they are combined with the characteristics particular to Chinese archeological lives.

The phrase 'obedient autonomy' is at first glance an uneasy mix of dishonourable and respectable meanings that makes no sense. The concept of obedience appears to negate the possibility of individual expression and autonomous behaviour. The humanist definition of autonomy, assuming as it does the concept of 'self-directing freedom' and 'moral independence,' is built on the foundational precept that resistance and struggle are required for self-actualization. The individual exists prior to social experience and must contest the demands of society to realize his or her[7] full potential. In this formulation, 'identity' assumes that the individual strives to be separate and distinct, whether in kind or degree, from others.[8] Autonomy's close cousin, agency, as the 'capacity, condition, or state of acting or of exerting power,'[9] is among the most valued of end-goals of humanistic philosophy. In its formulation of power, agency necessitates a specific kind of rationality dependent on binary bifurcations and the division of the social world into categories such as society, politics, economy, and religion.[10]

The imagined world that supports the agonistic struggle for autonomy is a harsh one of competition where one person's personal project of identity necessarily leads to a diminishing or even destruction of another's. Added to the competitive struggle to distinguish the self relative to others is the notion that rules are restrictive structures that must be twisted or broken to achieve a space for the distinctive self. Stereotypes and other ascribed roles and responsibilities are, like rules, necessarily perceived as controlling and limiting identity. Liberty thus becomes defined as freedom from the influence of others, from rules, a freedom best found in the private spaces carved out at considerable cost from the public sphere. Michel de Certeau gives us a vision of a world where the considerable resources of the Goliath of the state are strategically pitted against the weak tactics of the minuscule David.[11] The state is assumed to desire to overcome David by restricting or repositioning him in new identities more suitable to state projects; David, in turn, is determined to escape however he can. In such a world, we are most often expected to identify with the 'little guy,' the underdog, whose desperate attempts to resist the state are honourable in themselves even if they ultimately fail.[12]

Combined with this vision of a competitive field of interaction among individuals and structures is a moral vision of the world in which inner intention is emphasized as much as, or more than, actions. A person who acts consistently according to his principles achieves a state of moral virtue. Adherence to principles may be difficult, but it is foundational to a person's sense of self-esteem. Playing a role, being forced to play a role, indulging in performance, or otherwise misaligning intent with action becomes a sign of weakness (often of a feminine sort) or oppression. A man must *achieve* his identity and individuality through action. Whether or not a man has achieved these goals is a matter for him to decide, and he alone can judge his own success.

In such a worldview, the concept of obedience is preternaturally occluded. If what is meant by obedience is obedience to state, familial, social, or cultural projects of identity, then what is meant is collusion, giving in, a lack of principle or false consciousness, or slavery. At best, obedience is a signal of oppression, of someone too weak to help himself and who therefore needs 'our' help (we being those who appraise the situation); at worst, it is a signal that a person has fallen into such a state of moral decrepitude that he obeys consciously and willingly. The dichotomy is absolute: one *resists* the system, or one is no longer moral. It is, moreover, a dichotomy that slips into the work of even those (feminists, queer theorists, practitioners of ethnic and cultural studies) who consciously attempt to redefine the concepts of individuality and identity to diminish the David and Goliath vision of competitive struggle.[14]

Within Euro-American thought, to obey is to forgo one's own plans and projects in favour of those advanced by people superior in status or might. But it is more than this, for obedience is also a 'peculiar practice' of the 'East,' of those 'wily Orientals' who transgress in their written texts and interpersonal actions the entire complex of binary divisions, categories, and values upheld so consistently in Euro-American philosophical and economic texts. I need only turn to Wittfogel or Weber to be presented with a vision of a society of 'oriental despotism' that exacts obedience from its subjects at a terrible price.[15] Such visions are exemplary of the anthropological understanding that descriptions of the 'other' are exaggerated opposites that take characteristics that the self finds most important about the self, imagines appropriate opposites to them, and then exaggerates them for effect.[16]

Euro-American society and government are described as if they work in the ideal manner: living in a world based on the rule of law *(fazhi)*, contract, and a rational and effective system of checks and balances, enterprising individuals carve out spaces for themselves in the free market (in the sense of exercising identity choice, political choice, and consumer choice in the economic free market). Individuals might choose to cooperate in a free association to create a central government but only for the narrowest of purposes calculated to increase market efficiency and group protection and security. Asiatic society, in as stark a contrast as possible, is based on the rule of 'men' *(renzhi)*, of ascribed unchanging status structures, and of people forced by the control wielded by the totalitarian state over irrigated agriculture to obey and be enslaved. It is a society, moreover, mystified by a moral system of checks and balances in which the leaders are purported to be responsible for the well-being of the people in a paternalistic 'father knows best' manner. There is no free market, no freedom of identity, and no autonomy. The exaggeration is forced: the deficiencies of 'our' system are passed over in favour of unmitigated praise; the achievements of 'their' system are elided in preference for an emphasis on the negative.[17]

It may seem to be an exaggeration on my part to indulge in this sharp bifurcation of the concepts of obedience and autonomy. That bifurcation, unfortunately, is not merely my own theoretical construct but, in fact, shows up all too often in the scholarship of Euro-Americans when they turn their gaze on Chinese archeology. Anglo-North Americans, with their frontier traditions of rugged resistance and antigovernment libertarianism, are particularly prone to insisting that 'those' archeologists 'over there' are nationalist communists with ulterior motives. Whenever Chinese archeologists write something that sounds political, it is taken as a sign that either they lack archeological integrity and principle or that 'we' need to liberate them.[18] A preexisting suspicion of anything that smacks of submission is exacerbated by the superficiality of the analysis or the lack of data. And when a scholar does attempt to praise a Chinese archeologist, he tends to do so because he believes that he has found something resembling 'resistance' as defined by his own sensibilities.

One cannot expect, of course, that a busy archeologist can undertake the historical and ethnological study required to understand a 'foreign' archeology in context; but, one may well ask, why do so many archeologists continue to try?[19] It is particularly odd given that Euro-American archeologists pride themselves on their ability to reconstruct lifeways and meanings in the past.[20] Euro-American archeologists are painfully aware of the importance of context and combination in the creation of meaning – if not from their reading of Wittgenstein himself, then at least through his interpreters.[21] In addition, Euro-American archeologists have access to several ethnographies of academic disciplines since Bruno Latour and Steve Woolgar led the way with *Laboratory Life: The Social Construction of Scientific Facts*.[22] Nevertheless, Euro-American archeologists habitually assign motivations to behaviour without adequately grasping the different implications of that behaviour given a wildly distinct political, historical, economic, and social context.

Although this study seeks to understand obedient autonomy in China, a secondary goal is to temper our tendency to judge the actions of others as if they were like us. It is particularly important to be wary in discussing issues of autonomy. Such a discussion is likely to founder on moral condemnation, a faint sense of horror and disgust, and charges of ascribing faults of manipulation or corruption to my informants.[23] It is difficult to resist the instantaneous assumptions that spring to mind and try instead to 'see through a glass, darkly,'[24] in order to understand a very different context in which strategies of something called obedience, and the achievement of a life of order, combine to create autonomy.

The Intellectual's Burden and the Judgment of History

I therefore begin with the sorest of sore points causing friction between foreign and Chinese archeologists: the relationship between the archeologist and the Chinese state. That relationship is founded on the values pursuant to the role of the intellectual and to the importance of history as a source of judgment in the lives of intellectuals. It should come as no surprise that Chinese intellectuals, due to their particular combination of social and historical circumstances, have a view of their social position and political responsibilities distinct from that held by Anglo-North American academics.

Chinese archeologists consider themselves historians. While many archeologists of other countries also define archeology as properly a subdiscipline of history, many in North America and Great Britain define it as anthropology. Whenever there is debate over the relative merits of defining archeology as history or anthropology, it is usually accompanied by the claim that there are attendant methodological and epistemological differences in the archeology of cultural history and anthropological archeology.[25] When Chinese archeologists declare themselves historians, however, they are not referring to the differences in their archeological methodology. Mao's famous statement 'Let history serve the present' is not something new or unprecedented in Chinese thought, but it is something with which neither traditional scholars nor modern intellectuals would think to disagree.[26] To claim that archeology is history is to claim that archeologists belong to a particularly elite group of intellectuals *(zhishifenzi)* who, throughout recorded Chinese history, have had a special role to play with regard to the state.[27]

That elite group is comprised of the historian-scholars *(shi, shidaifu)* of imperial tradition. Traditionally, scholars studied the histories and classics for the sole purpose of being admitted to government service.[28] The proper relationship between a historian and the state can be illustrated by the life of Han historian Sima Qian, a famous scholar who served the Han Chinese people by rectifying the actions of the emperor. In the face of the emperor's attempt to force him to rewrite history in accordance with the emperor's wishes, Sima Qian politely 'resisted.' That is, he did not rebel, deny the emperor's right to rule, or attack the dynastic system; rather, he simply remained at court and continued to write history as it happened. He was eventually sentenced to death for his trouble, but his daughter and brother continued his work of writing an accurate account of the events in question. Faced with such a display of loyalty to the system, such a clear and correct example of duty and responsibility (and an impressive display of filial virtue to boot), the emperor eventually relented. It is a Chinese happy ending: the emperor rectified his actions by allowing the truth to be written and became a better ruler. Since at least the time of Sima Qian, there have been innumerable similar stories told about the contradictions that historians have faced in attempting to remain utterly loyal to the ideals of dynastic rule as well as faithful to the requirements of historical truth.[29]

Given that the stories of the great historians such as Sima Qian have been repeated endlessly in Chinese literature, philosophy, plays, and poetry, history has become something much more than stories from the past or a source of experience to guide the present. It is not going too far to insist that, if there is a transcendent arbiter of right and wrong in Chinese society, it will be found not in the notion of an omniscient God who knows whether 'you have been bad or good' but in the annals of history, which have recorded whether a person was perceived to have been acting correctly or incorrectly with regard to his or her duty. Thus, historians and, by extension, archeologists are aware that historical figures leave a legacy. A legacy lasts forever: a valuable longevity if one's actions are praised, an inescapable infamy if one's actions are judged lacking.[30]

Since an intellectual leaves a legacy, the practical question turns on what kind of legacy will last and be exemplary. Surely it is important to write down the truth of events. But what happens when, as is inevitable, new information is discovered showing that the historian misunderstood or did not have all the facts? If a reputation is based solely on 'truth,' then new information will destroy the historian's importance to subsequent generations. If reputation is instead based on living an exemplary life, then it can remain intact despite subsequent discoveries, because later generations can continue to remember a historian through an appreciation of his virtue. A morally exemplary scholar therefore works hard and writes the truth as he sees it but nevertheless expends equal amounts of energy in the pursuit of moral action with an eye to the ultimate judgment of history.[31]

Ideally, the state is expected to seek the advice of historians (the modern slogan is *xueshu dai tou:* 'Research Should Lead the Way'). Since at least the turn of the twentieth century, however, the willingness of state representatives to live up to this ideal has certainly been questionable. Moreover, the influx of European philosophical ideals, especially those concerning the nature of the autonomous individual and his relation to state institutions (in particular, the notion of human rights and democracy), has complicated the standards of proper and exemplary intellectual behaviour. Rebellion in the form of direct and open resistance can be justified as moral using the values of European philosophies, and as a result some intellectuals did rebel against the Qing; the Communists rebelled against the Kuomintang; and, currently, various intellectuals, including some archeologists, rebel openly against the Communists.[32]

While an individual intellectual may choose to espouse democracy or support communism, extol the virtues of Western nations, or scorn them as morally defunct, in all cases he will subscribe to a strong form of paternalism. Intellectuals are convinced that both the rulers and the people of China need their knowledge, guidance, and aid to be raised up from the darkness of ignorance and tradition into the light of modernity. The leaders need advice; the peasants require guidance and paternalistic care. If the needs of one conflict with those of the other, then it is the intellectual's responsibility to mediate and create a solution.[33] After the fall of the Qing Dynasty, intellectuals merely changed their allegiance from emperor to China and its people.[34] While this change opened the way for intellectuals to differentiate themselves on the question of who needs their aid the most (the masses, the Republicans, or the Communists), it is also important to realize that the vision of the intellectual as paternal guide is still foundational to the self-perception of most if not all intellectuals.[35]

Intellectuals thus subscribe to an 'intellectual's burden' regardless of political orientation. In using this vocabulary, I want to recall the notion of the 'white man's burden' to emphasize the hierarchical assumptions within the stereotype.[36] Just as white colonialists thought that they were bringing the light of civilization to the uneducated savages, so too intellectuals view the people whom they help as inferior; just as white colonialist governments saw differences in perspective or culture as being problematic, so too intellectuals view the opinions and customs of non-intellectuals as needing eradication if things are to change for the better.[37]

However, unlike colonized 'savages,' who eventually resisted and overthrew their oppressors to reclaim responsibility for the development of their societies, neither Chinese peasants nor bureaucrats resist the traditional role of the intellectuals. Members of the other classes seek the guidance of intellectuals even as the latter seek to provide it to them. For a brief period, Mao did make earnest attempts to reorder society by placing peasants and workers at the top of the social hierarchy – an attempt that can be seen not only as a reaction to traditional class hierarchies but also as driven by Marx's well-known suspicion of the bourgeois attitudes inherent in the intellectual class – but Mao's social order failed utterly to be maintained after his death.

That 'failure,' the return to an expectation that intellectuals both can and ought to provide paternalistic guidance to the nation, is distinctly due neither to the 'passive' nature of the Chinese peasant or bureaucrat nor to some imagined need of theirs for strong central governance, as is so often repeated in the musings of non-Chinese political theorists. Such theorists have forgotten to look at the *incentives* that make it beneficial for peasants and bureaucrats alike to maintain intellectuals in their paternalistic social position. Those said to be responsible for the well-being of the nation make, after all, excellent scapegoats if something goes awry; moreover, someone expected to serve, and trained throughout university in the language of service, is ripe for exploitation when an official or peasant needs a favour. It would be a grave error to assume that, just because an intellectual is approached by a politician for advice, the intellectual controls the relationship.[38]

The great majority of archeologists share this paternalistic notion of their role with regard to China, to both its leaders and the masses, and they seek to live up to the ideals of proper behaviour by serving China in whatever way they can.[39] Chinese archeologists have been forced to aid the state in the past. More often, however, they become involved with state representatives willingly and in response to a direct, usually polite, request. And they can just as easily be sought out by people who wish to resist the government as by those who support it. In both cases, a Chinese archeologist may well choose to become involved regardless of how he feels about the policies or plans presented. He becomes involved because it is his duty to provide a corrective, to model upright behaviour, to guide people into right actions.[40]

As we have seen, there are disciplinary incentives for an archeologist to develop and maintain a large Rolodex of contacts. The depth of experience in social interaction required to be an archeologist has not gone unnoticed by the officials and bureaucrats in charge of managing the government and the Chinese Communist Party (CCP). From the perspective of the CCP, archeologists are unusual among intellectuals because they embody a number of modern and traditional concepts of the 'good intellectual': they are 'good communists' in that they work with their hands (and most definitely get their hands dirty) alongside the peasants; they are 'good scholars' because they study the past in a culture where history is highly valued; they accumulate material artifacts to produce knowledge that seems, under the doctrine of empiricism, to be more 'true' than that produced by historians; they therefore produce knowledge about the Chinese past that can support Marxist historical materialism; and, last but never least, they know everyone from the top to the bottom of the government hierarchy.

These characteristics can be enormously useful. A bureaucrat with a budgetary problem who needs an economic prediction or a scientific result might as well begin by asking archeologists. Why? Because not only will the archeologists know the answer to the question – or at least know someone who would know – but also by asking them a politician can show that he honours good communists, proper scholars, and glorious Chinese history all at the same time. It must come as no surprise, then, that archeologists are inundated by requests for aid – sometimes by people who ask merely for the sake of asking, sometimes by people who need an answer, but almost always by people who ask in cheerful disregard whether the archeologist knows anything at all about the issue in question.

While in Beijing during the 15th Party Congress, I was visiting with an archeologist when a politician came calling ostensibly to bring the archeologist local goodies from Shandong. The two had met over thirty years earlier and since then had each worked his way up the hierarchy, although the archeologist had done better by working his way out of Shandong altogether. The politician came to the archeologist for help on a policy issue relating to the Shandong railway system. The archeologist did not know a great deal about the matter; luckily, it was not his knowledge that was sought but the names of other knowledgeable intellectuals and officials whom he might know. The politician additionally asked the archeologist to read a draft of the proposal and provide a cursory edit so that he could then use the archeologist's name as a stamp of approval on both himself and the proposal – the one because he could show others that he had friends in high places and the other to show that the proposal had been evaluated by an intellectual.

Why would the archeologist help the politician and, more importantly, allow his name to be placed on a political document? An outside observer might immediately assume that he must want the power derived from a deeper involvement in state affairs. Such power is certainly available. However, if the Shandong politician is criticized, or his work shown to be shoddy, then it is the archeologist who will be blamed for not having provided correct guidance. Those who become involved in state affairs have the potential for greater power yet also face a greater risk of punishment: indeed, it would be foolish to imagine that the potential for authority and influence in the political sphere is not equal to the potential for destruction of one's career, family, and ultimately self.

The question of motive is always a difficult one. Certainly, an individual can be motivated simultaneously by ideals and profit. Note, however, that, if self-interest were paramount, then there ought to be many more Chinese intellectuals who choose the path of Western-style resistance rather than remain obediently 'at court.' The great value placed by Euro-American nations on overt resistance of any kind, as long as it looks familiar to Western eyes,[41] means that the path of resistance now leads more often than not to exile and a comfortable life in Paris or New York.[42] If one's luck holds, riches can be made whether one chooses resistance or obedience. The difference between the resistant and the obedient, then, can cynically be said to consist of wanting rewards in the present versus waiting for the judgment of history to bestow rewards on one's memory and children. As for resisters who do not manage to be fruitfully exiled from China, they can always reposition themselves in the mould of traditional, long-suffering scholars sacrificing all for China and take heart in the idea that history will rehabilitate them.

Orthopraxy

This vision of Chinese archeologists still falls dangerously close to allowing readers to continue to accuse them of having collusionist political agendas (whether Nationalist, Maoist-Communist, Centralist, or Han Chinese chauvinist).[43] By now, it ought to be obvious that such accusations completely miss the point: the duty of the intellectual involves so much more than having opinions about present-day political issues. It primarily involves proper moral action as judged by history.

With judgment being assessed by history rather than policed by the individual, a radical break must be made between internal intent and external action. External action must be groomed to fit the standards of the people who will write history. Thus, if a person is classified as a historian, then he must present himself as a historian; that is, as a man of principle and loyalty who would willingly die before he sacrificed either duty to China or duty to archeology. In such a presentation of the self, a person must ensure that his actions are interpreted as intended; the intangibles of internal beliefs and intentions are simply less important than the apprehensible acts of moving and speaking.[44] Thus, a person can assist the state yet be firmly anticommunist, for being perceived as someone who will do what he must to uphold the nation is more important than personal opinion. Indeed, personal opinion is of little import, for what are the thoughts of an individual, limited as he is, compared to the judgment of history?

Ortho*praxy* describes a system that depends on 'orthodox practice': that is, on the express formulation of *action* to conform to commonly held standards.[45] In such a system, belief and intent may be important to a person's sense of character and self-esteem, but they cannot be the final arbiters of moral character, success, or satisfaction. For those, we must look to the audience who is witness to any action, for it is the audience who provides judgment. A person polices his actions, not his thoughts, in response to the presence of an audience. Ortho*doxy*, in contrast, depends on the attempt to align internal beliefs and external practices. The self is the source of ultimate judgment, or the relationship between the self and an omniscient God, such that, even if the audience insists that a person is incorrect, he can continue to insist within himself that he is correct. The final arbiter of character, success, and satisfaction is his perception of his ability to act in the world in a manner that conforms to his beliefs and intentions.

The difference between the two perspectives is not absolute, nor are they starkly opposed. Indeed, each includes the same elements, but they differ in combination and emphasis. Yet the seemingly minor difference in weighting has enormous implications. As each chapter in this book will show in its own way, that seemingly simple difference, of a recentring of focus on action rather than intent, leads to starkly different choices across all social relations.

Uncertainty

The worldviews implied by orthopraxy and orthodoxy entail very different kinds of uncertainty. Under the system of orthodoxy, if intent must be aligned with action, and the final judge of character is the self or God, then questions concerning the existence of God, the distinct and individual nature of the self, and the self's ability to control its circumstances all become highly problematic. It is no wonder, then, that in systems of orthodoxy scholars of deconstruction, standpoint, or relational identity have encountered great resistance outside the academy.[46] Their questioning of the nature and source of identity is seen as an attack on what bestows on people their sense of control, character, and satisfaction. There is not a person under orthodoxy, sometimes especially scholars immersed in the counternarratives of hermeneutics, constructivism, and practice theory, who does not have to struggle every day to avoid slipping back into the notion that he is in control, that his tastes are his own, and that his physical tics and distinctions have no source but his own unique individuality.

Orthodoxy, in other words, is an incorrigible system. It appears fragile, for the ontological and epistemological basis of each stark dichotomy has been ably deconstructed and decentred at every turn. Yet it persists; attacking the system of orthodoxy from within is a slow and arduous process hampered by the fact that beliefs about the self, God, race, class, or gender and the complexes of moral values pursuant to such categories, all beliefs long thought eradicated, will return in moments when attention is focused elsewhere.

The system of orthopraxy is similarly incorrigible despite appearing fragile on inspection. Its fragilities, unsurprisingly, take slightly different forms from those found in orthodoxy. If other people sit in ultimate judgment on the moral character, successes, or failures of the person, then the agent has a problem. How is he to figure out the standards that others will use to judge him? And how might these standards differ among people or, worse, across the kinds of space and time implied by a long-term vision of history? Will the people of tomorrow interpret the actions of today as we would now? These questions simply cannot be asked too often or pursued too strenuously, for they reveal the uncertainties that threaten to destroy the system of orthopraxy. Just as in daily life the system of orthodoxy remains impervious to critique, so too the questions that threaten orthopraxy are lost in the midst of the complexities of everyday social interactions.

It seems that the maintenance of everyday life is incompatible with constant, searching critique and requires instead certain shortcuts, which include assumptions, tastes, impulses, and other forms of 'common sense.' The predominant shortcut used by participants in orthopraxy is elegant in its simplicity: all Chinese people, over time, are the 'same' – that is, they share the same standards and interpret each other's actions in the same way. Such an assumption, which I call the *doctrine of similarity*, is manifestly untrue, even from the perspective of a Chinese person who has never left his or her village or met a stranger. Differences of opinion about what to do next or in response to some event arise relentlessly. Nevertheless, the doctrine must persist. Without the belief that everyone shares the same ideals about the intellectual, his role, and his responsibilities vis-à-vis others, the intellectual cannot act at all. He cannot plan his actions, devise a series of strategies, or predict the reactions of others in any given social situation. He is lost. Once the doctrine of similarity is accepted, all else falls into place: one knows who one is in the eyes of others, what they expect, and what one can or cannot do.

The doctrine thus achieves the status of 'social truth':[47] it may be manifestly untrue, it may be said openly to be untrue in any given encounter or by legions of academics, but its presence is inescapable. Much in the same way that an escape from racial thinking is impossible in the United States, the belief under orthopraxy that everyone is and has always been (and will always be) the same is unavoidable in China, for this belief underpins the conceptions of the self, guides social relations, interprets history, and is a source of character, satisfaction, and success. In the United States, it would not behoove people classed in certain racial groups to forget, even if they themselves are certain that race should not be a factor, that racial thinking inheres in their every social interaction. In the same way, an individual under orthopraxy who is suspicious, whether due to training or experience, about the ontological status of the doctrine of similarity has no choice but to assume that other people believe in it. By acting as if *they* believe in it, he de facto makes it true, since he chooses to act in conformity with what he thinks they believe in order to communicate with them. Under orthopraxy, when one's focus is constantly on what one predicts, hopes, or imagines other people to be thinking, and when one tailors one's actions to fit those imagined thoughts, social truth becomes more important to a person's plans and projects than any other kind of truth (statistical, physical, observational, experiential).

Under orthopraxy, identity must therefore be radically redefined. It can no longer be defined as something only fully achieved after an agonistic separation from others, nor as a personal project of self-actualization pursued in private space, nor as something carved out in competitive struggle with other people. Identity arises through the interaction between self and others – or, more complexly, in the interaction between the self, what the self imagines other people to be thinking, and the reinforcement received from the audience. The evaluation of an act depends on audience expectations. When there is little effective difference between what others think of a person and the identity of that person, issues of *reputation*, or what in Chinese studies is more often called 'face,' are foregrounded in social interaction.[48]

Interdependence

Reputation is an extraordinarily complex issue because the concept reveals how very differently the individual and identity are categorized in China. Under orthodoxy, the division of society into four categories (politics, religion, economy, and family) has a long tradition in the social sciences.[49] These categories are predicated on the dichotomies of public and private, rational and irrational, and emotional and instrumental. The family is imagined to be emblematic of the private sphere and the place of emotional, often irrational, affect; politics symbolizes the public sphere and is instrumental and irrational; the economy is public, instrumental, and rational; and religion is private, irrational, and emotional. The categorizations themselves, of course, occasionally come into question, but for the most part they continue to 'feel' natural, fit common sense, and persist despite all efforts to destroy them.

In the Chinese context, these divisions make little sense. No boundaries are required to distinguish corporation, religious group, political entity, and family.[50] The head of a corporation is the head of a family wielding as much political as economic influence. His control over his workers depends not simply on the threat of unemployment but also on paternal disapproval backed by the full force of emotional, moral, and religious affect. A boss disenchanted with one's ability to work well is one thing, but when that boss is also one's father it becomes impossible to separate one's identity within the family from that within the workplace. The separations between instrumentality and affect and between rationality and irrationality are similarly lost: a worker is simultaneously an instrument to be used for the greater good of the corporation as well as a beloved son or respected daughter.

What does this blurring of categories mean for ethnographic observation? Let us take the example of the role of the language of kinship under conditions of orthodoxy. When kinship language seeps into the Euro-American political sphere under orthodoxy, it is a move viewed with suspicion and labelled as a rhetorical strategy to mystify and seduce the electorate by calling on their irrational emotions. It is a linguistic crossing of boundaries that alerts the orthodox observer that something unusual is happening. When the orthodox observer turns to China and finds that the language of 'kinship' appears in Chinese 'political matters,' not surprisingly she might assume the politicians to have similarly aggressive intentions with regard to the masses and that, if the masses accept such rhetoric, they must have been duped by moral mystifications empty of meaning.

Unfortunately for the orthodox observer, identification of both the strategy (that kinship language is being used where it should not be) and the implications (that the government uses it to mystify the masses, that they are duped unless they cry out against the 'misuse' of kinship terms) is misguided. When words are moved from the contexts in which they are normally heard to new contexts, new meaning is indeed bestowed, and the question of motive must arise. But where there are no categories, the movement of words across categories is logically impossible. A kinship term showing up in the political sphere is an event perceptible only if there is a distinction drawn between kinship and politics. If whatever we might define as 'kinship terminology' is instead considered acceptable in any context at any time, then kinship terms are not marked but unremarkable, even imperceptible, and the act of using them is not endowed with special meaning.

It is interesting to compare the use of kinship terminology under orthopraxy with the use of the language of rationality under Euro-American orthodoxy. The language of rationality appears in every conceivable social interaction. The word *logic*, for example, has a meaning for philosophers very different from that used in everyday conversation. Yet the term has become so pervasive and acceptable in everyday speech that it would be utterly odd for someone to insist that we should qustion the moral intentions of the speaker. Terms like 'rationality' and 'efficiency' have made a similar transition into everyday speech and similarly excite no special notice. In China, kinship terminology enjoys a history of boundary crossings so numerous one could could say that there are no boundaries that kinship terms cannot cross.

'No boundaries' is, of course, an exaggeration for effect. The Chinese world is structured by its own set of categorizations and dichotomies. But where orthodox categories are predicated on classifying what people *do*, orthoprax categories are predicated on classifying what people *are*. When classification is based on what a person *does*, the individual remains whole and complete even as his actions are sorted into different categories; when classification is based on who a person *is*, the individual himself is chopped into categories.

To understand how the individual can be 'chopped up,' it is useful to compare the relationship ideally said to hold between the man and the position of the president of the United States. The office of the president existed before the present man arrived and will outlast him when he leaves.

When a given individual undertakes that office, he surely must follow certain procedures, given rules of formal behaviour, and structured forms of responsibility.

Under orthopraxy, the identities that preexist and outlast a person are not limited to political offices but extend to include *all roles*. Thus, the position of sister both preexists and outlasts any individual woman, in the sense that the role brings along with it certain procedures, behavioural rules, and structured responsibilities in relation to the other positions and offices in the family/corporation. That sense of potential bifurcation, between a person and any given 'office' of father, brother, archeologist, or bureaucrat, is what is implied whenever this book uses the phrase 'inhabiting a role' or 'an identity.'

The categories of orthopraxy are structurally similar to those of orthodoxy in that they form the boundaries that bifurcate the social world. Orthoprax categories are also held rigid over time and are believed to be 'natural' and matters of common sense. And, again like orthodox categories, when the language held natural to one category, such as that attributed to women, crosses into a category in which it sounds strange, it excites notice and engenders suspicions concerning reprehensible motives.

What happens when a person's identity is chopped into different categories? Reputation takes on unprecedented importance. To understand the role of 'reputation,' we can compare the role of 'culture' under orthodoxy. Culture under orthodoxy is a catchall concept that, on the one hand, takes a diverse set of (presumed) unique individuals and moulds them into an identifiable group and, on the other hand, dissolves radically into its constituent parts – ideas, grand narratives, habits, traditions, categories, signs, and symbols – that an observer would be hard put to knit into a coherent whole.

Reputation is as confusing and contradictory a concept as culture. On the one hand, it takes a diverse set of status roles and knits them into a single individual, and, on the other hand, it dissolves into as many different parts as there are audience members to perceive and judge a person's actions. When a person acts as father, head of the company, and boss, the audience must struggle to figure out how to judge that person's action, for the standards of appropriate action expected of the identity category 'father' are different indeed from those expected of the categories 'company head' and 'boss.' How can reputation mediate among these differing standards to create anything resembling a person?

The splintering of culture is reconstituted through an act of will that takes shape in the form of reification: in everyday speech, in literature and other cultural products, in education, politics, and economics, culture is spoken of as if it were something that a person 'has' that can be gained or lost. It is rhetorically conceived as unified, bounded, and, remarkably, affecting all of an individual's actions as well as those of all members of his group. That culture is said to affect all actions and be shared among members of the group is particularly remarkable under orthodoxy because the orthodox categories that break up the social world seem to preclude any unifying narrative. Nevertheless, despite the tendency to fracture the world into categories of activity, and despite efforts of anthropologists, psychologists, philosophers, and other specialists who struggle against these habits of thinking, the reified and holistic notion of culture persists.

Reputation is similarly a rhetorical construct. The doctrine of similarity is one of the main acts of will that reconstitutes reputation into a whole. Since the doctrine holds that all audience members are the same and hold to the same standards, possible conflicts between the available standards used to judge the actions of a man who is simultaneously father, company head, and boss are thus elided and ignored. One acts, makes choices, and assumes that others act *as if* all audience members would choose to emphasize one of a person's roles over another in the same context in the same way.

Equally important to the reconstitutive project of reputation is the role of audience memory. The audience remembers judgments made of a man's previous actions, and that memory will affect opinions of that man in the future. Audience memory creates reputation because it links a man's identity, when that man acts in the role of father, to his identity when he acts in his role of boss, friend, son, or politician. These fragments of events and roles are knit into a whole through the memory of the audience.

The rhetorical strategies of reification also come into play, for once reputation can be seen as holistic it can be reified. Identity becomes a thing that can be gained or lost, is vulnerable to attack, and can be both groomed and protected. Despite the tendency to fracture identity into different categories of moral character and proper action, the reified and holistic notion of reputation persists. Where culture under orthodoxy unifies a nation or society, however, reputation under orthopraxy unifies a person.

The practice of 'chopping up' individuals into roles, identities, and statuses is exacerbated by the Chinese *danwei* system. Although this system is in the process of being dismantled, intellectuals, particularly archeologists, remain under its influence. The *danwei* is not simply a place of work but also a system that manages every aspect of a person's life. One works, eats, and plays with one's colleagues and often lives only a few steps from one's office and above or below one's superior. When a person quarrels with a spouse, when children do badly in school, when family health is at issue, members of the *danwei* intervene, advise, and decide what to do. When a superior must make decisions concerning the housing, health, and education of the children of his inferiors, he is simultaneously making decisions about people who are his friends or enemies of long standing. These are the conditions of interdependence, as Andrew Walder so aptly termed it: one action in any part of one's life affects one's actions in every other part.[51]

Under conditions of interdependence, one's reputation in the eyes of others is important not just because the audience is the source of identity but also because, if one is judged to have acted badly in any particular social interaction, the harm done to one's identity can affect one's chances of success in every other interaction. The stakes are high indeed when an argument in one's home is overheard, judged, and results in being punished by having to go into the field despite one's wife being pregnant with one's first child or when one's careless excavation skills affect whether one's only child can attend a good school. Under interdependence, in which reputation is all-important, each action becomes fraught with uncertainty about its implications for and effects on every other aspect of one's life as well as those of one's spouse and children, colleagues and friends, and extended kin.

Autonomy and the Achievement of Order

What does the word *autonomy* mean when a person's actions are presented for the judgment of others, when success or satisfaction depends on conforming to the standards of others, when reputation – a person's very identity – is created in interaction with others? Autonomy cannot be, as it appears to be under orthodoxy, a kind of self-directed or selfish desire for freedom in the sense of wanting to be left alone to do as one pleases. The conceptualization of autonomy must be refocused on the person not as individual but as absorbed in interactions in the social world. Autonomy, in other words, must be redefined to mean something like the 'active intervention in the process of judgment undertaken by the audience.'

Intervention in a process cannot be undertaken unless the elements involved are known. A person concerned with his reputation must know not only the identity categories into which he may be placed by others but also whom these audience members are and the categories of identity into which they fit, which will recursively affect the judgments they make of him. Identity categories cut both ways: a person is fractured into many identities, as are the members of the audience. How can the plethora of potential identities be reduced to a manageable number?

The required reduction is achieved with 'scripts': a combination of habits related to contexts that guide both action and interpretation.[52] However many 'offices' a man may 'be,' when he carries his injured and sobbing child into the hospital after an accident, he is, above all, a father: the combination of context and event reduces his potential complexity in the eyes of the audience. Similarly, two archeologists arguing over an artifact metamorphose into a superior and his inferior when standing in the *danwei* office discussing next year's budget. Given the importance of audience as a source of identity, it is imperative to understand that these scripts include the reactions and identities of audience members. For example, the *danwei* audience watching the father take his child to the hospital has a very different stake in this event than in watching the superior and inferior argue over the budget that will affect the entire *danwei*'s well-being in the coming year. Similarly, imagine the differences of opinion of an audience of peasants viewing an argument between two archeologists over a piece of dirty pottery versus standing outside the hospital and witnessing the archeologist-cum-father bringing his child to the hospital.

Reductions in the number of potential standards of judgment used by a given audience can be actively achieved by the actor. The most important strategy used to intervene in the judgment of the audience is that of claiming, which refers to the judicious combination of scripts, contexts, and incentives used to seduce the audience into agreeing to use the particular script desired by the actor. If a man can convince the audience that he is acting as a father rather than as a *danwei* director, then the attention he pays to his child rather than to the protection of the *danwei* can at least be understood and subject to grudging approval; however, if he cannot convince the audience that it is appropriate for him to act as father rather than director, then he will indeed face censure. Since the success of any action requires that it be judged in a way beneficial to the actor, his only choice is to try to manipulate that judgment in whatever way he can.

It is therefore fundamental to any attempt to interfere in the process of audience judgment that order be both achieved and maintained. What is *order* under orthopraxy but a structured series of standard associations between preexisting identity categories and their attendant prescriptive norms and between contexts and certain habits of judgment (scripts)? Only once order is achieved can a person begin to plan interventions, devise strategies, predict outcomes, react to failures, and build on successes. It is not surprising, then, that the doctrine of similarity is maintained against all odds, that the categories of identity are protected from attack, and that rules, norms, and values are rarely disputed or resisted, for it is only with the achievement of orderly rules and structure that autonomy, that ability to intervene in the judgments of others, can be accomplished. Structure, rules, categories, norms – all the elements seen under orthodoxy to be oppressive and limiting of freedom – become under orthopraxy the very strategies required to accomplish autonomy.

Obedient Autonomy

The strategies that achieve and maintain order, while still intervening in the process of judgment, are those of obedient autonomy. Such strategies 'obey' because they maintain and even strengthen order. They lead to 'autonomy' because, once order is established, intervention, manipulation, and the management of reputation, and therefore of identity, may begin. Such practices are strategies because they take a great deal of effort to devise and execute. Order is not easily achieved, not simply because the sensory world is not naturally ordered in any consistent fashion and events occur out of turn, but also because other people are actively attempting to intervene in the ordering of action and identity. Strategies must accomplish a balancing act among the contradictory yet utterly necessary goals of upholding the structures and rules that enable one to intervene in the judgments made by others, intervening in the judgments of others to one's own benefit, fending off the attempts of others to ruin one's reputation, and, as if all that were not enough, neutralizing the threat to order that such strategies of intervention represent.

'Performance' is a metaphor useful in understanding the strategies of obedient autonomy under orthopraxy, in which the opinion of the audience takes on unprecedented importance. An actor on stage is not alone in his attempt to convey a story to the audience: he is aided by the stage and its decorations, by the other actors on stage, by the script and language used in it, and by the audience and its willingness to accept and react to the fictions produced. Each factor has its own signs and symbols, rules and traditions of meaning, that are multiple yet constrained through the judicious combination of decoration, language, costume, and all the other details of voice and physical movement used to convey meaning. There can be as many interpretations of the intended meaning as there are actors and audience members, but the fiction that there is only one, or ought to be only one, is maintained despite arguments that people have after the show or interpretations offered by drama critics.

The metaphor of performance is especially helpful in understanding the autonomy of the actor.[53] Despite having a script, such that even his stage directions are written out for him, and despite his desire for audience approval, an actor is hardly reduced to passively, *obediently*, following the rules. We admire actors who seem to infuse life anew into the oft-repeated lines of Hamlet and decry those whose wooden readings deflate imaginary worlds old or new. Let us not imagine that whatever has us admire one actor and despise another is something over which we have complete control, for we are not entirely in control of our reactions to what we perceive; however, let us also not imagine that the actors themselves have complete control, for our impressions of them are always based on the entirety of things – stage, script, and fellow actors – rather than simply focused on the actor out of context. Interpretation is a mutual act.

What the actor intends to convey can be any variation of the following four categories: he is 'right' for the role; he is, in fact, playing a role (some skill, in other words, must be perceived before someone can be praised for it); if he plays the role well, then he deserves reward; and if he plays it badly, then he seeks through justification and excuses to convert the negative press into something positive in the future or at least reduce its impact on his reputation and chances of being cast in other plays. The strategies of obedient autonomy are exactly these: they strive to measure, understand, and intervene in audience opinions, all the while submitting to the idea that the audience has the right to judge.

The actor lives for the approval of the audience: he is outward looking, concerned with appearance, apprehensive of gossip, and protective of his reputation. Following his lead, we too must remain concerned with the audience. Actors, of course, value the comments of some members of the audience more than others. It would surprise no one that a Hollywood actor is likely to give more weight to the opinion of critics working for the *New York Times* than to critics working at the *China Daily*. The phrase 'audience-that-matters' is used throughout this book as a reminder of the complex interaction between actor and audience. The audience-that-matters is one that matters not just because it has the power to matter but also because the actor allows it to matter: mattering, too, is a mutual matter.

Roles and Agency

It is in the discussion of roles that the metaphor of performance fails to convey the full impact of the combination of orthopraxy and interdependence in the lives of Chinese archeologists. The metaphor does remind us that the roles that an actor plays always take their shape and meaning only in relation to the stage, other actors, and the events (and order of events) defined by the script. What the metaphor of performance does not adequately emphasize, however, are three key characteristics of roles: that they are multiple, that they entail multiple motives and goals, and that they often take the form of hierarchical relations of authority.

First, on stage, the actor plays only one role in one script at any given time. The Chinese archeologist, in contrast, plays multiple roles, and his audience (particularly in the *danwei*) is well aware of the details of most if not all of those roles. A person can therefore be torn apart in the attempt to live up to the expectations that the various roles simultaneously demand of him. As we have seen, scripts – combinations of roles, contexts, and events – are the only way to avert such disaster. An actor must engage in strategies of claiming that convince the audience that just one script is applicable in a particular event or moment in time. Strategies of convincing the audience to agree to one script rather than another are in effect ways of helping the audience decide which set of standards to use when judging. By controlling the standards used to judge, a person knows how best to act to receive the rewards of audience approval.

Second, the actor in the metaphor of performance is motivated to convince the audience of his skill in acting a role and seeks its positive judgment; the Chinese archeologist seeks not only praise for his skill and a positive judgment of his character but also more material rewards. The notion that a performer seeks a salary and uses his fame to increase the salary that he can command is too simplistic a vision; it cannot address the kinds of rewards sought by archeologists under the conditions of interdependence in which their salaries are set and they are barred from leaving the *danwei* and looking for a position elsewhere. Both the strategies used to secure rewards and the kinds of rewards that are sought (money is in short supply) are remarkably different from what can be gained under the system of orthodoxy and its attendant structures of free-market capitalism.

Third, under orthopraxy, the rewards sought are those of hierarchical position with respect to others and/or authority in the sense of command over resources. A good reputation dialectically reinforces a person's ability to convince the audience that the person is acting correctly in most if not all contexts. That, in turn, leads to a repositioning in the hierarchy: one is promoted or otherwise enjoys increased access to and command over resources such that they can be redistributed as desired. Why is a change in hierarchical position so important? One answer is that once one adds the credentials of a higher position in the hierarchy to one's reputation, it becomes that much easier to convince an audience that one has the right and the skill to play a given role properly (somewhat in the same way that an A-list star is often praised whether the performance is perceived as good or not, while a B-list star suffers a much greater stringency of critique). A second answer is that once one has access to resources, especially the kinds of resources considered desirable in the eyes of the audience-that-matters, one can provide incentives to seduce the audience into accepting any claim to a role that he makes (somewhat in the way that an A-list star will agree to interviews, autographs, and whatever else fans want in order to give them reason to continue in their appreciation of the star).

Hierarchy is important not just because it provides credentials that enable one to convince an audience that much more easily but also because the roles played by people under orthopraxy are explicitly hierarchical in form. Roles-in-relation are always either subordinate or superordinate. Given that roles are multiple, it follows that a person has the experience of being superior to someone and inferior to someone else, often simultaneously.[54] To understand what it means to be senior or junior, and especially the contradictory and difficult position of being simultaneously senior and junior, under conditions of orthopraxy and interdependence, requires a very different understanding of agency.

The vision of agency common to orthodoxy is entirely instrumental and competitive. It is a zero-sum game: if someone gets 'more,' then someone else must have less. Agency seems to be imagined as a tool held by those in hierarchically superior positions and wielded aggressively against those who, being without such tools, are weaker by definition. Michel Foucault's visionary redefinition of power as arising out of the relationship between master and servant notwithstanding, the conception of power under orthodoxy persists in imagining people in higher positions in the hierarchy to be strong and powerful, flexing their muscles and using their superior might to overshadow, in a most foreboding and negative way, those weaklings crouched submissively in the lower, darker places.[55] In this world, there is no room for the cooperative creation of mutually beneficial ties.

The vision of agency in orthopraxy, concerned as it is with the judgments of moral character made about the self by other people, is rather different. It is neither a top-down instrumental relation nor, in contrast to Foucault, something that arises out of the relationship between master and servant. Rather, it is something bartered between junior and senior, a gift in constant exchange; at times, the junior is in charge, and at other times the senior takes control. The senior who issues an order receives the gift of obedience in return. As Marcel Mauss observed, once the gift of obedience is given, the senior (gift taker) becomes indebted to the junior (gift giver).[56] What constitutes the gifts passed between junior and senior, why they are considered worthwhile or important, how they are given, and the meanings attached to both the choosing of a gift and the manner in which it is given are all issues of consummate importance in understanding agency. Strategies of obedient autonomy can therefore be conceived not only as achievements of order that simultaneously intervene in the judgments made based on that order but equally as achievements of order that both maintain the rules of gift giving yet intervene in the judgments of the value of a gift. The term 'roles-in-relation' will be used to recall the complexity of multiple relational roles in which authority is constantly in flux.

Disintegrating *Guanxi*

The concepts of the intellectual's burden, the judgment of history, orthopraxy, and the uncertainties engendered by interdependence all combine to provide strong incentives for the use of strategies of obedient autonomy. Strategies require both resources and the rules for using those resources. The resources that we have encountered so far include the doctrine of similarity, the categorization of the social world into different identities with their attendant scripts to guide action, hierarchical positions and credentials, roles-in-relation, authority and access to resources, and reputation. Strategies drawing on these resources are used to convince an audience to agree with a person's version of events and otherwise to intervene in and attempt to guide their judgment of that person's actions.

To understand the complexity of these strategies of convincing and intervention, we must consider the notion of *guanxi* as it is normally used in analyses of Chinese society.[57] *Guanxi* is normally defined as 'social networking' and is therefore used as a catchall phrase to describe or explain social interactions. Unfortunately, much like the concept of 'culture,' the term has lost its analytic usefulness, for it simultaneously refers to too many things and smoothes over the distinctions in *guanxi* practice among the different identity categories. In an attempt to pinpoint the ways in which people of different identities interact with others, or with their audiences, I prefer to split *guanxi* into four related but distinct analytical concepts: trustworthiness, compatibility, hierarchy, and authority. These categories expressly do not appear in the theories, terminology, and practices common to everyday life in China. They are instead crutches for the observer of the Chinese social world, a way to trace a path through and over the pitfalls of orthodox thinking to arrive at some semblance of orthoprax perspectives.

Trustworthiness refers to judgments made of another person's moral character; compatibility refers to practices of positioning – both self-positioning and being positioned – that can bestow access to resources that others want or need; hierarchy refers simply to positioning in either hierarchical junior-senior relations or the formal bureaucratic hierarchy; and authority refers to the command, or the appearance of command, over the redistribution of resources. These four concepts will help to explain both how difficult it is to achieve an orderly life and the incentives in the form of opportunities to plan, predict, and achieve success that orderly life bestows.

An Apologia for Obedience?

Euro-American anthropologists, for a variety of reasons related to orthodox tradition and custom, tend to undertake projects examining the dispossessed and the tactics that they use to resist the state, doctors, patriarchs, imperialists, or other oppressors. Ethnographies of the bourgeois middle class, in this case represented by the Han Chinese male middle class with its access to traditional and modern forms of power, are thus atypical. This oversight is unfortunate. If we truly want to understand the dispossessed, then we need to understand the reasons why the 'oppressors' continue to oppress or why the dispossessed might participate in the very structures that maintain their oppression. For the most part, it seems we often simply assume that the oppressors are consciously perpetuating their hold on power, while the dispossessed, due to a lack of opportunity, either do not understand or cannot resist the conditions of their oppression.

All systems are unjust. This study intends to show that what is 'unjust' in the Chinese context is surprisingly distinct in form, content, and implication from what would be seen as unjust in the Euro-American context. Chinese forms of injustice certainly do not arise out of 'obedience' alone. Obedience is not essentially oppressive (or liberating); it can only become so in conjunction with other social structures and norms. Under orthopraxy, the disjoint between internal belief and external action leads to a focus on obedient action, rather than obedient thought, as the source of moral worth.

In the fashion of Rodney Needham, I will not seek to examine the *actual* motives, intentions, and beliefs that no doubt exist within the black boxes that comprise informants' heads.[58] When the terminology of motive and intent is used, it should be understood as the stereotypical interpretations of certain standard behaviours available for use by archeologists. Luckily, I am enabled by my informants' tendency to collect and use stock interpretations of action. Chinese intellectuals prefer a world where internal beliefs are not as important as whether a person acts *as if* he has such beliefs.[59] In other words, Chinese archeologists, like Needham, are not particularly interested in whether behaviour is 'actually' aligned with the beliefs of an actor; instead, they are intent on discovering the general standards by which action may be judged and the strategies by which one can modify that judgment. Our goals are different, for I want to understand these standards and strategies in themselves, while the archeologists need to learn them for use in everyday practice. Our understandings of the epistemological grounds of these standards are also different: although Chinese archeologists will question the doctrine of similarity from a logical standpoint, they must nevertheless slip back into their habit of acting *as if* everyone is the same, because it is that habit that allows them to engage in the highly beneficial strategies of obedient autonomy.

Chinese archeologists encounter a series of distinct contexts and categorize the world in a distinct way. They therefore identify both 'things' and which things can be compared to other things, and the implications of that comparison, in a manner very different from their Euro-American colleagues. Thus, even when a Chinese archeologist openly resists his government in a manner expected and revered by a Euro-American academic, his action means something (both to him and to the audience that matters to him) quite different from what similar actions would mean in the North American context. Before we can interpret – much less pass judgment on – the actions of others, we must ensure that we are not using definitions and habits of categorizing identity and autonomy that do not apply under the system of orthopraxy.

2
The Social Contract

We do not succeed in changing things according to our desire, but
gradually our desire changes.
— Marcel Proust, *Remembrance of Things Past*

What is the process of becoming an archeologist? One answer examines the
basic notions of uncertainty, interdependence, and 'orthopraxy' that comprise both contractual agreements between teachers and students and those
among students in their cohort. The phrase 'social contract' is meant to
recall the basic notion of contract: a private agreement between parties for
mutual benefit. Happily, teachers of archeology are as determined to teach
their students how to make and sustain such contracts as the students are
to learn how to do so.

Uncertainty and the Social Contract
To become an archeologist, students must, of course, study the names, dates,
artifacts, methods of excavation and analysis, and all the other details required to be accepted into the discipline by other practitioners. To be *welcomed* into the group of archeologists, however, students must learn to
translate and broaden what they already know of the principles of group
membership into this new context. Students begin learning these principles
through experiences in their families and in their elementary, middle, and
high school classrooms.

The prescriptive norms and principles that students learn are articulated
as common-sense ideals and expectations. Since discussions of common-
sense ideals are often misunderstood, a caveat is required at the outset: in
no way is this discussion meant to suggest that any person conforms to
each ideal and expectation discussed. The point of common-sense notions
is that they guide action, in the sense that they both enable and limit the
choices that people make, but they do not have the power to determine

action. Just as conformity in dress does not necessarily imply conformity in opinion or attitude, the mere existence of a set of shared ideals does not necessarily imply that everyone views such ideals the same way.[1]

It is important to deliver this warning at the outset because discussions of Chinese group behaviour have a history in Euro-American thought that can form a barrier to open discussion. Indeed, it is extraordinary that the claim that 'group conformism' is unique to the 'Asian' context persists despite innumerable studies of the pressures to conform in Euro-American societies. As Proust reminds us, the process of living among our fellow humans does change our desires, goals, and hopes for the future. Participation in any kind of group constitutes an educational experience as people, much like actual students, discover new information and possibilities, become aware of new role models, and are caught up in new friendships. Assimilation and incorporation are, after all, just negative terms for socialization and education, and to insist that a person, if he or she is to be defined as autonomous, can never learn or change seems odd indeed.

Yet negative claims regarding the fate of the individual in Chinese hierarchical group relations persist. Observers appear to believe that Chinese prescriptive norms, most of which do overtly insist on social conformity, are fundamentally different from Euro-American prescriptive norms. The Chinese form is considered somehow more effective. If the truth be told, Chinese students are like everyone else in that they are fully capable not only of reinterpreting social norms but also of benefiting from the rhetorical strategies of conforming, pretending to conform, believing that they conform, or insisting that they conform. They differ only in which culturally specific things constitute the 'benefits' that they receive from conformity.

The concept of 'benefits' or 'incentives' is key to understanding why Chinese students enter into social contracts with their elders and each other. Despite the number of scholars who have discussed the nature of mutual benefit in Chinese *guanxi* relations, mutuality is sadly often forgotten in the rush to characterize Chinese hierarchical group relations as oppressive to the individual.[2] Mutuality is expressed in explicitly contractual terms between people: 'If you scratch my back, I'll scratch yours.' Each participant is motivated to act according to expectations if and only if the expected returns are, in fact, received. To understand the returns that motivate Chinese students to enter into the social contract, we must begin with the conditions of uncertainty that affect their lives.

University students of any nation, leaving their families, friends, and hometowns for the first time, can be expected to feel uncertain. Chinese archeology students are no different, although both the uncertainties experienced and their reactions to them change over the four years of school. One can likely imagine the tensions felt by first years leaving home for the first time or the worries felt by fourth years as they prepare to find jobs, and it takes minimal effort to understand the effect on third-year archeology students of participating in their first excavation. Nevertheless, it should come as no surprise that the implications of uncertainty and the reactions to it are very different depending on social and cultural contexts.

In the case of Chinese students, the reaction to uncertainty is not to reinforce calls for rugged independence and individualism such that they cut ties to parents and authority figures and try to 'go it alone.' Instead, the reaction is to create strong and dependable relationships and groups in order to reduce uncertainty, forestall disaster, or help manage disaster if it strikes. These relationships are contractual because everyone who enters into them expects something in return; there would simply be no point in participating in such groups if the aid were not forthcoming. They are also hierarchical because it is beneficial for group members to know who has the responsibility to do what for whom. And they are diverse because one wants a group of members who have access to different kinds of resources, in order to benefit from what each member can bring to it.

Creating contractual, hierarchical, and diverse groups is no easy task. The creation of such a group requires members (or potential members) to share (or believe they share) the standards by which they can judge each other as worthy, that is, as people who can be relied upon to provide the protection that is the group's primary goal. The doctrine of similarity – the belief that all Chinese people share similar standards of judgment to interpret behaviour – is an immensely useful tool in the creation of the group. So, too, is the concept of orthopraxy, which is very similar to the Confucian concept of *li* in its emphasis on proper action and its disinterest in internal ideas or beliefs.[3] To be seen as an acceptable group member, then, one must perform 'being a good group member,' and perform well.[4] Luckily, the students have help in learning how to perform group membership. Both the doctrine of similarity and the precepts of orthopraxy are not only endlessly reinscribed in students' daily lives but are also explicitly taught to students by teachers, parents, and fellow students.[5]

The Junior-Senior Contract

Parent and Child

Uncertainty pervades the childhood of any person who wishes to become part of the intellectual class in China. It is difficult to survive the many exams that bar the way into university, and the sacrifices required by both parents and children cannot be overestimated. The outcome is highly uncertain: the number of places in university is small and governed by a strict regionally based quota (the dreaded *ming'e* system).[6] Yet if the gamble does succeed and the child does get into university, then future success is (or was until the changes in the late 1990s) guaranteed. The student will be assigned a job (or, nowadays, find a job) and likely have access to the benefits of not only a salary but also many other perquisites, such as housing, health coverage, and schooling for their own children.[7]

Competition is stiff because most members of Chinese society, whether already based in the urban environment or hoping to have their children leave the country for the city, are remarkably unified in their stated belief that education, in particular a university education, is the best way to ensure success. The definition of 'success' has changed over time, but education as the clearest and most dependable path to success has not. For some parents, themselves not of the intellectual class, belief in education is akin to religious fervour. Their fervour appears to be maintained by the media hype and personal stories and experiences continuously exchanged among friends and neighbours regarding the difficulties of preparing a child to pass the dreaded university entrance examination *(gaokao)*.

That fervour is particularly strong among parents of all classes (intellectual, worker, or peasant) of the right age to remember the Cultural Revolution.[8] In 1966, the university entrance exam was suspended, and senior and junior high school students were sent to the country to 'learn from the peasants,' a task that generally resulted in their living permanently there. In 1977, the exam was reinstated to the great excitement of most of the 'sent-down students,' who saw this as an opportunity to acquire the education that they had been denied and, most importantly, to enter the intellectual class and receive the benefits of belonging to it. The most important benefit, of course, was the right to return to the cities. Teacher Chen of Jilin University (JiDa) described studying to pass the exam as akin to 'eating after a long fast.' Others became inarticulate in their rush to explain that it was simply the most important event that had happened to them since 1966. Although many of these prospective students were already almost thirty years old, had jobs and families, and would likely have had to leave their families behind both during school and once jobs were assigned after graduation, many of them attempted the exam.

Members of this generation have been intent on giving their children similar educational opportunities. Several of them put it this way: 'If you go to university, you will wear leather shoes; if you do not, you will wear grass shoes' *(du daxue, chuan pixie; bu du, chuan caoxie)*. At that time, leather shoes were emblematic of urban living and of jobs in the *danwei*, while grass shoes represented the poverty of the uneducated, rural, jobless peasant. In 1990s China, urban living and secure *danwei* jobs were no longer the main definitions of success. The long and fitful transition from full Maoist socialism to a compromise with capitalism has led to the strange situation in which university-educated people with *danwei* jobs are no longer necessarily able to afford much of anything – much less the latest styles in leather shoes. The money now lies with the *geti hu:* independent entrepreneurs working within the new market system. Nonetheless, education remains important, for people with university degrees are still the most likely to become successful entrepreneurs or find other jobs in the economic sector. Whatever hopes for the future the child or parent might have, in other words, education is pivotal to success.

The university entrance exam represents the single most difficult barrier to the success of the child. A single-point difference between marks can decide whether a student will get into a first-level school *(zhongdian)* or a second-level one. That single point will also decide whether one can study a popular subject *(remen*, literally meaning 'hot door') or an unpopular one *(lengmen*, literally meaning 'cold door'). Depending on the province (and on particular years in some provinces), a student either lists his preferred school and discipline choices *(zhiyuan)* and then takes the exam or waits to see the results of the exam and then fills in his choices. The Central Bureau of Education then assigns him his place depending on how well other students did on the exam that year. Once that decision is made, little can be done to change it.

I discussed the university entrance exam with an archeologist by the name of Lou, who sighed, 'Yes, the exam is arbitrary. But still, this is the only way things can be objective in China; the exam can be nothing else but a correct assessment of the student's abilities. It cannot be manipulated by back-door corruption.' Lou was unhesitating in his opinion that tests are not ideal ways of measuring intelligence. Nevertheless, he was adamant that the exam must continue because it is the only way, in what he sees as the corrupt context of modern China at least, that students can be given a fair chance. That Chinese officials are 'corrupt' is a common refrain among anxious parents.

Wang, another archeologist in the same *danwei*, had a different opinion. Lou's use of the worn trope of 'corruption,' as far as she was concerned, is just another example of how government propaganda has blinded even intellectuals to the class barriers embedded within the education system. Her argument rested on the structure of the education system combined with the parent-child relationship: while the child on examination day may face her task alone, success is never the achievement of a single person. The path to university is long and difficult: an exam must be passed at the end of each of the three divisions (elementary, junior high, and senior high) to ensure a place in the next class.[9] China has a two-tiered system: key schools are singled out to receive the monetary and faculty support that will virtually guarantee that a child accepted to such a school will be able to pass each exam. The path begins, then, in kindergarten, in the competition to enter the best elementary schools, which will eventually lead to a successful pass of the university exam. The entire future of the child, and therefore of the family, depends on the parents' long-term economic and social wherewithal to prepare the child.

By referring to economic and social wherewithal, Wang meant that a successful candidate is one whose parents and extended kin have combined their efforts to create the perfect learning environment. Only certain children – often boys, though girls will be picked if there are no brothers and their intelligence is praised by a teacher – who fit the accepted model of a good or intelligent student will receive the help needed to pass the exam. Since the child must be entirely focused on his studies, he effectively becomes a nonproductive member of the household. Wang reminisced about her own experience – about how she was released from all chores on the family farm and how, in addition, her three younger siblings were removed from school in order to support the family and free up money for her tuition, books, and outside tutors. A child is released from more than just productive economic activity: Wang was also set free from banquets and other forms of reciprocal social activity among her extended family and neighbours. Her world was limited to classmates *(tongxue)*, the teacher, and her immediate family.

Wang added that, when a child fails to achieve the desired results, it is rare to try again the next year, simply because parents do not find it easy to put forth that kind of effort all over again. Indeed, many will not be able to invest so much effort into their children the first time around. Wang insisted that the exam maintains the social status quo since it favours children of already economically or socially well-off families and, therefore, is not a fair way to determine a child's merit.

The children who succeed may be the products of heroic family efforts, but the resulting burden on the child is equally great. Fan, a fortyish archeologist, reminisced about how in 1981 he, though first in his class at the best school in his province, was not given a place in university. He had been enrolled in the science curriculum in high school with the hope of one day working for the government (since science students often become officials in the agricultural sector). When he received the news that his name was not on the list of students who had passed, he lost his wits. As he put it, 'I became inhuman, I was an animal. I ran into the office [of the local Bureau of Education] and screamed at the official. He would do nothing for me. I ran into another office and began to throttle the man behind the desk. I don't remember how I got out of there. All I could think of was my parents and how they would feel.' Luckily, Fan's temper, combined with a lot of work by his parents, teacher, and an uncle, managed to get the bureau to change its decision. There was a single spot left in the whole country: in history at Zhongshan University (the student slated for the spot had died unexpectedly). It is not a good school; Fan had studied science rather than the humanities (into which history falls); he disliked history intensely and had not even studied it for the past two years – yet it was his only choice, and Zhongshan was where he ended up.[10]

Fan is now the assistant director of his archeology *danwei* and continues to work hard at archeology, a discipline that he despises, because he 'must repay [his] parents.' His experience is indicative of the sacrifices that parents must make on behalf of their children, and the exam reinforces notions of filial duty. Interestingly, his colleagues and superiors all know that he dislikes archeology; indeed, each had mentioned his vociferous criticism of archeology and history to me independently of each other. But Fan is nevertheless praised because he works hard at archeology despite his dislike, and this shows that he is a 'good son' acting out of a sense of responsibility to his parents. Filial duty posits that a person acting on behalf of his parents is always more praiseworthy than one acting on his own behalf. Both Lou and Wang, who belong to Fan's *danwei*, are certain that Fan is destined to rise high in the *danwei* hierarchy exactly because of his known sense of filial duty. As Wang put it: 'What official would not be happy to promote someone who has such a strong sense of duty?' She went so far as to suggest that Fan secretly does not mind archeology in the least but finds it better to be seen as filial than to be seen as enjoying his duties. The more he 'hates' his work, the more filial he is seen to be.

While Confucian and religious beliefs about filial duty are common in Chinese society, they are unusually prevalent – whether as beliefs, rhetorical tools, or guides to behaviour – among intellectuals. Traditionally (until 1905), scholar-officials had to pass the imperial civil service exam, a test that, like the modern university entrance exam, required grave sacrifices by parents and children. It is, I think, no coincidence that scholars then and intellectuals now have perpetuated a strong version of filial duty through repetition in stories, poems, and prescriptive literature.

In any case, one might as well depend on whatever praise one can get out of filial duty, because in a system of draconian university entrance exams there is little opportunity to be praised for success in or choice of career. In the North American context, an archeology student might be praised by others for making such an independent choice of career rather than going to law or medical school like so many others. In China, where a student who becomes an archeologist because he received fifty-five rather than fifty-six points on an exam, questions such as 'How did you choose archeology?' and 'How did you become interested?' and 'Why do you like it?' are nonsensical.

Archeology is considered an unpopular subject since practitioners have little likelihood of making money and are not taught the skills that bring success in the economic sector. Students cannot change disciplines once they have entered university, but they can choose electives in other disciplines in which they are more interested. The result is that, among students in archeology, a significant number do not intend to become archeologists. They do what they have to do to graduate and spend the rest of their time studying English and economics. If they have these subjects, then at least they have the hope of getting a job in the economic sector, even with a degree in archeology. Many of the students whom I met on excavations went so far as to say that they passionately despised archeology but were determined to do as well as possible to get the degree *(wenping)* that could still lead them somewhere useful. Education itself becomes reduced to the social contract between parent and child: there is an investment in the child by the parents, and the child responds by giving back a return to the parents.

The relationship, however, cannot be simplistically characterized as one of tyranny of parent over a defenceless child. It must be seen instead as following a paternalistic pattern in which the anxious parent gives everything that he or she thinks the child might need and the subsequent guilt of the child being enough to secure obedience. Yet there is ample room for the child to get what he or she wants out of the relationship: Wang, for example, describes herself as being 'held hostage' by her daughter, who insists that she cannot study for the exam (in her case, it is 'only' the senior high school exam) unless she has certain snack foods and, above all, an air conditioner. Who, here, is the tyrant? Similarly, Li, a vice director of a different *danwei*, has been forced to discover video games and computers due to his son's desires. The situation is exacerbated and intensified since archeologists, like most intellectuals, have only one child. The relationship is, above all, mutual: it becomes ever more tightly knit and intense as the university entrance exam draws near, yet paradoxically, the more intense it becomes, the greater the latitude for each side to compel the other to do his or her bidding by bartering gifts in the form of material goods (parents) or study hours and exam grades (children).

The number of children who get into elementary or secondary school is quite low, and the number of those who get into university lower still, so it must be understood that there are many other types of relationships between parents and children.[11] But this is an ethnography about educated children and their parents. The parents' values are saturated by the need to make intellectuals out of their children, and parents are driven by real and imagined fears about the educational system that might bar the success of their plans. The uncertainties of success drive them to create close-knit relations of dependency with their children; children, in turn, learn how to barter with their parents.[12] Having lived through this rather intense relationship, archeologists metaphorically extend the mutuality and barter aspects of the parent-child relationship to the two other hierarchical relationships of importance in their lives: teacher-student and superior-inferior relationships. We will examine the teacher-student relationship in this chapter and the superior-inferior relationship in Chapter 5.

High School Teacher and Student

Children are taught to relate to teachers from the moment that they step into school.[13] As the child grows up, each teacher along the way contributes to his success in the exams, but the senior high school teacher takes on the greatest importance and has the final say in all matters of the child's educational life. Given the difficulties of succeeding in the university entrance exam, the senior high school teacher can often take on a greater importance than the parents. The parents 'merely' feed and house the child, preparing the home environment to be the most conducive to studying as possible. The teacher, however, does most of the work of changing a child into a successful student. She – teachers are nearly always women at this stage – is a repository of all knowledge important to the exam, provides studying advice, and is a specialist in matters relating to exam bureaucracy and choosing a university. Both child and parents will therefore defer to the teacher's knowledge and opinion when it comes to deciding whether to invest in a child in the first place and, once the exam is taken, choosing a discipline or school.

Since the prestige of the university is always more important than the discipline, the senior high school teacher will decide to place a child in an unpopular subject in order to get him into a better school. A university student named Yao told me how he 'wanted to die' when he first heard that he had been assigned to the less than prestigious Xiamen University (XiaDa), a placement made all the more horrible since XiaDa is in the south, while his family lives in Beijing. Yao's dream had been to enter the Department of Chinese Language and Literature (Yao had never thought much about archeology), but had he insisted on studying literature he would have had to go to an even less prestigious university. It is important to understand that Yao's teacher had made this decision alone and without much more than a cursory consultation with Yao and his parents. Nevertheless, both Yao and his parents understood that his teacher had done the best she could to get him into the most prestigious university possible given his results and were grateful that she had helped him to pass the exam and get into a university in the first place. Yao's relationship with that teacher remains strong, and every time Yao goes home he makes a point of visiting her and bringing her gifts and news of university.

The strong relationship between teacher and student has its own traditions and values. These traditions have not been diminished by the attack on tradition undertaken during the Cultural Revolution that was so uncomfortable and often deadly for teachers.[14] If anything, it appears that, at least among archeologists of a certain age, the guilt people feel about what they did to their teachers during the Cultural Revolution has made them more 'filial' and obedient to those teachers.

That the word *filial* appears in discussions about the proper behaviour of students toward teachers is an indication of how easily the teacher-student and parent-child relationships are conflated. The parent-child relationship acts as what Victor Turner might call the 'root metaphor' for many other hierarchical relationships.[15] Even when it is not directly involved, its structure and value system affect, sometimes consciously and sometimes not, other mutual and unequal relationships. The teacher, especially in the lives of scholars and intellectuals, protects and guides the student just as a parent is supposed to protect and guide a child. Therefore, the teacher must be treated with the same sense of respect and honour as a parent. This is not to say that actual parents (or actual teachers or children) all live up to the ideals stated here but to say that a person who makes a significant effort to guide and protect a person will be treated *as if* he or she is a parent.

The ideal teacher-student relationship, then, imagines that a 'proper' teacher cares for and guides the student; in return, the student dutifully obeys the teacher. Again like the parent-child relationship, this one lasts forever. Strong connections are maintained between teachers and students, especially if a student is successful on the exam and becomes an intellectual. Of course, many students in China are not successful, do not become intellectuals, and have differing opinions, images, and expectations of their high school teachers. Once again, it is important to remember that this is an ethnography of successful students; it is therefore no coincidence that these relationships have such an important role to play among archeologists. Incidentally, given that the literati and scholarly class in pre-modern China faced the same uncertainties engendered by difficult entrance exams, and considering that Confucius himself was a teacher, it is also no coincidence that ideal teacher-student relationships are extolled and perpetuated in Chinese literary, philosophical, religious, and artistic productions.

Student and University Teacher

The relationship with the high school teacher differs from that with the university teacher[16] because the conditions of exchange in the relationship are limited. After all, the relationship between student and high school teacher is necessarily short term: if the student succeeds on the exam, then he leaves for university. Although he may come back once or twice a year, the relationship is attenuated. There is no incentive for either side to maintain a strong relationship. It is only when the relationship is expected to be long term and mutually beneficial, in a direct and obvious way not limited to the occasional food basket sent around New Year's, that either teacher or student will take more care to maintain it. When the teacher can see that a student will be valuable in the future, there is simply more reason to ensure that the student is happy, and the student therefore has the leverage to get whatever he may desire.

The relationship with the university teacher is indeed one of long-term mutual benefit and is worthy of the Chinese term *shitu guanxi* (relations between master and disciple). In Chapter 3, we will examine in greater depth which resources, material and immaterial, are bartered between university professors and their students and how the relationship can become increasingly beneficial over time. The discussion here is limited to the conditions of uncertainty that drive university students to police and enforce the social contract between themselves and their university teachers.

When the student arrives at university, he becomes a part of that year's cohort of students and meets the set of university teachers that will affect and guide all aspects of his subsequent career. That there is more than one teacher is important in itself, because for the first time a student is presented with a choice among teachers. Each teacher has his (teachers are nearly always men at this stage) own specialty in archeology, his own prestige in the discipline, his own personality, and his own strong likes and dislikes regarding appropriate student behaviour. Eventually, in their upper years, students will have to decide with whom they will pursue more intense and special relationships.

Nevertheless, at the beginning of the university experience, one teacher does have an immediate impact: the cohort teacher. Somewhat like a homeroom teacher, the cohort teacher takes care of the bureaucratic, health, and dormitory needs of the students. This teacher takes on the role of parent in an explicitly maternal way (the men themselves joke about their motherly role): it is his responsibility to teach the students how to take care of themselves.

Why would students at the age of seventeen or eighteen need to be instructed to take care of themselves? As we have seen, before arrival at university and regardless of class background, students are entirely shielded from the requirements of daily life. To be successful, students are raised to be utterly dependent on others and are nearly helpless without that close support network. In the first term of the first year, students are therefore enrolled in a six- to eight-week military-style course in which they are taught to do laundry, clean themselves and their rooms, and manage their personal belongings. The cohort teacher both ensures that the students have learned the basics of self-care and continues to watch over them after the course is finished. If a student looks sick, badly dressed, appears too thin or too fat, or otherwise shows signs of trouble, the cohort leader has the responsibility to address the issue.

Archeology students are rather different from other university students because they must be taken out on a practice excavation, or practicum *(shixi)*, in their third year (and sometimes again in the fourth year). One or two teachers are assigned to this task, and they have a different relationship with the student from that of the cohort teacher.[17] Yet even these teachers must ensure the safety of the students. Although these third-year students have had two years away from home, they still know very little about 'the real world' outside the university gates. Students' inexperience is not simply an assumption by the teachers but also a notion shared by the students themselves. As far as the students are concerned, they are inexperienced and are unnerved by the idea of learning how to plan, pack, negotiate a train station, find food, or otherwise prepare for the excavation. They are avowedly petrified of travelling, particularly into the Chinese countryside. It is traditional to imagine the countryside as some kind of backward and wild place filled with unknown dangers, and the students' fears are exacerbated not only by the tales that older students and teachers tell about what can go wrong during excavations but also by their anxious parents, who imagine that their precious children will encounter all sorts of dangers while travelling.[18]

University teachers, for their part, are in a difficult position with regard to the fears of the students and the requirement to lead them all into the countryside for a period of at least three months. The teachers must ensure not only that nothing actually goes wrong but also that the students feel as if they are well taken care of and protected. If the students perceive the field experience otherwise, then they will complain, and if those complaints are heard by the parents, the university administration, or the party secretary, then the repercussions on the individual teacher's career can be severe.

Both the students and the teachers are fully aware of the power of the students. The students feel free to demand that teachers do everything in their power to reassure them. In China, reassurance takes a visible and corporeal form: the students' environments and bodies must be seen as being under the complete control of the teachers. Both before and during the excavation, the teachers craft elaborate performances of control: the students are allowed to bring only a certain set of objects, wear certain clothing, and eat only certain foods. Since both teachers and students worry about injuries and accidents, students are not allowed to (and would not want to in any case) go for walks or otherwise leave either the excavation site or their living quarters. From the students' perspective, a 'well-run excavation' is one where every moment of spare time is organized for them. Each student must *feel* regulated as well as *be* regulated before he will describe himself as feeling secure. By being utterly dependent on the teachers, the students ensure that their environment is controlled in a way that they recognize as appropriate and acceptable.

As someone brought up to feel (or at least perform as if I feel) fiercely capable, who would be insulted and shocked by any teacher who dared to suggest what I ought to bring or eat as if I were a kid going off to summer camp, the regulated environment of the excavation appeared patronizing and invasive. For both students and teachers in China, however, the situation is seen as an expected and normal result of the ignorance and inexperience of the students. The students demand this treatment as their *right*. They speak about it explicitly in the language of contract: in return for a teacher's protection, the student feels it a duty to work hard and do whatever the teacher needs done. Students will also take on the burden of disciplining fellow students, if need be, to ensure that everyone in the group acts appropriately with regard to the teacher in order to maintain this contract between them. Obedience, the students believe, is the gift that will force the teacher to protect and guide them as he should.

I visited six practicum sites in the Three Gorges region of Sichuan Province, and it is instructive to compare the experiences of the students of a southern university (SoDa) to those of the students of a northern university (NoDa). The SoDa archeology department had not provided its practicum teacher with either a great deal of money or much help despite the fact that he was a single teacher: he was taking care of twenty-one students. SoDa's female students, all eleven of them, had to sleep in the same room, half on the floor under the beds of the other half, while their male classmates slept in the hall. Not incidentally, SoDa had also been assigned to a ridiculously barren archeological site that was yielding little of importance. NoDa, in contrast, was blessed with no fewer than three teachers, only twelve students, and lots of money. The students were three to a room and very well fed. To top it all off, they had been assigned a fairly interesting site. The SoDa students, however, could have cared less about all of that. They waxed wistful not about NoDa's comforts, or the rate at which the students were learning archeology, but about the excellence of NoDa's *teachers*.

SoDa students were wistful because they believed that they were saddled with what they considered the worst teacher in existence. Unlike the other teachers, Teacher Wu had some very bizarre ideas about teaching. He forced the students, for example, to make all of their own food, causing no little discomfort in the form of food poisoning nearly every other night. The students had never cooked before. They also had to go to the market to buy groceries and many of the tools and living items such as washbasins and blankets. And Teacher Wu did not accompany the students on these shopping trips. Nor did he send a graduate student, manager, or even technician with them. He did not even allow the peasant woman in whose house they lived to help them. She was as distressed as the students about the whole situation since, as she pointed out many a time, the students were being cheated in the market as well as buying inappropriate amounts and kinds of food. SoDa Teacher Wu did not make many friends among his students. He believed strongly that the students needed to learn to take care of themselves. The students, in return, firmly thought that his belief was utterly inappropriate. Wu was thus guilty of the worst crime: breaking the contract between teacher and student by refusing to protect the students.

One must feel only sympathy for the poor (metaphorically and economically) SoDa students, who, in addition to feeling the usual fears of encountering disaster and making mistakes, had to deal with a teacher who refused to protect them. The SoDa students had no idea how to behave with the peasants, cook food, organize their living quarters, or excavate the site. They also had no idea how to relate to such a strange teacher.

To understand what they should have been doing, we need only turn to the NoDa excavation. NoDa students were extraordinarily well behaved. They had nothing to complain about with regard to their teacher and spent most of their time policing each other. As we will see in the discussion of cohort behaviour below, students have a well-established structure for ensuring the discipline of the entire group. NoDa students were exemplary in both the obedience to their teachers and the harshness with which they punished any of their own who stepped out of line. Indeed, they had certain incentives to help the teacher ensure that the excavation ran smoothly: as one NoDa student, who had just told a fellow student to stop spending so much time talking to me (thereby slowing down the excavation), said with unusual fierceness, 'I just want to get home and never return to the countryside again. Anyone who interferes [with this plan] must be stopped.'

In contrast, SoDa students found themselves without structure. Since their teacher refused to accede to the duties incumbent on him as a teacher, the students did not feel the need to obey him or listen to him, nor did they see any reason to police each other. SoDa students were the only ones who went for walks, though even then they went in small groups. They once even came to visit me at the NoDa excavation, something that no other students or archeologists in the Three Gorges region did, even though I regularly walked the forty-five minutes that it took to reach four other university practicum sites. SoDa students also ate local junk food (they were hungry most of the time) and (most dangerous of all, as will be seen in Chapter 6) interacted with local peasants of their own age. They fought openly among themselves over their respective duties. Compared with those of NoDa, their living quarters were chaotic. Nevertheless, habit combined with a sense of trying to get whatever they could out of their teacher encouraged them to obey Wu in matters of archeological excavation. Wu, after all, was an excellent archeologist, and the students were happy to learn archeological techniques even if they were finding nothing of importance (not even a grave) at their site.

Unlike SoDa Teacher Wu, the teachers of all the other practicum sites that I visited took great pains to organize and regulate the experiences of their students. The teachers saw it as an arduous and complex project given that they had to manage all the aspects of student life and all the requirements of an archeological expedition. Many older teachers waxed highly nostalgic about the 'good old days' when the students were older, more mature, less afraid, and altogether more competent. They were referring to the latter part of the Cultural Revolution and just after the reinstatement of the university entrance exam, from 1972 to 1980. During this time, although there was no university entrance exam, the schools were not idle. Teachers had been brought back from their exile in the countryside or their near imprisonment in the cities to teach a whole different set of students from the traditional sort (who were still in the countryside): the *gong* (workers), *nong* (farmers), and *bing* (soldiers).

Students who attended the Schools for Workers, Peasants, and Soldiers (*Gong Nong Bing Xuexiao*, hereafter GNB) were chosen by their work units based on their political credentials and class backgrounds. They are remembered as being difficult to teach because of their diverse educational levels. Nevertheless, the burden on the teachers was much lighter simply because the students all came with a great deal of experience in taking care of themselves and their families (most were much older than the twenty-year-old third-year students of today). The group of students who took the exam when it was reinstated in 1977 and 1978 were seen to be even better than GNB students because they were highly skilled in taking care of themselves (and older than the norm), better educated than the GNB students (there had been no exam for those students), and therefore easier to teach. There was, then, a brief period of about three years during which the teachers had both skilled and well-educated students. To this day, teachers tell wistful stories about that thoroughly wonderful moment in archeological history.

In contrast, the youngsters of today are 'selfish, spoiled, and ignorant.' Their demands are many. Even though they give the teachers respect and obedience in return, the teachers still fear the tyranny of their demands. The more prestigious the school, the more power the students hold in this relationship since, as 'students of higher quality,' they have more power to make life difficult for the teachers by complaining.

The experience of the SoDa students helps to illustrate the effect of class and prestige on the power of the students in the social contract. All the SoDa students came from very poor backgrounds (SoDa was not a prestigious school). Their parents, as peasants, would not dare to criticize Wu. I heard the SoDa students angrily planning to attack Wu once they returned to the campus, but I do not know whether they could be successful without the support and guidance of someone more sophisticated than their parents, someone with more social clout. The archeology department at SoDa, given that Teacher Wu is the vice director there, was unlikely to support the students' claims.

In more prestigious schools, the only thing that stops the students, as the sons and daughters of more educated parents, from abusing their power is fear of breaking the social contract by making too many demands. The students are driven by their belief that they are inexperienced, by their fear of the countryside, and not incidentally, by their sincere desire to return to the city as soon as possible, so they will spend time and effort to maintain and police the social contract.

The Teachings of Orthopraxy

From the teacher's point of view, the contract between student and teacher requires something more than simply ensuring the students' protection and well-being. The teacher also takes it as his explicit duty to teach the students how to be adults – that is, how to take care of themselves both physically and socially in the Chinese context. A fully adult archeologist, after all, has to be able to take care of himself as well as plan and run an excavation. Given the need for archeologists to have significant interactions with local peasants, workers, and officials, the teacher is particularly worried about the fact that students are desperately ignorant about society and the finer points of social interaction. The younger students especially are incapable of understanding most of what the teacher tries to teach them about society. Even stories and analogies do not work. The students tend to take explanations and stories at the surface level: they do not hear the ironies or intended jokes, nor can they tell whether a story is meant to relay an exception or the norm. If the story is meant to illustrate some principle of social interaction, then the students might learn the principle but not realize that the implementation of principles is more context-dependent and flexible than a single story can possibly convey.

Since stories are clearly problematic as teaching tools, most of the teachers whom I met believed that the only way to learn how to be an archeologist/fully adult member of Chinese society is through experience and observation. Therefore, and once again in the explicit terminology of contract, the teacher accepts it as his responsibility to require students to accompany him in any number of activities. Students must go along with the teacher to the library, stand by while he deals with office personnel, go with him to buy train tickets, or tag along to the market. No matter is too small or mundane to be included in the day's lesson.

All students are given opportunities to watch their teachers in action, but only some students are brought fully into a teacher's life (we will examine how and why in Chapter 3). When a student is chosen to be a teacher's apprentice, the contract between teacher and student becomes stronger and more intimate. The teacher 'ups the stakes' in the contract by offering the student the chance to become ever more involved in every aspect of the teacher's life, thereby binding the student more closely to the teacher. Teacher Cao's chosen apprentice, for example, was often invited to accompany Cao to the local village. Along the way, there were ample opportunities for him to observe Cao's marvellous capacity to connect with boatmen on the river or sellers in the market. When I arrived at Cao's practicum site, for example, the apprentice came along with Cao to pick me up at the pier. The apprentice was therefore able to watch how Cao dealt with a foreigner (me), and we both saw Cao thank the ferry captain for my safe journey (I had never met or even seen the captain during the three-day trip). Cao explained to us that he was making connections through me to the ferry captain – the reason might not be immediately apparent, but, as he explained, we should always be prepared to make connections wherever we can. Cao's explicit analyses of social interactions were common to all of the teachers whom I met and were clearly believed to be an important aspect of the archeological education. Part of the teacher-student contract, then, is the teaching of civility, good manners, respect, and, above all, deference to the peasants, officials, and others whom students will encounter during their archeological careers.

These aspects of social interaction are important to the maintenance of smooth interpersonal relations. There are always good reasons to show respect, whether one actually feels it or not, and deference is part and parcel of being civil. Young, arrogant, and ignorant students, flushed with their success in getting into university, proud of the history and responsibilities of their class, and spoiled by their parents, must be given more reasons to discover the price of arrogance and the benefits of simple good manners. The students must also be taught that 'good manners' are judged by the audience for whom they are intended; if the audience does not think the behaviour appropriate, then, despite any or all of the good intentions of the person attempting to be polite, the audience will be insulted.

I was asked one day to accompany Cao to the market. We bought provisions and then decided to have his shoes (grass, not leather[19]) repaired. I was not feeling tired, so I remained standing while we waited for the shoemaker to finish. Cao asked me to sit down, and I refused. He reacted immediately by reprimanding me. He explained that it is important to show patience whenever waiting for someone else to do work. He criticized me for being so insensitive to the situation of the shoemaker that I would hover over him and make him feel rushed. I became embarrassed that Cao was reprimanding me in public and became even more so when he turned to the shoemaker to elicit his opinion on the matter.

Cao felt that it was his duty to lecture me. That we were in public had no bearing (for him) on the issue. I think back to my experiences in school and remember that teachers would only discipline a student in public if they wanted to inflict maximum humiliation. But Cao was not in any way attempting to humiliate me. He was only performing his appropriate role for all to see – and assumed that I would perform mine in return. The teacher is the one who lectures; the student is the one who learns. It is not humiliating for the student to be ignorant or to have to be told something a second or third time. It is only embarrassing if the student is inattentive or breaks the implicit contract between teacher and student: it turns out that it was Cao who felt humiliated and embarrassed by my refusal to sit down.

Moreover, I realized that my sense of shame was related to the fact that Cao was telling me, loudly and with frequent stops to get everyone around us to agree, how to act to make myself *look* like a better person. When Cao first criticized me, I replied that I was not feeling impatient and that it was not my *intention* to annoy the shoemaker. This excuse failed utterly to mollify Cao. In fact, I think that he thought I was being quite stupid. He did not care whether I was or was not tired, whether I was stretching my cramped legs, or whether some other little personal problem might explain why I was hovering over the shoemaker. The point is that I was hovering: clearly, my intent with regard to the shoemaker was unimportant; what mattered is that it was customary to sit and look relaxed while waiting in order to show respect for the work being undertaken.

My sense of shame when told by Cao to *act* like a better person arose out of my own education. I had been told by parents and teachers that there is a difference between 'pretending' to be a good person and 'being' a good person.[20] My training had posited a separation between an essential person and what everyone else perceives a person to be. So a person can be perceived as bad yet remain good (presumably, this notion of inner, invisible goodness is related to the idea of a transcendent, all-knowing God who will judge a person's quality). Not so for Cao and my many other teachers, who took such great pains to explain to me that there can be no difference between being and perception.

What Cao was doing, of course, was trying to teach me the concept of 'orthopraxy' in the negotiation of relations with other people. Being civil and polite requires understanding exactly what it is that will be considered civil and polite by the audience-that-matters. This audience must include the immediate person whom one does not want to insult (in my case, the shoemaker) as well as the bystanders or one's own friends, teachers, or family members who may have the opportunity to see the event in question. 'Every interaction,' said Cao, 'is an opportunity to show you understand society.'

One's motive in acting correctly cannot simply be because one wants to smooth relations with the person most immediately affected, such as the shoemaker, so that he might give a better price or do a better job fixing the shoes. Nor can it simply be because a student wants to make the teacher proud in front of everyone in the market. Nor can it be limited to the satisfaction arising from having interacted correctly and pleasing the shoemaker. A person's motives could include all of the above yet still be more complex: for example, part of a long-term plan to make the teacher proud so that he might work harder to find the student a good job after graduation. Or, more interestingly, a student might make a mistake to give the teacher the opportunity to show off his teaching skill in front of people in the market. A person's reasons for acting can be multiple and mixed; the point here, however, is that, regardless of the *substantive* nature of the incentive, there are strong reasons for acting appropriately in any given social interaction.

To act appropriately leaves what is going on inside a person's head – the motives or plans – entirely up to that person. People are free, and I use that word advisedly, to think what they wish. But they are not free to act as they please. In a later conversation about this incident, I brought up some of these ideas with Cao. He noted that the companion idea to *orthopraxy,* that of *orthodoxy,* has had of late a problematic history. Orthodoxy is the notion that people should believe in what they are doing when they are doing it. Cao referred to the attempt by Mao during the Cultural Revolution to ensure that people were thinking and feeling exactly what he wanted them to think and feel. Unfortunately, it is very difficult to work out whether people are actually feeling and believing what one wants them to feel and believe. Mao's attempt to judge whether others had proper intentions led to chaos and brutality as people accused each other of thinking incorrect thoughts. Since that time, the attempt to expose or direct other people's innermost thoughts has fallen out of favour in preference for an emphasis on orthopraxy. For Cao, the teacher's role was to engage in the socialization of the student such that he or she acts like a 'good student.' Matters of intention or internal worth ought to be left, said Cao with some disdain, to the party secretary.[21]

This incident marked the first time that I began to recognize that 'playing a role' not only is a safe, secure, and indeed predictable thing to do but also endows one with the freedom to think as one wishes in a way with which I was unfamiliar. No longer did I have to ensure that my actions and my intentions were in line. Once I knew the rules, being a student in relation to a teacher, and being good at it, was easy. When I met a new teacher, I knew what he expected me to do to show that I was ready to be obedient in the Chinese manner. As a result, he made sure to teach me what he thought I should know about archeology or Chinese society, would willingly correct me when I made mistakes, and would come to my aid if I inadvertently insulted another person. A student in China always has someone who will teach and protect him or her from the significant uncertainties of complex social interactions as well as from the more obvious physical dangers of life. Cao, Li, Bai, and other teachers whom I met taught me various things: when it was polite to wash my face and why sometimes it really was not, how much to drink at which kind of banquet, interesting tidbits about Chinese archeology and history, how to work with peasants or buy things at the market, and the proper kind of gift to give in which context. In other words, they did not separate bringing me up as a 'proper (civil) Chinese person' from bringing me up as a 'proper archeologist.'

Best of all, I was praised all the more as a good student the more I relied on their teachings and the more willing I was to follow their examples. Like every student, I was taught that, in return for my obedience, I would receive both material benefits in the form of protection from physical harm, and less tangible benefits in the form of praise, information, and guidance. The junior-senior contract persists exactly because it represents a combination of mutual incentives and freedoms.

In terms of incentives, the contract not only benefits both sides but also provides a variety and mixture of benefits such that in the group there must be at least one thing attractive to someone. A junior might, for example, seek the satisfaction of making others (parents, teachers) proud of him and enjoy the opportunities to show how well he has learned a lesson and to receive praise. Others might desire something more concrete, such as a job, a connection, a better deal on the goods being sold, or better services. Similarly, a senior might want the satisfaction of seeing a student do well, or he might want the more concrete benefits of obedience, such as loyalty and preferential treatment, as the student grows up and gains control over significant resources himself. In short, whatever it is that one wants, one can likely get it through the social contract.

For the second element of the combination, it must be understood here that 'freedom' refers to two things: the 'freedom from uncertainty' as well as the 'freedom from being forced to ally intent with action.' When the junior-senior contract is working correctly, everyone undertakes to perform the given roles as expected. Uncertainty about what to do in the event of disaster is mitigated by the notions that, from the junior's perspective, the senior will protect and guide the junior and, from the senior's perspective, that the junior will do as he is told even when under stress. Uncertainty about how to act or the predictability of the actions of others is also contained by the assumption that no one will try to surprise anyone else. Freedom from uncertainty is matched by freedom from moral governance, for there is no moral expectation that intent should match action. Thus, while the individual plans and goals that may motivate any individual junior or senior in any given relationship are truly legion and no doubt infinitely complex, no one really needs to think or worry about them. As long as the appropriate and expected actions are being bartered within the relation, both sides are satisfied.

The Cohort Contract and the Domestication of Difference

Orthopraxy requires the doctrine of similarity: the notion that all people, all over China, act and interpret each other's actions in similar ways *(datong xiaoyi)*. Only if there is a will to believe, maintain, and reinforce this doctrine can people imagine that they can predict or interpret other people's actions or be sure that their own actions will be interpreted as intended.

This will to believe is not 'natural' and must be learned. More importantly, there must be incentives such that people maintain their will to believe in the face of the manifest differences among Chinese people. In the course of learning civility and good manners, the differences among students are *domesticated:* that is, made unimportant or denied altogether. One of the many methods of domesticating difference that we will encounter throughout this book is the creation of the classmate cohort.[22] Much like the extension of the parent-child relationship to the teacher-student relationship, the cohort model, and the contractual relations that underlie it, are metaphorically extended to groups of friends that crosscut bureaucratic boundaries (as discussed in Chapter 4).[23]

Theoretically, the notion of a 'cohort' is contradictory. On the one hand, by definition, everyone within the group is equal. The students all share more or less the same age and, by virtue of having passed the entrance exam, the same status. The exam cannot lie: each student should end up precisely where his ability places him. There is therefore no hierarchy possible among these students since they are *supposed* to be at the same level and of the same intelligence and ability. Yet, on the other hand, each student comes to the group as a stranger to the others and has different regional, educational, and class backgrounds. To deal with the contradictions in the cohort concept, teachers must accomplish a double structural move: stripping *unacceptable* difference from the students and imposing *acceptable* difference on the students by structuring their relations with each other using the approved bureaucratic model.

Unacceptable differences are those of worldview, background, class, or experience that might subvert the doctrine of similarity. People can be differentiated from each other given that they come from different regions and social classes, are gendered, and possess different educational backgrounds and goals. Many of these differences are domesticated through widely disseminated stereotypes. For example, regional stereotypes insist that northerners are more community oriented and honest, while southerners are sly and more prone to selfish interests than the good of the community. These differences are not what is meant by unacceptable differences and are even reinforced among the students. These stereotypes, after all, are well known across China, and their purported impact on social interaction is equally well known. In my brief introduction of orthopraxy, I let the reader imagine that students are taught a general and simple notion of social interaction in China. In fact, they are made aware of regional and class differences from very early on so that they may easily typify the kinds of actions to be expected from each group and the appropriate responses to them. Chapter 5 will discuss stereotypes, or what I will call credentials, as both acceptable difference and the fracturing of identity, but here I want to return to the notion of unacceptable differences.

The first year of university marks the first time that students have been away from their families and schoolteachers, the people who have always made all decisions on their behalf. Students are thus often beset by the illusion that they are in control of their own lives. The relative freedom is significant enough for them to remark often on it. This belief in their ability to control their lives is woefully incorrect: as they move through university, they find a new set of people in their lives – their university teachers and their peers in the cohort administration – whose opinions will become ever more important to them. Although the four years of university yield close, fairly noncompetitive relationships among their peers, it is still a goal-oriented training session directed to the all-important end of getting a job. Teachers are very aware that they are training students to get the best jobs they can and that these jobs will throw the young students into a society of superiors and colleagues who are not as nice and noncompetitive as university classmates.

The first-year students in their innocence run a little 'wild' in university – not in the North American sense of drinking heavily, taking drugs, or dancing all night (these kinds of activities are extremely rare) but in the sense of making decisions without fully exploring all the options. They imagine that they can do whatever they want to do, even choosing classes based on personal interests, without regard for the hierarchical interpersonal relationships between them and their elders or more authoritative peers. Since most students are rarely interested in archeology anyway, they often take classes in business, economics, or English – skipping or ignoring archeology classes altogether. The result can be extremely negative if their parents and teachers decide that the student will have to become an archeologist in the end. Such students are then woefully ill prepared for archeological tasks and, worse, because they have not cultivated appropriate relations with their teachers, will be given unfortunate job placements. Students also 'run wild' by treating certain people as friends and potential marriage partners without asking for their parents' or teachers' approval: again, they can be dismally surprised when their parents, teachers, or peers step in and force them to break these ties in order to spend more time with the kind of people thought to be more beneficial to the cohort, family, or discipline of archeology.

Making choices based solely on self-interest is obviously one of the most unacceptable sources of difference among the students. It is in complete opposition to the social contract because it flouts the notion that a person's actions can be correctly predicted and interpreted. If people are acting on the basis of personal intent and impulse, then nothing can be certain, surprises are likely, and misunderstanding, insult, or some other disaster is that much greater. Last, but not least, the reaction of the student when he or she must finally be introduced to the realities of *danwei* life is likely to be that much more exacerbated and harmful.

Differences in attitude, temperament, and experience are also considered unacceptable unless they can be channelled into the activities for which they are appropriate. Some students arrive excited, some depressed, some unhappy, some arrogant: these are problems of attitude and must be corrected. Some students tend to talk too much; others are more quiet and shy: once again, these are issues of temperament and must be minimized and controlled. Some students come with more or less than the average experience or knowledge of school, archeology, or personal care: these differences, too, must be excised. They are unacceptable because they threaten the notion that everyone acts the same.

In many cultures, the socialization of students begins in grade school, during which time the classroom teacher must perforce deal with all of these issues.[24] The teacher must perform a balancing act by, for example, directing the material at the average student, forcing the untalkative students to speak while restraining the others, and intervening when students make fun of each other or become too proud or arrogant. The difference in China, perhaps, is simply the age at which students begin to learn how to behave among their peers. Chinese grade school teachers do not have the latitude to change their teaching techniques to suit their students or to intervene too much on behalf of the students' moral character. For one thing, they simply have no time: there is a set amount of material to cover, most of it requires rote memorization, and the students spend their time explicitly studying for exams. For another thing, the students themselves rarely have the time to relate to each other in any fashion beyond helping each other study for the exams. Chinese students are not as well practised in the art of human interaction as, say, students from countries in which high school is more about socialization than learning.

The cohort model accomplishes the socialization required remarkably rapidly and efficiently by replacing unacceptable differences with acceptable distinctions. First, students are organized into cohorts based on discipline and year of arrival at university. Chinese universities are residential, such that students room with cohort members from the same department (or closely related departments, such as history in the case of archeology, if the numbers do not work out). Six to eight students room together and will retain the same roommates for the next four years. Since classes are assigned and there are very few electives, everyone has almost the same class schedule and will go to class, eat, wash, and relax together. The combined effect of the close living quarters, same schedule, and especially the first six weeks of military training is to force students to see themselves as an interdependent group based on what appears to be an incontrovertible, 'essential' similarity: age. That there are different ages among the students (some take longer to pass the entrance exam) is ignored in favour of assuming that they all are more or less the same.[25] In the context of the cohort, then, all

regional, class, and gender differences are minimized in favour of the realization that, above all, they are students with similar clothes, food, lodging,
and leisure and class schedules.

Second, about halfway through the first year, the cohort teacher and students work together to re-create difference by structuring the group's relations hierarchically. A cohort leader, party secretary, social events coordinator,
and health manager are chosen. Students to fill these roles are chosen by
the cohort teacher, other teachers, and the students themselves. The choice
is usually based on a recognition of a student's sense of responsibility and
ability to socialize, and, for the most part, students who have the tempera-
ments of leaders or who are already familiar with taking care of themselves
are diverted into leading roles. The student can refuse the honour, but it is
exceedingly rare that a student who does not want these duties will be chosen in the first place.

The cohort leader organizes classroom homework assignments and con-
veys information from the teachers to the students; he or she is responsible
for the general well-being and organization of the class. The party secretary
runs the meetings and workshops that represent ongoing attempts to relate

Figure 1

Allocation of roles and duties in the student cohort

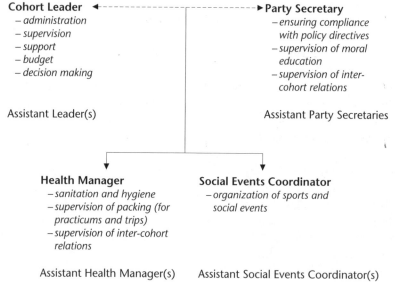

Student cohort

Cohort Leader
– administration
– supervision
– support
– budget
– decision making

Assistant Leader(s)

Party Secretary
– ensuring compliance
  with policy directives
– supervision of moral
  education
– supervision of inter-
  cohort relations

Assistant Party Secretaries

Health Manager
– sanitation and hygiene
– supervision of packing (for
  practicums and trips)
– supervision of inter-cohort
  relations

Assistant Health Manager(s)

Social Events Coordinator
– organization of sports and
  social events

Assistant Social Events Coordinator(s)

communist theory to practice and translate party directives into student activities. If there are any 'moral' problems – cohort members becoming romantically involved or quarrelling with each other – the party secretary and the cohort leader step in to mediate. The social events coordinator organizes sports events (often with other departments), movies, picnics, or shopping expeditions that are the main extracurricular activities of Chinese students. Finally, the health manager helps the rest of the cohort administration to organize the students, maintains hygiene, and ensures that students clean and manage their rooms and themselves properly. The manager reports health issues to the home-room teacher.

Differences of attitude, temperament, or ability are further domesticated as each of these bureaucratic leaders begins to choose among the remaining students those who will help them undertake their responsibilities. Like any *danwei*, the cohort hierarchy quickly becomes finely differentiated, with named leaders – including the four main leaders and their 'assistant' *(fu)* leaders (such that there is a cohort leader and one or two assistant cohort leaders, a health manager and assistant health manager, a social coordinator and assistant coordinator, and so on) – and a relatively small number of unnamed followers. Grades play an interesting role: often the students with the best grades remain part of the unnamed followers so that, much like a parent or teacher protecting the outstanding student likely to succeed, they can concentrate on their studies without being bothered by the needs of bureaucracy.

Assertion of the cohort model on what began simultaneously as an undifferentiated mass and a random collection of distinct individuals manages to remove any of the unacceptable differences and replace them with acceptable modes of interaction among the students. Once roles and responsibilities have been assigned, the students' interactions become increasingly structured according to the bureaucratic models that will be so important to them when they enter the *danwei*. The cohort model teaches the students how to make friends and how to break off friendships, how to negotiate despite petty grievances, and how to overcome differences. The primary way that students learn to cooperate and maintain relationships with others, despite any number of personal and political barriers, is, after all, through their relations with each other. This aspect of student life is considered so important that the cohort teacher will base grades on how well students appear to be interacting as a group. The need to be seen as acting correctly, to perform group behaviour, is necessarily intensified by having one's grades tied to performance.

While I was visiting a third-year practicum site run by a university in the midnorth region of China, for example, the students were called together by the teacher and criticized for being too 'scattered' *(san)*. The cohort party secretary and cohort leader were reproved for being incompetent in the mediation of disputes, and a new cohort leader was assigned to fix the problems among the group. Had this explicit restructuring of the cohort not occurred, and had the teachers not been so reproving of their students, I never would have noticed that the group was not cohesive. As far as I could tell, the students spent all their time together and did not appear to quarrel. I was completely at a loss to understand how anyone could have criticized them as being too scattered until I visited other sites and began to recognize how a properly cohesive cohort ought to behave.

One example of what proper cohesion looks like came from a group of older fourth-year students whom I met while on a practicum site in the south. Every waking moment that the girls were not eating, washing clothes, or undertaking archeology together, they huddled together knitting. The boys spent their leisure time in the incessant playing of a card game called *Hong Qi* (Red Flag), a boisterous game that appears to require the loud slapping down of cards, intense drinking, and generally yelling at the top of one's lungs. Sometimes the girls would join them in the common room, sitting around the sides and continuing to knit or even occasionally joining the fun. The teachers could also be found in the same room, usually doing work, though they would also occasionally join in the game. The noise and general excitement of the group as a whole were clearly a far better way to perform cohesiveness than the general quiet of the scattered students.

The NoDa site mentioned above was merely ten minutes away by foot from the Red Flag-playing group. Yet, recalling Lao Zi's ideal of two villages so close to each other that each could hear the dogs of the other yet not feel compelled to investigate the cause of the commotion, neither group of students ever visited the other.[26] There seemed to be little point in attempting any cross-university relations. NoDa students had the luck to be led by teachers Li and He, who had a rare ability to negotiate with the peasants and so had electricity at all times. The students thus spent their leisure time either playing Go with He, drinking with Li and the local peasant leader, or watching TV or videos in the common room. Once again, it was the noise that convinced the teachers of the proper cohesiveness of the group. NoDa students were also innovative in their performances in that they constantly discussed their cohesiveness and how proud they were of it with each other and in front of the teachers. In one skillful move, then, they convinced the teachers of their propriety and maintained, policed, and enforced cohesiveness among their cohorts.

I moved often between different student practica. It took a few moves before I noticed another method of performing cohesiveness among these groups. No matter which group I visited, as long as they had access to TV, the students and teachers were endlessly engaged in discussions about a certain soap opera. It was slightly surreal at first that every cohort member at every practicum site seemed to be enthralled with the same TV show: a rendition of the life of the great historian Si-Ma Qian. Students would discuss topics ranging from whether the show was historically accurate to whether or not the woman playing the daughter was pretty. Soon I was forced to watch it so often that I became confident enough to bring it up and trade opinions about it as one of my favourite strategies of showing that I knew how to behave.

I do not know whether the students really did care about the show, but they had certainly seized on it as excellent fodder in their quest to perform cohesiveness in front of their teachers. Having personally experienced the manner in which graduate students, brought together in the same dorm from all over the world, also seize on movies, TV, or music to make small talk and get to know each other, I should not have been too surprised. Surprising, however, were the energy and sheer creativity with which the students figured out how to use this show to perform cohesiveness. Small plays, group calligraphy, and fond nicknames taken from the show were all used. After months of observing these strategies, when I recall that the third-year students who were criticized as being scattered were not talking about the show *even though they were all watching it*, I can understand how their silence became a prime indicator for the teachers that something was awry within the cohort.

Cohesion is so important that it outweighs any consideration of personal comfort. I met two male students from a university in the west whom I will call the 'Wu boys.' They had been sent, for reasons of convenience and necessity, along with two girls and a single teacher to a site far away from the rest of their cohort. The Wu boys complained bitterly about this separation from their fellows, saying that they missed being part of the larger group and felt that life was rather unfair. Amazing to me was that this feeling persisted even though they were also fully aware that the rest of their cohort were living in very uncomfortable circumstances while they got to live well in a hotel. I had met the rest of the Wu students a month earlier and had observed their rather appalling living conditions. When I pointed this out, one Wu boy replied, 'To be sure, the best circumstance would be for everyone to be living well, but, failing that, it is better to be with a larger group and living poorly than part of a small group, even if living well.' I do not know what it was that the Wu boys feared about living in a smaller group or whether they knew something that I did not about the dangers of the area, nor do I know whether or not each one really felt what they said they felt, but they certainly spoke and acted as if, the more people there were, the safer and happier they became. In this way, and perhaps just out of sheer habit, they maintained the ideal of a cohesive group among themselves, even when they manifestly lived without one and, at least to an outside observer, were physically better off than the rest of the Wu students.

Of the more than 100 students I met, only one had a tendency to go off by herself (meaning, and this is important because of how slight a difference it seems, that she would sit apart from everyone else and not participate in the card games). She was certainly considered odd by her classmates. In her case, it was attributed to the fact that she was from Beijing, while all the other students in her cohort were southerners. One day she invited me, in front of everyone, to stay at her house in Beijing. I thought that she was arrogantly showing off her Beijing background and wondered if the students would criticize her for rudeness. Instead, to my surprise, the other students were pleased and praised her. She had made them anxious because they thought she was asocial; to see her finally attempt to begin a relationship was a relief. Moreover, the relationship so attempted was appropriate to her Beijing status: it was readily accepted that she, as a Beijinger, would want to make connections with foreigners rather than waste her time with people from the south. The party secretary of the class, who had been close to reporting her to the cohort teacher for asocial behaviour, was particularly relieved. Cohesion is too important to be left to chance or individual idiosyncrasy.

Cohesion is also effective in creating the cohort as an enduring institution that will affect students for the rest of their lives. After graduation, members of the cohort still imagine themselves to be part of a unified group of people who share the same salient characteristics. The differences among their backgrounds are minimized by having been raised during the same historical moment and educated at the same institution by the same teachers. Yet though the group is unified by these rather gross sociological similarities, it is structured such that each member differs from the others by occupying a certain place in the hierarchy. This hierarchy also remains intact over time, and the party secretary can always be called on to mediate disputes and the social secretary to organize events many years after graduation or even after retirement.

That crucial combination, of differentiated similarity, in which differences are domesticated and channelled into an appropriate organizational structure, provides a vision of both closeness based on shared experience and clarity bestowed by precise hierarchical positioning that is considered ideal. The cohort contract is clear: each member will minimize or hide his or her own idiosyncratic and therefore unpredictable differences in favour of the modes of difference that are accepted and expected. In return, social stability is attained, for it is only when the doctrine of similarity is realized in truth (or at least as much as possible) that human interaction can begin. Only when cohort members know the rules of interaction can they decide what to do next and, more importantly, interpret what everyone else is doing. Social interaction has its benefits during the four years of school –

how delightful to make friends – but in the Chinese context cohort bonds last a lifetime.

A final note on cohorts regards how different cohorts of the same school stand in relation to each other. The root narrative is once again kinship: those cohorts who entered before the present cohort are populated by 'older school brothers' *(xuezhang)* and 'older school sisters' *(xuejie)*, and those who come after are comprised of 'little school brothers' *(xuedi)* and 'little school sisters' *(xuemei)*. The relations are explicitly unequal and hierarchical. The same behaviours exhibited in the social contract between teacher and student are mirrored in the relationship between younger and older siblings. A single person has the experience of being both a junior and a senior depending on the other person in the relationship dyad – an older brother to a younger sister, a younger brother to an older sister. Students are therefore given the opportunity to learn how to be seniors themselves, at least in relation to their school juniors. These aspects of the cohort relationship reinscribe the teachings of orthopraxy and, most importantly, provide benefits in the form of protection and advice from elders and in the chance to guide and aid juniors.

The many benefits of the cohort help us to understand the tendency for students to police each other, ensuring not only that each student maintains the contract between student and teacher but also that each student maintains the social contract with cohorts. The teachers' emphasis on cohesion, especially by linking grades to the performance of cohesion, can be seen as a method of teaching students appropriate ways to police, enforce, and reinforce their cohort bonds.

Identity through Hierarchy and Mutuality

Proust notes that 'we do not succeed in changing things according to our desire, but gradually our desire changes.' University can be considered a training ground for new desires. To be sure, it provides information that the young archeologist needs to learn (artifact types, dates, site names, and methods), but it also teaches a student both how and why he should want to interact in junior-senior and cohort-like relations. He should want to enter into such relations because they are contractual, produce freedom from uncertainty and the need to align internal intent with visible behaviour, and allow him to reap the material and immaterial benefits of mutual association. He enters these relations by obeying – that is, performing actions that appear to conform with – the ideals and models of behaviour given throughout his elementary, middle, high school, and university experiences. The benefits of orthopraxy and mutual association are considered so important that, if he does not obey the rules of these relations, both his teachers and his fellow cohort members will take steps to ensure that he does. In short, the performance of obedience is enforced by both the carrot of benefits received and the stick of punishments endured.

The contractual model of relations that a student learns can also be understood to bestow identity on him by assigning him to a specific role. Roles can never be understood without reference to a particular relationship with another person. A person assigned to a role thus no longer faces the uncertainty of interacting with unknown others in just 'any old way.' He knows both who he is and who they are and thus that he must act as a student (in relation to a teacher), a cohort manager (in relation to the cohort), a father (in relation to a child), or whatever other role he may claim or be assigned. When he acts in a role, he may be said to *inhabit* that role, to live within it, such that the ways in which he performs and displays his opinions, goals, and actions change according to that role. Furthermore, as long as the doctrine of similarity holds, when he acts in a role he can be certain that his co-participants are also performing their roles-in-relation to his. If he acts as a student to another person in the role of teacher, then the corollary holds: he can be certain that his teacher is acting as a teacher to his student. It is in this way that a role may be said to help a person decide how to behave as well as how to define, categorize, interpret, and ultimately judge the behaviour of others.

These roles-in-relation are all the more useful because they are explicitly hierarchical. The imposition of hierarchy is useful because inequality means that participants have fundamentally *different* things to offer each other. Contractual relations are explicitly expected to create relations of mutual aid: if everyone is the same, and if no one has access to the resources that someone else needs, then there is little reason to enter into or maintain contractual relations. The theme that exchange requires things of value, things that someone has and someone else wants, will be emphasized throughout this book.

The imposition of hierarchy, however, should not be imagined to indicate that the person inhabiting the senior role has all the authority in the relationship. The senior role itself is an identity insisting that a person behave so as to protect and care for those juniors under his care; if he does not, then the contract is broken, and he can no longer expect the allegiance of his juniors. Whether he internally cares for or wants to protect his juniors is not at issue; what is at issue is that he makes sure to perform behaviour that will be perceived by his juniors as protective. The senior, too, is thus locked into the requirements of his role. In addition, since relations are mutual and for the most part expected to last a long time, any imbalance of power in a given context can shift along with changes in life circumstance, age, or experience, or whatever other changes may convert a lack of authority in the present to authority in the future. The concept of power here thus cannot be imagined as linked in any definitive way to the senior hierarchical position and does not flow necessarily in a top-down direction. Indeed, as we will see in Chapter 4 in particular, power can be radically divorced from hierarchy to the benefit of those in the junior position.

It is clear that identities in the form of roles are both enabling and limiting (for both juniors and seniors). Once a role is 'inhabited,' a person's unique, contingent, and particular experiences must be channelled and redefined for that person to live up to the identity represented by that role. There is no way to isolate any aspect of life from the relation as long as the relation holds. That is not to say that a person's unique nexus of experience disappears in his head when he inhabits a role: what a person believes or thinks, his intentions in performing a role, and what he hopes to achieve in the end cannot be determined and are therefore unimportant (to anyone other than him). Rather, it is to say that he must perform actions that he judges appropriate to his assigned role. Luckily, he is enabled in this task by the belief that roles-in-relation are unchanged and unchanging across time and space such that 'all Chinese people' are said to adhere to the same standards of behaviour. In his actions, he must always strive to follow the guidelines supplied by his identity in a hierarchical relation to ensure that they will be interpreted or judged in the manner that he desires by the audience-that-matters. In that sense, identities in the form of roles in hierarchical relations are double-edged swords: they enable both action and interpretation, yet they also limit and channel behaviour.

As we will soon see, neither the guidance provided by these identities nor the shared goal of social stability is all that is at work in the social contract. There are many more models of identity to obey, and a greater variety of benefits to be reaped from that obedience, than has been suggested so far. Although at first glance the existence of yet more roles and more hierarchical contracts might appear to inhibit creative behaviour, if they are seen instead as tools and materials, then their multiplicity can be understood to be generative of creative meaning and action. It is instructive in this regard to examine the meaning of the Chinese term *yuanfen*. *Yuanfen* can mean predestination, and in that sense summon up imagery dangerously close to the orientalist discourse of fate and fatalism, yet it can also mean luck or coincidence. *Yuanfen* is a happy thing, a moment in time when everything predestined comes together. The only way to understand the positive nature of the term is to realize that roles and relations may be predestined, but inhabiting such roles is a different matter open to creativity, cooperation, and competition.

In Chapter 3, we will learn how people compete for authority and change their positions in the junior-senior and cohort hierarchies. Their strategies of positioning require an understanding of the importance of reputation and interdependence. In later chapters, we will learn what it means to say that there are many identities and how choices among these multiple identities can be used in strategies of claiming and combination. A repeated theme throughout is that one of the most important benefits of obedience is order. The obedient inhabiting of identities in the form of roles-in-relation ensures that hierarchical relations and the standards for judging behaviour and exercising authority are unambiguous, obvious, and, above all, unchanging. In a manner similar to Edmund Leach's Kachin-Shan social structure, the people inhabiting the roles and wielding the authority may vary, but the hierarchical structure and the rules for interaction remain unscathed.[27]

3
The Rule of Law

Nor do they trust their tongue alone,
But speak a language of their own;
Can read a nod, a shrug, a look,
Far better than a printed book;
Convey a libel in a frown,
And wink a reputation down.
                    – Jonathan Swift, *The Journal of a Modern Lady*

Reputation, reputation, reputation! O, I have lost my reputation! I
have lost the immortal part of myself, and what remains is bestial.
                    – William Shakespeare, *Othello*

Available Discourses

One late afternoon, Teacher Cao and I went to the suburb of Xindian to
visit the HuaDa second-year archeology students. Since the main university
campus in Hua City cannot house all the students at once, first- and second-
year students live and take all their classes in a suburban campus. Since it is
rare that anyone actually makes the trek to Xindian, the students were excited to have guests. They scrambled to find enough chairs for everyone in
the girls' room, while two male students used makeshift plates and old glass
jars to serve us tea and snacks. They did not have much to offer, yet they
were deservedly proud of themselves for knowing how to take care of me in
front of their teacher. Cao took care to praise them for their attentiveness in
filling my tea jar. The two more attentive boys, it turned out, were the cohort leader and social events coordinator, and, although we were in the girls'
room, they clearly had the task of playing host and speaking for the group.

The students knew that I was there to ask questions and were prepared to be
talkative. They were particularly eager to know why I wanted to study students. I explained that I was interested in how students become archeologists

and in what they need to know to become one. When I then asked them what they thought should be the answer to that question, they each replied with merit-based arguments, insisting that all one really needs to be a good archeologist is the ability to withstand hardship *(chi ku)*, a clear grasp of archeological method, and a good memory for artifact types.

I was startled. I had already interviewed innumerable archeologists who had told me repeatedly that success in schooling relates to *guanxi* (social networking) and little else. I was thus at that time a devotee of the *guanxi* worldview and, like so many other scholars, vague about what 'it' was but nevertheless convinced that it was the sole governing principle of Chinese society. The rhetoric of *guanxi* cannot admit of the merit-based approach to success, instead envisioning a world run on kinship and friendship connections. Without recognizing how the discourse had captured my imagination, I could not restrain myself from commenting that I thought more than strict attention to archeological method was needed to become a successful archeologist. The students had no idea what I meant and looked to Cao for an explanation.

He must have been in an unusually expansive mood, because he began to describe all the things that would affect the students' success in archeology. He listed in vivid detail how they would need to learn to negotiate *danwei* politics, manage local peasant workers *(mingong)*, navigate publishing opportunities, and figure out how to be selected to participate in important excavations or conferences. I added some things that I thought Cao had left out, such as the need to deal with local officials and regional politics, even going so far as to point out gender disparities in the discipline. The students must have thought us crazy, throwing ideas and scenarios around and becoming increasingly exaggerated as our imaginations warmed to the task.

By the time we were winding down, I noticed that the students had become considerably more quiet and reserved. I asked one what she was thinking about, and she rebuked both Cao and me, saying that we were 'corrupt' and that the discussion of social networking for the sake of social networking was making her uncomfortable. Cao had little sympathy. He sternly urged the students to get used to it because there was no way to avoid *guanxi*. He relented only to add that, once they learned to do it, they would not be so frightened by it.

We ended the night with a group of sober and subdued students who walked us to the bus stop to the city in almost morose silence. After we boarded the bus and left the students behind, Cao asked me rather worriedly whether I thought he had been too harsh with the students. I said no. Since I believed that the *guanxi* perspective was more 'true' than not, I thought it imperative that the students start learning all about it earlier rather than later. But *guanxi* discourse, for all its insistence that it is the only way of looking at the Chinese world, is not the only available discourse. By the words *available discourse*, I mean to call to mind a store shelf stocked with products. When buying these products, the consumer chooses not only a product but also a *brand:* a complex of ideas and images that implicates a lifestyle. The choices that a consumer makes are limited to what is available on the shelf, but once she buys a product she is not limited in what she does with it. She can combine it with other products and contexts to produce assemblages imbued with her own meanings. She aims to have her creations interpreted by her audience. Yet that audience, depending on context and relationship to her, will interpret them very differently. Someone who knows her, someone who has different tastes, someone who wants to praise her, someone who has seen those objects used by someone else in a different assemblage: each of these people will interpret her creations differently and for different reasons. And so it goes: she is in an endless dance to combine and recombine in an attempt to constrain and direct the fickle and ever-changing opinions of the audience.[1]

Discourses are like brand-name products in that they are similarly both enabling and limiting: they are chosen to create meaning and are combined with context in ways that must satisfy both the actor and the audience-that-matters to the actor.[2] Each discourse is utterly similar in that it is an extreme and exaggerated vision that imposes order on a disordered and confused world. That order is an act of will, of social truth making: people act as if a particular discourse applies, so the categories and rules embedded in that discourse do end up ordering and clarifying social relations. The question is, if there is a will to believe in *guanxi* widely shared among adult archeologists, can *guanxi* describe everything that enters into social relations among them?

The answer to this question is negative because, while each discourse might insist that there is no other way of acting in the world except according to its principles and strategies and in pursuit of the goals that it heralds as the most important, each, in fact, coexists with a number of other discourses. Each can exist only so long as there are habits and traditions whereby certain contexts call up certain kinds of language, goals, and strategies, while other contexts call up different discourses entirely. The context in which the young HuaDa students find themselves clearly affects the types of discourse that they find useful. The notion of hard work and merit seems to be required when one enters an academic community for the first time. After all, the memorization of artifact types, archeological cultures, and techniques is integral to archeological success. Perhaps merit discourse is important in the school context because it convinces students to do the work of learning. Given the negative reactions incited by Cao and me saying that something different should apply, it seems to be detrimental to reveal too early in the game that memorization of types and techniques – already an overwhelming task – is not all there is to be learned about being an archeologist.

I later had the opportunity to meet a few of these students again during one of their rare trips to the main HuaDa campus. I was half relieved and half startled to discover that in the intervening time they had reverted almost entirely to their idealistic merit model of a good, hard-working archeologist. To succeed, one 'merely' needed to learn techniques and artifact types. They hastened to tell me that all that other 'stuff' we had talked about that night was much less important and that Cao and I were, simply, incorrect in our estimation of the relative lack of importance of memorization and studying in becoming a good archeologist. I was impressed as much with their willingness to disagree with Cao, their teacher, as with the tenacity of the model of merit-based success.

Note that Cao and I and the students had differed on which discourse most aptly described success in archeology. If the same context calls up two discourses with differing value systems, as it so often does, then the interpretation of events will be in dispute. Whose version of events prevails depends, of course, on a variety of contextual elements. I am certain, for example, that, when these young HuaDa students return from their first practicum excavation, they will have developed models of the successful archeologist that resemble Cao's. Not only is Cao their teacher and should be obeyed given the junior-senior contract, but also he will explain their every interaction in the field among the peasants using *guanxi* terminology. Consequently, the students will have learned only the vocabulary of *guanxi* and will perforce use it when discussing their practicum experiences among themselves or with friends and family. The terminology of the merit-based discourse will simply not be helpful.

The point here, however, is not to examine why in some contexts some people have the power to make certain discourses prevail more often than other people but to draw attention to the fact that disputes over interpretation often become heated exactly because each discourse refuses to admit that other value systems or worldviews have worth. It is the concerted effort of each discourse to insist that it and only it applies to any given situation that makes discourses useful: not as anthropologically 'true' descriptions of behaviour but as *gifts*.

How can a discourse be a gift? To answer that question, we must first work through the ways in which discourses have meaning in contexts, can be combined with roles and scripts, and, above all, can seduce someone else into doing what is wanted despite everything that person wants. To understand how it works, we might keep in mind that we do not strive for things that are freely available and likely to come our way without effort. If, under the discourse of *guanxi*, mutual aid and cooperation are *expected*, then why would a person bother to barter anything in return for someone's coopera-tion? Only in opposition to the discourse of merit, in which competition is the norm, can an act of cooperation take on value. What exactly consti-tutes a gift – its value, the methods by which it is given, and the expected returns – depends on the discourse claimed, whether the audience-that-matters accepts that claim, and the strategic combination of discourses and acts.

Judging from the skills observable in older students, the young HuaDa students, after their practicum, will be able to combine the rhetoric of merit with context and roles-in-relation to create gifts that can be exchanged in the pursuit of certain goals. Often, and somewhat paradoxically, the goals achieved are contrary to the very rhetoric deployed in their pursuit. The best examples are found in narratives of justification and excuse. One stu-dent, for example, used merit rhetoric to justify his unwillingness to inter-act with a certain person. He insisted that he was stupid and needed to work very hard not to fail, so he could not take any time to have fun. Since such merit rhetoric is common and acceptable in the school setting, it was thus easy to avoid the person without creating a rift that might foreclose a rela-tionship later. This student used the rhetoric of merit, which does not ad-mit of the importance of social relations, to maintain proper social relations. Similarly, another student excused his teacher's absence at an important event by explaining that his teacher was working very hard. In one fell swoop, the student thereby accomplished a series of goals: not only did he excuse his teacher, but he also reaped the benefits of first reinforcing the idea that the teacher is a 'great man' because he works so hard and second by implying that he himself is close enough to this great teacher to know his schedule and be his spokesperson.

Use of the rhetoric of *guanxi* to excuse or justify hard work also occurs, particularly in the *danwei* setting. One archeologist explained how he was able to examine a data set without revealing that he was, in fact, working on a paper involving those data. His trick was to insist that he had to exam-ine the data only because he was obeying the wishes of his superior, the implication being that he himself had no real interest in the data. The same archeologist even insinuated that he was a lazy man who hated archeology but was devoted to his social relationships with his superiors mainly to ensure that he would continue to receive his yearly bonus (as he put it, 'only interested in patting the horse's ass [*pai mapi*]'). In fact, he enjoys archeology and looks forward to a time when he can be more open about his interests.

These examples reveal that motives and goals are, as always, mixed and that meaning arises in the juxtaposition of discourse, action, and percep-tion. We see also that these discourses are incorrigible – that is, they cannot be corrected by experience. The merit worldview thus persists despite being used for reasons that directly contradict its central claim that the path to success is through hard work. It persists even though people have used it to cover up an unacceptable opinion about someone or to endow a gift with greater value. It persists because it is an *acceptable* excuse that, simply by being acceptable rather than 'true,' accomplishes goals far more complex than simply 'success through hard work.' The possible scenarios, motives, and implications of combinations of these discourses – and here I am discussing only two,[3] while there are several more – are endless; however, while lived experience and other discourses can be combined with any given discourse, none can be allowed to destroy the other, for, as we shall see, each is too useful as a resource in the strategies of gift giving.

Values and Acts: The Rule of Reciprocity

In Chapter 2, I briefly mentioned the rule of reciprocity as a kind of mutuality that exists in contractual relations. Juniors were seen to seek, maintain, and police the contract between themselves and their seniors, as well as between cohort members, because they gained something important from those relationships: freedom from uncertainty and freedom from the requirement of allying intent with action. There are, however, more concrete benefits to be gained from submitting oneself to the social contract. To understand the types of 'gifts' that can be exchanged in junior-senior relations, and to understand the strategies by which they are exchanged, we must further discuss the values, ideals, goals, and actions embedded in the rules of reciprocity. This chapter focuses on junior-senior relations; cohort relations, with their exquisite facility in the domestication of troublesome differences, will be discussed in Chapter 4 in relation to Chinese bureaucracy.

The rule of reciprocity is simply another take on *guanxi*, which has become a word too loosely defined to be of use.[4] What is particularly difficult about *guanxi* discourse is that it is explicitly discussed and repeatedly disseminated by both Chinese and non-Chinese people, in literature, mass media, philosophy, and scholarly work. It appears in anthropological studies, political treatises, historical research, and economic modelling, and it has become over time a social script with its own tradition of commentary, conventions, etiquette, and morality. This continuous reinforcement of *guanxi* discourse creates of it something analogous to a religious worldview – by which I mean that it has been discussed among both scholars and lay people, among those with the time and education to indulge in exegesis as well as those who use it in daily practice in the pursuit of other goals, and has often been conflated more or less correctly with Confucianism.

I am thus avoiding the term to make it clear that I am not focused on many of the issues so commonly associated with *guanxi:* I do not argue that *guanxi* underlies or subverts all other social forms in Chinese society; nor am I interested in how *guanxi* does or does not elaborate Marcel Mauss's understanding of gift giving; nor, finally, am I trying explain all the possible strategies and/or tactics of gift giving.[5] I am concerned instead to explain that autonomy cannot be achieved in any kind of relationship, whether dyadic or group in form, unless each participant has both wants and something to offer in exchange for those wants.[6] That crucial combination, of wants and things to exchange for such wants, in some sense underlies all social interactions among human beings. Therefore, it makes no sense to use the specific Mandarin term *guanxi* as if exchange is somehow peculiarly Chinese. What differentiates Chinese from other people is not their proclivity for exchange – for all people indulge in exchange – but what they exchange, how they exchange it, and the purposes of exchange.

As a discourse, the rule of reciprocity provides two kinds of knowledge: a set of values, ideals, and expectations and a set of acceptable strategies complete with generally approved excuses and justifications for actions. Both values and strategies can be finely differentiated depending on the authority claims of the speaker, the audience, and the events in question.[7] In practice, values and strategies are maintained and perpetuated through repetition in social interaction and combine to form a multilevel discourse that moves easily from action to justification to ideals to excuse and back again.

In unequal hierarchical relations, both junior and senior need to be able to assess the likelihood that the other is 'worth' the trouble of creating, maintaining, or strengthening the relationship. Two elements are important to the judgment of another person's worth: 'trustworthiness,' an assessment of whether or not he will act according to reciprocal values, and 'compatibility,' an assessment of whether he has anything to bring to the relationship. The *kind* of things that a person has to offer – not his *access* to resources – is emphasized by compatibility. Remember that, in making judgments of other people's worthiness, a person is well aware that he, too, is judged in return. The corollary to judging others, then, is the requirement that one must perform one's own worthiness for the consumption of others. I first examine reciprocal values out of context and then use examples drawn from the teacher-student relationship to illustrate how the judgments and performances of worthiness are used in strategies of autonomy in mutually beneficial hierarchical relations.

Reciprocal Values and Reputation

The roles taken by a person in junior-senior relations are necessarily tied to a particular point of view or identity. Much like a kinship chart, in which the terms used and the categories perceived cannot be understood unless the perspective of ego is chosen as a vantage point from which to begin, a person's moral duties are particularized depending on the specifics of his role, his position in a hierarchy, and the goals and responsibilities entailed by the roles and positions that he claims. Indeed, Fei Xiaotong goes so far as to suggest that this particular worldview as practised by the Chinese subject exists because of the emphasis on kinship and the resulting habit of seeing the self and others as constituted by where they stand in relation to lineage members.[8]

The most cardinal virtue in the junior-senior contract is reciprocity *(bao):* the notion that the moral person always repays his or her material and immaterial debts. Reciprocity is not limited to repaying debts in kind. It is understood instead that any balance of debt on one side of the equation will be generously overpaid, such that the burden of debt is transferred back across the relationship dyad.[9] People not only recognize that the balance of debt will shift in the future but also depend on it. Each social interaction becomes an investment: by doing something for another now, one ensures that the other will respond with something even more valuable later.

The concept of 'face' or 'reputation' combines both the value of reciprocity and the particular point of view inhering in roles-in-relation. Maintaining face is the attempt to maintain one's reputation as a moral person – that is, as someone both able and generous in the repayment of his social debts. Reputation is about three things at once: how a person judges himself, how he imagines himself to be judged by others, and how members of the audience-that-matters do judge him. Reputation is much like a biography: it is the set of things that people 'know' about a person, have heard said about him, or have experienced themselves that makes up their image of him. It is, in short, a person's *identity* in the eyes of the audience-that-matters.

Reputation is a difficult matter both because it must link a person's many possible roles-in-relation and because true control over one's reputation, and therefore identity, belongs in the hands of others, not the self. So far, we have discussed roles as if a person merely inhabits *one at a time*. Fortunately, and occasionally unfortunately, the situation is more complex. A person has available to him a series of roles: he can be a student, a cohort manager, a child, and an intellectual all more or less at the same time depending on who is present and on the context in which he finds himself. Each role has different required behaviours, performed attitudes, and acceptable goals and strategies that often conflict. If a person is unable to control the perceptions of his audience such that they judge him to be acting incorrectly according to the standards applied to the student role when he was trying to act according to the standards of a cohort manager, then he – and his reputation – are in trouble.

A person must therefore attempt to control the perception of his audience through the strategy of 'claiming,' which uses language and behaviour to seduce the audience into acting as if it agrees to interpret the situation in

the way that the actor wants. Reputation both limits and enables the interpretation of behaviour because the audience applies what it already knows
about a person in his other roles to his behaviour in a particular role. The
logic is simple: since a man has the reputation of acting correctly in one
role, he is likely to act correctly in his other roles. If his reputation is very
good, and audience sympathy is strong, then the audience might just give a
man the benefit of the doubt and not expend too much effort in investigating his actions, even if he seems to be acting improperly. Of course, if his
reputation is not so good, then even if he is acting correctly the audience
will subject his actions to scrutiny. This tendency to assume that, if a person
can act correctly in one role, then he can in all others is both limiting and
enabling: limiting because a person is always restrained by the history of his
past actions (and past mistakes), enabling because a person's claims can be
bolstered by the history of his past actions (and past successes).

Given that reputation is a person's identity in the eyes of the audience, it
is not surprising that a person spends much time and effort maintaining
face and warding off attempts by others (or by fate) to ruin his or her reputation.[10] Anthropological studies of *guanxi* and face have been mainly devoted to how someone maintains face and extends his or her social network.
The most common way to do both is, of course, through the time-honoured
practice of gift giving. In giving and receiving gifts, a person's ability to
repay debt and his generosity of spirit are continuously tested, measured,
judged, and, above all, performed. Gift giving simultaneously maintains
and strengthens a person's social ties and his reputation as a moral person.[11]

The rule of reciprocity must be examined with reference to two key aspects of the Chinese context: the problem of extreme interdependence and
the attempt to cure that problem through the mixing of what might at first
glance be considered contradictory values of instrumentality and affect in
social relations. To begin with interdependence: in China, when people insist that 'everything' is dependent on contractual junior-senior and cohort
relations, they really do mean *everything*. A person's plans, as well as those
of anyone connected to him or her, require an extended social network.
From something as small as getting a book out of the library to things such
as health, career, and education (of the archeologist, the archeologist's children, and the archeologist's extended kin), there is literally nothing that
can be negotiated independently of one's social network. Since access to
important resources is organized such that subordinates are utterly dependent on their superiors for all things, subordinates have no recourse except
to cultivate personal ties to superiors by showing loyalty, deference, and
obedience.[12] But where many scholars see interdependence as benefiting
only the superiors in any given relationship, I see it as also benefiting the
juniors. As we will soon see, interdependency means that both seniors and

juniors are dependent on the resources that each brings to the relationship.

That so much depends on personal ties creates a terrifying sense of uncertainty. As a result, people are constantly attempting to reduce uncertainty. This ethnography emphasizes those who deal with uncertainty through the social contract rather than those who take chances (both responses – and more – are possible). The social contract is preferred by archeologists because of the *danwei* context in combination with the circumstances of interdependency in Chinese society more generally. Since each person is affected by the actions of everybody else, each considers it his prerogative to intervene in the actions and choices of others.

The high stakes and constant change under interdependency demand both a way to ascertain who will be most likely to respond to a request for aid and a way to force or encourage others to repay their debts. One strategy can do both at once: the creation of a network of 'mixed-tie' relations.[13] To grasp the idea of the mixed-tie relationship, we need to understand the strength of the moral prescriptions underlying reciprocity and, most important of all, the conflation of morality with positive emotions. Simply put, we begin with the idea that 'a good person is one who reciprocates.' Person A gives person B something in compensation for person B having given something to person A and so on: the classic, unending Kula ring that links the past and the future through exchange. This idea is then combined with the notion that 'a good person is worthy of emotional investment.' A person who returns gifts or otherwise fulfills obligations appropriately is thus someone genial and likable, deserving of a certain warmth of attitude and, certainly, further aid. A mixed-tie relationship is a good way of reducing uncertainty on the assumption that someone who reciprocates = someone who is moral = someone who is likable = someone who is not going to renege on his or her obligations: each of these four attributes implies all the others. The term in Chinese is *renqing*, a concept that explicitly combines emotion and instrumental value.[14]

Emotional affect, then, arises out of exchange practices in the social contract. Note that the corollary also holds: to begin a relationship with a person who appears to be likable, one must offer aid, a gift, or some other indication that this relationship can also be instrumentally beneficial. The ideal that friendship ought to be simply 'friendship for friendship's sake' is often touted in Euro-American societies; in contrast, the junior-senior contract insists that any given interpersonal relation is both a good in itself and a resource that can provide both material and immaterial benefits to both ends of any given relationship dyad. Friendship must combine a strong emphasis on reciprocity: that is, on the creation of mutually (though at any given time unequally so) beneficial ties.[15]

Certainly, social ties that are more clearly instrumental exist, but they tend to be short lived and less productive since neither side feels the emotional commitment to the relationship that might lead the person to repay – generously – his or her debts. Without 'upping the ante' in each exchange, the tie is easily broken. At the other end of the scale, more clearly affective social ties are extremely unlikely to be broken. Family ties are, of course, the extreme example, although, as we saw at least with parents and their school-age children, even they are based on material and affective ties simultaneously. Unfortunately, more purely affective ties are also less likely to be instrumentally effective, since a person rarely has an extensive set of relatives who as a group have access to all the things required to satisfy the needs of one's family or career. As a result, the creation of mixed ties is simultaneously an attempt to maintain affective relations (affect used to increase the likelihood that the other will maintain instrumental ties) and instrumental relations (instrumentality used to increase the likelihood that the other will maintain emotional commitment). The two mutually reinforce each other: to have warm relations, one needs to reciprocate; to have reciprocal relations, one needs to have emotional attachment.[16]

Since in social interactions one can never know for certain what another person is thinking or feeling, it must be understood that emotional attachment, affect, and other concepts are meant to refer to *visible indicators*. Given orthopraxy, what a person actually thinks is rather unimportant as long as he is committed to acting – smiling, spending time, visiting, giving gifts, or whatever other actions he might perform – in a way appropriate to the mixed-tie relationship. Those behaviours are, as always, to be interpreted and judged by the audience-that-matters. A person must strive to display ideal standard behaviour in the hope that the audience will accept and praise that behaviour.

Reputation in the context of mixed-tie relations thus becomes rather complex: remembering that reputation is judged by the audience-that-matters, a person must 'appear' to be moral in the sense of being both likable and possessing something of instrumental benefit to bring to a relationship. The appearance of being someone who has access to resources is somewhat difficult to maintain unless one really does have such access. The system is therefore not solely about abstract appearances or beliefs: eventually, one must deliver the goods.

The emphasis here is on delivery, and that is key when we think about the relationship between juniors and seniors. Juniors deliver their services in the form of obedience to the wishes of their seniors and, at least in the case of students, in the grades and other indicators that they have put in the hard work required. Seniors, in their turn, are supposed to be able to take care of and guide their juniors; if they cannot, then there must be something wrong with their access to resources, and their reputation as being of instrumental benefit is severely damaged. In the marketplace of judgment, neither juniors nor seniors seen to fail at delivering benefits will

be considered worthy of relationships by other potential partners. It behooves people, then, to ensure that they both deliver the goods required of
them and figure out how to access more resources in order to deliver a
wider range of goods, for this is the main method of building and extending one's standing both morally and materially.

As a cure for the uncertainty that arises from the extreme interdependence in modern Chinese society, the creation of mixed-tie relations is effective. Unfortunately, such relations have their own measure of uncertainty:
since they depend on the attempts by the actor to seduce and intervene in
the judgment of the audience-that-matters, they are not easy to predict or
control. The purported cure does little but increase the need to figure out
the standards being used to judge one's performance of *compatibility* and
trustworthiness as well as to judge whether others themselves are living up to
those standards.

Trustworthiness is defined as a judgment made about who is behaving
such that he or she appears worthy of investment. It would seem logically
to come before compatibility, defined as judging whether or not a person
can provide the kinds of resources considered useful. However, in mixed-tie
relations, by definition relations that refuse to separate the instrumental
from the emotional, neither trustworthiness nor compatibility can be prior
to the other. In the interest of emphasizing not only the mutuality of relationships but also the things that junior archeologists have to offer to their
seniors, I begin with the discussion of instrumental compatibility and how
it is affected by and recursively affects the teacher-student relationship.

Compatibility: Placement as a Reciprocal Act

Judging a person's instrumental rating, one's compatibility quotient, is all
about deciding whether one has the things (material or not) that one might
need. I like to think of it as judging whether someone is 'placed' well –
that is, placed in a social network that can provide certain wanted resources.
Not just any resources, they must be things that the person sitting in judgment desires or needs. Compatibility, then, is all about the shared conventions of behaviour that can be used to create performances of being well
positioned.

In the teacher-student relationship, assessing compatibility is unusually
simple because the quality of having access to desirable resources is created
cooperatively by teacher and student. In particular, the student wants a job,
and the teacher helps him to get the 'right' job.[17] Both teacher and student
must decide together which job is the right one. The ideal outcome is when
the student has studied a topic important to the teacher and therefore can
be positioned in a job that will allow the two of them to enter into a fruitful
collaboration as the student grows into a fully-fledged archeologist.

To see how this works, we begin from the perspective of the teacher. In his analysis of his group of students, it must be clear that not all students are equal in ability. It is not at all about merit – that some of them are more intelligent or even more interested in archeology than the others. Nor is it about a student being more likable. There is nothing *essentially* right or wrong about any of the students. It is simply that the teacher can (says he can) predict that some students will not be successfully placed in a job or situation that will be mutually beneficial to both teacher and student. Such students are simply *incompatible* with the needs of the teacher, and in turn the abilities and expertise of the teacher are incompatible with the needs of the student. Neither is able to provide benefits that warrant a close relationship.

Archeologists necessarily decide the standards of compatibility based on very different criteria from, say, entrepreneurs, bridge engineers, or peasants. An 'archeologically compatible' person can help to get access to data or materials needed for research, is able to help set up a smooth-running excavation, or has certain outstanding abilities in excavation, analysis, or publication. From the teacher's point of view, a student working in the same region or time period as the teacher could be considered compatible. Recognition of compatibility is, of course, rarely that straightforward: an archeologist of Buddhism may have little interest in the data to which a Paleolithic archeologist has access yet might still consider his ties to a particular locale, one that happens also to yield Buddhist artifacts, enough to make him compatible indeed.

Which standards does a teacher use to judge the potential compatibility of any given student? Teachers classify their students into three main types. The first group of students could be called the 'good archeologists.' Teachers define them as students who can endure hardship, are good with the workers, and understand clearly the principles of excavation and artifact recovery. These students are often the ones who interact well with their cohort members and tend to be the cohort leaders, party secretaries, and the like. They are most often found discussing what they have found and learned with each other and the teacher and are encouraged to follow the teacher closely in his daily rounds. Most importantly, these students have clearly decided that they want to continue in archeology after graduation.

In contrast, the second group of students has little or no interest in archeology. We can call them the entrepreneurs. They come to the department solely because that is where they are placed and they are interested only in graduating with the BA degree. The legitimacy bestowed on them by the degree will likely help them to find a job in business or computing. These students spend most of their time taking extra classes such as business English or economics. They have a very different experience of their archeological practicum in that they are there simply to get it over with. They will (occasionally) complain and sometimes even be obstreperous with the teachers. Most of the time, they flirt outrageously with each other – but never too seriously since they do not actually want to marry an archeology student – and stop working the moment the order to rest is given. They also put energy into making contacts among students and teachers of other departments, since their archeology cohort members and teachers are, in their opinion, not particularly useful.

Despite their lack of interest in archeology, the relationship of the entrepreneurs with their teachers exhibits the same conventions of respect as shown by the 'good archeologists': they still pay close attention to what the teacher says, always show up where they are needed at the right time, and are always ready to drop everything and do whatever the teacher asks. We have seen, however, that this is very much a part of the protection that they seek from the junior-senior contract. Since they despise and fear the work of archeology, they are particularly anxious to get it over with as soon as possible, and the best way to accomplish that goal is to submit to the teacher. Despite their obedience, however, they do not go the extra step to become closer to the teacher, and in their turn, teachers make no extra effort with them. Everyone is congenial; the teachers show no anger toward these students even though they are perfectly aware that the students are not interested in archeology. The effect of so many students wanting to change professions seems only to be that the teachers are less committed to undergraduate education as a whole. Nowadays, many teachers wait until a student attains the graduate level before putting much effort into him or her. Some teachers claimed that there are even MA or PhD students pursuing archeology only for the degree!

A third group is made up of students who will continue in some form of archeology but not for 'the right reasons.' Students from small towns or counties often continue in archeology because the security of being part of the *danwei* outweighs any other consideration. They are satisfied having had the opportunity to attend university and happy that they will be able to live in the city. Anything is preferable to returning to the farm, even a discipline that effectively sends them to the countryside for at least six months of the year. Their children will still be urbanites, and that is enough. These students often explained that pursuing the discipline for which they had been trained is the only 'natural' and acceptable course of action. They tend to use the values inherent in the trope of patriotism as a justification for continuing in archeology: since China had spent money on them to send them to school, they must repay the favour by doing their jobs.

When asked if they like archeology, this third type of student insisted that 'like' and 'enjoyment' arise out of, not prior to, the performance of one's duty. Many said that they once dreamed of studying in some other discpline but insisted that 'grades never lie' and that each person ought to pursue a career in the profession for which exam results say he or she is best suited. Besides, they continued, how can a person like archeology before he has learned anything about it? Liking archeology is properly a feeling that arises out of familiarity. Interestingly, many used a concept borrowed from the mixed-tie relation to explain what they meant: just as you cannot know whether a person is likable or not until you have entered into a relationship with him, so too you cannot like archeology until you have become more familiar with what it can offer you. These students often repeated two traditional sayings: *gan yi hang, ai yi hang* ('You love the job you have') and *ze lai zhe, ze ai zhe* ('Since that is the job you were given, that is the job you will come to love').

The sense of duty and responsibility to the profession and to China performed by this third group of students is certainly applauded by the teachers. These 'patriots' are perceived to be very reliable and loyal. The assumption is that, if someone feels so strongly about duty to China as a patriot, he will probably be just as good about maintaining correct teacher-student relations. Unfortunately, it is also said of this kind of student that he will not rise to the top of his *danwei* anytime soon and may never climb the hierarchy to gain access to the data and opportunities that a teacher might need. Such students are simply not ambitious enough to become fully compatible and therefore do not necessarily warrant the teacher's attention.

I would not presume to say, however, that teachers always choose to develop close relations with 'the good archeologists.' Which student is chosen depends on the goals of the teacher. If teachers themselves are very interested in archeology, then it behooves them to surround themselves with a network of good archeologists. Yet an archeologist also has friends and family to protect, and it may be that a student from the second group, one who intends to leave archeology to become a computer programmer, may be exactly the type of person whom the archeologist needs to tutor or guide his child when it comes time for that child to study for the university entrance exam. Besides, the good archeologist group can be threatening to a teacher because the students may be good enough to become rivals and, therefore, may no longer maintain mutually beneficial ties with the teacher. As for the third group, they are, if nothing else, dependable and certainly not ambitious enough to consider striking out on their own and breaking their ties with the teacher. Deciding which student to choose, in other words, is a gamble balancing what the teacher (or the extended kin and friends of the teacher) might eventually need, prognostications of whether a student will remain 'filial,' and predictions about the likelihood that the student will be successful in whatever position he or she is eventually placed.

In the resolution of the uncertainties of choosing a student, the teacher, luckily, has the help of the student. In the determination of relative compatibility, it 'takes two to tango,' so to speak. The students are well aware of the potential benefits that a close relationship with a teacher might bring – a good job, introductions, guidance, to mention but a few – and are as interested as the teachers in pursuing such relationships. It is up to each student, then, to decide whether or not he wishes to perform his compatibility for any given teacher and seek a way to catch his attention and interest. Similarly, the teacher cannot just assume that he will be successful in building a relationship with a student simply by virtue of his status as a teacher; he, too, must perform compatibility for the student by showing that he does have the connections to get the student a job or access to data. Performance of compatibility is, above all, a mutual process: both teacher and student have to draw attention to what each has to offer the other.

Given the need for each side to highlight what it has to offer, the rule of reciprocity must include a guide for the *interpretation* of action as well as simply a guide for action. For a teacher, for example, to be able to distinguish between a student interested in a close relationship and one interested merely in the 'normal' teacher-student relationship, there must be a standard for the normal relationship that is widely shared by teachers and students of all kinds. Figuring out whether the student is going that 'extra' step is possible only when the norms associated with the teacher-student relationship are juxtaposed and compared to the norms and moral orientation of the rules of reciprocity. The values of the teacher-student relationship detail the duties of each role; the rules of reciprocity explain how to tell whether a person is performing his duties differently from the norm and how to react appropriately.

From the students' point of view, performing compatibility for the teachers requires constant attention. The student must be attentive to the teacher's every action, over and over again, every day. He must learn how the teacher thinks and how to emulate his patterns of thought. In so doing, he demonstrates *in practice* to the teacher that he is willing to submit himself to the teacher's point of view. Therefore, he indicates that, when he himself graduates and goes on to become an archeologist, he will both espouse the teacher's theories and ideas in publications and at conferences and aid the teacher to strengthen that point of view by helping him to do research and gain access to data and sites. Students will even emulate how their teacher negotiates with local officials and peasants.

If all students are pretty much expected to adhere to the methods of their teacher, then how can a student make himself stand out as *particularly* interested and filial? It can simply be a matter of intensity: a student who is careful to be consistent and constantly follow the precepts of being a good student is already quite remarkable. A special show of enthusiasm or energy in the enactment of the rules inhering in the teacher-student relationship will also stand out. Other methods do exist. For example, several students explained that a good strategy is to disagree with the teacher in a private discussion between student and teacher and then later agree with him in public. In this way, the teacher knows that the student is making a conscious choice to be filial to his ideas despite his own opinions. Another method is similar: to choose to disagree (carefully) in public, debate the point, and then come to agree with the teacher's point of view as a show of obedience in front of the whole group.

One method that is particularly efficacious, however, touches on one's identity or reputation. Being seen as compatible always requires the performance of, as Michael Herzfeld might say, 'being a proper Chinese person.'[18] Another way of saying this is that a student ought to maintain the kind of excellent reputation that leads to a 'shining' or 'bright' face.[19] Being proper means conforming to the teacher's notion of correct behaviour in *all* relevant social relations. That is, if a student is 'good at being a morally proper child' in regard to his parents, or an 'excellent inferior' in relation to his workplace supervisor, then the teacher will likely find it easier to assume that he will be a morally proper student as well.

For example, one of the fourth-year HuaDa students observed my interactions with Teacher Cao and found me lacking. He cautioned that I should present myself as missing my parents and being homesick more often. In other words, I was having too much of a good time and therefore not being filial enough. By 'missing my parents,' I could reassure Cao that I am filial with regard to my parents and, therefore, that I can act appropriately in other relations. Whether or not I did miss my parents was inconsequential. More importantly, no one ever questioned whether or not Cao would agree with this vision of the world in which children ought to be filial and show filial behaviour by 'being homesick.' It appeared to be impossible to imagine that Cao might disagree with tradition and distrust 'overly filial' children. Everyone simply 'knew' that he would agree that filial behaviour is proper and share the same standard of filial behaviour as everyone else.

Even choosing an archeological topic becomes a performance of compatibility: the more a student shows that he will defer to the advice of the teacher, the more obvious it is that he is willing to submit himself to being of service to the teacher in the future. Choosing a topic together with the teacher provides the opportunity for these performances to catch the eye of the teacher. Of course, motives are mixed: the student also wants to get himself a research topic and launch his career (and the teacher, like any advisor, wants to speed the student on to graduation), but making closer ties with the teacher along the way is certainly a benefit not to be taken lightly.

So far, we have considered the performance of compatibility by the student, a performance that requires obedience above and beyond the norms expected in the teacher-student relationship. The teacher must also perform compatibility but certainly not in the same manner as the student. Rather, he submits himself to the norms of the teacher-student relationship by performing being in control. Appropriate behaviour for a teacher is to take conclusive control over a student's life and pour his energy into guiding all aspects of the student's life. A teacher who can lead and command with clarity and efficiency, and who, above all, has access to the resources that mean he can make good on his promises, is by definition a worthy teacher. That requirement, to deliver the goods, means that guiding students' lives is not an easy task of privilege and power but arduous and exhausting.

Teacher Xu, the director of a practicum run out of a northern university, XinDa, exemplified how a teacher can fail to be considered a worthy teacher despite following the norms set out in the teacher-student relationship. Xu certainly took care of his students and ensured their safety by controlling their bodily and academic lives as appropriate. But Xu is a relaxed man who does not care all that much about archeology or really anything other than having a good time. He got along very well with his students, and everyone liked him. Even the peasants and local officials liked him. But none of these people bothered much with him, and, when 'push came to shove,' he could not ask them for favours since he himself had made no attempt to offer anyone anything. He made no investment in the relations with the peasants or local officials or even his fellow archeologists in the area. What kind of teacher is that? Certainly not one who will, in the future, rise up the ladder in archeology, become an official or leader in his own right, or get to a position where he commands access to resources that might help the XinDa students.

Since part of a teacher's perceived worthiness depends on his ability to position his students in situations beneficial both to the student and to himself, students will pay careful attention to the ways in which teachers teach and interact with peasants and colleagues. Students endlessly discuss the rumours and truths about a teacher's social network (whether performed, intimated, or demonstrated) and attempt to evaluate his ability to position them in good jobs. Teachers are well aware of the evaluations made of them as they go through their daily rounds. Each interaction reinforces or erodes their reputations with the students, and each interaction is thus important not merely for its most obvious goal (the buying of provisions, the solving of a dispute) but also for its many implications for the teacher's worthiness and compatibility in the eyes of his students.

Both student and teacher, then, must ensure that his abilities, his positioning in the hierarchy and ability to position others, and his understanding of morality flag him as compatible both now and in the future. The examples used here were drawn from the teacher-student relationship, but the need to flag oneself as well placed and compatible is part of all social relations. Even in familial relations, some children adhere to the expected norms of filial behaviour, while other children make it their life goal to become very involved in a parent's life or career (the model here being the child of a high party member who aligns himself closely with his father). Similarly, there are normatively good parents, and then there are those who put all their energy into ensuring that their child gets the best preparation for the future as is humanly possible.

As a final example of compatibility, I turn to the superior-inferior relations common to the archeological *danwei*. The story of an archeologist named Li is exemplary. To increase his compatibility, Li decided to pursue environmental archeology upon arrival in his *danwei*. He did not much like the topic but chose it because he would then be the only person in his *danwei* that understood that form of archeology. Whenever the opportunity came to go to a conference on environmental archeology, he was the one who was sent. At each conference, he met a wide variety of people and dramatically extended his social network. His *danwei* superior, the director, was pleased indeed because Li was now that much more useful to the director and, by extension, to the *danwei*. The director and Li continue to cooperate: the director ensures that Li continues to receive the kinds of perquisites associated with being an expert in his topic, and Li responds by using his new social connections on behalf of the director and *danwei*. Neither could have reached the present situation without the cooperation of the other.

The story of a different archeologist, Chen, reveals another way to become differentiated from one's peers and increase compatibility. Frustrated by a lack of ability to rise within the archeological hierarchy or to distinguish himself through excavation or research topic, an archeologist will often leave archeology to become an official. Chen, after working hard for many years for his *danwei*, eventually realized that the arrival of a new, young professor with a PhD degree had put an end to his plan to become the director of the *danwei*. As a result, Chen decided to become an official in the Bureau of Cultural Relics. The present director of Chen's former *danwei* is quite excited by this move because, now that Archeologist Chen has become Official Chen, the director sees Chen as far more impressive in the kinds of resources he now commands. The director now expends more energy in maintaining good ties to Chen in the hope that one day Chen will be willing to help his former *danwei*. In this case, Chen made the move himself, but certainly a director can decide to move one of the archeologists into an official's job as a strategy for extending his and, by extension, his *danwei*'s network.

These stories exemplify how the need to be compatible requires the capacity to constantly reevaluate how one is positioned, how to change positions, and how to perform one's positioning (or potential to be positioned) to others. Under these circumstances, hierarchical relations do not entail the oppression of one side by the other or the privilege of one side with respect to the other. The teacher does not enjoy a more privileged lifestyle because of his control over the student. Instead, being a teacher requires enormous effort and personal sacrifice to ensure that the student knows that the teacher cares, is willing to put in the effort, and has the where-withal to do so. It gets worse when it is understood that people are always seniors to some and juniors to others. Imagine, then, being middle-aged: required to take care of relationships between both juniors and seniors (as the proverb goes, 'Once in middle age, one must manage both young and old' [*ren dao zhongnian, xia yao guan xiao, shang yao guan lao*]). The effort expended is significant. It may be 'only' orthopraxy – that is, the teacher may only be required to act *as if* he cares – but when, as in China, actions must entail material and immaterial benefits, the difference between caring and acting as if one cares is small indeed.

Acts of Trustworthiness

Compatibility requires, first, the ability to place oneself, or be placed, in an advantageous position (advantageous in the eyes of the audience-that-matters) and, second, the performance of that positioning or potential. In addition to the requirements of compatibility, that a person perform instru-mental morality, a person must indicate that he is *trustworthy* in the sense of adhering to the norm of reciprocity by repaying (generously) the favours done him. If he is not deemed trustworthy, then, as one senior archeologist pointed out, even if he is 'the son of the Chairman himself,' there is really no point in trying to enter into a relationship with him. He might be rich; however, if he cannot be trusted to reciprocate, then interacting with him is a waste of time.

I separate trust from compatibility, despite their connections, because the separation allows me to discuss those cases in which a person's moral behav-iour is enough to cause others to maintain and strengthen social relationships with him *whether or not he has access to resources*. In other words, someone who has nothing at all can still maintain and strengthen social relations with people simply because he is able to show himself utterly trustworthy. Often, however, this requires that he has a history (reputation) of access to resources, which, due to present vagaries of fate, are no longer available to him. Or that he has potential, such that someday he will be well placed again (or the opportunity to help him into such a position will arise). Either way, a person would do well to maintain relations with this trustworthy man even if he presently has nothing to offer in return, in the hope that the future will make him compatible again.

That trustworthiness can be independent of present access to resources is exemplified by the story of a prominent archeologist in Beijing. This man, Hu, thought that it was his duty and responsibility, as an intellectual and a teacher, to aid the students in Tiananmen Square during the events of May-June 1989. Hu did not at all agree with what the students were trying to do in the square. Not that he is against democracy, change, or increased economic prosperity, but in his opinion the methods being used were inappropriate and unlikely to succeed. Hu insists that the only way to deal with the truly powerful is to treat them gently and try to get them to see the light without ever suggesting, as the students were doing, that they are old, behind the times, or otherwise incapable. 'One must ensure,' he said, 'that the leaders retain their face whether you agree with them or not.'

Despite his reservations, Hu helped the students as much as he could and, of course, lost his job and position as a result. Yet by aiding the students, he maintained and strengthened his own reputation. He acted appropriately, as a model teacher and intellectual, and is therefore esteemed by the audience-that-matters: the historians and future readers of history as well as the people within the archeological world in the present. As a result, although Hu no longer has a formal position in any *danwei*, he remains one of the most powerful and authoritative archeologists in China, continues to travel (all over the world), publishes constantly, and has a large and loyal following of students. It is the highly public fact that he was willing to sacrifice himself to live up to the moral standards that accrue to his role as intellectual and teacher that maintains him in a position of considerable, even if informal, authority and influence. Even with a loss of placement – in that he no longer has access to the authority of the bureaucratic position that he once held – Hu has retained his trustworthiness.

A cynic might suggest that Hu helped the students because he knew that he would benefit from his actions. Perhaps. Who knows his motives, whether they were pure or mixed, or whether his own understanding of his motives has changed in reaction to events? Did anyone know in April 1989 how things would turn out? The search for motives is futile: we cannot get into the heads of other people to read their motives even if they were clear on all the impulses that led to their actions. In a worldview depending on reciprocity and mutual aid, Hu's narrative is expected to be read less as self-serving but rather as a story of astute judgment and praiseworthy behaviour. Certainly, Hu's colleagues and students read it this way, with no attempt to separate the selfish from the unselfish motive: for them, Hu's loss of material wealth and well-being from losing his job is the concrete expression of his morality, and it is enough.

Another way of understanding the notion of trustworthiness is to examine what happens when it is *not* achieved. I had the opportunity to visit two practicum sites of the same university, one in the north for third-year students and one in the south for fourth-year students. While visiting the third-year students, I heard them speak of two foreign visitors, one female and one male, who had participated that year in their excavation. The woman was praised because she was a *Zhongguo tong:* someone who knew and understood China. This praise was bestowed on her because she lived in close contact with the students and did everything with them (even though she was much older). Strangely enough, when I visited the fourth-year students a few weeks later, I discovered that they had also met this woman during their own third-year practicum the year before. The fourth-year students had a very negative opinion of her: she was called a 'manipulator' (described as someone who has a hidden agenda: *xinli you shu*) who 'uses' people *(yong ren)*. They too had been enamoured of her at first because she had spent all her time with them and at the end of the excavation had promised to write and send pictures. But she never did. This breaking of her promise would have been fine, said one of the students, had she not *appeared* to be so trustworthy. The combination of pursuing friendship without following through (revealing herself as untrustworthy) was read by the students as immoral, as related to her needs of the moment. She was not someone willing to undertake the responsibility of a real, long-term relationship.

In contrast to the manipulative woman, the male foreigner was neither condemned nor insulted. The students never used the words *Zhongguo tong* to describe him because he, as he himself told me, had privacy and noise issues and could not be around the students for very long before he had to go out for a walk. Walking – especially alone – is neither a common nor a sanctioned activity because it invites accident and suggests a lack of cohesiveness. Each student whom I asked about him brought up his apparent lack of interest in getting to know the students or becoming part of the team. In this case, his foreignness, which can usually be used as a good excuse to explain away any oddities, was almost not enough for the students to get over his asocial behaviour. Nevertheless, while the students disapproved of his behaviour, they never labelled him a manipulator: he may not have been fully socialized, but at least he was being straightforward about his lack of interest in the students.

Analysis of the different moral language used to describe these two foreigners leads us to understand the contradiction and uncertainty at the core of the rule of reciprocity: even as trustworthiness must be judged based on present and past actions, it depends on *future* actions. That is, the quality of trustworthiness assumes long-term, repeated, and repeatable interactions. If the system is to work, then the investment in a present relationship must lead to dividends paid out in the future. Who knows whether a person is really as trustworthy as he seems? He could take what is given to him and leave, never to repay his debts. The uncertainties over a person's trustworthiness seem to be reducible only over time and through experience, which is why long-term, well-known relationships are preferable to new ones, even if the new relationship appears to have more instrumental benefits to offer. Uncertainty over trustworthiness drives people to expend great efforts on proving themselves by maintaining face (somewhat like maintaining a good consumer rating) or investigating the reputations of others (through gossip, background checks, or judging the quality of their other relationships). In such a context, especially in a small discipline such as archeology, in which almost everyone knows everyone else, maintaining a good reputation requires paying attention to every social relationship by guarding it, maintaining it, and, above all, strengthening it over time.

Maintenance and Intensification as Reciprocal Acts

Strategies of performing, maintaining, and intensifying one's face and reputation, and therefore one's trustworthiness, are legion. The most celebrated strategies relate, of course, to the giving of gifts. From the perspective of trustworthiness and compatibility, gift giving can be seen as a technique of both performance and judgment. Giving gifts shows one's willingness to invest in a relationship by generously repaying any debts owed; at the same time, doing so is a test to see if the other person will react in an appropriate, and appropriately generous, manner. The quality and worth of the gifts passed back and forth also both perform and test compatibility. Given the norm of reciprocity combined with the mixed-tie relation, the giving of gifts is only justified if the relationship has a future.

Exactly what constitutes a gift depends on a variety of issues. First, the gift itself may be material or immaterial. It can be something claimed to be rare or difficult to get, since this implies special effort by the gift giver, or it can be something common but made special by the circumstances in which it is given. Regardless, what is particularly important is that the gift be perceived as a gift by the receiver: that is, it must be something that he wants (or the giver thinks he wants) or something defined by tradition as a gift (e.g., a New Year's box of candy, a moon cake for the moon festival, etc.).

All gifts take their meanings from their histories as 'objects.' As Arjun Appadurai points out, things have biographies and reputations just like people: an object's implications and meaning change depending on who has used the object, performed it, promoted it, written about it, sold it, or otherwise done something to it – or the class of objects to which it belongs – in the past.[20] Gifts similarly take meanings from the comparison of the present gift-exchange event with past gift-exchange events that have involved the same class of objects and persons. Meaning thus arises out of combinations: of history, context, event, and the particular circumstances of the persons involved.

The potential meanings of gifts appear to be innumerable from the perspective of the outside observer. Luckily, within actual communities of gift exchange, the interpretation of a gift's meaning is facilitated by habits and histories of past gift exchanges. This is not to say that the choosing of a gift and its reception are not fraught with uncertainty and worry. Both gift giver and receiver, at different times, must figure out what was meant by the gift, its value, and how to repay the debt that it represents. However, given socialization (in the form of more or less conscious instruction by parents, community members, and even, at least in the case of intellectuals, actual teachers) and the tendency to emulate the actions of others, especially people with high moral standing, community members limit the information that they believe they must take into account. No description of gift giving, then, can be removed from the specific community in which it is undertaken.[21]

The specifics of the community in which gift exchanges are to be analyzed are important because much of the interpretation of the meanings of gifts depends on a comparison between a specific gift-exchange event and the 'norms' of gift giving that have already been established for that type of gift exchanged with that type of person. Only by comparing the specific to the expected can one determine whether the gift giver has taken that extra step or is merely engaging in the minimum in response to the social contract.

It thus becomes important to analyze the *manner* in which any gift is given. The prescriptive norms insist that a teacher must provide protection to the student, but nowhere do they require that he provide it well or badly, quickly or slowly, with great pomp and ceremony or quietly and reservedly. Each variation in manner, timing, or attitude reveals something about the teacher and his opinion about his students. But that variation can only be noticed and interpreted if there is a widely shared standard of behaviour against which it can be compared. The unusual can only be defined in relation to the norm. Whether the norm in question is widely shared is a different problem altogether; what is important here is that the immediate community believes that there is a norm and has detected a variation of it.

Note, therefore, that there are two kinds of gift giving: the giving of gifts in a manner required by the norms of any given relationship – these are 'gifts of maintenance' – and the giving of gifts in an unusual manner in order to strengthen and augment (or destroy) a relationship – these are 'gifts of intensification.' The characteristics of the gifts themselves do not differentiate between these two categories so much as the manners in which the gifts are given. That the manner of giving gifts radically changes the value of the gifts is well known and was a subject that vexed the minds of Marx and Mauss and continues to vex scholars of consumption, economics, and social interaction today.[22] It is unfortunate that analysis of methods of gift giving and their implications is a far more imprecise science than, say, analyzing the merits of the gifts *qua* things themselves. I might point out here that Chinese archeologists, of all intellectuals, are readily prepared to analyze (and perhaps over-analyze) the implications of gifts, events, and combinations of the two; it may be that their peculiarly well-developed systems of gift giving are related to their training in the analysis of artifacts, assemblages, and site contexts.

Given the need to compare a specific gift-giving event with the norm, it becomes important to pay attention to the particular relationship context (parent-child? teacher-student?) in which a gift is given. Archeologists, for the most part, exchange gifts among themselves and their teachers, *danwei* superiors, and cohort mates. The cohort will be addressed far more thoroughly in Chapter 4; for now, I will limit the discussion to teacher-student and superior-inferior relations.

When I insist that no gift can be judged apart from the relationship in which it is exchanged, I am particularly interested in how it cannot be judged apart from the constant need to maintain balance within the hierarchical relations of teacher-student and superior-inferior. As we have seen, juniors and seniors will go to great lengths to position the junior advantageously. In so doing, however, juniors risk being too well placed. Being too successful by rising too fast and too high is problematic for the senior, who may find the junior beginning to outcommand him. If the senior is no longer needed, then there is the danger that the (former) junior will no longer maintain a mutually beneficial relationship with the senior: the senior's original investment in the junior will never be recouped. It is thus incumbent on juniors to walk a fine line between submission and compatibility. Being too submissive means that one is not all that useful to the teacher; being too compatible means that one begins to threaten the structure of the relationship such that the formerly junior person no longer needs the senior person.

Teacher Lan, for example, faces exactly this situation. In recent years, he has become increasingly well positioned by having received many important and useful opportunities. One of those opportunities was to travel to the United States and meet many of the American archeologists. As a result of that trip, he has been able to buy a computer and is the only person in his present *danwei* to own one. Other opportunities include escaping his responsibilities to his original *danwei*, located in a far-off western province, to be assigned to a much better *danwei* on the (much more comfortable) coast. He has also received various publishing and conference opportunities. Lan, in other words, is in danger of being entirely too successful. The Chinese phrase for someone like him is *chu tou niao*. It has the literal meaning of 'a bird with its head stuck out' and implies that the bird is in danger of having its head cut off. In other words, it is perilous to be noticed, especially if one has received more than one's share of luck or opportunity.

Lan has recognized his perilous position and has begun to lay low. He now spends a great deal of time doing *exactly* what his department director wants him to do. Lan volunteered for the job of leading a practicum (a job universally considered annoying and difficult) in such a bad region (the excavation is being undertaken as a result of a construction project and is devoid of archeological value because it is too rushed) so that his director will see him as a man who knows his place and, therefore, is a moral person who upholds the implicit values of reciprocity as well as the maintenance of balance in the superior-inferior relationship. Lan's gift is one of obedience: by submitting, Lan performs his trustworthiness to his director and anyone else who is watching. He is willing to submit to the junior role in order to maintain the social contract.

But Lan went further than just giving a gift of maintenance. He also played with the way in which it was given in order to intensify his relationship with his director yet without acquiring more opportunities or material benefits that would negate the attempted intensification. Lan played an elaborate game: he volunteered to lead the practicum before being asked, but he did so only after two crucial factors had been made clear. First, it had become obvious that the director was having trouble figuring out whom to send on the practicum; second, the co-leader of the practicum had already been chosen. Why was it important that someone had already been chosen to colead the practicum? It turned out that the man chosen, Teacher Xu, disliked Teacher Lan, and Lan appeared to dislike Xu in return. That they 'really' did hate each other seemed to be obvious to everyone who watched these events unfold, so, when Lan chose voluntarily to accompany Xu on a three-month trip to the countryside, it was considered to be a 'true' sacrifice, a really useful gift to the long-suffering director. Lan's gift thus clearly indicates that this teacher is prepared to do anything to guard his relations with his director.

The Effects of Class on Gifts and Gift Giving

Lan's gift was a case of a usual gift being given in an unusual manner to intensify its meaning. One can also manipulate matters by doing something usual for an unexpected person or something unusual for an expected person. To make possible the oppositional choreography of matching the expected and the unexpected, there must always be a finely differentiated and widely shared notion of who normally should do which tasks for whom. In other words, gift-giving strategies simply cannot work unless the division of labour is finely articulated in relation to widely shared models of appropriate behaviour. Only then can an action be defined as 'odd' behaviour for the 'wrong' person and, therefore, be interpreted as conveying an unusual and relationship-intensifying meaning.

Being part of a class[23] – intellectual, peasant, merchant, worker, et cetera – means that one is assumed to display a set of characteristics commonly attributed to members of one's group. Members of a class are expected to be more comfortable around their own kind because they are more likely to be able to judge, interpret, and predict each other's behaviour.[24] Being a member of a class is just another form of a role-in-relation – a role defined in relation to others who share a set of characteristics, standards, and expected behaviours that influence and guide interactions, reduce uncertainties, and increase the chance that mistakes and misunderstandings will be avoided.[25] Class can also be seen as a discourse that provides a variety of different foundational assumptions about people and how they should interact. Class boundaries are believed to be 'natural' and 'essential' and, therefore, extremely difficult to cross. Not only do people think that they belong to a group and should stay within that group, but they also think that a person should excel according to the standards of his or her class. A really good peasant is not necessarily strong, filial, ethical, or smart *in general* but strong, according to the expectations of his or her class. A peasant woman who attempts to dress up in a sophisticated urban manner is in danger of being derided not for looking bad (she may look very 'attractive' by city standards) but for acting unusually for a woman of her class. 'Being beautiful' or 'being intelligent' is a judgment that gains meaning only when it is shared between the actor and the audience.

This manner of judgment is rather different from the North American 'country bumpkin' concept. When a North American classifies another person as a country bumpkin, he assumes that everyone shares his hierarchical ordering of the social world that highly values the city sophisticate and further assumes that anyone in his or her right mind should want and, according to the American Dream, has the ability to become a city sophisticate. Individuals in North America are thus supposed to be competing for the same things – liberty and the pursuit of happiness, broadly conceived – regardless of race, class, and sex.

The corresponding Chinese Dream does not appear to require that everyone become a city sophisticate to be respected. Respect can arise from being a good model for the people of one's class. A peasant, in other words, should not aspire to become a worker; a soldier's child should not aspire to become a great farmer. Women should never aspire to be men: their greatest hope is to raise a good and filial child and maintain health and well-being in the home. There is no shame in aspiring to the ideals appropriate to one's group; rather, there are praise and accolades for being a good role model for others in the group. It is not a completely static class hierarchy because there is much to strive for within each particular class; there are, however, relatively few ways to cross class boundaries.

The only really acceptable method to cross class boundaries is, of course, to become an intellectual. Theoretically, any child, whether of peasant, merchant, or worker class, can get into school and be set on the path to becoming an intellectual. Once the child succeeds, the elders of his family have the right to be proud, for his success is their success. Indeed, the key to becoming a truly successful peasant (merchant, worker, etc.) is to have a child succeed in becoming an intellectual; that status increases the reputation of the family, for the parents must have been good in helping their child (trustworthy) and, through their child, now have access to increased resources (compatible). The intellectual class is thus the mediator between all classes: it is a category whose permeable borders seem to mock the notion of fixed class categories and whose promise of change and potential mollifies and deflates class resentment.

In any discussion of class discourse, it is important to understand that there is a hierarchy of classes. Both intellectuals and peasants see the intellectual class as at the top of the heap, the most important class not only in China's present but also in its past and future. The reason is the high value placed on knowledge and the ability to guide and advise others. In Chapter 6, we will investigate the many reasons for intellectuals to maintain their class predominance as well as the many reasons for peasants, workers, and others to help maintain the dominance of the intellectuals. Nevertheless, we already know one reason why class inferiors might want to keep class superiors in that position: as juniors in the junior-senior social contract, they can benefit greatly from exchanging obedience for protection.

Our task here, however, is to understand how the relationship between class and gift giving, as well as the discussion of labour, defines both what can be given as gifts and how those gifts ought to be given. Archeologists have brought the division of labour *(fen gong)* to a high art. At any excavation, it is virtually impossible to tell simply by visual inspection who is an archeologist and who is not. The reason, as discussed at length in Chapter 6, is that most archeologists attempt to minimize their differences from the locals by looking more or less like peasants themselves. But if one takes note of which tasks are done by which persons, the observer can distinguish between peasants and archeologists soon enough. A short list of the tasks that archeologists will and will not do reads like Claude Lévi-Strauss's imaginary list of Chinese dictionary terms that defy the imposition of an obvious system of classification by an outside observer:[26] archeologists will shovel the first levels of pits; do the finer trowel work; observe the workers; take notes; map a wall profile or site (if pressed); tidy up a pit, tomb, or feature; walk survey; host banquets; write reports and articles; and sketch artifacts. They will not fetch water; drive a car; carry certain tools; cook on site; build protective restraining walls on the sides of pits; take photographs (unless pressed); clean the first layers of tombs; take core samples; make drawings of artifacts; or edit publications (unless severely pressed and/or female).

Any archeological excavation, in any country, requires most if not all of the tasks listed above. During my own training, for example, I was taught that an ideal archeologist performs every one of these tasks. Even if we have learned little of a highly technical task, we are expected at least to understand what each task requires so that we can converse with the technicians analyzing our soils, drawing our maps, or processing our C-14 samples. Still, it is considered more or less ideal for an archeologist to be a combination of chemist, physicist, cartographer, and statistician – the implicit value system being that, the more tasks the archeologist masters, the better that archeologist is.

Not so in China. A good archeologist masters a set series of jobs and leaves the rest of the work to others. The cast of characters on a typical dig includes the site manager, whose job consists of managing the living needs of the archeologists *(houqin)*; the peasant worker *(mingong)*, whose tasks include crude digging, carrying tools, and heavy labour; and the technician *(jigong)*, who manages special activities such as survey test digging (e.g., using a coring tool), drawing profiles, photographing and mapping sites, and sketching and restoring artifacts. The key to the division of labour cannot be found in a different relationship to physical labour; while much of the more physical labour is left to the peasant workers, not all of it is. Nor can the tasks be classified by expertise, since to produce good drawings of artifacts, take good pictures, or take core samples requires no small amount of training and skill.

For my archeological colleagues, the classificatory key distinguishing among tasks is clear: work that archeologists do is distinguished by requiring that they think, that they use their brains (literally, *dong naozi*). Work such as heavy digging or photography (regardless of what some of my photographer friends might say) is not considered brain work: it is merely physical labour or technical work without merit beyond how it helps the archeologist. There is a class arrogance in the scholar-archeologist who fully believes that the work of direction and interpretation is far more important than good maps and plans, driving safety, or clear photographs and drawings.

The division of labour appears to be rigidly maintained. The discourse of class makes it clear that class members must limit themselves to the behaviours designated as appropriate for their class. Luckily, like most structured sets of rules, the very rigidity of class discourse ends up presenting opportunities for people to step outside their expected roles. Of course, and again as holds for all roles, there are rules guiding when and how one can step outside the expected class roles.

The consequences of stepping out of one's role are not the same for all classes. In the junior-senior contract, it is easier for a junior to break from the norm than for the senior. Since the classes are also related in unequal role relations of junior (peasants) and senior (intellectuals), it follows that it is relatively easier for site managers, peasants, or technicians to step outside their roles than it is for archeologists. That is, it is easy as long as the right balance is struck between deviating from the norm and maintaining one's role as a proper member of a class. For the most part, peasants strike that balance by capitalizing on the division of labour itself: since they are supposed to know about certain things, they can offer to teach that information to the archeologists (who, as intellectuals, are not expected to know about such things). Or they can transform some already acceptable skill into something more useful to the archeologists (the paradigm being the peasant who appropriately modifies his tilling skills for the excavation). Peasants and technical workers are immeasurably enabled in this strategy because, much like trustworthiness or reputation, physical skill is assumed to transfer well across roles. Thus, a driver can become an excavator on the assumption that he can likely wield a trowel as well as he steers the wheel. Under special circumstances – and this may be particular to archeology because of the discipline's unusually strong link between excavation (practice) and archeological thinking (theory) – physical skill can become so apparent that it blends into mental skill. Thus, one or two technical workers have gone so far as to become archeologists themselves, and at least one, to my knowledge, is now the vice director of a provincial institute of archeology. Not bad in a society where changing classes is not only difficult but also carries with it a kind of moral stigma.

When peasants, drivers, and technicians – class inferiors relative to intellectuals – step outside their roles, it is more acceptable and, concomitantly, less important. For them to step outside their roles is, therefore, rarely a gift-giving strategy. Indeed, it is usually perceived as the opposite: the peasant or technician is believed to have been *permitted* by the archeologist to step out of his role. Doing a different task is thus interpreted as a gift from the archeologist to the class inferior (regardless of who actually initiated the situation). Other archeologists or students will interpret the interaction as one in which the archeologist must have decided that it was worth his effort to indulge the inferior. I once 'caught' an archeologist in the act of taking driving lessons from the site driver; they were a good mile or so from the site, and, had I not decided to go for a walk at lunchtime, they would not have been discovered. The archeologist was clearly discombobulated by my unexpected arrival and immediately walked me back to the site, explaining at length that he was 'merely indulging the driver' by letting him 'act like a teacher' for a while. The archeologist insisted, of course, that he did not *really* want to learn to drive.

The audience, then, can rarely imagine a situation in which the inferior steps out of his expected tasks as an attempt to give a gift to his superior: it seems ludicrous, in a society where the division of labour is strictly maintained, to imagine that a driver would have taught an archeologist how to drive because the driver wanted to give the archeologist a gift. The latter, after all, will never actually drive and should ensure that he is never seen as wanting to drive in the first place.

Rather than manipulating the rules of the division of labour to give gifts, then, class inferiors tend to give class superiors gifts in the form of aid, such as making connections with local leaders or smoothing over troubled relations, or in the form of hospitality, such as hosting and participating in banquets. Open resistance to local custom or the orders of a local official or *danwei* leader, in order to help an archeologist, is also a potential gift. Between class juniors and seniors, only acts of aid or resistance to some other superior will be correctly perceived and interpreted as gifts in the eyes of the archeologists and other members of the relevant audience.

What makes it so risky for an archeologist to do a task not in his job description? Given the hierarchy that maintains mental skill over physical skill, the thinker risks contempt if he tries to engage in physical activity. An archeologist thus risks the contempt not only of his colleagues, who would not understand why he would stoop to the specialized tasks of a technician, but also of his class inferiors, who would no longer see him as emblematic of his class. Such an archeologist endangers his reputation of being trustworthy and compatible. Class inferiors, moreover, are entirely proud of their physical skills and would dismiss as foolish any weak scholar trying to dig as well as a farmer or take photos as well as a professional photographer.

Since so much risk is involved, the intellectual who does step outside his role likely does so for a calculated reason, one probably related to the strengthening of a social relationship. Perhaps the archeologist learning how to drive, then, was intent on making closer ties with the driver because of the latter's personal ties to a local official or peasant leader. The driver might have perceived the archeologist's interest in his profession as a gift of respect, made more meaningful because of the risks that the archeologist took in giving that gift. Once again it is clear that these kinds of interpretations of and opportunities for gift exchange cannot occur without the prior existence of strongly delineated standards of behaviour and the contexts in which certain behaviours are expected to be done.

Acts of Entrapment

Among archeologists, within their own class, the manipulation of the division of labour can be devious and clever indeed. Junior archeologists, like class juniors, risk less by stepping out of their expected roles than do their seniors (teachers or workplace superiors). Given the moral implications of being a senior in any senior-junior relationship, the senior who does the unexpected, especially by 'slumming' and doing the job reserved for someone else, risks not only the contempt of his or her fellows but also the ruin of his or her reputation as a trustworthy and compatible person. Within a certain class it is perfectly acceptable, after all, for juniors to want to do the 'better' jobs usually reserved for their seniors; it is inexplicable to the extent of being an affront to the 'way things are' if a senior suddenly starts doing the 'worse' jobs reserved for his or her juniors.

That need for seniors to maintain their reputation as trustworthy and compatible is what allows juniors to *entrap* their seniors. Entrapment here means that superiors can be forced into gift-exchange relations that are unwanted and become ever more onerous as the debt burden passed back and forth becomes incrementally greater over time. As the debt increases, the senior may simply not have the wherewithal to hold up his end of the relationship. Yet he *must* maintain that relationship: if one fails to act appropriately even in one relationship, then that failure will affect one's face and reputation and therefore every other relationship. Mutually reciprocal relations, then, can become strategies to check and balance the relationship between juniors and seniors: the junior can often force a senior to act or to stop acting. This aspect of mutually reciprocal relations is a remarkable source of agency for the junior, depending on how well the junior succeeds in getting the senior to accept increasingly valuable gifts. Yet we will also see that the creative senior can entrap the junior right back.

Entrapment is effective because, given the need to maintain reputation, people will act as if they are always being watched by either an actual or an imagined audience. A person must maintain proper behaviour in all his roles to continue to be deemed compatible and trustworthy in any given one. Yan Yunxiang's work provides a particularly detailed description of the impact of gossip on the success of gift exchange and relationship maintenance and how the fear of 'losing face' can be a formidable incentive to act appropriately given local norms.[27] The goal is to get the audience, especially the audience-that-matters – which, as we shall see, can be further broken down – to agree to an actor's claim that his actions are appropriate, moral, or otherwise worthy of respect.

Entrapment of seniors by juniors is possible because gift-giving exchanges are never simple 'gifts given and gifts received' events but continuous, back-and-forth exchanges during which gift giver and gift receiver change places. When a gift is given, the giver is in a morally superior position and has the greater agency in the exchange, since in choosing the gift and method of giving he can control and guide the behaviour of the receiver.[28] Yet, in the next exchange, he loses both moral superiority and agency by accepting the return gift. Both gift giver and gift receiver are aware that whatever plans accompanied the first exchange can be manipulated or converted by the return gift. Moral superiority and agency are exchanged between giver and receiver even as much as they exchange debt, and, when the junior is in the position of being the gift giver, his ability to control and manipulate a given situation more than overcomes his hierarchically inferior role with regard to his superior.

The entrapment of seniors by juniors that involves the manipulation of expected duties and roles in the context of a rigid division of labour is best examined by stories drawn from the interaction between director and archeologist in the workplace. If the workplace director must ask the archeologist to do some unusual task, then the archeologist can expect that, the more unusual the task, the more compensation can be expected in return for compliance. Since 'everyone knows' and 'everyone agrees' on who should do which jobs, the director will be aware that everyone who sees the archeologist do this task will know that the director must have ordered it done (since it is impossible to imagine the archeologist choosing to do it on his own). Once the task is done, the archeologist, having had his actions judged to be moral or appropriate by the audience, has the right to demand that the director do something unusual for him in return.

Imagine if a director, forced by circumstance, had to ask one of his older and more experienced archeologists to 'waste' his time helping the local university lead a student practicum. The archeologist, in agreeing to do so, is as aware as the director that 'people will talk' when they see him on the dig. The director is therefore asking the archeologist to risk his reputation as a senior archeologist, since it cannot be totally certain that the relevant audience members will immediately understand that the archeologist is 'helping out' the director as opposed to, say, 'being punished' by the director. Asking someone to risk his reputation is, as one might imagine, asking a lot. The archeologist now has a choice: should he respond happily, with reluctance, or with refusal and undermine the excavation? His choice depends on his own reading of the potential audience reaction to any of the choices and whether his reputation would be enhanced or further impacted. Obedience to the director and an air of martyrdom are the preferred reactions: obedience indicates that he is someone who follows the rules of the junior-senior contract and therefore can be trusted to shoulder the responsibilities of his roles in other relationships; the air of martyrdom indicates that he does not feel all that junior in relation to the director and therefore intensifies the importance of his act of obedience in the eyes of both the director and other members of the audience.

If the director does not give something of corresponding value in return for this 'selfless' act by the archeologist, then he will find that his own reputation as a compatible partner, as someone who can be trusted to have access to the resources that make him useful in a junior-senior relation, is at risk. Depending on how well the archeologist played his part, the director may find himself required to give something far larger in return than he bargained for. Of course, the director remains the superior of the archeologist, and therefore this kind of entrapment by the archeologist is a risky business. If the audience does not judge the archeologist's actions as justifiable, then the archeologist will be severely criticized as having stepped outside his proper place. Successfully gaining the approval of any given audience is not a simple task but depends, unsurprisingly, on how the archeologist's trustworthiness and compatibility are perceived by each audience member, each of whom has reasons for supporting, or not supporting, the archeologist.

Both archeologist and director are aware of the role of the audience in determining what the director should give the archeologist as a reward for participating in the practicum. As a result, even as the archeologist is determining how he should act to further entrap the director, he is also using the occasion to maintain or intensify his relations with members of the audience. For example, the archeologist might ask a junior archeologist, who normally would not be asked to participate in leading a practicum because of his inexperience, to go along and help him with the leadership activities. The junior receives the honour of being asked to help and is bound more tightly to the senior archeologist. The director, for his part, can mitigate his own situation by using the fact that he is sending such a senior and experienced archeologist to lead the practicum as a way to intensify his relations with members of the local university. He may have to give something valuable to the archeologist – indeed, in the case in question, he had to help the archeologist visit the United States – but at least he will manage to secure closer ties with the academics at the university.

As director and archeologist contemplate securing the support of different audience members, they must be aware of their differing hierarchical relations with regard to each person. That is, the archeologist, though enjoying the seniority of being relatively experienced, must be aware that he is not the director and therefore cannot command his colleagues as senior to junior in the same way as the director. Each member of the audience will also always consider his or her own reactions depending on where he or she stands relative to everyone else. The rule is that each person must always weigh the merits of one relationship against those of every other relationship. The implications of any actual act are therefore complex.

It would be too simplistic to imagine that face and reputation alone constrain the participants in this interaction. Under conditions of extreme interdependence in the *danwei*, a troubled reputation can have an immediate impact on one's own, and one's family's, material well-being. The *danwei* is in charge of all aspects of an archeologist's career and family life. Thus, the assessment of a person's behaviour affects promotions, opportunities to publish or excavate, access to better housing or hospital care, and/or the health and education of his children. The opinions of any member of the audience, then, whether the director or the most junior archeologist of the bunch, can have drastic effects on a person's life in the *danwei* context.

For example, Qi, currently the vice director of an archeology *danwei* near Hong Kong, remembers a time (long before Hong Kong's return in 1997) when his director at that time forced him to abruptly end all relations with

Hong Kong archeologists. The reason given was that Qi had mistakenly become embroiled in a conflict among his co-workers and had taken sides. He had helped his friend, a librarian, catalogue some books to get it done in time to forestall the librarian from being criticized by others. The aid went terribly awry, the books were miscatalogued, and the director blamed Qi – not so much for getting involved as for doing a bad job and unintentionally injuring the librarian further. Other members of the *danwei* sided with the director because, after all, a librarian (a technical worker) making mistakes is not as shameful as an intellectual making mistakes. The punishment levelled at Qi forced him to end his lucrative and useful relations with the archeologists from Hong Kong. Qi feels embarrassed to this day because part of the punishment was that he was not allowed to explain to the Hong Kong people why he had to stop returning their calls; moreover, he had to change his archeological specialty because he no longer had access to the data that he needed from Hong Kong.

Acts of Manipulation?

'Reputation, reputation, reputation,' cries a maddened Othello, whose love for Desdemona cannot be sustained in the face of the destruction of his good name by what he believes to be her betrayal. Whoever Othello thinks he is has been separated from his identity in the eyes of others. Whatever may exist of him other than reputation is but an inhuman beast whose right to rule among the people is in question; thus it is that a reputation under attack is an identity under attack.

There are as many ways to attack or threaten the reputations of others as there are to protect and develop one's own reputation. An encyclopedia of such strategies cannot be written, for strategies are utterly dependent on combinations – of contexts, discourses, roles – that in every permutation create different meanings and implications. That profusion of difference and creativity in meaning, however, is channelled by a set of unchanging standards, fixed ideals, strongly worded prescriptive rules, and the stock contexts and situations in which such things apply. Without such structures, or at least the will to behave as if they exist, communication becomes impossible.[29] Without predetermined categories and rules, we cannot begin to perceive behaviour, much less interpret or respond to it.[30]

Roles and reputations in combination with the law of reciprocity provide opportunities for actors to 'manipulate' each other as they struggle over the relations of power that move with gifts back and forth across relations of inequality. These acts of manipulation include gift giving to maintain, intensify, and channel relations among people. They can also be used to attack, break off, or destroy relations among people. In short, acts of manipulation are merely strategies of moving 'things' around among people; whether such strategies are cooperative or competitive, positive or negative, mutually enabling or individually limiting depends on the pursuits of the people who use such strategies. The strategies are merely tools; meanings and goals are supplied from the identities and contexts claimed or ascribed.

It is a pity that the word *manipulation* has such negative implications under the system of orthodoxy. Under this orthodoxy, the 'misalignment' of internal belief and external action is so determinedly condemned that it is hard to imagine that a person could 'play a role' and have good intentions. Manipulation refers to shameful strategies whispered behind closed doors. 'Petty politics,' 'the old boys' network,' or 'It's not what you do but whom you know' are considered (or at least people act as if they are so considered) embarrassing or discomfiting intimations of corruption or attacks on the ways in which things 'should' work.

Under orthopraxy, the moral condemnation of manipulation makes no sense. A person is very aware of the strategic practices of other people. Such strategies are *openly* taught and discussed by friends, family members, and teachers. A person knows he does it, knows others do it, and even teaches his children and students to do it, to act as if they do it, or at least to expect to be treated as if they are acting as if they do it. He receives benefits if he acts according to widely shared standards, and he is punished if he does not live up to them. All the while, what he is 'really' thinking is left up to him.

Nevertheless, orthopraxy also defines certain behaviours as unacceptable, and terms as negative as 'manipulation' are indeed used to describe them. A person is thought to have a hidden agenda not because he engages in strategies of maintaining and strengthening relations but when he does not live up to the prescriptive norms ascribed to the role that he has chosen to play. Therefore, there is no essentially bad behaviour in a role as is often assumed under orthodoxy. Any given act can only be judged according to the situation at hand – who has successfully claimed which role and what discourse – and 'good' and 'bad' are values that *do not inhere* in actions alone.

The 'rule of law' at work under orthopraxy guides the deployment of reciprocal values and acts. Those who act according to widely shared rules benefit; those who do not are punished. Social interaction is checked and balanced by issues of reputation. Because the benefits of the social contract are themselves fundamentally associative, it is also a system in which cooperation is favoured over competition. The student should surpass his teacher *(qing chu yu lan)*, not for his own sake, but because his success enhances the reputation of his teacher and his own situation in a mutual association enhanced over time. Competition would break the cycle. Therefore, it is a strategy best left to the creation of factions and cliques in which one wants to snap off relations with some people – converting them into enemies – to strengthen relations among one's group of friends. Such strategies will be further discussed in Chapters 4, 6, and 7.

The 'rule of reciprocity' is manipulated like any other set of rules, and, again like any other system, it tends to benefit some people more than others. What makes it unique are the manner of manipulation and the type of people who benefit. One of its more interesting characteristics is that the people who benefit more than others are not necessarily in senior positions. Hierarchical position is quite different from authority (command over and access to resources), and this theme is broadened in Chapter 4 by examining formal bureaucratic hierarchies and their impact on strategies of obedient autonomy.

4
The Separation of Powers

The bureaucracy is a circle from which one cannot escape. Its hierarchy is a hierarchy of knowledge. The top entrusts the understanding of detail to the lower levels, whilst the lower levels credit the top with understanding of the general, and so all are mutually deceived.

– Karl Marx, *Kapital*

The only thing that saves us from the bureaucracy is its inefficiency.
– Eugene McCarthy, *The Limits of Power*

Hierarchy and Authority

'Checks and balances' is the North American term for constitutional controls ensuring equity of power among the separate branches of government. Judicial review of executive and legislative enactments is expected to maintain equilibrium. In contrast, under conditions of interdependence, orthopraxy, and the law of reciprocity, the goal is an *inequality* of power as long as it is kept in constant flux across the asymmetrical relations of the social contract. Debt in the present is thus converted into an investment in the future. Now we turn to yet another system of checks and (im)balances that strives to limit the supremacy of any one person or group: a system based on what I will cheekily call the separation of powers.

I use the term here to refer to the curious fact that hierarchical position can be separated from authority. Hierarchy refers to position in junior-senior relations or in the formal bureaucracy imposed and enforced by the state. In the formal bureaucracy, it is assumed that each position is associated with a certain command, or authority, over resources in the sense of being responsible for their orderly distribution to the expected recipients. This authority implies the ability to decide to distribute resources to the expected recipients or to divert them into the hands of others. If all worked as intended, then there could be no separation between hierarchical position and authority. This chapter is devoted to showing the incentives to divorce command from position and the strategies used to wrest authority away from others.

'Archeology Is *Bureaucracy,* or It Is Nothing'

So far, I have concentrated on the teacher-student relationship, avoiding any real discussion of what is perhaps the most complex and convoluted aspect of archeological lives: the *danwei*. I touched on the importance of formal hierarchy through a brief description of the cohort structure imposed on students nearly from the moment that they arrive at university. This structure is a strategy of domesticating difference by suppressing (or channelling) unacceptable difference in favour of acceptable difference. I return to the notion of the cohort in this chapter as one of the most important strategies of separating authority from hierarchy through the creative use of that multitude of formal, explicit, written, and state-enforced rules that is 'bureaucracy.'

After only a brief time in China, I began to wonder whether it would not be going too far to modify Lewis Binford's famous statement that 'archeology is anthropology or it is nothing'[1] to read 'Chinese archeology is *bureaucracy,* or it is nothing.' My Chinese colleagues would (quite rightly) be insulted by that phrase. My archeological colleagues are committed scholars interested in archeology as the history of the Chinese people, the evolution of their culture, and the progress of their relations with the people on their frontiers. Yet, as my Chinese colleagues would be the first to admit, their lives as intellectuals are deeply affected by their relationship with the Chinese state and its present and future well-being.

I once found myself giving a lecture on the topic of 'The Bureaucratic Framework of American Archeology' to students and archeologists present at a university practicum. Teacher Zhang, my host, had requested the lecture; at the time, the last thing I could think of as particularly important to the understanding of archeology was the nature of government control over it. I spent an anxious afternoon trying to figure out what I actually knew about the relationship between the state and archeology in the United States and was convinced, since the topic, in my opinion, was so perfectly tedious, that no one would be able to stay awake through the lecture. When I arrived at the appointed time, I surmised that the number of people present was due more to the novelty of watching a foreigner lecture in Chinese than to interest in the topic.

Instead, I found that my lecture produced, of all things, an atmosphere of confusion and excitement. The audience had innumerable questions, many of which I could not answer and some of which made no sense to me. What control does the American government have over publishing? Which government office controls the travel opportunities of which level of archeologist? How do government officials control the distribution and display of artifacts? My answers clearly frustrated my audience. It was difficult for them to believe that American government officials do not control the everyday practices of the archeological community – publishing opportunities, the quality of accommodations and travel arrangements for individual archeologists, choosing objects for museum display – to the extent prevalent in China.

Members of my audience began to question whether I was not simply falling into the old 'West versus East' or 'intellectual freedom versus regimented control' dichotomy so prevalent in many comparisons of the United States to China. It was a slow process, but eventually I had to admit that I was obviously incorrect to say that the American government has little control over or impact on the practice of archeology. It certainly has an indirect effect in the sense of supporting the educational and legal institutions on which archeology relies, as well as regulating the university budgets and taxes that, in the 'trickle-down effect,' affect the salaries and therefore the travel arrangements and life possibilities of individual archeologists. The government also has a direct effect by issuing permits, promulgating applicable law, and, above all, providing sources of funding for archeological projects. We finally ended up agreeing that the only difference between the United States and China – concerning the role of government in archeology at least – is more a matter of 'visibility' than any substantive difference in the strength of the relationship. That is, as Teacher Sun put it, 'American officials like the people to imagine their government is uninvolved, despite the impact the government does have on archeology; our officials like us to imagine that the government is in complete and thorough control despite, regrettably, not having much control at all.'

It is the visibility of government in Chinese archeological (and intellectual) lives, combined with the invisibility of government control in Euro-American systems, that has caused so many of the misunderstandings that have marred relations between Chinese and particularly American archeologists.[2] Although Americans often write articles detailing the complex effects of their own government and Anglo-American cultural perspectives on the methods and interpretations of archeology,[3] the same sophistication of review is not extended to the Chinese context. Two extraordinarily simplistic visions are often produced: that of the 'archeologist as collusionist,' which casts suspicion on 'those' archeologists who willingly promote the nationalistic schemes of an oppressive state, and that of the 'archeologist as martyr,' which garners sympathy for our archeological 'brothers' who suffer so much in their resistance to the schemes of that state. While it is more or less acceptable to be 'guided by a cultural worldview,' as the post-modern Euro-American theorists at least see themselves to be, it is unquestionably bad to be openly affected and influenced by the government, as Euro-Americans (often) see Chinese archeologists to be.

Such simplistic visions of the Chinese world say a great deal more about Euro-American culture than they do about the relationship between Chinese archeologists and the Chinese state. Clearly, Euro-Americans define government intervention, guidance, and control as self-evidently corrupt. They are suspicious of their government and despise the bureaucratic 'red tape' that is seen as restricting personal freedom by being the prime method by which the state extends its already nearly limitless power into every aspect of human life. Bureaucracy is the butt of endless jokes, a source of infinite frustration, and derided as the 'scourge' of good government.[4] Given their almost 'instinctive' distrust of government, Euro-Americans seem to be unable to maintain a discussion of bureaucratic control without slipping into the assumption that its impact on people must always be unwanted and oppressive; or, if it is wanted, then there must be something wrong with the people who want it.

In contrast to the simplistic images of Chinese as collusive or victimized, there is a remarkable sophistication to the ways in which Chinese archeologists respond to the prevalence of bureaucracy in their daily lives. For one thing, simply by the open acknowledgment of the integration of bureaucracy in every aspect of their lives, they have changed their relationship with it. They have learned how to use its prevalence to their own advantage and, most importantly, *teach* those methods to their juniors. As opposed to being engaged in an individual struggle against a monolithic state, Chinese archeologists work both singly and together to outmanoeuvre bureaucracy and use it against itself. That is not to say that Chinese archeologists do not have their own share of jokes and stories indicating their frustrations with bureaucracy. It is merely to say that, by talking about it and being creative in their responses to it, they maintain their autonomy – that is, their ability to devise and execute their plans despite the prevalence and importance of bureaucratic control in their lives.

Karl Wittfogel believes bureaucracy in the totalitarian state to be so successful in its suppression of the masses that its people cannot resist it (he assumes, of course, that they want to be free of state control).[5] He promotes an image of government and individual locked in competitive struggle, in which the state's success is necessarily the individual's defeat and vice versa. In contrast, the Chinese archeologist, surrounded by rules, has no need to attack or resist them, for it is in obedience to them that he achieves what he sets out to achieve. Without rules, how would he know who is his junior or senior? How would he know who is in his group and who is not without some way to define the group in the first place? Strategies of competition

and attack, or cooperation and mutual aid, all require the structure of bureaucracy to remain in place before goals may first be defined and then
achieved.

Whether any given strategy is cooperative or competitive, it never attempts to attack the idea of hierarchy itself. The discourse of hierarchy, and
in particular the idea that hierarchy and authority ought to be linked, must
be maintained at all costs and despite all experience or reasoning to the
contrary. Just as in the case of the discourse of merit or reciprocity, so too
maintaining a discourse of hierarchy provides opportunities to predict, plan,
and otherwise reduce uncertainty. Far from being a tedious subject, the
methods that Chinese archeologists use to negotiate the demands of bureaucracy are key to understanding obedient autonomy.[6]

Bureaucratic Integrations

All archeologists are part of a *danwei*.[7] Just how deeply involved is the *danwei*
in a person's life? Han, the director of a provincial institute of archeology,
joked that he must take care of '*chi he la niao shui*.' The phrase is deliberately
rude in order to convey the feelings of frustration that a *danwei* leader feels
by being required to take care of the eating, drinking, defecating, urinating,
and sleeping of everyone in the *danwei*.

In other words, salary, archeological topics chosen, housing, marriage,
sites excavated, funerals, children's schooling, health, articles published,
interpersonal relations, a child's job and future career, retirement, remar-
riage, conferences attended: all of these aspects must be organized, managed, and dealt with by the *danwei* director. I wrote this list in a deliberately
confusing manner, without trying to split what a Euro-American might define as 'private' and 'public' because those categories simply do not hold in
the *danwei* context. When an inferior gets a divorce, it is the director who
will take on the duty of finding him another spouse and advising him on
what kind of woman he needs. It is the director, too, who will advise his
juniors on whom their children should marry, where they should go to
school, which doctor they should see, and how they should be punished if
they have become unruly.

In my own vocabulary, predicated as it is on that categorical distinction
between public and private, what a *danwei* director does is 'interfere.' In this
vocabulary, the level of involvement of the director and *danwei* colleagues
in one's life could be described either as the expansion of the public sphere
to subsume that of the private or as the expansion of the private sphere to
include the *danwei* in the category of the family. I prefer the latter description since the superior-inferior relationship is based on the model of parent-child relations. As we saw with teacher-student relations, *danwei* superiors
have the responsibility to care for their inferiors much as parents do for
their children.

A person finds it difficult, save by being adopted or disowned, to leave his or her family. The *danwei* shares that aspect of the family: in the same way as the family patriarch might refuse the request of a younger son to leave the family compound, it is very difficult for a *danwei* member to convince his director to allow him to leave to find another job. Although the question must be asked, even if a director were to agree to let a worker leave the *danwei*, where would the worker go? It is extraordinarily difficult to get into another *danwei,* and the economy is such that non-*danwei* jobs are rare. As a consequence, regardless of personal desire or ability, people tend to stay together throughout their lives in the same *danwei.* And since the director controls all aspects of the worker's life, he can ensure considerable compliance from his juniors through the threat of withholding housing or schooling opportunities as well as refusing to sign funeral, marriage, divorce, or birth documents.

As of 1999, *danwei* leaders were able to fire people for the first time. Yet at the time when I was visiting, in 1997, *danwei* directors did not hold out much hope for a quick change in the system. Firing anyone after so many years of the 'iron rice bowl' would be exceedingly difficult, especially when *danwei* leaders were fully aware that, at least in the present, there are so few social aid systems in place that to fire someone is tantamount to putting him in a situation of real economic hardship. Given the contract between superior and inferior, in which protection is due the inferior as a reward for his obedience, the act of firing a worker simply due to economic concerns, especially if the worker has served long and dutifully within the *danwei*, directly contradicts the ideal image of the director as a person who is both willing and able to provide for his inferiors.

Although it appears from a Euro-American perspective that the director has too much control over his workers' lives, this level of control, in fact, engenders in the director a strong sense of responsibility for the welfare of his workers. The burden of bureaucracy lies heaviest on the *danwei* director, who, on the one hand, must negotiate the complex system in order to acquire the best resources that he can and, on the other hand, must continuously care for and protect his inferiors. Worse, while bureaucracy is relatively faceless, especially the further away one gets, the director in contrast is face to face with his colleagues every day, and they are not too shy to demand their rights from him whenever they deem it appropriate to do so. After all, it is their *right* to be given certain benefits in return for their having *ting hua* – that is, having obeyed orders. Life does not get easier as a person climbs the hierarchy. On the contrary, the more juniors, the more mouths to feed and the more frantic the manipulations of the system required to keep everything from falling into chaos.

The *Xitong* Ladder
Archeological *danwei* are organized into vertical institutional hierarchies

called *xitong*. They are somewhat like the English concept of 'industry,' as in the steel industry, in which administrative bureaus manage the many corporations that mine and smelt steel, fashion it into products, and sell those products. In the Chinese case, *xitong* take the form of vertically organized 'lineages' that extend from the lowest bureaucratic level all the way up to the highest levels of the central government in Beijing. For the sake of clarity, I will use the Culture *Xitong* – the largest and most extensive of the *xitong* controlling archeology – to explain the concept.

All museums, institutes of archeology, archeology teams, cultural management teams, management teams of cultural sites, cultural relics shops, and any arts, dance, or music *danwei* – and the myriad of officials who control them all – constitute the Culture *Xitong*. Each *danwei* within the *xitong* is categorized by level: village, county, county seat, provincial capital, provincial, and central government (marked by *Zhongguo* or *Zhonghua* ['Chinese'] in the *danwei* name that I render as 'Central' in English). Much as there must be a point of view, an ego, in any kinship chart to define exactly who is included in the word *family*, exactly which *danwei* are included in any utterance of the term 'Culture *Xitong*' changes depending on the context and goal of the speaker. A person trying to explain how China as a whole manages its cultural relics would include the entire *xitong* from the top level in Beijing to the bottom level – I call this the 'National Culture *Xitong*.' Someone trying to explain only what happens in his or her province uses the same term to refer solely to those *danwei* that include and are inferior to the provincial level – I will distinguish this as the 'Provincial Culture *Xitong*.' Although it is relatively rare, since it is so easily subsumed within the provincial *xitong*, it is nevertheless possible to speak also of the 'County Culture *Xitong*.'

Taking our cue from E.E. Evans-Pritchard's notion of 'social distance,'[8] where two places geographically close to each other may be socially quite distant due to ethnic or other differences, the most obvious way to ascertain the status of a particular *danwei* is by examining its 'bureaucratic distance' from the central government. The greater the number of steps it takes to get to the highest level, the lower the status of that *danwei*. Lower-level *danwei* must deal with a greater number of superiors than those of higher status. For example, if requesting money, a low-level *danwei* director must worry about all the officials at each different step of the ladder reaching all the way from his *danwei* to the money-granting *danwei* at the top; he cannot simply leap over these steps and go straight to the top. Higher-level directors, of course, have to worry only about one or two steps between themselves and the top. The number of steps is significant because it is not only money but also a wide variety of resources that must be requested through this step-by-step application process. If a *danwei* wants to excavate, send an archeologist to a conference, publish an article, or hire or promote personnel, then it must request permission from its immediate officials, who in turn must request permission from their immediate officials, and so on all the way to Beijing.

A Multitude of Leaders

Until now, I have been playing somewhat fast and loose with the terms 'leader,' 'director,' and 'official.' All, just to be confusing, are referred to using the generic term *lingdao* in Chinese, meaning 'someone who leads.' I will use the term 'leader' to refer to the entire category of people who control archeological lives. Leaders can be broken down into three different kinds, each of whom has authority over different aspects of a *danwei*. First, we have already met the director of the *danwei*. The directors and vice directors of archeological *danwei* at any *xitong* level are always themselves archeologists who have risen through the ranks. The director is chosen by the officials, who use the phrase *kan zhong*, literally meaning 'to see and hit the target.' Once targeted, an archeologist can try to avoid his fate by petition or otherwise squirm out of sight of the officials. He is rarely successful.

I use the term 'official' to indicate the bureaucrats. These people have their own *danwei* different from the archeological one in the same *xitong*. At the top of the Culture *Xitong*, all official *danwei* are controlled by the *Guojia Wenwu Ju*, the Central Bureau of Cultural Relics, which in turn is directly under the control of the central government. The bureau's job is to oversee the entire country's cultural resource management system, to lobby for and publicize policy directives from the central government, and to organize the archeological budget for the entire country. At the next level down, a province can have a *Wenhua Ting*, a Hall of Culture. The *ting* is larger than a bureau and includes many departments, such as the Departments of Film, Dance, Music, Calligraphy, and so on. One of these departments, the *Wenwu Bu*, the Department of Cultural Relics, has control over the archeologists. Other provinces have a provincial *Wenwu Ju*, a Provincial Bureau of Cultural Relics, instead. The distinction between a *bu* (department) and a *ju* (bureau) is crucial: the *ju* must have somehow become independent from the Hall of Culture and, therefore, has an unusual amount of bureaucratic autonomy. We will return to this question of independence later, but here all we need to know is that, whether it be a *bu* or a *ju*, each has the task of overseeing all activity within its province and allocating funds from the central government to the different *danwei*. At the next level down, each municipal and county government also has its version of a Department of Cultural Relics that, in its turn, oversees the *danwei* within its jurisdiction.

Officials of the *ju* or *bu* do not simply supervise archeologists. Some also shoulder the burden of what I would consider archeological tasks. They survey sites, draw architecturally interesting buildings, and investigate reports of sites or odd discoveries by locals. The only thing that they cannot do is actually excavate or store artifacts; for those tasks, they must call on the archeologists. A good number of the officials working in the *ju* or *bu* of any level are themselves graduates of archeology or museology programs who, for one reason or another, were sent to bureaucratic rather than archeological *danwei*. In a fashion similar to archeological *danwei*-bound students, graduates of the better schools end up at higher-level government departments. Beijing and Jilin University graduates 'naturally' end up at the Central Bureau of Cultural Relics itself.

So far, I have described archeologists as having two forms of control: a director and an official. Both, just to confuse things, often have archeological training and end up doing cooperative archeological work together. Nevertheless, the two have different tasks and authorities: the *danwei* director organizes and chooses which sites to excavate, which reports to publish, and who does what analysis and goes to which site. In other words, he deals with the *yewu* or 'work' directly related to archeology as a profession. The official deals with the *zhiwu* or 'management' of the *danwei:* he appoints the *danwei* leader, clears the budget, expects yearly reports, and does the paperwork to approve changes in *danwei* structure, including the hiring of new people or the promotion of those within the *danwei*.

To confuse things even further, note that the officials themselves have both a director and an official. The officials' director decides who among his workers do which jobs: this can be considered the *yewu* of the bureaucrat, the work directly related to bureaucracy as a profession. Above him is the *tingzhang* or director of the Hall of Culture, who appointed the official's director to his post. The director of the Hall of Culture will monitor the budget of the Department of Cultural Relics, expect yearly reports, and approve changes within the department concerning the hiring and promotion of personnel: this is the *zhiwu* or management of the bureaucratic *danwei*.

I have not yet mentioned the third line of control: the party secretary. In China, there is both a government (populated by officials) and a party (populated by cadres, the most important of whom are the party secretaries [*shu ji*]). I had always before simply conflated the government *(zhengfu)* and the Communist Party *(Gongchan Dang)*: since at the highest level there is not more than one party in China, it had never occurred to me that there might be differences in the ways in which the two affect archeology. From an archeologist's point of view, however, there is an immense distinction to be made between his official and his party secretary. His party secretary's authority (command over resources) waxes and wanes depending on high-level political struggles among the leaders in Beijing. When the leftist ideologues are strong, the party secretary has more authority; when the rightist pragmatists are strong, the authority of the party secretary is equal to that of the directors and officials.

The role of the party secretary is to ensure compliance with policy directives from the central government as passed step by step down the ladder of party secretaries beginning with the top party leaders in Beijing. When Deng Xiaoping called in the early 1980s for the masses to 'Seek Truth from Facts' *(shishi qiu shi)*, it was the party secretary's job to hold meetings to discuss what this might mean for the practice of archeology in particular and how archeologists should change their daily behaviour, modify the language of publications and reports, and rethink excavation methods in conformity with the slogan. In other words, the party secretary is the key link between theory and practice.

The party secretary is chosen from the pool of cadres (party members) in the *danwei* and, perforce, is an archeologist (unlike leaders and officials, the party secretary is often a woman). Most archeologists are members of the party; as educated people, they are already considered cadres *(ganbu)* and are eligible to become party members.[9] It is the party secretary of the official's *danwei* who chooses the party secretary of the archeology *danwei*. Just as the officials have their own directors and officials, so too do they have their own party secretary.

An individual archeologist, unless he is somehow privy to the negotiations among officials and leaders, generally perceives only the united front performed by the official's *danwei*. An archeologist thus often speaks of juggling only *three* lines of control: his director, his party secretary, and his *danwei's* official. Since the official himself must negotiate with three lines of control, however, the archeologist is in practice affected by at least six different people: his *danwei* director (that's one), his *danwei's* party secretary (one more), and his *danwei's* official with his director, party secretary, and official (four more). Inevitably, the official's director himself has a director, party secretary, and official. Like infinitely repeated images in a three-way mirror, the individual archeologist faces a plethora of leaders.

While the exact details of Chinese bureaucracy may not be clear, I hope that the sheer number of people involved is apparent. More importantly, I hope it is clear that there are many different possible junior-senior relations, and many opportunities to play one off against the other. Let us examine the issue of promotion. Archeologists are categorized into different levels within a *danwei*: the new recruit arrives as an assistant *(zhuli)* and rises through the rungs of assistant researcher *(yanjiu zhuli)*, associate researcher *(fu yanjiu yuan)*, and researcher *(yanjiu yuan)*. A change in rank has a direct and material impact on the archeologist's life. A higher rank has a higher salary, of course, but also carries the right to better housing, to a hard sleeper rather than a hard seat on the trains, to a middle-level hotel rather than a cheap flophouse, to more conference and publishing opportunities, to be in charge of better or more important archeological sites, and to be involved in *danwei* research decisions. Even an archeologist's child's future – which

Figure 2

Culture *Xitong*

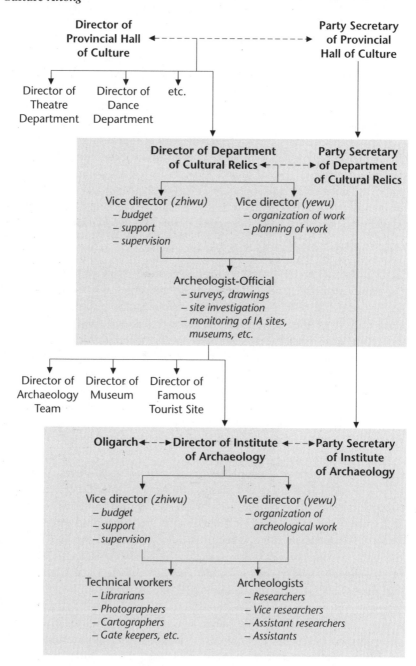

Figure 3

Education *Xitong*

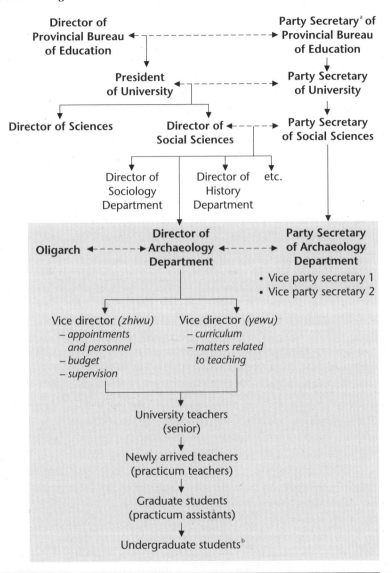

---

a   It is the party secretary's job to interpret CCP directives for the leadership of the *danwei* and to supervise the moral cultivation of *danwei* members.

b   The Academy *Xitong* structure differs from the Education *Xitong*: the vocabulary is different (e.g., *researchers*, not *teachers*) and the CASS has no undergraduate students.

school, the quality of tutors, the possibility of getting a job in the parent's *danwei* – is affected by the parent's job title.

Ranking and promotion of personnel are controlled by the leaders. At the least, all six people become involved, and an archeologist's fate can change wildly depending on who has relative authority over whom. What if his director respects his work but the official does not? Or what if everyone likes the archeologist except the official's party secretary when he or she is in a period of strength? Or what if only his director respects him but, luckily, is extremely powerful because of his social links to Beijing and therefore can outrank everyone else? The outcome of any attempted change in an archeologist's life is never predictable because it is based on too many uncertain factors. As Teacher Wu once said, 'A person cannot control anything; [he] can only hope to be in the right place at the right time' – that is, he can only hope to be well liked by at least one director, official, or party secretary who supports him and has the authority to back up that support.

To add to the uncertainty, archeologists are nearly always married. If an archeologist's spouse works in a different *danwei*, then she also has six leaders controlling her housing, food, salary, promotion, children's future, et cetera. These are things shared by the archeologist-husband. In effect, then, each nuclear family has at least *twelve* people who have direct, concrete, visible, face-to-face control over the 'bread-and-butter' infrastructure of their lives. The six on his side and the six on hers may not know each other well or clearly understand the situation in each other's *danwei*. Yet each side makes decisions based on what it 'knows' about the other *danwei*, knowledge that may have little to do with reality: if the one side imagines the other to be rich, and it is not, then it can have a grave effect on the salaries or opportunities offered. Alternatively, the two sides may actually know each other all too well and use the opportunity presented by the request of the archeologist or spouse to engage in their own battles.

The interdependence of directors, officials, and party secretaries means that rifts between individuals at the bottom of the bureaucratic hierarchy can cause altercations to ripple through all the levels of the *xitong* hierarchy. In the event of marital strife, for example, directors and party secretaries from both *danwei* are called in to mediate. If the mediation goes badly, disagreements can start among the twelve different leaders that can then be played out in the budgetary and personnel decisions of the leaders of those leaders. In short, everyone is so tied together that a movement at any level of the web ripples both higher and lower and can affect people very distant from the original event.

A Tale of Three *Xitong*

I have so far restricted myself to examples drawn from the combined Culture

Xitong because it employs the greatest number of people and stretches from the top of the government/party hierarchy to the very local. At each level, there is a way to manage cultural relics and people whose lives are, literally, devoted to that task. I say 'devoted' not in the sense of passionately interested (for who knows how they feel about their work?) but in the sense of their lives being utterly subsumed within the goals and structures of their tasks. There is simply no way to imagine a part of one's life that is not affected by the *danwei*. A person inhabiting – not 'working in,' because that would assume there is a life outside work – the Culture *Xitong* has very different expectations about access to education, housing, and opportunities for travel than someone who works within any other *xitong*.

Given the tendency toward complexity of Chinese bureaucracy, it will come as no surprise to learn that there are, in fact, two more *xitong* that affect the practice of archeology. The Education *Xitong* is comprised of the eleven universities that have archeology as a separate course of study and the multitude of universities that must include an 'Introduction to Archeology' class as part of history department requirements. The Academy *Xitong* is a complex of research institutes separated into the Academies of Science, Humanities, and Social Sciences. Archeology is placed within the Chinese Academy of Social Sciences (CASS) as a distinct unit called the Institute of Archaeology. The tradition is to call the institute CASS in order to distinguish it from the provincial institutes of archeology that, despite their titles, have no formal bureaucratic relationship with the academy but are included in the Culture *Xitong*.

Each of the three *xitong* – Culture, Education, and Academy – has its own distinct links to the top of the governing hierarchy, answers to different leaders, and has a different budget source: that is, each has its own kinds of authority. That authority is also differentiated by the kinds of status that the *xitong* have relative to each other, their ways of life, their standards for judging who fits the ideal of a good archeologist, and the life-career goals held by the archeologists who live within them. Education, Academy, and Culture archeologists are thus quite potentially different from each other.

Yet all three *xitong* do have similar structures with regard to the number of leaders with whom any one archeologist must negotiate: each has its own structure of leaders (the director and vice directors), its party secretary, and its own set of bureaucrats, the officials. Each also has a similar system to deal with requests for permission to engage in collaborative excavations, reports, and budget proposals: each request must be passed up the ladder rung by rung to the top of the *xitong*. The main structural distinction among the *xitong* is that the Academy and Education *Xitong* do not extend nearly as far as the Culture *Xitong*. From one perspective, the relative shortness of their ladders is beneficial, if only because the number of rungs to the top is considerably decreased.

Unfortunately, for the Education and Academy *Xitong* at least, there is something peculiar to archeologists that makes a short ladder detrimental. Due to their need to excavate and their desire for material data, archeologists cannot afford to be too far removed from the peasant workers and local officials[10] with whom they must work so closely. Because their *xitong* alone extends to the local level, only the Culture *Xitong* archeologists have the connections to work well at the local level. Education and Academy archeologists must therefore rely on the Culture archeologists – the least well paid, least educated, and most exploited of archeologists – to help them mount an excavation. This situation breeds ample opportunities and motives for sabotage in the form of holding seniors hostage and otherwise wresting authority from hierarchical position and is, with good reason, contemplated with dread by most archeologists.

Conflicts of Hierarchy and Authority

The success of any action depends entirely on the relationships among the people involved. Unfortunately, many people are involved, and each has his own perspective on the situation, his own definitions of compatibility and trustworthiness, his own goals as determined by his relative status and responsibilities, and his own hatreds and allegiances. The uncertainties produced by this situation are clearly correlated with the number and variety of different leaders whom an archeologist faces. There are no easy answers to the questions of which leader should be approached before another leader, which leader will react more favourably to one's request, and which leader actually has the authority to get things done.

It is under these circumstances that the separation of *hierarchy*, the formal structures and rules of the bureaucracy, from *authority*, the access to resources and right to redistribute them by an individual leader, comes into its own. It is the primary tool used to evade the relentless control of the hierarchy and/or the problem of a recalcitrant leader. The conflict between authority and hierarchy is not limited to a vision of authority pitted against bureaucratic hierarchy. The situation is far more complex, for authority can be pitted against authority, hierarchy against hierarchy. The possible permutations are many. Authority is a fleeting matter of reputation that bestows access to resources; bureaucracy is not a singular, consistent entity but in constant conflict with itself. Bureaucratic hierarchies conflict with themselves because *danwei* large and small are pitted against *danwei* of other *xitong* as well as against *danwei* within their own *xitong*. Status among *xitong* is not predetermined. Who can say whether someone in the Agricultural *Xitong* (the peasants) is hierarchically superior to someone in the Culture *Xitong* (the archeologists)? Who can say whether an archeologist working in an archeological *danwei* is hierarchically superior to an archeologist working in an official *danwei*? The bureaucracy itself cannot answer these questions, no matter how often it tries to promulgate policies, and these questions get more confused the more we understand the kinds of status games that individual *danwei* can play to change their access to the resources of authority and hierarchy.

Obedient Aggression: Changing Access to Authority and Hierarchy

The practice and the analysis of archeology depend, after all, on things large and small. It is no coincidence that artifacts and sites are collectively named using the Chinese term for economic resources *(caichan)* and occasionally by the kinship term for inheritance *(yichan)*, for it is by finding things and distributing them among themselves that archeologists can radically increase their compatibility (access to things valued or wanted) in the eyes of higher-ranked archeologists. It is these resources that break the link between hierarchical position and authority, such that a bureaucratically low-level *danwei* can wield authority (have access to resources and choose whom to distribute those resources to) over much higher-level *danwei*.

If any *danwei* needs to examine the artifacts or sites found by another *danwei*, it must first enter into serious negotiations. The more hierarchically inferior a *danwei*, the more it controls access to its artifacts, for that is its only bargaining chip with higher-level *danwei*. In return for allowing access to their data, lower-level archeologists seek connections through the higher-level archeologists to their high-level officials, who can then order the lower-level officials to provide the lower-level archeologists with a variety of resources. The perquisites asked for the most include being allowed to hire or promote certain *danwei* members, allotted a special budget for publications or conferences, provided with quotas to attend conferences, or given opportunities to attend classes to increase hierarchical position by attaining advanced degrees. In addition, since only provincial-level (or higher) institutes have the right to make direct contact with non-Chinese institutions, the lower-level *danwei* can also use their connections to gain access to the outside world.

In other words, once a lower-level *danwei* finds something important, its compatibility increases. It can then begin to increase its authority in ways that reinforce each other in an ever-upward spiral. Once something is found, more money and more opportunities are awarded. More money, more opportunities, and connections to higher-level archeologists and officials mean a better reputation. With a better reputation, the lower-level *danwei* can attract students from better schools. The students themselves bring more connections in the form of access to the famous teachers of archeology in the rarefied air of Beijing or Jilin. These students and their connections to famous universities mean that those universities might decide to send their students on a practicum in the lower-level *danwei*'s region. The arrival of all those students and teachers represents an infinity of new opportunities to create, maintain, and intensify connections with the university. At the same time, all those mouths to feed and bodies to house mean that the lower-level archeologists have more opportunities to strengthen relations with the local peasants who provide the food and housing. Choosing to house the students in one person's house rather than another, or asking a certain family to provide and cook the food rather than another, establishes the archeologists in their local community as people with resources who can parcel those resources out to their friends. And people with resources soon make friends.

Clearly, the key to authority despite hierarchical position is *finding something*. Making a discovery disrupts the stability of the hierarchy, unmasks it as nothing more than a series of empty rules, and allows low-level *danwei* to reap significant rewards. As can well be imagined, this situation has not gone unnoticed by the higher-level archeologists, particularly those at the provincial level, who resent the authority that lower-level, low-status *danwei* can command over them. The provincial-level archeologists have therefore expended much energy in convincing the even higher-level archeologists, in Beijing, to realign authority with hierarchy. Unfortunately, while higher-level archeologists have been somewhat successful in limiting the control that lower-level archeologists have over data, they have perforce increased the resentment felt by lower-level archeologists and incited them to be that much more clever in their attempts to work the system. Paradoxically, the attempt to rigidify the structure has but increased the opportunities for intrigue.

Higher-level archeologists have sometimes realigned authority with hierarchy by 'poaching' or even stealing the resources found by lower-level *danwei*. One method is to assert control over who is allowed to excavate and, therefore, whose name is published on the report. The regulation of excavation rights *(fajue zige)* was codified into law in the early 1980s by the Central Bureau of Cultural Relics. The 'right to excavate' was assigned to *danwei* based on the number of people in that *danwei* who had undergone a special practicum of four to six months. Every archeologist, regardless of age, status, or previous excavation experience, was forced to participate in one of these practicums. If a *danwei* could boast at least three such people, then it had the right to excavate. Unfortunately for lower-level *danwei*, there were strict quotas to control attendance at these all-important special practicums, and these quotas were parcelled out by high-level archeologists in Beijing. A *danwei* had to be invited to send people to the practicum. A lower-level *danwei* without serious ties to the top, or one that had caused trouble for higher-level archeologists by limiting access to data, perhaps found that its archeologists were never invited to attend these classes.

About halfway through the 1980s, these practicums were concluded on the assumption that they were no longer needed because all existing archeologists had been retrained. While it is true that archeologists of the higher-level *danwei* had all been retrained, unfortunately lower-level *danwei* archeologists had not. Worse, being at a lower level means that rarely is a university student (who would already have the right to excavate simply by virtue of graduation) assigned to that *danwei*, especially if it does not have the right to excavate. So low-level *danwei* are doubly cut off from excavation. In some provinces (Henan, Shanxi, and Shaanxi), even very low-level *danwei* have the right to excavate because the archeological yield of the province is so large and deemed so important that many archeologists are needed to manage it all. In most provinces, however, the right to excavate is most effective in ensuring that higher-level *danwei* gain control over the best archeological materials.

The situation appears dire: when a lower-level *danwei* finds something, it must call in higher-level archeologists to excavate; as the main excavators, the higher-level archeologists get to publish the report under their own names. The lower-level *danwei* disappears almost entirely from the written record and gains little benefit from the excavation even though it likely found the site and was integral to the excavation itself. On the other hand, if a lower-level *danwei* were somehow to be awarded the right to excavate, it can be amazingly beneficial. Because the benefits are so obvious and so immediate, I never found lower-level *danwei* attempting to change the rules regulating the right to excavate. Rather than complaining that the judgment of who has the right to excavate is biased from the beginning and openly resisting the system, the lower-level *danwei* prefer to concentrate on figuring out ways to secure access to that right and the benefits of authority that it brings.

The right to excavate is only one of the ways that higher-level *danwei* attempt to maintain their stranglehold on the best archeology. Another way is through the allocation of 'regional control.' Each *danwei* has a certain geographical region over which it has jurisdiction. Unfortunately, for the lower-level *danwei* at least, these regions overlap. For example, Jiangsu provincial-level archeologists can excavate anywhere within the province, including anywhere in Suzhou county. Suzhou county-level archeologists are limited to the administrative region around Suzhou City. Since the provincial-level archeologists have a higher status in the *xitong* and are therefore assumed to be better (more skillful) archeologists, they are often assigned to excavate the good sites even if those sites are located within Suzhou county. Of course, they must cooperate with Suzhou county archeologists, but they are able to use their superior position to ensure that their names come first on any publication and that they control any artifacts found. When questioned on this point, provincial-level archeologists defend themselves by pointing out that their facilities are better funded than county-level ones and that good sites would be ruined by bad methods and inadequate facilities. Like many generalizations, this one has some basis in fact. The problem is that the lower-level archeology *danwei* are never given the chance to start the arduous process of becoming more famous and thus better funded and educated.

Lower-level *danwei* react to these attempts to restrict them using methods that depend on their local ties. Most local-level *danwei* are related by blood to local peasants. They can thus obtain workers from their kinship networks provided that they are well treated in return. They can also, in a particularly nasty fashion, use their connections with local workers and officials to cause so much trouble for those high-and-mighty provincial-level archeologists that they find it more convenient to leave the artifacts or publishing to the local *danwei*. Lower-level *danwei* use their connections to local peasants to gain knowledge about archeological resources in the region and can refuse to report (but continue to protect) sites that they know are particularly good in the hope that someday they will have the power to excavate the site on their own. Similarly, they can hide data in their archives until they can be used in bartering; the hope is that someday they will have the opportunity to exchange that knowledge/data with top-level archeologists far off in Beijing. They try to bypass their own provincial officials and directly superior archeologists because the Beijing archeologists are so bureaucratically distant that they do not feel threatened by a tiny, bottom-level *danwei* and will give it any number of opportunities out of a sense of pity or even their own privilege. Provincial-level archeologists are far more resistant to creating a competitor out of a *danwei* that is too close for comfort. These methods are 'successful': that is, lower-level archeologists control the data to such an extent that higher-level archeologists will deploy ever-harsher rules in the attempt to wrest the data from them. Higher- and lower-level archeologists are therefore locked in a never-ending struggle in which neither can completely control the other.

Deposing Judgment

I noted above that finding things is the path to success in archeology. However, not all 'things' are equal. It it not every site that is interesting enough to command the attention of higher-level archeologists. The standards that arbitrate what is noteworthy and what is not are themselves tools in the constant struggle for authority despite the formal bureaucratic hierarchy.

Historic and cultural value (the two are often conflated) is ostensibly the main arbiter of relative importance in the standards applied to artifacts or sites. Cultural sites *(wenhua dian)* are arranged in a hierarchy throughout China; some are categorized as 'merely' county quality, others as good enough to be provincial-level sites. Others, such as the Terra Cotta Warriors, the Buddhist caves at Dunhuang, or the Great Wall, are judged as 'first-level' national treasures *(guobao)*. The benefits of receiving a high grade for the quality of artifacts are legion: for example, a county seat such as

Zhenjiang, a tiny city lost in the sea of Jiangsu provincial counties, can, because of the deemed quality of its history and the artifacts found there, become quite a player within the Jiangsu Provincial Culture *Xitong*. Individual artifacts are also subject to the standardized judgment system. A county-level museum that in bureaucratic theory ought to be inferior to a provincial-level museum can use the fact that it has a great number of first-level national treasures in its collection to increase its authority, and, through the judicious redistribution of those treasures, it can gain more money for renovations and excavations than the bureaucratically superior *danwei*.

High-level archeologists attempt to maintain an alliance between authority and hierarchy by instituting a strict quota system *(ming'e)* that ensures that there are only so many of each kind of national treasure allowed to be designated for each province or region each year. These quotas exist regardless of what might actually have been found: if one province or county has a bonanza year, it has to wait several years to get everything correctly classified. Yet again we see the expected response: by attempting to reassert hierarchy, the top-level archeologists have only increased the incentives for lower-level *danwei* to disrupt and destabilize the hierarchy. Indeed, these attempts by high-level archeologists to crack down only encourage lower-level archeologists to feel justified in their disruptions. One lower-level archeologist argued, 'The higher-level archeologists are so unfair. They are not acting as proper superiors; why should we be proper inferiors?' This statement sounds like resistance in the Euro-American sense, but it is not. The lower-level archeologists do not resist the system, nor do they dislike the idea of hierarchy and authority. Their goal is not to destroy the system but to work with it, even if they have to go against their superiors, to increase their own authority and access to the benefits of the system.

Destabilization at the lower level is also produced because, inadvertently, the imposition of a single standard of judgment on artifacts causes grave problems for lower-level archeologists in their negotiations with their own lower-level officials. Before a site or artifact can even get into the running for one of the quota spots, it has to be designated as important first by local officials, then by provincial officials, and only then will it be presented to the 'great archeologists' on the Archaeological Council in Beijing. Unfortunately, lower-level officials and the archeologists often disagree on importance. The latter are specialists who have been taught to judge sites and artifacts according to archeological reasoning; the former, unlike many at the higher level of officialdom, are not specialists and have no idea why the archeologists make the decisions they do. Nor do they care. They have their own interests in artifacts and sites based on whether a site will make a good tourist attraction or a well-stocked museum will bring money into the region. They judge an artifact on whether it fits their naïve ideas of what is attractive or representative of the past and are emphatic in their demands for beautiful artifacts that will bring them, the officials, fame among other officials. It is, therefore, extremely difficult for an archeologist to convince an official that a Paleolithic site – essentially a bunch of cracked stone tools – is of any importance when the official wants things such as bronze and jade artifacts to increase his own reputation among his fellows.

Local and lower-level archeologists might like to agree with the archeo-logical standards set by the Archaeological Council, then, but between them and that exalted group stands the ignorant official. The *danwei* director is faced with immense pressures levied by officials who will not give money, help out with the housing situation, or even help a child of a *danwei* member get into school unless the *danwei* finds a 'national treasure.' At the same time, the director is faced by a multitude of *danwei* members clamouring for help in every aspect of their lives. It is thus no wonder that lower-level *danwei* directors often opt to excavate the grand tomb rather than the gar-bage pit, even though the latter is immensely more valuable from an ar-cheological perspective. There is too much at stake – too many people's lives – to be rigid about archeological standards.

A single official also often has authority over many different archeologi-cal *danwei* at once. With everyone trying to get the attention of the official, the resulting intrigue among the *danwei* is intense. Their struggles can be harmful to archeologists' attempts to attain their archeological goals. In using the word *intrigue*, I do not mean to suggest that the *danwei* are neces-sarily in competition. It is more likely that several *danwei* will cooperate to have one site designated a national treasure in the hope that it will benefit them all. *Danwei* will often plan together how to approach the official, how to explain the archeology without sounding boring and/or patronizing, and which gifts to offer to smooth their requests. The attempt, then, to promote archeological standards by regulating the classificatory system of sites and artifacts at the top has led both to increased difficulties in applying archeo-logical standards and to increased manipulations of the system at the low-est levels of the hierarchy.

The use of a regulated standard of classification has, also inadvertently, created opportunities for intrigue at the top levels of the archeological hier-archy as well. Here we must ask the all-important questions: Who gets to decide which sites or artifacts are 'important'? Who gets to create the stan-dards that are literally codified in law? The classificatory system of artifacts was created by the highest-level archeologists: Beijing-based BeiDa and CASS archeologists. Both BeiDa and CASS are *danwei* at the top of their respective *xitong*. So close are they to the central government that they might as well be the central government, for it is they who advise and create the laws promulgated by that government. These archeologists are called together once a year into the Archaeological Council that is then sent all over the country to judge finds made in the previous year. As we have seen, their judgments can have enormous effects on the daily lives and prospective futures of archeologists all over the country: one decision made by this group and a *danwei* is either doomed to obscurity for another year or jump-started to fame and wealth.

However, the authority of the council is open to subtle strategies of redirection. Remember that the 'resources' over which a person has authority – that is, to which he has access and over which he has the command to redistribute as he wishes – include personal connections in the form of contractual junior-senior relations. Authority thus also means command over a personal network. The struggle over access to these immaterial resources can affect who is chosen to participate in the top councils and thereby indirectly affect the regulations used to judge artifacts and sites as well as the substantive judgments themselves.

Members of the council are chosen by officials of the Central Bureau of Cultural Relics *(Guojia Wenwu Ju)*. Most of these high-level officials are former students of the teachers at BeiDa and CASS. There is a fierce struggle among the officials over which of these teachers get to be on the council each year. These officials struggle so hard because each one's reputation is linked to that of a particular teacher: the more famous and powerful the teacher, the more compatible an official with close ties to that teacher is seen to be. The official's reputation will be immensely improved – at least for a year but usually much longer – by the appointment of his teacher to the council.

While the officials struggle over the appointment of their teachers, the rest of the country watches with bated breath. Each appointment ripples down the *xitong* ladder to affect the authority commanded by each archeologist. Each is, after all, a former student, a graduate of the same institution, has friends who are former students, or is somehow connected in a junior-senior relationship to one of the teachers on the council. As the fame of a teacher increases, so do the reputations of his students. As the students' fame increases, the reputations of their respective *danwei* increase as well. As a result, a director who has several students of the same teacher in his *danwei* will try to get that teacher promoted to the council. Even if the director has no direct connection to the teacher himself, he can help the reputation of his *danwei* by increasing the 'compatibility index' of the archeologists who work for him.

I made the point that the people who have direct control over appointments made to the council, the officials at the Central Bureau of Cultural Relics, are themselves former students and will benefit from their teacher being so honoured. They have personal stakes in getting a teacher, or at least someone from their alma mater, on the council. Yet it is also important to remember that these officials have cohort mates scattered around the country. Cohort mates will approach their former classmate, the official, in an attempt to influence the nomination of a certain teacher.

An archeologist named Cai once spent an afternoon explaining the ins and outs of his attempts to influence the council in its appointment of a teacher. Cai was the only student of a certain BeiDa teacher in his *danwei*, but there were four students of a different BeiDa teacher present. Cai was doing everything he could to block the teacher of those four students from gaining a position on the council since, if their teacher was appointed, their authority in his *danwei* would become too great for comfort. Unfortunately, his only personal connection to the officials making the decision that year was to the one who shared the same teacher with the four students, and Cai was expecting certain defeat. Fortunately, in the end, the official had his own reasons to agree with Cai that the teacher should not be appointed.

Even such a short description shows how many complex permutations are possible. The reasons why an official might want to help a cohort mate, a former teacher, or even a *danwei* director from his hometown are so convoluted that it becomes clear (or, rather, it remains entirely murky) that one cannot predict whom among the BeiDa and CASS teachers will be nominated or accepted to the council. Nomination is the result of a great number of strategies and interactions at a number of different levels. Interactions at the face-to-face level within an individual *danwei* far down the ladder can in this way influence the top of the hierarchy. Since the categorization of sites and artifacts can affect the relative authority wielded by a *danwei*, the attempts to gain influence and change the makeup of the council destabilize and undermine the entire bureaucratic system, from the lower levels all the way through to the top archeologists and officials themselves.

Fictive Cohorts and Commensality

Cohorts, it may be remembered, are groups of students who have been brought together for the purpose of education and, in order to achieve cohesiveness and group loyalty, have denied, suppressed, or channelled their interpersonal differences by accepting the imposition of a bureaucratic hierarchy. After graduation, these original cohorts are split up by the vagaries of fate as people take up their jobs all over the country. However, the bonds of group loyalty as well as the hierarchical structure are maintained such that cohort mates will help each other when they can or, if need be, ask for advice or aid from the cohort leader, party secretary, or health manager. Interestingly, the conflict between authority and hierarchy affects the cohort as well, since the status of some cohort members may increase far beyond that of their hierarchically superior cohort leader. Even as the ties to teachers or other famous archeologists reflect back on even the lowest archeologists, as members of a cohort gain compatibility in the eyes of the audiences that matter in the form of access to valued resources, the rest of the cohort benefits from their success. Trustworthiness, too, comes into play in the concept of the cohort since it is assumed that someone who was trustworthy in university is likely still to be so. As cohort members are scattered throughout the country, the cohort relations so important during school become even more important later as tools to subvert hierarchy and gain authority.

'Actual' cohorts are also and more importantly useful as models for the establishment of 'fictive' cohorts: groups of people tied together by friendship and loyalty for the purpose of managing and subverting bureaucratic hierarchy. These groups are fictive only in the sense that they, unlike real cohorts, are not based on a common experience of the educational system. The analogy with actual cohorts is not absolute, for now the 'unacceptable differences' are not those of regional background or social attitude (as they are among first-year students). For the most part, people are given jobs that lead them back to their hometowns, or at least home provinces, so those differences are mitigated in any case. The differences here are created instead by disparities in hierarchical positioning. Some members of the group are higher in status than others (some are officials, while others are archeologists), and some are in a different *xitong* altogether.

The fictive cohort created by these diverse people, therefore, is contingent and unstable. There is simply no official bureaucratic reason or tradition for any of these people to help each other: none is of the same *xitong* or *danwei*; none is a cohort mate or in a teacher-student relationship; and none is related by kinship. Most worrisomely, at any time each member can be forced through ties to teacher, superior, official, or actual cohort mate to leave the group or harm someone in the group. This group cannot and does not exist except in the actions of the people involved. To bring these people together, and keep them together, there must be a surefire method to proclaim one's continuing allegiance to the group, that one is still trustworthy, that one still belongs and is worthy of belonging.

The domestication of disparities in social or bureaucratic status is an extremely complex matter requiring the combination of instrumental friendship (people have to act as if they both like each other and are useful to one another), mutually agreed upon goals (material and immaterial benefits, including a sense of security from being part of a group), and tradition/habit (the methods of determining and performing instrumental friendship drive the creation of these cohorts as much as do the ostensible objectives). The banquet is frequently the site at which the instabilities of diverse bureaucratic and social allegiances are continually combatted by members of the clique. By appearing at the banquet and performing mutual displays of respect, each member signals that he has allegiance to the others present and will continue to be trustworthy.

Banquets draw their importance from being the stage on which each participant gets a chance to perform his trustworthiness and compatibility and to test those of others. Such cooperative performances/tests aside, banquets can also be places of noncooperative struggle and outright competition, of showing each other up, or of indicating that a person does not consider the others worthy of further effort. Indeed, a banquet can serve many goals at once. It can show respect or insult, or, more often, both at the same time. Matters can become truly convoluted: an insult to one person can be a way to strengthen the relationship with that person by showing that the two are close enough to share a joke, or it can be a way to forge a relationship with someone else, on the principle of 'The enemy of my enemy is my friend.'

The banquet can be seen as a field, in Pierre Bourdieu's sense, as a context in which there are habits of interaction.[11] These habits impel people to act in certain ways or to use certain encoded methods to attain their goals. There is nothing determinant about a field: its rules for action are no more and no less influential than any other set of rules. An appropriate analogy might be the way that one feels impelled to act in a church. One could run about shouting at the top of one's lungs, for there is apparently nothing to stop such behaviour; however, even if one is not a member of that church, or is an atheist, one still feels impelled to straighten the back, restrain one's language, and speak even criticism in hushed tones.

Banquets have a similar set of unwritten codes for behaviour.[12] Although each banquet unfolds differently due to context and participants, certain patterns of behaviour may still be discerned. Banquets are spaces structured by habit and etiquette: each archeologist or official has no doubt participated in literally thousands of banquets by the time that he has reached middle age. There are many ways to classify banquets. I will concentrate on two here, relating to cohort creation, and introduce a third, creating ties between social classes, in Chapter 6. The first type that I discuss is the full formal banquet: a tense event held in a relatively expensive restaurant on behalf of local or visiting officials and directors. These are tense affairs because people do not 'know' each other. That is, they have all sorts of preconceptions about each other but do not know whether the other is friend or foe. That uncertainty means that one cannot predict how a person might interact. The second type of banquet is informal and held among friends, members of a fictive cohort, but there are manners to be followed even among friends. During my fieldwork, I attended far too many of both kinds of banquets; two that I attended in the same day exemplify the differences between the formal and the informal banquet.

Both banquets were held in celebration of the visit of Director Hao, of a prestigious institute of archeology from a different province, who had come to visit on his way back home from a conference (his train conveniently stopped in this city). He had been invited to visit by Director Wang of the local archeology team (a *danwei* lower in status than an institute). The first banquet, at lunch, was in the formal mode and held at a local museum set up near a key archeological site. The host, the director of the museum, en-sured that there was a huge amount of food and drink, and we were served by very quiet waitresses. Guests were on their best behaviour and used their faces and voices to indicate grave seriousness. The toasting and drinking were restrained: toasts were offered only to the host, Hao, and Wang, and no one got drunk. No one spoke unless the host or guest spoke first. The hierarchy at the table was obvious because everyone was working very hard, by using elaborate performances of formal respect, to show that he or she understood and respected that hierarchy. As for conversation, the host seemed to be intent on making sure that Hao understood that the host's museum was extremely wealthy and had been visited by many famous ar-cheologists. The room in which the banquet was held, the host boasted, had been used to entertain Su Bingqi and Su Bai, two famous archeologists, and their calligraphy praising the museum was displayed prominently on the wall. When that topic had been exhausted, Hao and the host discussed archeology in an extremely polite fashion. 'Polite' here means asking ques-tions about logistics and facts while avoiding any discussion of controver-sial topics such as interpretation or theory.

Once the banquet was over, Hao, Wang, members of Wang's *danwei,* some of his *danwei*'s officials, and I all climbed into a minibus. Instantly, the op-pressive quiet was broken by everyone talking at once. Wang went on at length about how the site had been excavated very badly and that the inter-pretations promoted by the museum were incorrect. The official complained about the food, scoffing at the purported budget of the museum and won-dering if the food had been intended to be an insult or if the museum sim-ply had no taste. I said that I thought the food had been pretty good but was sharply corrected. I also learned at this point that I had inadvertently been a part of Hao's subtle attempt to discombobulate our host. Hao and the museum director had been involved in a subtle struggle for status by manipulating the norms regulating when a person can stop eating. The physical act of eating – the amount eaten, the time taken to eat, or the kinds of food eaten – is expressly not about personal pleasure or feelings of hunger. One does not stop eating when one is no longer hungry; rather, one must wait until the chopsticks of the person with the highest status at the table are placed on his rice bowl. Clearly, deciding when to stop eating is a useful way to flag one's allegiance to and understanding of the hierar-chy at the table. If one stops when one's director stops, then one is support-ing the director's claim to superior status. I had indeed stopped eating when Hao put his chopsticks down (simply because I had thought we were get-ting ready to leave). Hao proceeded to thank me, saying that it was very pleasing to be supported by a foreigner. I regret to say that I did not disabuse him of the notion that I had consciously helped him to insult the host.

That night there was another banquet for Hao hosted by Director Wang. Other than me, and two unnamed party officials who sat off by themselves and never said a word, everyone at the banquet knew each other. It was attended by luminaries such as the vice directors from the Institute of Archaeology, the director of a different archeology team from Wang's, and the vice director of the Provincial Bureau of Cultural Relics.

The guest list of an informal banquet is the result of strategies whereby respect has been shown, deals and allegiances made, and a certain number of enemies made. The existence of enemies both maintains a cohort and gives it a purpose. In this case, the enemies were Niu, the director of both the provincial museum and the Institute of Archaeology, and Fan, the director of the Provincial Bureau of Cultural Relics.

Fan and Niu both hold high positions in the hierarchy. In contrast, everyone present at the banquet was either young or of bureaucratically lower status, being merely vice directors of their *danwei* or directors of (lowly) archeological teams. The formal authority of Fan's and Niu's high bureaucratic positions was collectively subverted by the creation of a larger group of people in lesser bureaucratic positions. None of these people could ever individually or openly have resisted Fan and Niu. Their resistance was much more subtle: it was the performance of being in each other's company and helping each other by intervening in issues of promotion, making introductions to other people, mentioning each other's name in certain contexts, and promoting each other's work.

In the days before this banquet, I had spent time with Chen, the vice director of the Provincial Bureau of Cultural Relics, and had asked him to be my teacher in matters of Chinese bureaucracy. He had spent several hours drawing family trees of different *xitong* and explaining how the government and the party work together. Being my teacher in one context, he thus took it upon himself to be my teacher in the banquet context. He sat beside me at the table despite having to sit with his back to the door (one of the least important seats at the table). Chen told me that the restaurant we were in is one of the most expensive in the city and is owned by Wang's sister's husband. The waiters clearly liked Wang: they smiled a lot and treated all of us as friends. Wang had ordered an extravagant spread, but the waiters added more (for free) as a way of showing their appreciation that Wang had chosen their restaurant. Everyone seemed to be in a supremely good mood, and it was very noisy with people talking over each other and laughing. There was no attempt to allow each other to speak in any formal order, and nobody, whether of lower or higher status, waited for anyone else to finish speaking. The cacophony, chaos, and clear lack of interest in formal bureaucratic status were emblematic of a cohort-type group whose formal differences could be elided in favour of shared allegiance.

Since Wang had invited me to join in the day's festivities, I tried, ineffectually, to get his attention to offer him a toast. Seeing that I was clearly incompetent, Chen began to teach me the rules of toasting. He was not quite sure whether it would be acceptable for me, as a foreign woman, indeed the only woman at this banquet, to toast anyone, so he decided that I could be taught but should not put any of it into practice. Since Hao was Wang's guest of honour, explained Chen, I ought to toast Hao first in order to honour Wang. Moreover, since one of the unnamed but presumably powerful party men was seated in the next important seat, it would be a good idea to toast him too. Chen went on to explain that how much I drink during a toast is very important. If I toast someone, I have to finish my glass and show the empty glass to the toastee as a mark of respect. If I am toasted by someone, it is up to me how much I want to drink – but, of course, how much one drinks is clearly another opportunity to show insult or respect, so, unless insult is intended, it is always safest to drink it all.

Banqueting advice often stipulates that one be overly cautious and conservative. Chen noted that, if he were unsure about who was who, all marks of respect, all decisions about how much to eat, how much to drink, whom to follow in amounts of food eaten, and when to stop eating, would be made according to the most conservative analysis of the situation. For example, if he had no idea how everyone else at the banquet felt about each other, then he would stick closely to the seating rule and toast everyone in proper order. He would thereby consciously place himself in a deliberately inferior position to the most obviously hierarchically superordinate person present. Even if that person were not the one with the most authority, by toasting him according to conventional rules Chen would still show himself to be someone who understands and respects the rules of hierarchy and therefore can be trusted. The person with the most authority may thus think it safe at some point to entrust Chen with information about who actually has the most authority in the situation and how it differs from who has the hierarchically superordinate position.

It is only when Chen does know everyone else at a banquet that he will leave off being conservative and begin to play deliberately with the seating order, or even try to insult or mistoast his friends, just to catch them off guard and play a joke on them. By making them feel, just for a moment, that he was not acting appropriately given their relationship, he opens up the opportunity to reassure them that he is still their friend. 'You have to upset people,' said Chen cheerfully, 'before you can set them right again.' As the banquet wore on, Chen kept bringing up more rules and discussing how and when to make exceptions. He also tried to mistoast Wang to show what he meant by annoying someone – he toasted Wang very peremptorily and did not drink down his glass – but Wang just grinned at him and continued to talk to Hao. Chen shrugged; he and Wang are old friends, and that tactic hardly works anymore.

I never did manage to toast Wang at that banquet because I was never important enough to get his attention. Chen made it clear, however, that, just because both of us were seated in very low-status seats, neither of us should take it personally. It is not an indication of any fixed notion of our status held by Wang. At this banquet, Wang was engaging in his own particular project. His success was important for all of us because we were part of his group. If he wanted to impress Hao and the two party men, bringing them into the clique, then we should have done what we could to help him. Wang expected us to help in this way because we were part of his cohort but not because he in any way led the cohort. He would do the same in return if Chen were hosting a banquet.

One's seating position and relative status at a banquet, then, while always indications of one's relationship with the host, are not obvious or simple. The person with the most authority who takes the least high-status seat in deference to his cohort mate, student, or inferior who is hosting the banquet presents a valuable gift in the form of respect. But these games occur not only between a person of authority and the host but also among audience members. Chen noted that, if he had tried to sit where I sat, in the least of all the seats, other people at the banquet would likely have interfered and stopped him from sitting there. Chen has a great deal of authority, and his friends really ought to show him respect by trying, even if ineffectually (because he in fact wanted to sit next to me), to offer him their seats.

In other words, there is a plethora of possible strategies involved in the banquet that will change depending on who is present and which goals people have. People behave very differently depending on their relationship with the host and/or other guests in the past and on their hopes for those relationships in the future. Both formal and informal banquets are filled with uncertainties and instabilities. At the formal banquet, when no one really knows each other, conventions of etiquette can become weapons of insult. At a different formal banquet, the same conventions can merely be habits showing that one knows how to behave. At an informal banquet, the same conventions can be used as insults that turn out to be good-natured jokes.

These are subtle differences and changes, and to an outsider like me it seems impossible to tell when someone will interpret a gesture as meaningful, when it will go unnoticed, or when it will be seen as an insult or a compliment. My inability is not all that surprising, since even insiders, as anyone who has attended a formal dinner party among colleagues can attest, can overinterpret certain actions and miss other performances of insult or support altogether. The difference, I think, is merely one of expectation: in

China, it is well known and openly discussed that negotiations over status and authority are played out in the banquet setting. Students, for example, are taught from an early age how to show support to their teachers during a banquet: by arguing on their teacher's behalf, by emulating his eating habits, or even by formally expressing the wish to drink to any toasts given on the teacher's behalf (the logic being that, if the teacher does not want to drink all that much, the student will drink himself silly to protect the teacher). Those early lessons are integral in the quest to create a cohort out of whole cloth, so to speak, a clique of people whose differences in hierarchical standing are converted into something useful through the constant maintenance and intensifying strategies of the exchanges of material and immaterial benefits.

Danwei Divorce

Immaterial benefits of the cohort-like group include exchanges of respect, certainties created by strong mixed-tie relations, and opportunities to meet people and benefit from their advice. The material benefits produced, especially of a cohort clique that includes members from many different *xitong* or *danwei* at different levels, can be legion. Here I will concentrate on the ways by which these cohort-like groups can openly subvert the formal bureaucracy.

I mentioned above the crucial difference between the concepts of *bu* and *ju* in the Culture *Xitong* hierarchy. Director Zhang, of the Department of Culture (a mere *bu*) of his Provincial Hall of Culture, would greatly like to gain independence from the hall and become a bureau *(ju)*. Despite having only five people working for him, Zhang is charged with a great number of duties, including surveying, mapping, photographing, and drawing sites and buildings throughout the province. His staff barely have the time and energy to deal with cultural artifacts within the capital, much less manage those found in the rest of the province. Moreover, Zhang's authority over the archeologists in the *danwei* under his command (the Provincial and County Institutes) is extremely weak since Zhang can hardly get access to resources to benefit his own people, much less provide resources to the *danwei* directors whom he ought to be helping.

Unfortunately for Zhang, his province, Inner Mongolia, does not yield artifacts that excite the central authorities enough for them to support his bid for bureaucratic independence. Provinces such as Shaanxi and Henan, each of which does have a successfully independent Bureau of Cultural Relics, are extremely rich in archeological remains with a direct relationship to Han Chinese history. Inner Mongolian archeological remains, in contrast, are not Han Chinese. As a result, Zhang's *danwei* will remain subsumed within the Hall of Culture, and his authority over the archeologists will remain weak.

Zhang is helpless because he does not have the aid of archeologists in Beijing, who outrank his superiors in the Inner Mongolian Hall of Culture. There have been, however, successful cases of *danwei* divorce, and the tales of those accomplishments illuminate the potential for manipulation inherent in multiple bureaucratic structures. For the most part, a *danwei* such as Zhang's, subsumed as it is within a much larger *danwei*, must maintain its inferior position with regard to the director of the larger *danwei*. However, periods of intense competition and change from the outside can ravage these superior-inferior relations, and the performance of obedience to that director is no longer an option. The uncertainty engendered by changing structures of authority in the rest of society provides the opportunity for the inferiors to claim both authority and full structural bureaucratic independence.

The example presented here is the divorce between archeologists and museologists that resulted in the creation of provincial-level Institutes of Archaeology *(sheng kaogu suo)*. The creation of these independent institutes out of the remains of the provincial museums *(sheng bowuguan)* shook the archeological world in the 1980s. Before the 1980s, Culture *Xitong* archeologists were fully subsumed within the larger museum *danwei* in Departments of Archeology. Some provinces (Jiangsu) and cities under special administration (Chongqing) still maintain this bureaucratic structure. Most regions, however, have changed to a situation in which the archeologists are now in *danwei* completely independent of the museum. The two are fully separate but equal *danwei* with different tasks and therefore different authorities: the museum is supposed to study and display artifacts, while the institute is charged with handling all excavation and data analysis.

The creation of a new *danwei* is logistically difficult: it requires the establishment of an administrative building, the reallocation or building of housing units, and the hiring of librarians, artifact and site draftspeople, editors, specialized workers *(jigong)*, accountants, secretaries, office managers, gatekeepers, night watchmen, janitors, drivers, and sundry management personnel. Some statistics might help. In one institute, I recorded a total of eighty-two people associated with the *danwei*. Of that number, nineteen are retirees, five of whom are archeologists. Of the sixty-three working members, only nineteen are archeologists (and three of the nineteen are directors and vice directors and do not excavate at present). The remaining forty-four people do the various different jobs that maintain the economic and physical health of the *danwei*. Housing units in more modern buildings are given to the archeologists and the more important technical workers, such as the office manager, while red-brick structures are often temporarily thrown together for drivers or lower-level workers who, after all, are usually uneducated peasants presumed (by the archeologists) to be happy just to have the opportunity to live in a city and be associated with a *danwei*.

Since setting up a new physical space for the *danwei* is an administrative and logistical nightmare, one might assume that no one in his or her right mind would undertake the task. As a result, some museums and institutes continue, as in Gansu and Yinchuan provinces, to share physical facilities and even some management personnel, such as gatekeepers and the like, to mitigate the administrative and financial burden. However, every institute director, as the 'little brother' who wants to leave the family compound, feels the limitations of being too close to the physical space where 'elder brother's' authority still reigns supreme. To get the budget that would allow him to leave, the director must impress the relevant officials with how important his *danwei* is, how much work it has to do, and how worthy it is of the bureaucratic and financial aid needed to move into its own space.

The split from the museum, then, creates nightmares for the director of the new *danwei* for years to come. Yet archeological *danwei* persist in their attempts to divorce from the museums. One of the most important reasons stems from the control over artifacts: there is a law stating that the institute must give all artifacts to the museum after the former has finished analyzing them. Of course, as any archeologist knows full well, one is 'never quite finished' analyzing collections. There is always a new technique to try, and, in any case, most archeological *danwei* do not have the time or the funds even to begin analyzing most of their collections, much less publish reports. Therefore, archeologists have gained effective control over the artifacts, a goal worthy of the struggle to become an independent *danwei* with its independent headaches. Once the archeologists become their own *danwei*, the museum can no longer order them to hand over data and artifacts but must ask politely and give something in return.

The museum is severely handicapped by the lack of artifacts and not just because they are needed for display. Most provincial capital-level or higher museums have a history department, whose members are art historians or specialists in the history of a specific kind of artifact and rely heavily on archeologists for new data. Archeologists, after all, are theoretically not specialists in any one type of artifact; rather, they are supposed to specialize simply in the recovery of artifacts. Unfortunately (for the museum scholars), each archeologist wants to become a specialist. If the archeologist allows the museum historian access, then the latter will be able to publish articles faster. As a result, archeologists, as a tactic of subversion, simply do not analyze their artifacts until they have time to write articles on them.

Budgetary concerns are also a major incentive for the establishment of an independent *danwei*. The museum has a relatively large budget, but it can also have ten or eleven different departments – for history, archeology, exhibitions, artifact storage, propaganda and public education, archives, et cetera. The budget and energies of the museum director must be split among all these different departments. Archeologists must engage in a series of anxious activities to attain the favour of the museum leader in order to get any useful amount of money. An independent *danwei* consisting solely of archeologists and their support workers does not have to compete with such a large number of people for favour and has more control over its budgetary fate.

Much like budgetary issues, opportunities are also important resources for which archeologists must compete. The museum has links to places beyond its allocated region. It can arrange contracts for exhibitions to be sent to other provinces within China or even to foreign nations. At first glance, the independent *danwei* of archeologists will lose these opportunities. In practice, however, the archeologists had rarely managed to benefit from these opportunities anyway. The museum director chooses who accompanies exhibitions: that choice is always made on seniority and the social networking projects of the director rather than on ability or merit. As a result, as one Japanese archeologist once explained in reference to an exhibition sent from Beijing to Tokyo, most exhibitions are accompanied by a bunch of ignorant (at least of the artifacts in the exhibit) party members, officials, and perhaps even an aged driver or secretary being rewarded for years of faithful service or in compensation for opportunities lost in some other context (or compensation for historical wrongs during political upheavals such as the Cultural Revolution). Rarely are archeologists or specialists sent along.

Unlike a museum, an archeological institute cannot mount exhibitions, but as an independent *danwei* it does have the right to make contacts to entice foreign archeologists to engage in cooperative expeditions or in research on the collections. Independent institutes at the provincial level can also send certain people abroad to participate in conferences or apply for foreign grants to publish articles or build better facilities. While the opportunity to accompany exhibitions might be lost, then, opportunities to travel in China or abroad are actually increased for archeologists once they have their own *danwei*.

An independent *danwei* can also make its own decisions about how it will attempt to raise money. Recent economic changes have meant that the budget allocated to each *danwei* by the central government is no longer enough to cover expenses. As a result, the government is encouraging *danwei* to figure out their own ways of making ends meet – as long as these ways are legal, of course. A short list of some of the enterprises that I have seen *danwei* use to raise money include restaurants and/or karaoke clubs, day-care centres, antique shops, art and school supply stores, tourist attractions such as parks with cultural events, and *zhaodai suo* – lower-end hotels that have few amenities beyond a room and a bed meant to house visitors from within the same *xitong* but that can also house anyone who finds out about them (though they are restricted from advertising independently). Archeologists are particularly good at setting up profitable enterprises since they are able to use their connections among peasants and rural leaders to provide both cheap labour and the clientele. When working for the museum, the archeologists had to do all the work of setting up such enterprises (because the non-archeologists in the museum do not have these connections at the local level) but received only some of the profit. When they are an independent *danwei*, freed from the need to share the money with everyone in the museum, they can become quite affluent indeed.

The split from the museum, then, is excellent from the perspective of the archeologists and not particularly beneficial for the museum. Since the museum is much more powerful at first glance than one small department within it, it is valid to wonder how the archeologists managed to divorce themselves from the museum so successfully. The answer to this question lies once again in the strategic playing of the multitude of leaders against each other. If archeologists can craft a cohort of like-minded people who cross *danwei*, *xitong*, and official lines, then they can open up the space for a tiny subdepartment of ten people to become an independent *danwei* of eighty with its own clear hierarchical status and command over considerable resources.

We have seen some of the tactics, mainly of banqueting, that *maintain* this kind of cobbled-together group. *Creating* the group is equally difficult. The strategies involved are, of course, entirely contingent on the people involved. The only way to convey the combination of contingent, contextual luck and tactical thinking that goes into the creation of such a group is to relate a story. Director Liu, of an independent institute, related to me what is, I am sure, only a small part of the story of how he accomplished the divorce of his *danwei* from the powerful provincial museum. Yet even so truncated a story illustrates the tactical, contingent methods that he used to create a new *danwei* in which he is at the top in terms of hierarchy and authority.

We must understand first that Liu is a fairly well-known Culture *Xitong* archeologist who graduated from BeiDa in the early 1960s. He is also well known because the museum that he used to work for is itself quite famous. The director of the museum was also a BeiDa man and had considered Liu his 'little brother' *(xuedi)* because they had shared the same BeiDa teacher. As a result, when Liu first arrived at the museum as a new recruit, the director treated him well by offering him many opportunities, including excavating important sites and returning to BeiDa to complete his MA. At the time, the MA degree was considered prestigious since PhD degrees were extremely rare (nowadays, the PhD is much more common and no longer inspires so much awe).

Liu advanced rapidly in the *danwei* hierarchy until the Cultural Revolution. He and his colleagues spent the next thirteen years surviving the chaos. Living in a large city made this somewhat more difficult. Even after the Red

Guards were cleared out in 1969, the chaos continued. While it was less difficult after Mao's death and the fall of the Gang of Four in 1976, the chaos continued within the *danwei* as people continued to struggle with each other, often in revenge for how they had been treated during the height of the revolution. It was only by about 1980 that the museum returned to relative normalcy with the appointment of a new director from outside the *danwei* who, as an outsider, remained beyond the power struggles and forced them all to work again.

While the museum went back to work, the situation was no longer beneficial for Liu and the other archeologists. The new director was not a BeiDa man and had no connections to Liu or anyone whom he knew. The director had, in fact, been imported from another county so that no one could use previous connections to sway him. The archeology department was no longer given special consideration compared with other departments. Liu had already been appointed department head, but there was nowhere to go from there, and he was not being allowed to do the kinds of things that he, as a fairly well-known archeologist, thought he ought to be able to do.

Liu began to think about divorce. He had the support of most of the archeologists within the department, who told him that, as their leader and superior, he had the duty to lead them out of this dead-end situation. However, one person did not agree: Liu's vice director. This man was extremely good friends with many of the historians and did not want to be separated from what was effectively his own cohort-like group. Liu also faced an obstinate refusal to help from the director of the Department of Cultural Relics of the Hall of Culture. The director was against the divorce because he knew that he would be dealing with struggles between the archeologists and museologists for the rest of his bureaucratic career. It goes without saying, of course, that the museum director was also completely against the idea.

Liu began his approach with the problem of the vice director. First, he began to ruin the man's reputation as much as possible with the museum director so that none of the already diminished opportunities and quotas would be allotted to the vice director. Second, Liu had the colleagues and, especially, the two cohort mates of the vice director in the archeology department try to talk sense into him. And third, he promised the vice director that he would retain his post in the new *danwei*. The vice director, reluctantly, began to throw his lot in with Liu – his 'lot' including the friends whom he had among the officials in the Hall of Culture who could help to change the mind of the director of the Department of Cultural Relics.

Unfortunately, none among this nascent cohort-like group had direct relations with the director of that department. Luckily, Liu had several friends with whom he had formed a mutual aid group during the Cultural Revolution. Among these friends was a man who had been a low-level official in the 1960s. Liu had asked his own eldest child to take care of the considerably younger children of this friend when he was sent into the camps early on in the revolution. Although Liu's children were no longer openly acknowledging their father at that time, they still carried out his wishes by taking care of these 'abandoned' children. That low-level official survived the chaos eventually to become the vice director of the Provincial Hall of Culture *(Sheng Wenhua Ting)* itself. In other words, he was the *direct superior* to the director of the Department of Cultural Relics who oversaw the museum. Taking care of this man's children was not enough, perhaps, to single-handedly ensure the success of the proposed divorce, but it certainly helped.

Liu was also able to capitalize on the fact that he was a local boy with various connections, while the museum director was an outsider. When Liu started to campaign for an independent *danwei*, he was able to stress the outsider status of the museum director in order to encourage a form of regional nationalism among the officials at the Hall of Culture. He also called up his teachers at BeiDa and asked them to work on the situation at a level much higher than the Provincial Hall of Culture. On his behalf, the BeiDa teachers put forth the idea to the officials of the Central Bureau of Cultural Relics. While this bureau does not have direct authority over the Provincial Hall of Culture, it is certainly one among the several leaders to which the Provincial Hall of Culture must listen. And, finally, what likely had the most impact on Liu's campaign was the successful divorce between the museum and archeologists of Shaanxi province. Shaanxi, being such a 'wealthy' province (in terms of archeology), was one of the earliest to achieve a successful divorce. Once that divorce was made final, a precedent was set for other provinces.

Liu had started his attempt to divorce from his museum in late 1980, and it took him four full years to manage the deed. Even now, he is still trying to get the sole right to excavate in the province since, for some reason probably the result of negotiations by the museum director, the museum has retained that right. This result is unusual. It means that museum and institute are fighting over excavations in the same geographical space, and the situation remains tense. The competition between the two *danwei* to create ties to the peasants and lower-level archeologists, strengthen the ties that they already have, and weaken the ties that the other *danwei* has with the locals still takes up a lot of Liu's time. Liu also expends efforts, of course, to encourage the Central Bureau of Cultural Relics to take away the museum's right to excavate completely. This effort is utterly necessary, as we have seen, because control over data is key to fame and further negotiations with other archeologists and officials at different levels.

In this story, we see Liu creating cohort-like connections across bureaucratic divides in order to accomplish something that, theoretically, goes against everything for which a *danwei* stands. *Danwei* relations are ideally cooperative, and people ought to work together for a common goal. One subgroup trying to leave the *danwei* ought to be immoral. How can Liu avoid being seen as acting improperly relative to his junior role? The answer lies in unpacking his rhetoric. In telling his tale, Liu never spoke of doing anything for his own benefit. Everything was instead for the benefit of his inferiors, his archeological colleagues in the *danwei*. Liu further called on the trope of being a good patriot, seeing himself as helping China better manage its cultural relics. He also saw himself as helping archeology as a discipline, given that, in his view, the more independence garnered by archeological *danwei*, the more authority and influence (compatibility) archeology will be seen by non-archeologists to have. Finally, he also mentioned his goal of making the bureaucratic system more efficient. What does Liu really think? How does he really feel about the people, his goals, and his motives? What he thinks or feels is not important. What is important is to see that he does not rely on narratives of resistance, of smashing the system, or of individual rights to justify his actions; instead, he narrates his agency through tropes of cooperation and obedience. As an agent, he may speak of his autonomy differently, justify it differently, but the result is the same: he achieved what he set out to do.

Benefits of (the Performance of) Obedience

Teacher Li once said that '*Guanxi* is just like archeology. Both can only be learned through experience. No matter how often I tell my students what to do in some situation, the next moment they are calling me again to ask about a new situation even I have never experienced before.' Given that social relations are about making judgments based on events as they happen, there logically can be no such thing as a single method of social networking that affects all people similarly. Teacher Cao noted that students become fearful when they begin to realize how difficult social relations can be, because they are too young and inexperienced to understand social networking. They are right to be fearful, says Cao, precisely because social networking is so intricate, and there are no hard and fast principles to guide behaviour.

From an anthropological point of view, one abstract principle underlies all these different interactions: the more rules, and the more stringent the rules, the more opportunities there appear to be for people to use the separation between authority and hierarchy to get around the rules. The rules are *required* for everything else to work: they do limit some behaviour, but on the whole they appear to enable or even impel behaviour much more often. It makes sense, then, that Chinese agents in the *danwei* and *xitong* systems do not resist those systems but perform their obedience to them, even while they engage in a variety of strategies to achieve what they really want or need.

It could be said, in the manner of Wittfogel, that lower-level archeologists do not resist the system openly because they are oppressed by their superiors. Indeed, there is grave danger in angering higher-level archeologists and – by the law of extension of social networks – the officials of those archeologists. Such officials, after all, are also the directors of the officials who control the lower-level archeologists. The lines of control are too many and too interlocking; any open resistance would result in swift and wide-ranging punishment of the rebellious *danwei*.

Yet it is too simplistic to focus only on that aspect of the *danwei* and *xitong* systems. The separation of hierarchy from authority means that the system is not only multiple but also has so many inconsistencies that it generates more opportunities the more high-level archeologists attempt to crack down on lower-level colleagues. Moreover, top-level archeologists are as affected by the machinations engendered by the system as are the lower-level ones: there is mutual pain even as there is mutual benefit. Most importantly, however, the benefits of the system are so potentially great that even the most suppressed of lower-level archeologists would never think to change it. County- and other lower-level archeologists are fully aware of how higher-level colleagues oppress them to maintain the present hierarchy, but they are even more aware that increasing one's authority is the key way to mitigate the harsher effects of the system. If everyone in the *danwei* works together to increase its authority as a whole – and that goal might include, much like the parent who chooses one among his children to become an intellectual, cooperating to support one member's becoming famous – then life becomes much more comfortable for everyone in the *danwei*. Whether the benefits are individual or collective, the point is that the system is what provides those benefits, so it must be policed by both juniors and seniors to protect it from open resistance or attack.

Manipulations of the system by archeologists, particularly in their separation between authority and hierarchy, may be strategies peculiar to them. It may be that, in a non-archeological *danwei*, the lower levels yield their resources to their superiors and are rewarded appropriately. I doubt that the system ever works as it is intended, but I am at least certain that it does not work that way in the archeological case. The problem in archeology is that there is simply no way that a hierarchically superior *danwei* can reward a lower-level one for being dutiful in as lucrative a manner as the lower-level *danwei* receives by maintaining authority over the redistribution of its resources. There is therefore no incentive to act according to the bureaucratic model and every incentive to act against it. I hope that I have made it clear that bureaucracy is not a magical system of totalitarian control.[13] Instead, it is one structure among many, one that both limits and, by being productive of that many more opportunities to manipulate the disjuncture between hierarchy and authority, enables the plans and strategies of individuals and groups of archeologists.

There are lower-level *danwei* whose situations are such that they do not feel the need to increase their authority. Some of these *danwei* are comfortable, wealthy, and relaxed places to work. Such *danwei* are often out in the provinces where no one wants to live (the Qinghai Provincial Archaeology Institute in Xining, for example, is a beautiful, comfortable place). Since these areas are considered hardship posts, they are surprisingly wealthy due to the subsidies given by the central government. Meanwhile, life in a high-level *danwei* is not necessarily all that much more comfortable or happy. *Danwei* in the refined Beijing ether are often in such extreme competition that they offer only cramped, cold housing, little budgetary excess, and a tense, competitive environment. Moreover, being in such a high position means that everyone below expects them to have a great deal of wealth and power. If people think that the high-level archeologist is highly compatible, then they will place many demands on him, many of which are outrageously inappropriate to his access to and command over the redistribution of resources.

Finally, I might add that the *danwei* at the lowest levels of the Culture *Xitong* – far down in the depths of a tiny county village – are of a different sort altogether. I do not include these people when I refer to lower-level archeologists because they are placed even lower in the hierarchy. These people do not pay much attention to events going on higher up because they have no hope of becoming involved. They occasionally engage in what might objectively be called archeology (excavation); however, since everyone else thinks that their work is so unimportant or unskillful, they do not have the incentives to do much work at all. Instead, they become involved in other projects. I cannot describe their lives in detail here: suffice it to say that, at the lowest levels, the stories of social relations, individual machinations, and intrigue appear to be similar, in that there are struggles over personal authority versus bureaucratic hierarchy, yet different because the goals, gifts exchanged, and contexts in which such gifts are exchanged take forms different from those among the intellectuals.

5
Majority Rule

We fill the physical appearance of the person we see with all the
notions we have about him, and in the totality of our impressions
about him, these notions play the most important role.
　　　　　　　　　– Marcel Proust, *Swann's Way*

Claiming and Credentials
We have encountered to this point a number of strategies used in maintaining and strengthening the junior-senior contracts and cohort-like groups.
Most of those strategies have to do with performing trustworthiness and
compatibility – or testing the trustworthiness and compatibility of others –
and the exploitation of inconsistencies in formal bureaucratic structures
that allow the separation of authority from hierarchy. The key to all of these
strategies is the performance of obedience in the form of submission to the
responsibilities and acts expected of any given role. So far, we have concentrated on dyadic relations (how juniors interrelate with seniors) or group
relations (in cohorts). Now we must turn our attention to that all-important
third party who stands as witness to junior-senior and cohort relations: the
audience-that-matters. This chapter thus examines the strategies by which
an actor prompts sympathy from his audience to entice it into accepting
that he has the right to play his chosen role in a certain way.

An intervention in audience judgment requires that audience members
have certain preconceptions about how the role that the actor is playing ought
to be played. The role brings with it a set of expected behaviours, moral
judgments, and goals. An individual inhabiting the role of father, for example, has certain responsibilities with respect to his child. He will be judged
as a good or bad father according to how well he lives up to the set of rules
that fathers are to follow. In short, the role of father is a stereotype that
individuals use to guide their behaviour even as the audience uses it to
measure the behaviour of others.

It is when addressing stereotypes that I stray the furthest from the way in which autonomy has been theorized in the Euro-American literature. The word *stereotype* is defined in orthodox contexts as 'a standardized mental picture that is held in common by members of a group and that represents an oversimplified opinion, prejudiced attitude, or uncritical judgment of a group.'[1] Much of the scholarship treating stereotypes examines their use and abuse in conjunction with a criticism of racism, sexism, and other negative forms of prejudice.[2] As a result, intolerant acts of discrimination have come to stand for all acts of stereotyping. In other words, stereotypes themselves have all too often been negatively stereoptyped in the minds of Euro-American scholars and readers.

Critical theory, in particular hermeneutics, stands out in Euro-American thought as a rare attempt to rehabilitate the reputation of stereotypes. Hans Georg Gadamer points out that, in order to perceive, we must have preconceptions; we cannot even begin to think without preexisting models of how things are or ought to be.[3] Michel Foucault's 'archeology' has similarly been focused on how knowledge is deeply structured by preexisting (accumulated through the habits of lifetimes) paradigms, discourses, traditions, or institutions.[4] Theorists of epistemology have many goals, but for my purposes two must be highlighted: (1) to deconstruct the hegemonic discourses that have maintained the status quo by bestowing the most effective kinds of agency (strategic, interpellatory, and hegemonic) on an elite minority[5] and (2) to show that certain groups in society – the poor, women, non-whites, et cetera – have always had a kind of (tactical, *bricoleur*, consumer) agency at the margins of these discourses.[6]

Although well intentioned, neither of these goals makes sense in the context of orthopraxy. Under this system, dominant discourses – whether they be the rhetoric of *guanxi*, class, merit, or otherwise – are available for use for all, and their benefits are not enjoyed solely by an elite minority. Moreover, a differentiation between strategies used by the elite and tactics deployed by the 'weak' is nonsensical.[7] Instead, juniors engage with seniors using the same strategies that seniors use to engage with them. Power, authority, and even hierarchical position are subject to constant flux in a system based on the law of reciprocity. If gifts are constantly shifting debt back and forth across unequal hierarchical social relations, then it is very difficult to sustain a fixed oppositional worldview of the 'weak' pitted against the 'strong.' Any given individual may be weak at one moment relative to some person yet strong relative to someone else at some other time. A person who tastes the benefits of being in a dominant position is not likely to destroy any chance that he might return to that position again. That some people receive different (lesser) benefits, and are often told to be satisfied with what they receive, are issues worthy of critical analysis and concerted efforts for change. Yet such efforts will surely fail if it is not realized that the system provides resources and benefits for both juniors and seniors such that both have good reason to believe that they will continue to receive benefits and resources only if the system is maintained.

The advantages and disadvantages of the Chinese system are nowhere as clear as in the use of stereotypes. Since the word *stereotype* has been irretrievably tainted in the literature, I use the word *credential* instead. This word incorporates both the idea of a role and the rights and duties attendant on that role. Credentials thus accomplish 'things': that is, they allow the person exhibiting them to entail action, force events, and guide interpretation. In that sense, credentials are 'speech acts.'[8] Speech acts are (at least) triple in form: they ostensibly 'say' things following the rules of the language; they are intended to have certain meanings and effects by the speaker; and they do have certain (often unintended) effects after utterance. The term 'credential' is also meant to embrace 'felicity conditions,' defined as the conventions, rules, and rules for breaking those rules that impact on the success of any given speech act.[9]

It is the audience-that-matters who judges whether any attempt to 'do something with words' is acceptable, and it is that interpretation that the speaker so artfully seeks to influence and control. Understanding what credentials do – as well as why they do different things under different circumstances – requires an understanding of how interpretation is a matter of tacking back and forth between the specific (the particular goals of a speaker in the context of a particular event) and the rules (the norms and conventions that guide speakers in a certain context) in the attempt to motivate the interpretations of the audience-that-matters.[10]

To do anything, credentials must, much like roles and discourses, resist correction by experience. No matter how often a person encounters someone whose behaviour flouts all expectations, the credential must revert to its original form the next time it comes into play. Without such incorrigibility, the credential is useless as a tool to measure the actions of others. Yet while the rules and characteristics that comprise a credential do not change, what does change is its application: how, when, by whom, and in what context it has been deployed in the past guide its subsequent use.

Four types of credentialling strategies are presented here: (1) the art of motivation – that is, of using incentives to seduce the audience-that-matters; (2) the art of reinterpretation, used most often to justify or excuse behaviour; (3) the art of conversion, in which present failures are converted into future successes; and (4) the art of combination, in which the combination of roles is used to entrap co-participants in junior-senior relations. Along the way, we will learn more about the credentials related to school background, regional background, and class as they affect the strategies of Chinese archeologists.

School Credentials and the Art of Motivation

There are ten universities and one graduate institute (the Chinese Academy of Social Sciences, or CASS) in China that teach archeology.[11] Any group of students who has shared the same teachers and school is expected to share similar attitudes, career goals, and abilities – that is, to exhibit a school-related credential. Every graduate of JiDa, for example, is expected to be a technically proficient archeologist who follows the preeminent scholar at JiDa, Zhang Zhongpei, in his theoretical, methodological, and even political positions. There can only be one truly preeminent scholar at each school. Other teachers might be important in their subfields but will not have the authority commanded by that one scholar.[12] For example, a student may have had a close relationship with another venerable JiDa professor, Lin Yun, and would be assumed after graduation to emulate many of Lin's attributes. Nevertheless, since the most famous teacher at JiDa remains Zhang, the student will still be expected – as Lin himself ought – to follow Zhang's lead.

With the exception of BeiDa and CASS, graduates of the other eight schools suffer in their reputations as archeologists because their credentials are assumed to be geographically narrow. Students of ChuanDa in Sichuan, for example, are said to excel at Sichuan and Yunnan archeologies, especially the famous Sanxingdui Culture and the southern silk route, but are not expected to know anything about the northern or coastal regions. Since ChuanDa teachers also happen to have the reputation of being good documentary historians, ChuanDa graduates are likewise expected to be good at reading documents but not technically proficient in other archeological tasks. The reputations of these eight schools also suffer because archeology is offered only as a subdivision of the Department of History (with two exceptions), and therefore the students are not expected to be well educated. Graduates of the regionally based schools are expected to get jobs only in the regions immediately surrounding their alma maters and are assumed to do well only in lower-level jobs.

JiDa is somewhat different in that it is a regionally based school that also boasts a full and flourishing department with a long tradition of its own and a number of MA and PhD students. JiDa students are expected to be limited in their substantive knowledge of the past to the northern regions; however, since they have had the benefits of an intense methodological training from the renowned Zhang, they are believed to have the capacity to learn about other regions fairly quickly. These students, therefore, are believed to have more flexibility than those of the other regionally based schools and can rise high in the bureaucratic hierarchy.

In contrast to the limitations placed on the eight regional schools, the teachers and students at BeiDa and CASS are allowed to excavate anywhere in China. Each institution has a full complement of scholars who specialize in each region and time period. BeiDa students, in particular, are supposed to be good all-round archeologists, with the best teachers and broadest education. Even so, they are expected to be particularly good at Neolithic and *San Dai* (Three Dynasties or Bronze Age) archeology (not incidentally, these are also the most prestigious time periods to study). CASS students are a little different because they are all graduate students. As a result, they are said to be more narrowly specialized than even the graduate students at BeiDa. Given that both CASS and BeiDa are extremely prestigious institutions, their graduates are widely believed to be arrogant and to demand special treatment by people who did not study at either school.

The impact of school credentials can be exemplified by the situation faced by XiaDa and ZhongshanDa graduates. These two institutions are (or were) different from all other universities because they classify archeology *(kaogu)* as anthropology *(renlei xue)* rather than history *(lishi)*. In 1997, archeology was reclassified as history at XiaDa, and there is much talk of ZhongshanDa following suit. The reason for the reclassification is that its graduates were not getting hired. Most people in China have either never heard of anthropology or continue to entertain the traditional Marxist belief that it is a bourgeois pursuit. Those who do take a chance and hire these graduates usually do so because they expect them to be somehow different or strange. They are often vocal in their disappointment that the graduates turn out to be pretty much like all other archeology graduates. It's a classic catch-22: graduates either are not hired because difference is not wanted by a certain *danwei* or are hired because they are expected to be different and inevitably disappoint their superiors when they turn out to be indistinguishable from the 'norm.'

The catch-22 of credentials is what makes them so interesting to study. Credentials are clearly intended to reduce uncertainty. When the director of a *danwei* decides whom to hire, he must base his decision on something. If interviews are involved (rare in China), then he might make instant inferences on visual contact: dress, hair style, and body language can all affect a director's opinion of the student. For the most part, however, decisions to hire candidates are based on the reputation of school and teacher, with little attention paid to candidates' experiences. And a candidate's decision to accept a job is similarly based on *danwei* locale and reputation.

Theoretically, widely shared sets of credentials help us to make decisions, and to act on those decisions, because they inspire confidence in our capacity to understand people around us. Unfortunately, at least from the perspective of people interested in the reduction of uncertainty, credentials create new types of uncertainty even as they purport to reduce it. No one is so foolish, or so confident, to imagine that, just because something appears to be fairly certain, it will be in any particular instance. When director and graduate finally do meet, it is therefore the unknown that occupies their attention as they establish how each *differs* from expectations. Not all differences, of course, are equally important. When people are interdependent, and where the success of any personal plan depends on their social relations with others, the potential differences of interest relate almost entirely to a person's compatibility and trustworthiness. Will he be competitor or cooperator, useful or worthless? These questions are nowhere more important, and nowhere more problematic, than in the transition that an archeology student undergoes as he leaves the comforts of the university for the trials of the *danwei*.

'I used to be happy. I was never sad ... until I arrived here,' said Hua, now the vice director of a smallish regional museum, as he morosely smoked cigarette after cigarette and stared at the empty walls of his airless office. Over the next four hours, Hua related the story of how the naïve ideals of his youth had been destroyed by intrigue and Machiavellian machinations. Mirroring Hua's fractured picture of the world, the museum under his care is in a state of disarray, its potential for becoming a place of beauty unrealized, and his workers without motivation or hope. Yet even if Hua is not personally happy, for our purposes his use of the arts of motivation to intervene in audience perceptions is exemplary of the way in which school credentials both use and abuse students as they enter the *danwei* setting.

Hua got high enough scores on the university entrance exam to get into BeiDa. Getting into BeiDa was truly a crowning moment. His parents had been the children of intellectuals but had been sent down from Shanghai to the countryside early on, in 1964, and had therefore missed their chance to have an education. From Hua's perspective, then, getting into BeiDa was a vindication of Hua family tradition as well as the sweetest moment of his and his parents' lives.

His undergraduate experience was good despite the consternation of his parents when they discovered what archeology actually entails. The irony of putting all that effort into the child's education only to have Hua sent back to the countryside to dig holes was a bit rich. There was some debate whether Hua should become an entrepreneur or not, but in the end the security represented by the *danwei* job was too enticing, and they decided that he should become an archeologist. Hua did well, made good friends among his cohort members and his teachers, and became the vice director of his cohort.

As graduation neared, Hua's teachers were dismayed to discover that there were no jobs available in good *danwei* in his home region. The choice was to send Hua to a good *danwei* far away from his home or to a lower-level *danwei* close to his home, in fact, in the same county in which his parents live. On the principle that it is always better to be a 'chicken's head' than a 'phoenix's tail' (i.e., to be a 'big frog in a little pond'), his teachers decided to send him home. Theoretically, his BeiDa education would make him a hot commodity in the village.

When Hua arrived in the *danwei*, however, the situation was, to put it bluntly, awful. That is not to say that his situation was more awful than anyone else's. *Every* youngish archeologist whom I have met was distressed by his first experiences in the *danwei*. The primary complaint is about the difficulties of creating a personal space within the complex of *danwei* social relations. The attempt to conform and become part of the group is called *cha dui* or 'entering the team.' Entering a team already in existence is obviously difficult because the newcomer must change the things on which others rely or have come to consider natural or essential to their own well-being. But it is also difficult, at least in the narratives of younger archeologists, because the newcomer has very little understanding of why he is being treated so badly, exactly how he is unnerving his colleagues, or for which benefits he is supposed to be competing. Young people are, in other words, out of their depth.

In Hua's case, much of the hostility related to his credentials as a BeiDa graduate. Hua's new colleagues – especially those who had been barred from a chance to go to BeiDa because of the Cultural Revolution – clearly resented his BeiDa education. Worse, the *danwei* had never before hired a student from such a prestigious institution. Hua's new colleagues had an exaggerated picture of the benefits of being a BeiDa student. They expected Hua to be spoiled and, therefore, to complain about the way in which the *danwei* was being managed, its lack of resources, and its relaxed attitude toward its responsibilities. Plus he was assumed (as an inexperienced archeologist) to be completely useless at archeology yet, being arrogant, would no doubt imagine himself too good to learn from the old-timers. Worst of all, Hua's credentials caused uncertainty: colleagues worried about what Hua might do, whether he would upset their lives, and which resources he would take away from each of them. Before he even walked through the doors of the *danwei* for the first time, his future colleagues already 'knew' everything about him and were ready to teach him a lesson in manners and hard work.

While his colleague's preconceptions strained the situation, Hua's arrival in the *danwei* was also made difficult by his own preconceptions. Hua arrived believing that *danwei* relations work the way that they are ideally said to work. The ideal model of the *danwei* is based on cooperation, teamwork, and mutual aid. Colleagues are supposed to be like cohort mates – working, living, and playing together. Unfortunately, unlike in the cohort, everyone in a *danwei* is forced to compete for the same resources. Everyone wants opportunities to excavate and money to write up the reports; housing and health benefits; to get married and raise a family; to position himself in the best possible manner to rise up the ladder; and to do himself and his teachers, cohort mates, and family proud. Competition is fierce. Worse, given that everyone is interdependent, one wrong move can shatter the lives of many people at once. And there is no way to leave the *danwei* to start with a clean slate somewhere else. There can be no feeling of cooperation within a group of people who are forced to live together yet compete for access to resources. Only when faced with enemies from without will this group willingly cooperate.

Hua was certainly disheartened by his reception. But he was smart. Or at least his parents were smart, for once he and his family had figured out that something was wrong they told him to call up his teachers for advice and help. The teachers' advice could be summed up as follows: first, Hua should do everything that his director ordered; second, he should use the local ties of his parents and family; and third, his teacher promised to call up an old cohort mate, now an official in the county, and ask for help.

The reasoning behind the first piece of advice relates to the performance of compatibility and trustworthiness. Hua had to ensure that he was humble only before his proper, bureaucratic superior. For everyone else, he should continue to mention and take pride in being a BeiDa graduate, even elaborating all the connections and resources that his school credentials entailed and being arrogant about his experiences. In this way, he would perform his compatibility in his access to significant resources despite his youth. But there was much more going on: by combining BeiDa arrogance with a performance of obedience to his director, Hua would endow his submission to the director (not a BeiDa graduate) with new meaning. His actions would become a gift to the director to show his trustworthiness as well as a performance for the audience-that-matters to show that he respects hierarchy. If he were seen as respecting the hierarchy of the *danwei*, then it would be easier to make the leap of faith to perceive him as being respectful of the hierarchies of age and experience that are even more important to his audience. He might be arrogant, but at least he would be respectful at the same time.

Hua had been sent to this *danwei* because his family had local connections. The teacher's second piece of advice was to invite his parents and close kin to the *danwei* as often as possible. Doing so would accomplish two things at once. First, it would remind the *danwei* audience that Hua was a filial son who had returned home to take care of his parents. His colleagues need not know that Hua had few other options; all they need know is that he probably could have become rich in the big city with a BeiDa background. His eminently filial behaviour would therefore be reinterpreted to mean that he knows how to act properly in other relations as well. Second, bringing his family to the *danwei* would remind people that, although Hua was a BeiDa man, he was also one of their own, a local boy made good, and therefore someone in whose BeiDa education everyone could take pride. Hua's accomplishment could therefore become their accomplishment; what was his would become by extension the group's. The group would be reminded that Hua's existence enhances the reputation of their *danwei* and could therefore become a resource to use to increase their own compatibility in the eyes of others.

Meanwhile, in response to Hua's teacher's call for help, the local official was working on the case from the other end. He began to praise the director of the *danwei* for being so eminently capable and well positioned that he was able to secure a BeiDa graduate. The director, of course, had nothing to do with the assignment and had even resisted accepting a BeiDa graduate. Now, however, he found that his official was acting as if having a BeiDa graduate made the director himself more compatible. As a result, the director was immediately predisposed to appear as if he accepted and even wanted Hua in the *danwei*. In this context, Hua's constant deference to the director's authority was certainly gratifying since it showed others in the *danwei*, the audience-that-matters, that the director was important enough to command the allegiance of the BeiDa graduate. Ever quick to capitalize on a mutually beneficial relationship, the director used Hua's overt filial behaviour as a reason to praise and promote Hua even as that performance enhanced the director's own reputation in other people's eyes.

The teachers' advice had excellent results. Within six years of graduation, a startlingly short time, Hua became the vice director of his *danwei*. Among archeologists, the vice director always has more authority over resources than the hierarchically superior director: not only does he do the actual work of running the *danwei*, but the vice director also advises the director on promotions, budget allocations, opportunities, and punishments. Hua may not be very happy, but at least he holds authority over almost everyone else in his *danwei*. He also has good relations with his director and official (and the relations between those two have also been strengthened).

Hua feels, however, that the costs of success were too dear. He appears to have been quite the idealist in university and really thought that the *danwei* would be an exciting place where he could enjoy doing what he was trained to do. Instead, he had to expend much more energy thinking about how to achieve a good reputation in the eyes of his colleagues than he had been prepared or trained to do. He was surprised at how difficult it is always to be thinking about which gifts can be given and how they should be given and other strategies used in the motivation of others, all undertaken under stressful circumstances in which his children, his wife, and his parents all depend on his success. As his colleagues have warmed to him, he feels that much more responsibility, because now *their* success depends on his success as well.

A new recruit, from WuDa, was being foisted on Hua's *danwei* that year. Since Hua has become more familiar over the years with the *danwei* situation by reading the budgets and understanding the terrible constraints under which the *danwei* works, he now knows exactly why his colleagues were so discombobulated by his arrival all those years ago. The *danwei* really does not need another mouth to feed, yet another person whose housing, health, marriage, and family must be taken care of, yet another person with whom to compete. 'It really would,' he said, 'just be best for everyone concerned if the newcomer would just simply go away.' His bitterness only increased as he realized that uncertainty, desperation, and constant worry have created in him the same hostile attitude toward the newcomer that he had faced upon arrival. Nevertheless, although Hua has had a painful personal experience of the negative impact of school credentials, he still, without apparent irony, fell into the habit of predicting that the new recruit would be more trouble than he was worth based on his (assumed) narrow WuDa training. The poor WuDa recruit: life would not be easy for him upon his arrival.

What is important is that at no point did Hua attempt to resist or openly contradict the negative aspects of the credentials applied to him. He does not try to undermine his BeiDa credentials by hastening to reassure people that the school is not as great as its reputation would suggest, nor does he protest that he is not arrogant and spoiled, and he certainly does not attempt to smooth things over by being friendly. Rather, he accepts the preconceptions made of him and then provides good incentives to impel the audience-that-matters to accept him anyway.

In short, Hua uses the art of motivation to claim that he is useful to his colleagues and director. The director and the rest of the *danwei* decide whether a new arrival fits their expectations or not; they thereby set the stage and define the vocabulary that will be used in subsequent struggles to control meaning and interpretation. The onus then lies on the student to claim that 'who he is' is, in fact, beneficial to each of them. Hua put it succinctly: 'You need to *kai wei*' (open the stomach). *Kai wei* is basically the act of giving someone appetizers good enough that he or she looks forward to the main meal. Hua had to show what his colleagues could gain from association with him (a strategy that depended on his colleagues continuing to believe that BeiDa graduates have unusual access to resources) and to indicate that he himself was a trustworthy man who would share his privileges with them. Once that task had been accomplished, his colleagues, director, and official all had incentives to accept him as one of their group and exploit him and his reputation in plans and projects of their own. The act of reinterpretation is accomplished by the audience; Hua merely provides each member of the audience with a reason to reinterpret who he is and what he has to offer.

Regional Credentials and the Art of Reinterpretation

Much like school credentials, regional credentials determine which characteristics a person should exhibit in the eyes of the audience. For example, a married couple whom I met in the north, where she is from Shandong and he from Gansu, are still – twenty years later – criticized by their families and *danwei* colleagues for having gotten married. Deciding something so simple as what to eat for supper still causes strife between husband, wife, and now daughter (who is often, through her food choices, forced to choose whose daughter she wants to be). After I witnessed a particularly intense discussion about what to make for dinner, the archeologist-husband turned to me and explained with no little annoyance that, although he and his wife share many experiences (both having been sent down to the same place during the Cultural Revolution), it still was probably a mistake to have married her. His wife, sitting by his side, emphatically agreed, adding that in her opinion the worst legacy of the Cultural Revolution is these 'bad' marriages. That night we ended up eating Gansu-style dumplings only because the daughter wanted them; husband and wife never did come to an agreement.

The characteristics of a certain region are spoken about as being fixed and unchangeable and are upheld by a person as a mark of pride. Even a wife, who theoretically should concede to a husband, does not necessarily do so when it comes to matters of this sort. Or, if she does relinquish her regional tastes in favour of his, it is considered a great sacrifice, a truly valuable gift, a sign of how properly obedient a wife she is, and an indication of the strength of their marriage. In other words, regional credentials are in structure like all other roles: they both guide action and provide the context in which certain actions are expected and against which actions undertaken are measured.

Knowing someone's regional credentials allows one to assume a great deal about a person's tastes, needs, and wants. Regional credentials are why it is said to be 'mere common sense' that a southerner should be barred from attending a northern school. The student is expected to be unhappy in the north because of his need for a certain climate and particular foods and customs. When teachers are looking for jobs for their students, then, it is assumed that students want to be as close to their respective hometowns as possible. Great pains are taken to accomplish this task without ever asking the student whether this assumption is correct in his or her case. Nevertheless, students barred from a certain school or sent back to their home regions do appear to expect and appreciate the efforts by teachers to make them comfortable in these ways.

Returning home also has its practical advantages. I met a student, Chen, who, on a whim ('I just wanted to see something different!' he interjected in a mournful refrain throughout the conversation), decided to take a job in Chongqing rather than in his hometown of Nanjing. He ignored the concerns of teachers and parents, who told him that it would be extremely inconvenient and/or unfilial for him to move to Chongqing. By the time I met him, three months into his new job, he was beginning to realize that their warnings were justified. He was much thinner than he wanted to be and lived in an uncomfortable and dirty dormitory. He received only 400 yuan a month, which, despite being the standard salary for a first-level archeologist, is an absurdly tiny amount. The salary is low because the government expects it to be supplemented with aid from parents or the moonlighting job opportunities acquired through family networks. Since this young man was both alone and a stranger in Chongqing, he had none of the resources needed to ameliorate his situation.

Worse, Chen's situation was causing others to worry. I later had the opportunity to interview his teachers at his alma mater. They mentioned Chen (independently of my urging) because they wanted to use his case as an example of how teachers can fail in their responsibilities toward students. They thought that they should never have let Chen move to Chongqing: they worried about him, his family worried about him, even his *danwei* worried about him. As for Chen, realizing how much upset he has caused others causes him daily worry as he tries to figure out how to do well while simultaneously reassuring everyone that he is doing well. It is exactly this kind of inconvenience or stress that everyone seeks to avoid by sending a student back home.

Are all people from a region alike in their tastes? Do all students have a family that will or can help them in the expected ways? These questions are simply pointless; the point, instead, is to understand that the system assumes these things to be true (by having policies of paying salaries below a living wage) and that the people who maintain and perpetuate the system assume it to be true (by continuing to send most students home). In a practical and physical way, what people and systems assume to be true becomes true. Of course, exceptions such as Chen exist and can even survive despite the assumptions of others and the rules of the system. Chen may even make a successful career despite his situation, but his exceptional success will not influence the foundational assumptions of the system.

Regional credentials can be manipulated by what I call the 'art of reinterpretation.' It is achieved through the juxtaposition of words, norms, events, and actions to gain control over interpretations of the credential.[13] The reinterpretation does not attempt to disrupt the link between region of origin and personal characteristics. Instead, the speaker twists interpretations and repositions them such that he presents a picture of himself that neither breaks with his regional credentials nor allows such credentials to impede the achievement of his goals. His performance of reinterpretation must be a fine balancing act: he must twist meaning but only in a way that 'makes enough sense' to the audience that they will accept his reinterpretation. His goal is to intervene in the 'usual' interpretations to create something else; the adroit manipulation of meaning is not an end in itself but a strategy in the pursuit of other goals. The goals pursued can be many, but here I will examine how the art of reinterpretation can be a by-product of the goals and intentions that attend narratives of justification and excuse.

Zhang is a Culture *Xitong* archeologist who, having been born in the southwest, works at a southwestern provincial institute of archeology. According to him, his entire life would have been better had he been assigned to a job in the Central Plains region in the north. He does not particularly care for the Bronze Age archeology practised in the Central Plains and, in fact, both prefers and is proud of the work that he has done on the southern silk road. Nevertheless, he is convinced that, had he been a Bronze Age archeologist, he would now live in Beijing and be a member of the top committees that control archeology's future. He would, in other words, have had a better life – in the context of archeology, 'better' being defined as having more opportunities to publish, excavate, or go abroad, all of which lead to promotions and an increased standard of living for an archeologist and his family.

To attain a better life, an archeologist must be part of a hierarchically well-positioned *danwei* with actual authority. Zhang insisted that archeologists of the south suffer because they lack access to the authority that is supplied by tradition, fame of teachers, and data. Archeology, after all, began in the north, where techniques of archeological and geological survey were worked out, where the Swedes began introducing Li Chi and Xia Nai to archeological method, and, in the Central Plains in particular, where all of Chinese civilization was supposed to have begun.[14] Zhang had a point: no matter how often archeologists of other regions proclaim the beauty of their artifacts and the fine craftsmanship of their bronzes and jades, the Central Plains remain the ancestral cradle in the opinion of most Chinese people. Indeed, this theory of cultural origins has long been official Communist Party policy. Even after ideas in archeological circles changed to suggest that China's origins are far more diverse, money and effort continue to be poured into the region.

Zhang also noted that, in addition to having resources and traditions of research, northerners have the privilege of studying Han remains, while he and other southerners are consigned to study one or another of the fifty-six or so 'minorities' (he called them 'barbarians' after the terminology of the historical texts). It is a privilege to study Han culture because the study of minorities is comparatively difficult. Chinese archeologists believe that they know how the 'Han' people of even the distant past lived, including their religious and family values, because it is believed that Han customs have not changed much over the intervening 3,000 years. The minority cultures of the south, however, are believed to be very different from Han culture. As a result, an archeologist has to analyze the data carefully, compare them to data from Vietnam and elsewhere, and engage in ethno-archeology to try to figure out questions of worldviews and lifeways. As far as Zhang is concerned, then, the northerners 'have it easy': they study data that are easier to understand and can therefore publish more articles without having to do as much work. Northerners also have it easy because the officials consider their data to be more prestigious and valuable. Note that Zhang was not saying that the data in themselves are more prestigious. He himself is a committed regionalist who believes that there are many origins to Chinese culture, and he even goes so far as to include Central Asian influences; nevertheless, he recognizes that nonspecialists such as the officials still hold to old beliefs and, therefore, tend to support (monetarily) archeology of the Central Plains more than other kinds.

Finally, Zhang went on to say that northerners have a very different personality from southerners, and this personality is the main reason for their success. Northerners are said to be more political, honest, and straightforward *(pushi)* than southerners. By 'political,' he meant that they are far more interested in issues of party policy and Chinese nationalism. Southerners are usually too 'lazy' *(lan),* self-involved, and relaxed to get involved in such issues. Zhang noted that northerners seem to be so straightforward and honest with him because they make their goals – upholding the Chinese spirit, maintaining China's present borders, et cetera – clear and do not appear to have any hidden agendas. Northerners are, said Zhang, 'like you Westerners. They lead simple, direct lives with obvious goals.' They are somewhat dull and plodding and so are probably not capable of scheming to use every event for personal gain, as do southerners. For Zhang, this means that northerners are easygoing and work together well; meanwhile, in the south, people are craftier and put their own needs above those of the group. Northerners are therefore able, through their superior ability to unite together *(tuanjie),* to bully the scattered, disjointed southerners and keep them from power.

Zhang's goal here was clear: to excuse his lack of success and insist that his failures are not his fault but a result of northern oppression. We could also read his excuse as an insult, for he was clearly insisting that the success of northerners is due simply to regional affinity rather than personal ability. His claims succeed in the Chinese context because Zhang takes readily available credentials and twists the meanings in ways that inspire recognition: everything that Zhang said about archeology in the north is pretty much what I have read in the histories of the discipline and makes immediate 'sense.' To an outsider, though, the credentials of the honest, political, straightforward, and unified north make less sense, but in my readings of Chinese history the impulse toward unification and dynastic rule is always placed in the north, while southerners are described as introspective, literary, and rebellious types who could never get themselves together enough to resist northern conquest (the typical example being the southern Song). It is a trope of Chinese history: whether it is strictly true is not at issue; what is important is that these concepts are as widely shared and socially useful in explaining one's life history as they are in outlining national history. As long as Zhang's use of vocabulary and examples drawn from history or pop culture continues to make sense, his claim to reinterpretation will be successful.

Let us turn now to Han, a northern, Beijing-based, BeiDa graduate archeologist working at CASS. From Zhang's standpoint, Han really should be happy since he works in the north and, better yet, studies Bronze Age archeology. I was rather startled, then, to be subjected to a litany of complaints about how southerners are 'lucky,' have everything they need to succeed, and are using their advantages to harass *(qifu)* northerners. Han insists that southerners are 'always' more successful than northerners simply because there is more freedom due to the lack of older and established archeologists in the region. There is also so much more to be found and so many more exciting sites to excavate (Han also supports the theory of the multiple origins of Chinese culture). In contrast, in the north, everything has basically already been found and catalogued, and the chronological mysteries have been solved. Archeology in the north is therefore much more difficult because northerners have to transfer their energies to unimpressive, detailed topics such as the stylistic sequences of roofing tiles. Meanwhile, southerners get to do the exciting, groundbreaking research of finding whole new archeological cultures and, better yet, establishing their theories on chronological issues and cultural origins. Nobody can become famous researching roofing tiles; fame comes from the unearthing of new sites such as Sanxingdui or previously unknown southern silk route sites. For Han, then, fame, tradition, and data mean nothing in comparison to unbroken ground where anything might be found. He feels confined by famous teachers, oppressed by tradition, and overwhelmed by data. There is no way to make the broad statements and the startling discoveries that can even overturn whole theories.

In the end, Han relates all his problems to deficiencies of the northern character: northerners are too straightforward, honest, and wrapped up in Chinese tradition and politics. They are dutiful such that no student would ever rebel or openly disagree with a teacher and research new topics or even old topics in new ways. The north is thus a centre not of change but of continuity and tradition. Southerners, says Han, are in contrast smart, sly *(jiaohua)*, and always thinking about how to turn any situation to their own advantage: these features cause the somewhat 'dull' northerners no end of distress because they find it all a little hard to follow. If archeology had not begun in the north and had not had enough time to establish roots, there is no way that the northerners could withstand the intelligence and scheming of those wily southerners. As it is, Han's own failures are clearly the fault of young, smart, and devious southerners.

Han and Zhang use the same credentials. Southerners are intelligent (sly), complex, and lack the ability to *tuanjie;* northerners are traditionalists and straightforward (dull), honest folk who clump together well. Neither man resists or disputes these regional credentials. Han does not, for example, maintain that northerners are actually sly and manipulative and that their constant scheming (hidden behind the characteristic of honesty) caused his lack of success. Nor does Zhang complain that northerners are deviously perpetuating the regional credential of the 'wily southerner' in order to ruin their reputations as trustworthy folk and therefore bar them from social networks that would allow them access to more resources.

Instead, Zhang says that northerners are naïve, dull, political folk, better at political and party matters, who can unite to oppress the south. Han begs to disagree: he thinks that northern naïveté, dullness, and political traditionalism are the reasons for their failure, while he imagines that southerners are smart and have the space to develop their archeology. Zhang disagrees: southern intelligence is what keeps the south divided. And so it goes, back and forth: the same characteristics and oppositions are maintained, while the evaluation (positive or negative flavour) and interpretation of their effects on archeology is contested.

It is clear that the shared credentials assumed to apply to northerners and southerners are not much of a hindrance to either Han's or Zhang's strategies of avoiding responsibility in their explanations of why they are not successful. The only effort really needed is a little reworking of the meaning and implications of any one of the characteristics believed to be essential to members of each group. A word such as 'dull' needs only a slight reemphasis to mean straightforward and honest; a word such as 'intelligent' needs only a little twist to mean sly or wily. No word is limited to its ostensible dictionary definition: its meanings flex with events. Words are not just linked to other words but also submerged in entire assemblages of words combined to create images. Such assemblages themselves exist only transiently, for certain reasons. Once a particular goal has been achieved, assemblages dissolve once again into small groups or pairs of words, even into single words, to allow them to be spun into different groupings in the light of new goals.

We see the recombinations of words, meanings, and implications in regional credentials when Han and Zhang turned the conversation away from their personal success or failure. Suddenly, the same credentials used to excuse their failures only moments earlier became reasons for regional allegiance and pride. Han could *never* move to the south, he said, because northerners are so nice, have excellent food, are efficient, and have concepts of fun that he enjoys. Han feels that he understands the north. He described himself as being too straightforward and honest to understand the complexities of southerners. For his part, Zhang insisted that he could *never* move to the north. The south is rich with difference, people are mercurial in their thinking yet also relaxed (he used 'lazy' again as well), the food is excellent, and he understands why people do the things they do. Northerners are too simple and straightforward for his tastes, and they are far too easily manipulated.

I do not know whether the credentials that Han and Zhang share are, in any way, accurate in their descriptions of southerners and northerners. Can it really be true that all people south of the Yangtze are all the same, despite repeated migration and subregional differences (not to mention the fifty or so non-Han groups who make their homes in the south)? The question is unanswerable. Han and Zhang are certain that the credentials are accurate or, to put it more interestingly, are especially certain when they need the credentials to be accurate for reasons of their own. Certainly, exceptions to the credentials (a wily northerner, a straightforward southerner) must have been encountered, but either their exceptionality went unnoticed (since it did not 'fit' with expectations) or it was blamed on something other than the notion that the credential might be incorrect. It is belief, or at least the overt performance of belief, in a credential that gives it life.

The belief in the existence of credentials, and their broad dissemination and sheer repetition, are what make them so useful in struggles over the interpretation of an event. It is indeed difficult to resist a credential that everyone thinks is self-evident, yet it must still be understood that credentials create opportunities for the agent. Credentials, after all, *guarantee* instant recognition and agreement by the audience-that-matters. When audience reactions are predictable, and the audience is reassured by the use of familiar tropes and ideas, the implications and meanings of those ideas can be manipulated. An alienated and confused audience is likely to react negatively to attempts to change something that everyone wants to believe, and thereby becomes unpredictable and untrustworthy.

Han and Zhang also use regional background to reassure themselves about the relative trustworthiness and compatibility of members of their own group. Since Zhang belongs to a certain group that he assumes exhibits certain characteristics, when he meets a member of that group, he feels confident that the person is as trustworthy as he is himself. Moreover, since the person comes from the same region, his access to resources, what he can bring to any relationship, is probably more useful and compatible than that of someone who lives far away. If there is any choice of relationship partner, then it is always 'better' to choose the man who comes from the same region rather than the one who does not.

That feeling of belonging to a group also precludes Han and Zhang from feeling insulted by the negative characteristics attributed to their respective groups. There is nothing shameful about being 'dull' if one's entire group is dull in the same way, just as there is nothing wrong with being 'sly' if everyone is sly together. Han explained it this way: 'a northerner in the south is a fish out of water, but when he swims in his own pond he can compare his speed and agility to others of his kind. A southerner, more like a monkey than a fish, can only be judged in comparison to other monkeys and can never be judged using the standards of fish.' In other words, while northerners and southerners need each other for comparative purposes in their struggles to establish who and what they are (and are not), they are not expected to *compete* with each other. The northern fish competes with other fish in his own pond, while the southern monkey competes with his own kind; competing across the boundary that separates the two is simply pointless.

As we have seen before in our discussion of a similar situation with regard to class boundaries, the existence of generally agreed upon attitudes creates new opportunities for the giving of gifts, especially gifts of submission or obedience, in junior-senior relations. After all, if 'everyone knows' and 'everyone agrees' that every person hates to be in a strange place among strangers, then it becomes much more valuable when a junior agrees to go to a strange place on behalf of his senior. The southerner who dutifully goes to the north on his superior's behalf can expect a great deal of compensation in return. And so he should: after all, what can be more unfortunate than a monkey falling into a pond and trying to swim with the fish? The opportunities for the entrapment of seniors by juniors, or even vice versa, are, as always, endlessly produced by the play of action within a context of rigid rules and credentialling and other discourses.

Class and the Art of Converting Failure into Success

Each archeologist wants to be the best archeologist that he thinks he can, should, or ought to be. Clearly, many factors go into what an archeologist will do to promote his career, including whether he will put other matters such as family, friends, or personal inclinations above the needs of archeology, and it is neither my intent nor within my ability to list all the possible goals that a particular archeologist may be juggling at any given time. It is more interesting to examine the goals that are available and among which a person can choose as circumstances warrant. In China, being the 'best archeologist one can be' means a great deal more than simply being good at excavation and having an extensive knowledge of the archeological and historical record. It also means that one must be an intellectual and act in accordance with all the duties and social responsibilities that class status entails.

Class intersects with other credentials in complex ways. Class discourse expects each class member to live up to the intersection between a given role-in-relation (say a northerner) and his class (peasant). There is no shame in being a northern peasant; there is shame only if a northern peasant attempts to act like a southern peasant. How, then, would two intellectuals, one from the south and one from the north, interact with a southern peasant? The answer is dependent on circumstances: if there is reason for the southern peasant and the southern intellectual to unite against the northerner, then narratives of the importance of trusting someone from one's own region can be used to unite the two and exclude the third. If the two intellectuals have reason to unite against the peasant, then class narratives will come to the fore. The situation becomes more difficult and more interesting if there is reason for the southern peasant and the northern intellectual to unite: since there is no clear, broadly disseminated model to guide their behaviour, they may have to use narratives of friendship, interpersonal trust, or some other (notably weaker) discourse that can unite them but exclude the southern intellectual.

From the perspective of the archeologist, it is both a privilege and a burden to be credentialled as an intellectual. The intellectual's opinions are given great weight by other people, and they tend to come to him for advice. Being asked for advice, and thereby becoming involved in local or even national politics, is a concrete symbol that an intellectual can use to enhance his reputation as an eminent (and compatible) intellectual worthy of further social relations. Being an intellectual, however, can also be dangerous: the archeologist asked for help by the peasants might find himself too heavily involved. Like all people placed in the senior position, he must walk a fine line between responding to the responsibilities inherent in the paternalistic junior-senior contract and being trapped into doing things that he ought not to do or into projects that cannot possibly succeed.

Not only must an intellectual mediate between the state and the masses, but he must also uphold the principles of his discipline. In the traditions of imperial China, the most celebrated scholars were those who sacrificed themselves in an attempt to remain true to their discipline and use it to 'speak truth to power.' Scholars' attempts to correct the actions of the emperor were usually spectacularly unsuccessful, but they nevertheless were, and continue to be, held up as models for other scholars to follow. So, whether an archeologist is supposed to be sacrificing himself for China, his superiors, juniors and class inferiors, family, *danwei* colleagues, or discipline, the point is that he is supposed to sacrifice. Duty must be put above and beyond personal goals. The intellectual is indeed at the top of the social hierarchy, and we can scoff at his tendency to act in a paternal, superior manner that assumes he knows best; yet we must also remember that the discourses of his class place him in the role of the long-suffering father who sacrifices what he must, perhaps even inflicting bodily harm on himself, to protect his children.

The duties of the intellectual therefore often conflict: sometimes the needs of the country require sacrifice of the duty to archeology, or the needs of the students necessitate sacrifice of one's duty to the state; sometimes, too, the needs of archeology involve sacrifice of the duty to the peasants. It is in such a situation, in which something almost always requires the sacrifice of something that really should not be sacrificed, that an archeologist learns the art of conversion.

Conversion, in this case, refers to the conversion of a failure – the failure to live up to one duty because one is too busy living up to another – in the present to a success in the future. Given that relations are reciprocal, one may always assume that, if one does what is required in the present, even if it is distasteful (or especially if it is distasteful, because then the doing of it becomes more valuable), then one can 'live to fight another day,' so to speak. Thus, being forced to act in a manner detrimental to the state in the present can be converted into the resources, hierarchical position, or authority that will make it that much easier to protect China in the future. It is very difficult to convey how these differences of social, historical, and political positioning affect the actions taken by the archeologist as he negotiates among the conflicting responsibilities to the Chinese state, the Chinese people, and the discipline of archeology. The following story is an attempt to convey both the complex interactions of moral values and expectations guiding archeologists and the use of the art of conversion under difficult and conflicting circumstances.

The book *The Dead Suffered Too: The Excavation of a Ming Tomb* presents the story of Xia Nai, one of the most powerful archeologists of the Maoist era, and how he was forced, against his better archeological judgment, to excavate the imperial Ming tomb of Ding Ling during the Great Leap Forward.[15] The book was written with the express approval of the Chinese government and published by the official Chinese Literature Press. It presents an official version of what happened at Ding Ling and makes an analogy between the insanity of the Great Leap Forward and the actions of present-day industrialists (who destroy archeological sites in the rush to build) and peasants (who smuggle artifacts for economic benefit): whatever destroys China's cultural relics is considered an attack on China, *even if ordered by the Chinese state itself.* Xia's actions are presented as exemplary of the proper response of an intellectual to a state that has gone temporarily insane.

Xia is the consummate scholar-hero: he works day and night, rarely seeing his family, much in the manner of Yu, the lauded official of the Xia Dynasty, said to have worked so hard at controlling the Yellow River that for years he passed the entrance of his house yet never entered therein. Unlike those who work for him, Xia does not show excitement about imminent success or distress at apparent failure but acts always in the image of a wise old man unaffected by immediate circumstance. Most importantly, Xia never complains or openly resists the orders of the state despite knowing full well that the excavation of Ding Ling requires far more expertise and resources than CASS had at the time.

In the book's narration of the conversation in which Xia finally agrees to excavate, the tension is high.[16] During the Great Leap Forward, the emphasis was on 'catching up' with the West, with the result that everything had to be done according to ridiculously shortened schedules. Archeologists were expected to excavate bigger sites in shorter time periods. As a result of Mao's desire for the opening of the Ding Ling tomb, widely assumed to be filled with the most exquisite artifacts, Wu Han, the vice mayor of Beijing at the time,[17] gives Xia only two months to excavate.

Xia makes it clear that he vehemently disagrees not only with the task that he has been set but also with the time limit that he has been given. Two months to excavate any large site is wildly unrealistic, and Ding Ling was a tomb built expressly to counter such attempts. Were this an American novel, one could imagine that the hero would respond aggressively and obstructively to state directives that violate his sense of disciplinary integrity. But Xia is not American, and never once does the book suggest that the American concept of direct resistance crosses his mind. Xia is indeed careful to present his concerns to Wu Han and even argues strenuously with him. Nevertheless, in the end Xia submits to the inevitable and agrees to excavate.

Upon his submission to Wu, smiles break out, and the tension is relieved. Never imagine, however, that Xia is simply obeying Wu. From that moment on, Xia pours his energies into prying as much time and as many resources from Wu as he can. Wu, as a proper superior whose job is to take care of dutiful inferiors, does all that he can to help Xia. Indeed, before Xia even begins to detail exactly what he is going to need, Wu is the first to give aid by offering to use his position to secure food and housing from local peasants in the counties near the Ming tombs.

Xia had no choice but to follow orders. He knew full well that, if he had not agreed to open the tomb, someone else would have been forced to do so. Given that he was the most experienced and the most senior archeologist available, he had no choice but to take up the responsibilities thrust upon him by his position in the archeological community. That is not to say that Xia acted out of a heightened sense of self-importance or that he was arrogant. Rather, since Xia held the highest position within the archeological community, he, his colleagues, and state officials would simply have assumed that it was his responsibility to take care of the matter.

Throughout the book, Xia is presented as achieving 'success' even though he accomplishes few of his assigned tasks. Originally, he was expected to excavate both Chang Ling and Ding Ling, but in the end he only opens Ding Ling. Originally, he is given two months, but in the end he manages to draw out the excavation process for more than two years. In other words, as an archeologist, Xia does not allow overt submission in a single conversation to get in the way of his actual goal of avoiding, as long as possible, opening the tomb. Yet as a patriotic Chinese, Xia must simultaneously uphold the right of the state to govern, even if it appears to have gone astray. His true heroism, from the perspective of the book, becomes manifest in his ability to accomplish both goals at the same time: negotiating for more time and resources on behalf of archeology while presenting himself as ever dutiful and saving the faces of his officials and his nation.

The book is frank about the kinds of problems that Xia encountered during the excavation, including ignorance among local workers and their reluctance to participate, a great deal of trouble and miscommunication among his colleagues, and the tendency of his superiors to keep changing posts in response to political events. The project was ongoing during the 1957 Anti-Rightist campaigns, and, while Xia himself survived, nearly everyone who understood and could supervise his work or secure resources on his behalf was labelled a rightist and removed from his position. In this context of severe hardship, Xia is presented as being all the more heroic because he enlists the help of more reluctant (i.e., less heroic) intellectuals as well as local officials and peasants in his quest to satisfy state directives. He clearly understands how to motivate other people. Much like the trope of the American cowboy-hero exhorting the frightened and trembling young man to gather his courage and take up arms in the fight for justice, here we see the Chinese intellectual-hero urging his reluctant colleagues and workers to gather their courage and continue to be obedient to the directives of the state in the fight to protect China's heritage and its future.

Last (but never least), Xia is praised for overcoming some of the more interesting techniques of tomb construction that made Ding Ling a particularly severe intellectual and archeological challenge. As Xia himself knew full well, he did not have the resources to excavate properly and, as predicted, could not stop the disintegration of the wooden and cloth remains during the initial opening of the tomb. As the years pass, Xia organizes a museum to be built for the surviving artifacts, but they, too, are doomed to be destroyed by events during the Cultural Revolution. Indeed, the only time that Xia Nai is shown to allow emotion to break through his wise, all-knowing demeanour is when he arrives in the local village near the tomb in time to witness the Red Guard-led destruction by fire of the museum and the rest of the artifacts.

The book has this to say about the destruction of the Ding Ling artifacts: 'This was highly unexpected. To our regret and grief, the loss was irreparable. There are many causes – interference by political movements, damage done unwittingly, and, chiefly, the lack of knowledge and responsibility of the people involved. If a cultural worker does not have adequate understanding and knowledge, or at least a love for historical culture, losses are inevitable.'[18] In this single comment, we see education, as a source of understanding and knowledge, promoted as something that will clear up social and political problems as easily as it cures those resulting from ignorance. We also see a microcosm of the moral values of the intellectual: if the archeologist-intellectual does not have knowledge, a sense of responsibility, or a love of history, then 'losses are inevitable,' and the archeological record (and China) will suffer.

The ideal Chinese archeologist embodied by Xia cannot be described using the language of coercion. He is compelled and coerced by the state, certainly, but he does not do exactly what he is told to do. Xia is a fully capable agent who has both memory of past events and plans for the future. He is not simply thinking about what is happening in the present: he knows that the strong ties that he creates by being obedient to officials in the present can be used to help (or protect) other archeological projects or archeologists in the future. The damage that he does now to Ding Ling is appalling, but with quick wits and heroic behaviour the Chinese agent can convert even the worst of events into future archeological benefit.

It is also clearly inappropriate to describe Xia using the figure of the 'resistant rebel.' Instead, Xia compromises with the state and maintains appropriate relations with its representatives. After all, if Xia is to be successful in converting the ruin of Ding Ling in the present into archeological benefit in the future, he absolutely requires the maintenance of state hierarchy as well as the continuing existence of the junior-senior contract that binds him to the state. As long as the archeologist obeys the state, it is assumed that at some point the state will come to its senses and reward the archeologist appropriately for his obedience. Besides, an archeologist requires the stability offered by a strong state in order to secure opportunities to excavate. Xia's attempt, then, to help the state maintain its hold on power, by submitting to it and convincing others to obey its directives, is an example of behaviour that is positively valued both because of the degree of difficulty that it entails and because of the stable society that it helps to produce.

Under conditions of interdependency and the vagaries of fate, one cannot control whether conditions will always be ideal. As many an archeologist has replied, when asked why we so suddenly had to change plans or even leave a site suddenly, 'one can encounter things, but one cannot control things' *(ke yu, bu ke zhi)*. The appropriate response under such circumstances is to be flexible, roll with the punches, and, above all, make sure that one does not, 'because of one thing going wrong, lose ten things' *(yin yi fei shi)*. Xia is an ideal archeologist because he is skilled at the conversion of a bad situation in the present into a resource for success in the future.

Roles and the Art of Combination

The strategy of entrapment is immeasurably enabled by credentialling. It is considered honourable and praiseworthy to live up to the credentials of one's class, regional background, school allegiance, and, of course, role in a junior-senior relationship or cohort. If one is perceived to be acting appropriately according to the applicable credential, then two benefits are realized: first, the agent's own reputation (as trustworthy and compatible) is enhanced; second, his morally praiseworthy action instigates others to act in a way appropriate to their own positions. What links action to benefits is, of course, the opinion of the audience-that-matters.

Entrapment thrives under such conditions because it is the audience-that-matters who decides whether a person's behaviour is exemplary, and it is the fear of audience opinion that causes others to modify their own actions.[19] Only with that combination, of benefit and punishment, can the strategy of entrapment be used to check the authority of co-participants in contractual relations and cause people to modify their behaviour. Whatever the agent may think about his own actions is relatively unimportant except insofar as it influences his behaviour; it is the audience reaction that shapes his future opportunities to act and defines the rules, vocabulary, and goals of those future actions.

Although the attributes of the stock figures whom we have examined so far – exemplary intellectual, good archeologist, obedient junior, or caring teacher – are widely shared among both actors and audience, the way in which an actual person 'inhabits' one of these roles, or the interpretation of that 'inhabiting' by the audience, will not necessarily be the same in any given instance. Clearly, appropriate action in one instance can, for innumerable reasons of context, be considered inappropriate in the next, but it is also important to understand, as we saw with Hua, that each member of the audience has his or her own incentives to praise or criticize the actions of others. Especially in the *danwei* context, where interdependence is the norm, it is difficult to tell when an audience member will support the claims made by a person out of an interest in that person or on behalf of the *danwei* and, of course, whether the criticism of actions is related to the member's opinion of the person or to fear of the impact on the *danwei*. Just because credentials are widely shared, then, does not mean that their implementation or interpretation is in any way predictable.

So far, I have examined the stock figures available to archeologists as archeologists, but that emphasis has been misleading. To understand an archeologist by looking only at a subset of his available roles makes little sense. Two issues are important: first, a person never inhabits only one role at a time; second, an archeologist is not limited to any particular credential or set of credentials. An archeologist has access to an entire series of roles, for he is simultaneously father, brother, son, classmate, friend, inferior, and superior. Each role cannot be understood in isolation, for his actions in any one context are influenced by his, and audience members', memories of his actions in other contexts (i.e., by his reputation). In the *danwei* context, we must remember, everyone lives and works together such that judgments of the behaviour of an archeologist-father toward his son in his own home can influence opinions about his obedience to his superior in the office.

The audience does not randomly decide, out of the blue, to recall that an archeologist is a 'bad father' while observing him in the office relating to his superior. Clearly, it is a combination of audience goals and context that influences which behaviours will be considered worthy of comment and which behaviours in other contexts will be recalled in the present. It is easiest to explain the impact of goals and context using an example. From the point of view of an observing audience, if an archeologist – we will call him Guo – is speaking to his archeological director in the office, then he will be judged according to the expectations held of a subordinate. If an official is also present – and he is disliked or considered an enemy by the audience – then Guo's actions will be judged according to whether Guo is protecting the interests of the *danwei* against the official (including whether he is adequately protecting the reputation of the director in front of the official). If Guo's mother arrives on the scene, her presence will recall his responsibilities as a filial son, though how those responsibilities will play out in audience judgments of Guo while he speaks with the director and official are unpredictable. Perhaps his filial behaviour in the past will help to mollify an audience beginning to wonder if he is acting appropriately in the present; perhaps her appearance will cause audience members to inter-pret his actions in a negative light because they remember how badly he has treated her in the past.

If the entire scene is moved from the *danwei* to the countryside, then the concept of audience itself becomes multiple. The *danwei* audience contin-ues to see Guo as one of 'their' people in opposition to the peasants and official, as simultaneously subordinate to his director, and, since his mother is still there, as a filial son; however, the audience is likely to be more con-cerned about Guo's behaviour because of the uncertainties caused by the rural context, where the archeologists are strangers and 'bad' things often happen. Yet since they are now in the countryside, there is another audi-ence that Guo must take into consideration: the peasants themselves. They see the entire group of archeologists, even the mother, collectively as urban dwellers who have access to more resources than they do. Yet they are also trained to perceive distinctions of hierarchy within the group as a whole and will expect Guo to be appropriately subordinate to his mother, his director, and his official. Since they lack key information about the enmity between the archeologists (the group including the director and the mother) and the official, they are more than likely to be confused by or misinterpret the interactions between Guo and the official; if Guo acts insubordinately, while he and his *danwei* audience know why he is doing it, the peasants do not have the information required to see the situation as anything more than improper conduct.

We saw above how there are grave conflicts among the duties of an intellectual. Now we must understand that there is more than one credential in play and that they also tend to conflict. An archeologist is child to his parents, inferior to his superior, parent to his own child, and intellectual to officials, peasants, and workers all at the same time. Each role that Guo is seen to have can create conflict: the filial son must pay attention to the needs of the mother, but her needs may well conflict with those of his director; those needs may further conflict with the needs of his *danwei* colleagues and probably with the needs of his official; and all of these duties may conflict with the needs of his relationship as an archeologist and intellectual with the peasants.

In light of the potential for conflict, it is interesting that the stock figures available to archeologists paint a picture of the world in which roles do not conflict. The ideal interactions embodied in the credentials of the parent-child relationship, for example, simply neglect the issue of what to do if those ideals conflict with the ideals of a superior-inferior relationship in the workplace. Given this lack of guidance, how do archeologists navigate the kind of situation in which we find Guo? It is clear that he cannot resist: that is, he cannot attempt to defy the imposition of the ideals and expectations attendant on any one of his roles, redefine what constitutes appropriate 'filial' or subordinate behaviour, or begin lengthy arguments on the benefits of reducing class conflict between intellectual and peasant. Despite having read the work of Gramsci, Foucault, and Bourdieu (as have most of the younger archeologists), he simply does not have the time or authorization to arrest events while explaining issues of interpellation, doxa, perspective, and authority to the observing audience. Unfortunately, all that Guo can really do is try to minimize the times when these complex situations arise. If he fails to stop his mother from coming to work or does find himself in the (admittedly unusual) situation of confronting both his director and his official in front of the peasants, then he must act as best he can in the moment and engage in the arts of motivation, reinterpretation, and conversion to repair any cracks in his reputation at a later date.

Yet all is not so dire. As with all the resources that we have discussed so far, conflicts among roles can be both limiting and enabling. While role conflicts can create something like Guo's dangerous situation, those conflicts can also be used creatively by agents. If archeologists are able to choose the time and the place in which roles are to be combined, then they have a better chance to control the outcomes. The goal is to sway the audience through the creative use of role combination. The agent can but try, and the reasons why he might want to use such an apparently dangerous tool are due, of course, to the incentives of success. If the art of role combination works as planned, the impact on the agent's career and family can be beneficial indeed.

'The most important thing to remember,' said Cai one day while we were discussing my soon-to-be-reoriented perception of the rigid nature of archeological lives, is that 'a person is never simply an archeologist. One is only an archeologist at certain times and for certain reasons.' Cai then proceeded to tell me how his calculated combination of his different roles and duties in relation to the event of his son's birth catapulted him to the exalted position of vice director of his provincial institute at the age of thirty-two.

When Cai arrived at his *danwei*, just after graduation from university, he was already engaged to be married. He lived with his wife a few days after their marriage but otherwise spent his first two years in the field excavating (save for returning briefly at New Year's). This lengthy stint in the field is believed appropriate for young archeologists because they need training and experience. And, in any case, there was no place ready for the couple to live together, so he lived at the field site, while she continued to live with her parents. Eventually, her *danwei*, the railway *danwei* (much better financed than the archeologists'), managed to get her a flat, and Cai returned and moved in for a few months, during which time she became pregnant.

Near the end of her pregnancy, however, Cai was once again sent out into the field. He was not able to be present for the birth of the child and was given only one opportunity to phone his wife after the event (to find out the sex of the child). The child was a boy and the birth particularly difficult. Yet at no time did Cai complain to his director about not being allowed to go to see his wife and son. Rather, he relayed the news to his director with apparent cheer and a happy martyrdom. Cai made sure that his director understood that he was clearly putting the needs of work above the needs of his family. More importantly, he made sure that everyone in the *danwei*, including the party secretary and officials, knew that he was being a 'bad' father in order to be a 'good' junior.

Cai was counting on the idea that his commitment to work, appropriate given his age and the ideal of being a good (hardworking) archeologist, would maintain his reputation in the eyes of the audience and convince it that he was being *forced* to act as a bad father, not that he *was* a bad father. Once he had the sympathy of audience members, he could be sure that they would start to question how his superior could allow such a thing to occur. The ideal superior, after all, has the responsibility to take care of the needs of his inferiors. One of those needs is clearly related to enabling his inferior's duties as father and husband. By interfering with those time-honoured roles, the superior opens himself up to the criticism that he is not a good superior. The audience notices and comments; gossip leads to a loss of reputation; a loss of reputation, in turn, leads to a loss of ability to be considered either trustworthy (if he cannot even live up to his responsibilities as a superior, then how can he be trusted to enter responsibly into a social relationship of any kind?) or compatible (he has a bad reputation, so why would someone chance becoming involved with him when he probably has no access to important people?).

Cai played the dutiful inferior as submissively and as close as possible to the ideal characteristics of a good inferior. In so doing, he fought to control the interpretations of his actions by the audience. His success was not certain: his director, for example, could have fought to convince the *danwei* audience that his duty as director, to place the needs of the many over the needs of the few, justified his actions. It was impossible for the director to react in this way, however, not just because of Cai's clever performance of submission but also because of luck. Cai was simply lucky that the difficult birth and a male child called up sympathy from the audience. Such was the sympathy for his predicament that the director was rendered helpless. Only if the *danwei* had been in some immediate crisis could the director have convinced anyone that Cai's failure to attend his child's birth was required to protect the *danwei*.

Had Cai complained, resisted, or criticized his director in person in front of other people, the director could indeed have used all the authority of his senior position in the hierarchy to back up his treatment of Cai. Criticizing a director in public transgresses an important aspect of a person's role both as inferior and as *danwei* colleague: that person ruins the reputation of his leader. Morally speaking, juniors are not supposed to do that, but, more importantly, ruining the reputation of the leader of the *danwei* is a little like shooting oneself, and certainly one's colleagues, in the foot. The officials would be utterly pleased to have the reputation of the director ruined, for it makes their task of refusing to give him important resources (e.g., the budget) that much easier. *Danwei* audience members, whether or not they like or respect their director, certainly want him to have all the tools needed to negotiate for the resources they need. Had Cai criticized his superior's actions, the *danwei* director could probably have had the audience sympathizing with him and criticizing Cai for being a bad comrade, a bad father, a bad archeologist, and an insubordinate besides.

Cai, however, played his cards correctly. He did not get to see his son until seven months after his birth. That kind of sacrifice requires some fairly substantial recompense. The director responded by giving Cai multiple opportunities, including the chance to take a special course to secure the right to excavate. That right is considered a plum benefit since only when one can direct one's own excavation can one also publish. Moreover, only then does one have the authority to invite others to join the excavation and to control access to the data, both of which represent important resources in the struggle to build a career. Later Cai was even offered the opportunity to return to university to finish his MA degree. By providing him with such rare opportunities, the director felt satisfied that he had done his best to compensate Cai and would be seen by the audience to have acted appropriately toward his junior. Not only would he therefore be above criticism, but also any success Cai attained would be considered as much the director's doing as Cai's. Cai, in return, was happy to tell anyone who would listen about the excellence of his director. By associative logic, the two can continue to benefit from each other's reputation of being trustworthy (such dutiful seniors and juniors) and compatible (both clearly able to access considerable resources).

By the time that Cai was thirty, he was perfectly positioned – in a system that rewards the accumulation of academic degrees and pays close attention to excavation experience – to be chosen by the officials to become the vice director of the *danwei*. Over the same time period, the 'virtuous' director himself had been promoted from his post as director of the institute to the height of officialdom as the vice director of the Ministry of Culture. Given the new position that each has, and the new resources that each represents, Cai and his (formerly archeological but now bureaucratic) superior maintain their relationship and explore the new kinds of mutual benefit that each can expect from the other.

Not every junior can make the sacrifices needed to get audience sympathy and, therefore, control audience interpretation of his actions. It takes a certain kind of will, or incentive, for a person to undertake the kinds of actions and endure the short-term criticism that might, if everything goes well, lead to long-term success. Cai, by his own admission, is a callous, thick-skinned man. He needed a thick skin to endure the criticisms heaped on him by his mother (and his parents-in-law) for not having defied his director just a little and returned to help his wife. He had to be strong over the intervening years that it took him to complete both the special classes and the master's degree in the face of continuing criticism by his family. Had it not worked out so well – now he is the darling of the household, of course – he would be criticized for the rest of his life as a bad husband. After all, a husband's duty is to protect and help his wife in the same way that the superior's duty is to protect and help his inferior. If things had not gone well, Cai could have lost all his trustworthiness and compatibility within his family. Worse, once he has a bad reputation, by associative logic, his families' (both his and his wife's) reputations would also have suffered. Cai took a big chance.

Others in a similar situation might choose a way to remain submissive enough to the director yet still put family first. Perhaps the result would not be so beneficial for one's future career, but it would make home life more comfortable. Had Cai decided to emphasize his role as husband rather than inferior, he could have gone about it in ways that would not have completely destroyed his relationship with his director. When I asked how he could have done things differently, Cai said, with a big grin, that one of the best ways would have been to have his mother travel the great distance to the site and personally beg the director to let Cai return. It would be difficult for a director to go against the wishes of a mother importuning him on her daughter-in-law's behalf.

Note that, in this hypothetical situation, Cai never described his mother as requesting anything for herself (she does not say that *she* wants to see Cai) or for him (she leaves him out of it and takes all responsibility for the situation on herself; he could even beg her to go home in front of the director); rather, her request is on behalf of her daughter-in-law alone. Moreover, she never blames the director for taking Cai into the field at the wrong time. The best thing is for her to blame everything on herself. She could express her sorrow at how she did not plan the marriage or pregnancy properly and how terrible she feels about having to ask for the director's help in this way. Her role as an inferior woman and mother gives the director both a moral impetus to act (males should guide and aid females) and a way to avoid being blamed for getting Cai into such a situation in the first place. It is, after all, a perfectly acceptable trope in Chinese society to blame everything on a woman.[20]

Cai noted that these strategies would certainly have succeeded in allowing him to see his son yet insisted that they would have been bad for both him and his son in the long term. By doing his mother a favour, the director would escape being beholden to Cai. Instead, Cai would be in debt to the director for the favour of cleaning up a messy situation brought down on Cai by the women in his family. As a result, Cai would not receive all the opportunities that have helped him in his career in such a stellar fashion – opportunities, he added, that will lead his son to better educational and job-related opportunities.

The art of combination is often used by female archeologists to avoid going into the field. There are few female archeologists for a number of reasons, many of which are explored in Chapter 7. Suffice it to say here that young, unmarried, female archeologists are, in fact, expected to excavate as often as any young man. Some women, of course, are perfectly happy to go into the field, enjoy excavation, and look forward to it. Others, however, are horrified at the very thought of leaving the city for the country.

Huang is a graduate of WuDa and was assigned several years ago to an archeology *danwei* in Wuhan. She had wanted to become a tour guide for the provincial museum: a nice, clean, and steady job in the city that would allow her to learn English and maybe even meet some foreigners (I was her first foreigner). Her teachers, for some reason that she refused to discuss, assigned her instead to an archeology *danwei*. Huang told me that she is *never* going into the field again because she hates dirt and finds bones and garbage repulsive. I had to ask: how will she avoid what appears to be the universal fate of all new recruits to an archeology *danwei*?

She could, of course, get married and become pregnant: once she becomes a wife and a mother, no self-respecting director, both as a man and as her superior, would send her away from her children. Even if her husband works in the city and is actually wonderful with children, he will be assumed by the *danwei* and official audience to be useless when it comes to children, and, therefore, to send a mother away from her children is almost criminal. After marriage, it is hard for a woman to be sent into the field even if she *wants* to go precisely because the director (and possibly her husband) fear the gossip that would result from her leaving her child 'alone.'

Huang was not so tacky as to tell her director explicitly that she hated archeology. Instead, she used the fact that she was single to get her director to let her stay in the city. Since directors ought to be involved in all aspects of the well-being of their inferiors, she was perfectly in the right to subject her director to lengthy complaints about her ugly looks, how lonely she was, and how she worried that she would never get married because men simply did not like her or want her as a wife. She emphasized the fact that 'everyone knows' that a woman or her family is not happy until she is married. She felt terrible that she was not upholding her family's face. She wept. A few conversations along these lines, with one or two calculated to be overheard by others, had her director scrambling, as Huang related to me with considerable glee, to introduce her to suitable men.

The director set Huang up with an easy archival job to keep her in the city, all the better to meet the men whom he spent quite a bit of time finding for her. Indeed, her director took a great deal of pride in being seen as the type of person to help find marriage partners for the young people under his care. The *danwei* audience, sharing as it does the assumption that women need to be married, had sympathy for Huang and pride in the director, who took such interest in the well-being of his inferiors. Huang's lack of interest in archeology did not go unnoticed. Her colleagues expected Huang to sacrifice her own needs for those of archeology but thought that her needs as a woman trumped her responsibility as an archeologist. Their judgment was not automatic: Huang needed many more lachrymose discussions with a number of people to get the audience to see things her way.

The director took quite the fatherly interest in her quest. Huang was entertained by innumerable invitations by potential matches made all the more suitable because she could simultaneously please her director by choosing one of his candidates, get married, and still never have to go into the field. Huang, as far as I am concerned, is clearly brilliant: as of our last conversation, she was happily married to the youngest nephew of her director, bringing her into a close kin relationship with one of the most powerful men in her life, and has still never gone to work in the field. She only leaves the city occasionally to bring food or other gifts to her hard-working *danwei* colleagues.

Archeologists such as Cai and Huang may appear to be confined rigidly to their roles, but they can always choose which people to be from among the roles available to them: loving husband or dutiful inferior, new archeological recruit or unmarried, unhappy woman. The claims made to essential nature must be close enough to the credentials already ascribed by the audience yet different enough to intervene in the judgments of that audience. The claims must also be made in front of certain people in order to remind them of their responsibilities in the particular case set before them. The trick, then, is to control which roles the director will play in response to the junior's own role choice: it is a chancy game that can fall apart if the director chooses a different response than the one expected. Huang's director, for example, could have sent Huang into the field 'for her own good' and justified his actions by insisting that, if she wanted to be married, then she had better be a worthy match with the potential for a future promotion and increased compatibility, values that in archeology are entirely dependent on excavation. Claiming in the form of acts of combination, then, is perilous yet persists because the potential benefits are great.

Achieving Identity

All roles are achieved. Even if they appear to be as ascribed as they could possibly be – such as a person's birth position in the family – they must still be achieved. They are achieved because the way in which a person inhabits a role is very different from the model itself (and attendant rules for behaviour). Being born the third son is one thing, claiming what it means to be a third son in the light of a particular discourse is quite another, and being a third son in combination with one's credentials as a member of a class, region, or school is something different again. The deviation from the norms of expected behaviour are as governed by rules and guidelines as is straightforward conformity. The key to success in this system is the actor's ability to seduce the audience-that-matters into judging his actions as deviant or conformist and to interpret that deviance or conformity in a way beneficial to the actor.

The key to success, in other words, is the deployment of 'identity.' What is identity? To understand it, we must begin with the three models of prescriptive behaviour: 'roles-in-relation' is a term meant to apply to how a person acts in relation to co-participants in a hierarchical relationship;

'credentials' are visions of a person's essential nature that affect how his behaviour in roles-in-relation will be judged; and 'discourse' applies to the worldview claimed to be at work in the context in which a given relationship occurs. Together a person's actions in light of these three models of prescriptive behaviour combine in the eyes of the audience-that-matters to compose a person's reputation; that reputation includes his biography (the history of what he is known to have done) and his identity (the likelihood that he will act in expected ways in the future). Identity is fractured and multiple because the likelihood that he will act in expected ways in the future depends, always, on which roles, discourses, or credentials will be ascribed to him or claimed by him. Note that identity here conflates what a person is with how he behaves: the 'good' man behaves like a good man.

We have seen a variety of strategies by which an actor can achieve the identity that he desires, by motivating or even forcing the audience into judging his actions in a way that he desires. The audience-that-matters need not be an actual audience. People can be goaded into action simply by imagining the potential punishments of deviance (attacks on one's identity entailed by not conforming to expectations) or the potential benefits of conformity (material or immaterial enhancement of identity) on their own without others present.

While the possible permutations in audience judgment seem to be overwhelming, interpretation is, in fact, limited by the doctrine of similarity, the will to believe that 'everyone agrees' on what is 'appropriate' behaviour. Whether or not each interpretation is the same often does not matter because, by assuming that it is the same, and by using the same language, differences of opinion simply disappear. Disagreements are either not perceived or interpreted to mean something other than what they might mean about the prevalence of difference in Chinese society. It is rare that people actually sit down and work out whether their uses of a word have the same meaning. And, if a difference of opinion is perceived, then the logic of the junior-senior contract and the gift-giving strategies in which audience members themselves are enmeshed will help them to work out among themselves whose interpretation ought to prevail.

The strategies of claiming and credentialling described here differ with regard to informants' awareness of them. The arts of motivation, conversion, and combination are widely understood, discussed, and taught among archeologists. Although they might not have used the exact language and definitions that I used for the heuristic purpose of ordering the information, people do speak about marshalling incentives to modify the opinions of others, how to give the gifts of submission and obedience that can support one's claim to be acting one role rather than another, how to use failure in the present for success in the future, and how to use reputation and the threat of gossip to entrap others. Indeed, my teachers delighted in telling me their successes and failures in using these strategies.

The art of conversion deserves particular emphasis in this regard. Since one cannot control circumstances, one can only hope to be as flexible and creative as possible in order to convert anything bad (or good, for that matter) into something good (or better) in the future. In an unfortunate clash of behavioural expectations, the resulting relaxed attitude in reaction to difficult circumstances is often misinterpreted by Euro-American observers as indicative of resignation and passivity. Much ink has thus been spilled on the topic of 'Oriental fatalism.' What is perceived as passivity by outsiders is more likely to be perceived by insiders as one of any number of strategies by which someone converts a bad situation not by struggling but by 'bending in the wind' and 'coming back to live another day.' Given the difficulties of interdependency and the benefits represented by mutual mixed-tie relations, it is no wonder that the art of conversion is so often discussed and analyzed among archeologists.

In contrast, the art of reinterpretation is not explicitly discussed. It appears that when a speaker reinterprets the characteristics of the credentials ascribed to or claimed by him, he is unable to articulate what it is he does. Neither Zhang nor Han analyzed how they juxtaposed and reinterpreted their regional credentials, nor did they discuss or use any language of manipulation, planning, or strategy while using these credentials. I suppose it is because the contradiction between the rhetoric of essentialism that underlies credentialism and the language of flexible and strategic role playing is simply too great. While I observed credentials being manipulated and creatively reinterpreted, then, I did not have conversations detailing the rules for the appropriate use of the strategy of reinterpretation or the goals that can be achieved through its use, details that are so common when talking about the arts of motivation, conversion, and combination.

It is interesting that the speaker often uses a different model of the individual when *describing* as opposed to *justifying* his actions. When describing what he has done, the speaker will often speak as if everything is centred on him and his desires. Especially when telling stories of how he entraps others or convinces an audience to support him, the speaker sounds for all the world like a rugged individual in the Euro-American mode: he is in complete control of all actions and acts only out of self-interest. However, if asked to justify his subversion of the system, the speaker will change his tune. He will insist that he was doing everything on behalf of someone or something else, perhaps for his parents, wife, superior, *danwei* colleagues, or even China and the Chinese people – for anyone, in fact, other than himself. So strong is the anxiety produced when one is asked to justify acting like an individual that it suggests there is a strong moral injunction to present the self as 'sacrificing' rather than 'selfish.' Nevertheless, that discourse of sacrifice of personal desires for those of the group is just that: an available discourse. As a discourse, it guides behaviour and evokes certain goals and motives, but, as with all rules, it cannot determine a person's choice of acts or the manner of acting.

There is (among archeologists) only one group whose members do not pay much attention to context and who tend to act and speak as if they are selfish individuals most of the time. These are the members of the age co-hort called the 'lost generation.' The concept of age cohort is another kind of credential that insists all members of any given generation share similar essential characteristics and behaviours.[21] Members of the lost generation were teenagers in 1966 and thus had the experience of being Red Guards, of being sent down to the country, and of making it back to the city by any means after 1977. Strangely enough, these accidents of history have 'caused' the lost generation to inhabit the role of selfish, autonomous individuals regardless of context and without suffering audience disapproval. They always speak as if they act independently of others for their own selfish goals and tend to describe themselves, and be described by others, as rebellious mavericks. They can take risks that people not of their generation would not contemplate. In the face of age, for example, a young person should show respect by not expressing a contrary opinion; in contrast, a member of the lost generation is more likely to speak his mind (though he is still expected to obey the older person – individuality goes only so far, and he desires the benefits of obedience just as much as anyone else). Yet he is not punished because, after all, he is simply acting true to his nature. I do not know whether it is true that this generation lives or acts differently from others. What does appear to be social truth, however, is that 'everyone knows' that members of the lost generation are rebels. Their rebellion is domesti-cated as predictable, appropriate, expected, and understood (within limits, of course) due to their particular age cohort credential.

Nevertheless, most credentials differ from those of the lost generation in that they require group members to justify their actions according to the discourse of the sacrificing individual. The self-sacrificing discourse is more prevalent because it supports the law of reciprocity. The model of the sacri-ficing individual emphasizes the need to relate to others and to submit one's behaviour to the needs of that relationship. One's very identity is fractured by being controlled by the audience and co-participants in rela-tions rather than by a person himself. Were the model of the self-interested individual to be stressed instead, the incentives for people to care about the opinions of others disappear. Identity becomes singular and whole because it is governed simply by the self (a self not in relation to anyone else) rather than tied to the audience-that-matters. A main reason to engage in strate-gies of intervention or gift giving – the protection of identity and the use of that identity to gain access to and command over resources – thus no longer applies. Given the importance of identity and the conditions of material and moral interdependence in China, it is unlikely that the rhetoric of the self-interested individual will be expanded beyond the limited number of contexts in which its use is presently considered acceptable by the audience-that-matters.

6
Interest Groups

They want to eat others and at the same time they're afraid that
other people are going to eat them. That's why they're always
watching each other with such suspicious looks in their eyes.
  – Lu Xun, *Diary of a Madman*

A doubtful friend is worse than a certain enemy. Let a man be one
thing or the other, and we then know how to meet him.
  – Aesop

Given the generative conflict between hierarchy and authority, excavation
takes on supreme importance in archeological life quite beyond what con-
tributions it may make to archeological knowledge. Both preparing for and
undertaking an excavation provide the opportunities (by necessitating the
cooperation of many different institutional entities) and the resources (artifacts, sites, and information) that supply archeologists with ample fodder
to create the fictive cohort groups that can cross almost any gulf of bureaucratic or social divide. As we have seen, strict formal rules, multiple models
of behaviour, and conflicting lines of command generally can be turned to
almost any individual purpose depending on the skill of the actor and the
sympathies of the audience.

Unfortunately, excavation also forces archeologists into the countryside
and into contact with the peasants. That is an unfortunate situation because the archeologist-peasant relationship is doomed before it is begun by
the discourse of the 'urban-rural divide.' It is believed that the division between urban and rural society in China is so deep that it necessarily precludes the creation of mutually beneficial reciprocal bonds. The motives,
essential moral nature, and goals of peasants and archeologists are believed
to be so distinct that neither has anything but trouble to offer the other.[1]

The discourse opposes the educated and sophisticated *(you wenhua)*, high-quality *(suzhi)* urbanite living in luxury to the conservative, traditional, and naïve *(pushi)* country peasant living in deep poverty. This worldview persists, as all credentials do, in the face of all personal, historical, political, and economic facts that should have destroyed it. It is certainly not my intention to use research and statistics to 'prove' how 'wrong' or at least misguided are the assumptions made of Chinese urban and rural spaces. Rather, I recognize that the persistence of the belief makes it 'true': that is, as true as it needs to be in order to have an effect – a substantial effect – on the creation and maintenance of social relationships between urban and rural dwellers. This belief affects archeologists because they must make these 'inconceivable' connections under circumstances where they are dependent on the goodwill of the peasants to provide shelter, food and water, electricity, and, above all, the permission to excavate and the workers to dig.

The urban-rural divide is, at least in one sense, beneficial to teachers of archeology. To ensure that students feel protected, and that the social contract between teacher and student is duly strengthened, teachers often first cause them to feel endangered and then step in to 'protect' them from that 'danger.' A judicious use of the myths and tales of the terrible countryside is an excellent method to ensure docility and dependence among the students. Occasionally, older students use similar strategies on their younger peers (perhaps for practice but more likely just for the sheer delight of making the younger ones squeal).

To create a sense of danger, teachers combine the general fear of strangers (regardless of locale), substantive worries about peasants in particular, and uncertainties about the future to keep their students in line. Before students arrive in the countryside, they have had ample opportunities to hear exciting tales such as the 'teacher who was caught under a collapsing wall,' the 'discovery and subsequent struggle to prevent the looting of a tomb,' the 'student who was forced to marry a local girl,' and other horror stories. Often these tales incorporate myths of ghosts or curses (a time-worn favourite: 'the teacher – and/or students – who died mysteriously [horribly] after opening a grave') related to deeply held fears of death and the afterlife that appear to be entailed by the nature of archeology as an activity. Archeology students appear to be simultaneously attracted to and repulsed by these stories. Yet such is their power that even the students who are utterly uninterested in archeology and who prefer to ignore their teachers and take classes in economics and law can easily and effectively be quelled into submission by a few tales about what might happen to them while disturbing the dead in the deep, dark countryside.

The telling of stories is a strategy fruitfully combined with narratives of hardship. The concept of hardship comes up when asking archeologists (teachers, students, and professionals) to state the single most important attribute needed for a person to succeed at archeology. To a man, all replied that the ideal archeologist must be able to *chi ku,* which means 'to eat bitterness' – that is, to endure both physical and emotional hardship. It is because the definition of 'hardship' changes depending on one's experience with the countryside that it becomes so useful in the strategies of control and reputation enhancement.

From a non-archeologist urbanite's point of view, since he has little experience of the Chinese countryside, hardship is not so much *chi ku,* with its overtones of emotional stress, but *jian ku,* which can be defined as deprivation: lack of favourite foods, lack of shopping or other entertainment opportunities, and lack of family and friends. The imagined rural space contains nothing that any self-respecting urbanite would recognize as comfortable, healthy, or entertaining. A librarian from one of the universities, who had become close to the third-year students before they left for their practicum, felt so sorry for them that she actually made the long and difficult journey into the countryside to bring them a care package of food and tidbits. The package included meat strips since she was convinced that the students did not have access to meat in the country. More the fool, then, when she arrived to find the students physically in good health and enjoying their fine meals of meat and vegetables.

The tenacity of the notion of physical hardship in the countryside incidentally allows archeologists to use narratives of hardship to enhance their reputations among fellow intellectuals. By emphasizing the need for archeologists to be able to endure hardship they flag themselves as more hardworking and deserving than other members of the academic community. These tales also help to perform an archeologist's sense of duty: the more difficult archeology is perceived to be, the more valuable the gift that archeologists give (to the nation, to knowledge, or just to the relevant official) and the easier it becomes to access important resources in return.

The definition of 'hardship' used to maintain control among students *(chi ku)* is dissimilar from that used to garner sympathy among urbanites *(jian ku).* After all, archeologists know, and students soon find out, that the countryside hardly lacks meat or other physical comforts. Students did not describe themselves as uncomfortable. Most mentioned that they were better fed than in the school cafeterias. Many of the boys thought that it was fun not to wash, and, since the girls were always given the opportunity to wash much more often than the boys, they were also satisfied. Far from lacking entertainment, the students had access to TV and videos, a luxury they did not have at school, and some students from schools where the campus is far away from the city found that there were even more opportunities for fun during the practicum than at school. Given the luxuries that they enjoy, it would be difficult to convince them (for long) that hardship has anything to do with physical lack.

It is probably necessary to point out here that the conditions in the countryside before the early 1980s were indeed such that physical lack was a large part of the definition of 'hardship.' Older archeologists are fond of telling tales of their truly amazing physical feats in the pursuit of archeology. As one might expect, these tales increase the audience's respect for their experiences. Interestingly, older archeologists also insist that 'back in the old days' the feeling of shared national identity and the shared goals of communism were also enough to overcome any resistance by the peasants. These archeologists have a great sense of nostalgia for a time when peasants were said to be far less greedy and resentful. Whether peasants really were so kind or the old days so great is not important. What is important is the startling fact that older archeologists would rather return to the grand old days of physical pain and hardship than face the hardship represented by recalcitrant and demanding peasants in the present.

'Hardship' is thus defined by archeologists for archeologists as having to manage the peasants. Occasionally, the practices involved do require physical endurance, particularly the ability to drink and eat large amounts at banquets; however, since banqueting is a fact of Chinese social life regardless of context, students are not particularly intimidated by this physical requirement. Instead, they are aware, and are made infinitely more aware by the conscious actions of their teachers, that they are ignorant and therefore vulnerable when it comes to interactions with the peasants. Since all archeological practicum participants live together in the homes of peasants, some of the students' fear stems from being perceived as rude or arrogant or unknowingly breaking some rule of etiquette and thereby causing the entire excavation to come to a halt until the teachers figure out how to fix the situation. Most of their fear, however, arises from the oft-repeated tales of greed, graft, and corruption of the 'cheating peasant' told both at school and during the practicum.

The best way to thoroughly frighten – and teach – the student is to allow him to observe the teachers in negotiations with the locals. The student sees with his own eyes how his teachers, whom until now he had thought both omnipotent and omniscient, can fail to negotiate successfully. That failure makes the student uncomfortably aware of the capacity of the peasants to control the situation. It is a teaching opportunity in that the student begins to recognize the possible strategies available to deal with peasants, but in the main what the student learns is that he had better support, enable, and otherwise help his teachers in every way he can. A student can ensure his own protection only by supporting his teachers in whatever way they require for success in their negotiations with the peasants. The common enemy, as always, provides the incentives to strengthen group cohesion and the social contract.

The Peasant Enemy

Despite its usefulness for keeping students in line, the urban-rural divide is, for the most part, the most problematic and challenging aspect of excavation in China. To understand why, we need only recognize that the word *peasant* refers in general to all members of the Agriculture *Xitong*: the farmers and their leaders. Like archeologists, farmers have directors,[2] officials,[3] and party secretaries.[4] If an archeologist enters the realm of the farmer, then he enters a world as interdependent as his own where the ripple effect can reach far indeed. Gossip about an archeologist who exchanged harsh words with a farmer's child in one county can race through the complex network of peasant junior-senior and cohort relations and end up affecting the prices of vegetables and meat offered to a different archeologist in a neighbouring county.

When archeologists go into the field, they leave behind their families and friends, their hometowns, and their colleagues. Their familiar routines – domestic duties, kinship obligations, and collegial responsibilities – and the familiar standards by which they are judged and can judge others are suspended. Archeologists enter a context in which, more often than not, they know no one, in which the local routines are not immediately obvious, in which the work that they need to do is considered disruptive by local inhabitants, and in which they must depend on often disgruntled (or expected to be disgruntled) peasants for all their living needs. This situation is not exciting or appreciated and is not commonly cited as an incentive to become an archeologist. It is not embraced as an adventure. The countryside is contemplated with horror, the peasants are viewed with distrust and some disgust, and the effects on archeology of the actions of rural people are universally condemned.

Archeologists, in addition, are considered 'crazy' *(shenjing bing)* by many non-archeologists. Many are the academics of other disciplines, bus drivers, hotel maids, and fellow travellers I met, who, once they understood that I was researching the lives of archeologists, marvelled about the lives of extreme hardship that archeologists are assumed to lead since they must work and travel in rural areas. To a man, the archeologists whom I interviewed agreed that the vast majority of difficulties they face stem from having to work among the peasants. Even those who like to excavate admitted that they are unusual among their fellows. Most simply detest this aspect of archeology.

Trustworthiness and Compatibility across the Urban-Rural Divide

Strategies of performing trustworthiness and compatibility must change their implications and meanings in crossing the urban-rural divide. Trustworthiness, as a performance of reciprocal morality, requires that all participants, especially the audience, share the standards by which behaviour may be judged as moral (and deviations from the standard understood as the gifts they are intended to be). Compatibility requires that each participant be perceived as having something that others want or need.

Archeologists and peasants are equally uncertain about which standards of judgment should be used in assessing trustworthiness. With regard to compatibility, however, their positions are radically different: the peasant knows exactly what the archeologist needs and wants, while the archeologist has no idea what the peasant might want that he can actually deliver. Worse, the peasant thinks that the archeologist is better positioned, more compatible, than he actually is. The archeologist faces a catch-22: peasant demands can become outrageous, while any refusal to deliver is misread as an insult. Without shared standards to judge moral worth, or an accurate understanding of the other's access to resources, it is extraordinarily difficult for peasants and archeologists to engage in the gift-giving and positioning strategies that they are perfectly able to use in their own contexts.

The possible responses to this situation are many. As archeologists often tell their students, possibly as another tactic to increase student dependency, these responses are contingent and constantly in flux and can only be learned through experience. Nevertheless, some general principles may be discerned. In the following two cases, we will consider the creations of fictive peasant-archeologist cohorts and the use of credentialling as a strategy of claiming similarity. In both cases, we will encounter many of the patterns and strategies prevalent among teachers and students, especially the tactic of using fear to increase dependency and strengthen the social contract.

Case 1: Class and Increasing Uncertainty

The difficulties of crossing the divide are exacerbated by a brute structural fact: the short-term and unrepeatable nature of peasant-archeologist relations. The basic tenet of the rule of reciprocity, the very foundation of mutually beneficial yet hierarchically unequal relations, is continuity. If a person invests in a relationship by giving a gift, then the debt is transferred to the recipient until such time as the recipient returns the gift (in, one hopes, a generous manner). At that point, the debt shifts back across the relationship. When a third gift is given, the debt is transferred once again. At any moment in time, then, the balance of benefit is asymmetrical. If the relationship is suddenly broken off, then one person gains disproportionately to the other; while some people might wish to be on the side that gains, most dread the notion that they will be on the side that loses. Both sides thus share the same goal: the creation of a mutually but in the end *unequally* beneficial relationship with the other.

Given the short-term nature of the archeologist-peasant relationship, it is understandable that the peasant spends a great deal of time attempting to manipulate the archeologists in ways that will provide benefit even after they have returned home. Generally speaking, the peasant wants to make the archeologist more dependent on him so that he can control the ways in which the archeologist spends money. Controlling spending means that the peasant can decide who gets the money. The peasant tries to make the archeologist hire certain labourers rather than others, live in certain locations rather than others, buy food and drink from certain people in the market rather than others, and excavate certain sites rather than others. In this way, the peasant can redirect the money that archeologists bring to the region to his kin or friends and divert it from the friends and kin of his enemies or those people whom he wants to punish.

The peasants, of course, are in competition over the resources represented by the archeologists, and therefore each peasant must strive to make the archeologists ever more dependent on him and more willing to follow his advice than that of any other peasant. In his competition with other peasants, the peasant is enormously enabled by the persistence of the credential that labels his class greedy and untrustworthy. He is happy to live up to the credential because it so easily increases the sense of uncertainty and danger among archeologists. One method that he can use is the withholding (or the threat of withholding) of something that the archeologist needs. Unfortunately, there are often other peasants, or at least the peasant imagines that there are others, willing to give the archeologist what he needs for a better price. In such a buyer's market, the peasant must therefore figure out a way to ensure that the archeologist buys only from him. It is in this context that the peasant can most adroitly enter into a campaign to threaten the archeologist. When there are only professional archeologists in the group, there is not much opportunity to scare or unnerve such experienced men. When there are students around, however, peasants can threaten the archeologists by constantly reminding them of how vulnerable the students are to attack.

To understand how this strategy works, let us examine the situation of the Wu girls, two young women sharing the practicum with the two Wu boys whom we first met back in Chapter 2. The Wu boys, despite the difficult circumstances that they knew their fellow cohort mates to be in, were upset that they were not with the rest of their group. They were not with their fellows because they had been chosen to accompany the Wu girls on this practicum. The Wu class had only two girls, and, once it was determined that the original excavation site was too physically taxing for girls, the class was split up so that the girls could go somewhere more comfortable. Two male students had to accompany the girls for their own protection, and the Wu boys volunteered in the hope of gaining considerable value in the eyes of their teachers.

The Wu girls insisted that it is 'absolutely true' that they require better treatment than boys. Better treatment means bathing facilities, a secure and protected toilet, and more protection provided by their teachers. In the Wu girls' case, ample protection was also provided by the female proprietor of the hotel in which they stayed; she ensured that the girls followed a strict schedule of bathing and were insulated from other guests at the hotel. Their room was even decorated for them with old magazine photos of beautiful women, while the rooms of teacher Lu and the Wu boys, on the top floor reached only by a rickety ladder, were left bare.

While the Wu girls were assumed to 'absolutely' require these things, the female peasant workers, who make up the majority of people who work for the archeologists, were not. Female peasant workers engage in heavy labour and live without significantly different standards of protection and facilities from male peasants. Clearly, the needs of the Wu girls arose not simply because they were female but also because they were university students. The traditional credential applied to intellectuals is that they will not or cannot do hard physical labour. Even the Wu boys and the older archeologists were assumed to be much weaker than the peasants, even female peasants. Being weak and unable to handle the daily workload of a peasant is a mark that the person is intelligent (he or she got into school) and secured the highly valued chance to live in a city and have a job. As such, being weak can be a source of considerable pride. None of the male students or archeologists feels an urge to compete with the peasants: physical activity is clearly where the peasants excel, while mental activity is where the intellectuals excel. Both the Wu boys and the Wu girls considered their weakness a mark of distinction in Bourdieu's sense: their weakness proves that they are essentially different from the peasants.[5]

A female member of the intellectual class is assumed to be at great risk from the unspecified dangers of the countryside. The Wu girls, and many other young women on excavations, complain about the peasants taking great pleasure in telling stories and making comments that increase the apparent threat to the girls. In these stories, the 'trouble' is never said to arise from the local peasant workers themselves; rather, it is always the unidentified and nebulous 'stranger' who is at fault. The peasants also comment on all aspects of the arrangements made for girls, making it clear that they know when and where the girls bathe and go to the toilet. The girls are targeted in almost every interaction with the peasants and have their heads filled with the most horrible stories of what might happen to them if they were to walk outside alone or if their teacher were to take his eyes off them for a minute.

Occasionally, female students encounter something more concrete than the telling of stories. The source of such harassment is most often a local older male peasant worker with whom they are already well acquainted. Some men tend to drink heavily, even during the day, and once drunk make inappropriate comments about the bodies of the female students. While making comments about one's weight and 'beauty' – including comments on facial features and skin or hair colour – is acceptable in China from relatives or teachers (male or female), it is not acceptable from members of the opposite sex who have no accepted hierarchical relationship with the young woman. The same comment made by a peasant as opposed to a teacher can have a very different effect on the comfort level of the girl. The offence is only compounded when peasants use colloquial terms that the students do not know or slang words that they do know and find embarrassing. The girls with whom I spoke felt physically threatened and knew that these comments undermined their authority and importance in the eyes of the peasant workers, male or female, and therefore affected their grades because they could not manage their workers as well as the boys could.

The boys have their own gender-specific form of harassment to negotiate. There is always the worry that a male student might get involved with a local peasant girl. It has, or so it is said, happened in the past that a pregnant peasant girl has shown up along with family members to badger a student into marriage. In a campaign of attack more active than simply telling stories, peasants often send their daughters to work for the archeologists, all the while making sly jokes about how marriage to a university student would be nice indeed. Archeologists and peasants share the assumption that any peasant father would consider a male university student a good catch, though archeologists make fun of this assumption among themselves since they know full well that archeology students do not have a comfortable or rich future ahead of them.

Although some of this verbal and physical harassment may be undertaken for the sheer fun of watching at least the girls react, which they always do very satisfactorily by squealing or looking scared, for the most part the targeting of both male and female students is aimed at the teachers. The desired outcomes are several. The most immediate is that it encourages the students to put pressure on their teachers to provide more protection, but the strengthening of social contracts among the archeologists is not important to the peasant. For him, the most important outcome is how these threats can control the actions of the archeologists. The peasant who tells these stories simultaneously acts as solicitously as possible to show that he himself is unlike those other 'uncultured' *(meiyou wenhua, meiyou suzhi)* peasants. The teacher ends up relying on the one peasant to keep the other (assumed evil) peasants at bay, and the 'good' peasant then directs the archeologist to spend money in certain places and hire certain workers.

The ideal outcome, then, is something like a peasant-archeologist cohort, driven by economic necessity on the part of the peasant and cemented by fear on the part of the archeologist. Once the group is even half formed, it paradoxically gains strength from the efforts of nonsanctioned peasants to make friends with the archeologists. The more peasants try to befriend the archeologists, the more suspicious the archeologists become, and the more effort they put into maintaining the group of peasants that they already have. Ironically, of course, the individual peasant whom the archeologist relies on the most tends to be the same man who has spread the rumours and gossip that have frightened the students, has caused water or electricity to be withheld, or has incited the workers to strike for more money. Whatever awareness of these matters the archeologist has, it is still a matter of 'better the devil you know than the one you don't.' Besides, over several months of such close association, the peasant does end up becoming enmeshed in the logic of the mixed-tie relationship and often becomes the champion of the archeologists not only in word but also in deed.

Despite archeologists' considerable experience in the countryside, these strategies of increasing fear and uncertainty work as intended. The archeologists are aware enough of these tactics that they can discuss and analyze them (especially when discussing the abilities of archeologists other than themselves to control the peasants), yet they do not appear to be able to resist acting much as the peasants would have them act. Two main reasons can explain the archeologists' inability to avoid the entrapment: the interdependence of the *danwei* system and the need to protect one's reputation. Archeologists know that if something happens to their students on the excavation, then their own reputations and careers can be ruined. Even one mistake can have catastrophic consequences since one's family's health, education, and accommodation all depend on success in one's job. Fear of such consequences drives even the most experienced of archeologists and teachers to do whatever is required to protect themselves and the students. The needs of the excavation itself are therefore often secondary to the needs of the people involved.

The archeologist protects his reputation for a number of reasons. He must compete with other teachers to be seen as more compatible and trustworthy than they are in the eyes of his students as well as his colleagues. To compete, he must perform being a good teacher as well as a capable leader and a protector of his student flock. The difference is subtle but important. The experienced teacher is not stupid; he is aware that the peasants inflame the fears of the female students and is fairly certain that his fears about the countryside are irrational. Theoretically, he could protect the students with minimal supervision and expense. He could even break out of the mould entirely and require female students to take leadership positions and interact more with the peasants until the students overcome their city-bred fear of lewd jokes.

Unfortunately, a teacher's private assessment of the situation does not matter. It is the audience that matters. A teacher must take every opportunity to emphasize in a *recognizable* manner how important he considers his role and spend considerable energy planning when and how to highlight his exemplary behaviour. The driving force behind ensuring that one's behaviour is recognizably 'good' is the fear of gossip arising from any perceived loss of control over the students' safety. If anything happens, then a man's reputation is affected, and his students, colleagues, and peasants are less likely to perceive that man as compatible or trustworthy, less likely to invest in a relationship with him, and certainly less likely to react sympathetically to any of his attempts to claim or otherwise intervene in their judgments of him. No one dares to initiate that vicious spiral into ineffectuality and weakness.

The relationships among students, teachers, and peasants have different attributes depending on the perspective taken. The girls are primarily worried about being strangers in a land known to be dangerous. They demand protection. As women of the intellectual class, they accept that their obligations are different from those of the peasant women. The teachers, meanwhile, are worried about the future of archeology in this region: if they endanger their reputations with the locals by mishandling the students, then they will be in a weak position when they ask for future favours. They are also worried about their own careers and the maintenance of strong reputations in the eyes of their students and colleagues. The peasants aim to increase the business done with the archeologists. In so doing, however, they seek to keep the balance of power on their side and ensure that the teachers become ever more dependent on them as opposed to some other peasant. The boys are clearly the luckiest: they just want to get the practicum over with and are allowed, for the most part, to pursue that goal unhampered by considerations of gender, class, or reputation.

I do not intend to imply that these groups, or the individuals who comprise them, break down the situation as I have done here. Instead, each individual defines goals and behaviours by what he or she has been taught is appropriate as the representative of a certain role-in-relation and in light of his or her sex-class credential in that context. The cycles of back-and-forth negotiation and entrapment are maintained because there are strong incentives upholding certain goals. Perhaps the cycle would be disrupted if female students could stop caring about their physical safety and reputations as proper women, the teachers about their careers or the excavation, and the peasants about their status and alleviation of poverty. Unfortunately, these are difficult goals to relinquish. Perhaps, then, the cycle could be disrupted if the methods by which these goals are attained are modified. Unfortunately, while the performances of identity and the strategies of social interaction are rendered problematic and twisted by contingent tactics of withholding and increasing fear across the urban-rural divide, they are still successful enough that it would be hard to convince people to stop using them.

Case 2: Withholding and Claims to Similarity

In contexts not affected by the urban-rural divide, credentialling and other performances of identity are strategies of maintaining and intensifying mutually beneficial social relations. Those strategies require a basis of trust in the form of the belief that all participants share the same standards of judgment. What are peasants and archeologists to do, then, to create shared standards of judgment when none is admitted to exist?

One strategy is to claim similarity *(tong)*. Such claiming posits first that there is something shared between interlocutors and second that this characteristic, simply by being shared, can be used as a basis for judgments of trustworthiness and compatibility.[6] Not just any similarity will do. It is best to claim some kind of recognized, and therefore widely shared, characteristic, the more 'essential' (therefore natural, unchanging, and, above all, incontrovertible) in appearance the better. The logic is that of credentialling: if someone shares something of the same essence, he can therefore be trusted to act correctly in a given relationship. The essentialist rhetoric embedded in credentialling does not allow for the questioning of whether shared essence really does lead to the same moral outlook. Claiming similarity enables the judgment of compatibility as well, since credentialling also makes the claim that two people with similar backgrounds are thereby able to understand each other's needs and positioning relative to useful resources. Exactly which attribute can be chosen at any given time depends, of course, on context and on the juxtaposition of roles, discourses, and credentials in play. In the following case, I examine the use of the claim of similarity in response to the aggression of the peasants.

Teacher Hong, having decided that I definitely needed his instruction, often required that I accompany him on his daily rounds during my stay at his practicum. One morning we awoke to find our water pipes empty. That evening Hong ordered me to accompany him to the home of Zhang, the local peasant leader. Zhang had no official position in the party or state bureaucracy yet was somehow in control of the water and electricity for the farmhouse in which the practicum participants were staying. Prior to entering Zhang's large house, Hong commanded me to be a 'charming foreigner' and to be unusually chatty.

Upon entry, we found a group of women and children sitting on carpets on the floor watching TV while Zhang sat off to the side in one of the two chairs in the room. Hong unhurriedly sat in the other chair, and the two men commenced watching TV with morose and silent intensity. I was left surrounded by the women and children, who found everything about me fascinating and worthy of comment. I did my best to be charming and chatty. It seemed to work, because after about thirty minutes they had determined my gender[7] and discovered that I was unmarried yet had strong and childbearing hips, and they were beginning to trade crude jokes about what might constitute a handsome or otherwise suitable match for me. Both men appeared to be utterly ignoring our conversation.

After about an hour, and in response to something that I could not quite determine, Zhang was finally moved to participate in our joke fest and began to explain to me the meaning and implications of a particularly crude proverb. Only then did Hong step in to make an elaborate show of coming to the rescue of my presumably shocked sensibilities. Zhang and Hong then shared a laugh at my 'embarrassment' and began to chat about nothing in particular. The women quieted down and restrained themselves to holding my hands and commenting on my hair. We did not stop talking completely, but we all had one ear on what the men were saying.

Eventually, Zhang got around to mentioning the water problem. He explained that there had been a break in the piping system and that someone would have to walk along the length of the pipe to find it. Hong nodded sagely. They then discussed agricultural yields and recent rainfall statistics. Hong nodded some more. We finally left some two hours later, without Hong once asking Zhang for anything to be done or mentioning the water issue a second time. The women were sorry to see me go and loaded us up with a bag of tasty local oranges. We returned to a silent and sleeping farmhouse, added the oranges to the common pile, and went to bed as quietly as we could. The next morning we had water.

It might be imagined that Hong and Zhang were able to use their gender to break the ice between them. In fact, it was gender combined with the proclivity to be amused (rather than embarrassed) by crude jokes that helped them to bond. Their bond was fleeting because it was based on a particular combination of gender and class that occurred on that particular night in that particular room. Male intellectuals, by virtue of their sex, are assumed to be able to handle crude sexual jokes. This attribute they share with peasants of both sexes. Female intellectuals, a category into which I apparently fall, are in contrast expected to find such jokes distasteful, and a 'good' female intellectual ought to take every chance to feign horror in response to the ribald jokes of peasant women and men.

Had I been a male student, Hong and Zhang could not have used the same claim to similarity; at the same time, it is clear that neither the men nor the women had planned to create this concatenation of events. Claiming similarity is a strategy that seizes on the moment. What is most fascinating is that, despite sharing a similar logic of class and gender in that moment, the very logic that allowed them to make jokes and protect me from those jokes, the situation reverted to uncertainty instantly. Both men, as rural peasant and urban archeologist, returned to insisting that they shared nothing in common and, therefore, in their next interaction would be forced to figure out some other tactical method of establishing a common ground.

Indeed, this incident had its repercussions. Hong believed that Zhang had 'broken' the water pipe to get his attention. Hong was now aware that he had not made his proper respects to Zhang when the practicum had first arrived in the area (since he had not fully understood that it was Zhang who controlled the water to the farmhouse). Zhang was simply informing Hong of the local power structure in this direct (we could not help but notice) and politely indirect (nothing was said outright, so no insult was given) manner. Hong and his co-teacher Li spent the next few days trying to figure out what they could offer Zhang that he might want from them in order to maintain a healthy water flow. Eventually, it was determined that Zhang's second son needed money to go to the local school (in that province, second children could go to school only if they paid a fee). Teacher Li decided that he had the money and the interest in the boy, whom Li had determined was quite bright, to pay for his schooling. Moreover, an intellectual paying for the education of a peasant's son fits quite well with the approved role of intellectuals. Although Li could have capitalized on his performance of being a 'good' (paternal) intellectual, he in fact wanted to ensure that Zhang would not broadcast this favour to others, for then innumerable other peasants would try to manoeuvre Li into paying for their children. It was difficult for Li to get Zhang to be quiet about the transaction because, of course, Zhang wanted to broadcast to his community that he was being aided by, and therefore had connections to, an intellectual from the city.

Zhang's desire to tell everyone about the benefits from Li exemplifies how archeologists can interrupt relations among peasants that are prior to and will outlast the excavation. Zhang had to figure out a way for his interactions with the archeologists to enhance his reputation among the audience that mattered most to him, the other peasants. That Li offered the chance for his child to go to school was attractive to Zhang exactly because it was concrete and incontrovertible proof of his having outmanoeuvred the archeologists. Zhang's prowess in negotiation would prove his ability in matters of social interaction and, therefore, enhance his compatibility in the eyes of his peers. Li's attempt to make Zhang stay quiet about the matter made the whole exchange much less valuable to Zhang, and for a while there we risked losing our water yet again. A compromise was finally worked out: since Li knew that he was retiring upon returning to the city, he figured that he would never return to this region and thus did not mind if Zhang used his name; in return, Zhang promised to wait until the archeologists left before broadcasting the interaction.

The claim to similarity is a tactic used by both peasants and archeologists in their attempts to provide a basis for interaction. Which claim is made depends entirely, as we have seen, on context, but the incentive is always the same: to set up the standards by which subsequent behaviour will be interpreted and judged. Whether or not peasant and archeologist actually share such standards is less important than the belief that their similarities 'prove' they do. Only once the standards are set up can every action be placed and interpreted as a strategy by a teacher, a filial sacrifice by a student, a proper action by a woman, a logical though aggressive attack by a peasant.

The Establishment of Hierarchy

Trustworthiness and compatibility are necessary but not sufficient for the success of relations across the urban-rural divide. The other component to success is the establishment of clear hierarchical relations in which everyone knows which role he or she is supposed to play. Hierarchy refers to inequality in social relations in the sense of both junior-senior imbalance and formal, state-sanctioned, bureaucratic structures. In junior-senior relations, for the junior's gifts to be properly perceived, his interlocutor must not only accept that he (the interlocutor) is the senior in the relationship but also share the same standards by which to judge the behaviour of his junior. Hierarchies are also necessary to the creation of cohort-like groups. After all, there must be a way to decide who is bureaucratically well positioned before he can be approached as a possible member of the cohort; it may be a truism, but nevertheless apposite, to say that there must be a strong sense of hierarchy before there can be an incentive to climb or disrupt those barriers.

Moreover, the standards that the audience-that-matters uses to judge the behaviour of junior and senior, inferior and superior, must more or less match the standards that junior and senior are using. Unfortunately, as we have seen, peasants and archeologists lack that all-important fundamental belief that they share similar judgments of behaviour. As seen above, the tactic of claiming similarity can establish the sense of shared judgment that allows further interaction, but the claim is only momentary and does not last.

In addition to a failing of belief, the bureaucratic hierarchy between peasants and archeologists is uncomfortably confused and contradictory. There is nothing in the formal written rules to indicate who is the junior and who is the senior; neither side, therefore, is quite sure how to act in relation to the other. Archeologists have the permits and policies of the central authorities to support them, often in the form of letters ordering the locals to give the archeologists whatever aid is required. As archeologists are fond of saying, however, 'While above there are official orders, below there are coun-termeasures' *(shang you zhengce, xia you duice)*. When the peasants were or-ganized into strongly policed hierarchies in the communes of the early 1950s, the central government likely did have the authority whereby its orders were followed. Since establishment of the land responsibility system, how-ever, the centralized government in Beijing has lost that authority, and the peasants are unimpressed by the orders from the directors of the Culture or Education *Xitong*. Peasants are more inspired to create relations with the leaders of their own Agriculture *Xitong*, men who clearly have access to desirable resources, than with archeologists of unknown compatibility.

The response to this confusion of hierarchical position, by both archeolo-gists and peasants, is to convert the situation into one of momentary clar-ity: one side must claim to be junior or senior in such a way that it makes sense for the other side to allow the claim to succeed. Like the claim to similarity, claims to junior or senior positioning are necessarily contingent, rarely last long, and take a great deal of effort and creativity to reassert in new situations.

The most common strategy is for archeologists to claim the subordinate position relative to the peasant. 'Being placed' or 'positioned' is what hap-pens to a person once he has accepted the other side's claim to juniority or seniority: the claim puts him in his place. 'To claim' means, then, 'to posi-tion' both the self and the other. Who is commanding enough to put whom in which position is a delicate issue, the key to which is timing. Archeolo-gists must make their claim to juniority *first* (before the peasants stake their claim), or at least have it accepted first, before peasant and archeologist can be positioned in a manner that archeologists find beneficial.

To ensure that a claim to juniority is accepted, archeologists engage in acts of motivation to show the benefits of seniority for the peasants. It is best, insisted Teacher Wu, to act subservient and respectful in the first meet-ing with the peasants, praising and complimenting them in front of their fellows, so that they can get a taste of the benefits of a position of seniority relative to the archeologists. Wu used the same image that we saw in Chap-ter 5 from Hua: one must give the peasants a few appetizers in order to get their stomach juices flowing *(kai wei)*. Once the peasant understands that the acceptance of the positioning can be beneficial, the archeologists are relieved: they know what strategies they, as juniors, can use in the struggle for control in a junior-senior relationship and are more confident that they can predict the strategies that the peasants, as seniors, will use. As juniors, archeologists can threaten the peasant through a reputation requiring that he perform 'being a good superior' seriously. In typical mixed-tie fashion, and if the archeologists perform obedience to the peasant correctly, the peas-ant will find not only that he rather likes these submissive, non-arrogant, and potentially compatible visitors from the city but also that he had better treat them correctly or the audience-that-matters to him will question his abilities as a leader.

Claims to Juniority: Flexibility and Respect

One of the most common ways to claim the subordinate position is to be flexible. The apparent disregard for following the exact details of previously drawn-up plans and contracts has been a considerable cause for concern for Euro-American archeologists. The academic Euro-American archeologist expects the logistical components of the excavation – location, personnel, number of days, methods and tools, and goals – to be planned with considerable care. Untoward events are expected but are allowed to affect the excavation only within certain parameters. If such events exceed those parameters, then the excavation shuts down. Only under very strange circumstances would a Euro-American archeologist decide to excavate a completely different site with different methodological requirements.

Chinese archeologists, in contrast, are trained to be flexible. Flexibility is not only explicitly taught, as part of their classes in archeological method and ethics, but also reinforced because of the implications of flexibility in junior-senior relations. To begin with professional ethics, we must understand that China is a developing country where building projects of huge scale are ongoing. 'Protect and Salvage!' is the slogan *(baohu wei zhu, qiangjiu di yi)*. Both the archeologists and their government consider it reasonable that cultural heritage management be first on the archeological agenda; thus, salvage excavations – saving sites from immediate danger – are considered more important than excavating just any site. If tales of a site recently uncovered by a bulldozer or during the planting season come to the ear of an archeologist, particularly one working with the Culture or Education *Xitong*, he is likely to drop everything to excavate it.

In addition to ethical considerations, Chinese archeologists are trained by habit and past success to expect that flexibility can be given as a gift of submission and obedience to their superiors. If a junior is undertaking a project that the superior has decided no longer benefits the *danwei*, then by all rights he should change the project as required. As we have seen, he may perform reluctance even as he obeys, since reluctance followed by obedience is seen as a more valuable gift than immediate submission, but regardless of motive he must obey. In obeying his senior, he may no longer reap the intellectual information that the project may have yielded, but, as we learned in Chapter 5, he can achieve benefits of a different kind: perhaps opportunities for himself or his family, the protection of the *danwei* and/or his cohort-clique, or the enabling of more interesting projects in the future. Archeologists who suddenly stop excavating and head off to a different county, for example, are, in fact, often embarking on a plan to attack or undermine other archeological *danwei*. By arriving first at a site, even if they have no permit to excavate, archeologists can be the first to make strong relations with the local peasants. In this way, a low-level *danwei* can seriously inconvenience the higher-level *danwei* eventually sent to excavate the site. Peasant-archeologist relations are already difficult but can become much worse once archeologists begin to use the peasants to attack each other. Thus, a project ended before its time may not represent a failure so much as an opportunity to embark on other projects limited only by the creativity of the archeologist.

Further to this, flexibility can be a protection against cheating peasants. Any real archeologist knows to be careful about revealing anything of his plans to the peasants and to avoid being seen as inflexible. Otherwise, the peasants will find a way to use that inflexibility to wring out more money from the archeologist. Someone who does not accept modification can be forced to pay for his attachment to his goals. The old adage *jihua bu ru bianhua* says it best: 'It is far better to be flexible than to make plans.' Or, at the least, it is wise to *appear* ready and willing to accept change so that the peasants are given no reason to believe that the archeologist is wedded to any particular plan. Even if an archeologist truly desires to excavate a certain site, he will maintain his 'cool,' acting as if he could hardly care one way or another. By implying that he is ready to wander off to a place where the peasants are more friendly and prices are more reasonable, the archeologist forces the peasants to be careful, lower their prices, and appear friendly themselves. Hence the many Chinese complaints about foreigners who naïvely reveal all their plans to the peasants that we encountered at the beginning of Chapter 1.

Flexibility can also be used to claim the subordinate position. The archeologist must position himself not only as the dutiful junior who needs help but also as the *respectful* junior. The performance of respect as well as instrumental need is key to the mixed-tie relationship. Given that stepping outside one's class is frowned upon, the archeologist must make it clear that the peasant is worthy of respect because he is an exceptional peasant and avoid any intimation that the peasant is attempting to be an intellectual or otherwise act unbecoming to his class. The best way to perform class-related respect and subordination all at once is to ask questions and follow (or seem to follow) the advice and guidance of the peasant in a variety of matters.

As Teacher Wu put it, it is all a matter of 'knowing nothing.' Asking questions and seeking guidance rather than drawing up one's own plan and sticking to it are techniques that archeologists have learned in other contexts. The same technique works for students with their teachers and for inferiors with their workplace superiors. The strategy is simple: have a problem (or create one appropriate to one's position), ask for the senior's advice, and be careful to be seen to follow the advice or at least not head in a completely different direction. As always, the performance of obedience has very little to do with any actual obedience: it is surprisingly easy, as both Wang and Huang taught us in Chapter 5, to find ways of not following someone's advice, but making it appear that one is, or following it for very different reasons from those intended by the senior. Luckily for archeologists in the countryside, it is relatively easy to create reasonably apposite problems and seek the advice of the peasants. Such performances often occur when peasants and archeologists are discussing excavation logistics: whom to hire as labourers or as cooks, where to live, and from whom to buy tools and food.

It might seem contradictory that archeologists, of the intellectual and therefore educated class, will often ask 'dumb' questions about the lives and work of peasants. But archeologists are not expected to understand the lives of the peasants; indeed, they should know nothing of the orange harvest or how to tell the ripeness of fruit on the tree. Archeologists who may actually have grown up in the country and know exactly how to plant rice or oranges will still ask all sorts of 'silly' questions of the farmers. If an archeologist came to the countryside and acted as if he already knew everything there is to know about peasant life, then he would be stepping on the peasants' toes, in a sense, and expropriating what is theirs (which answers the other question posed in Chapter 1 of why it is problematic when foreign archeologists presume to tell the peasants how to do their job).

An educated man from the city will find many peasants willing to take up the responsibility of being a teacher to his student. First, there is simply a matter of personal comfort on the part of the peasant. Peasants often say that they find it embarrassing to talk to people from the city in the stated belief that they have 'nothing of importance' to say to urbanites. Urbanites are assumed to be more sophisticated and therefore uninterested in the lives of the peasants. By asking the peasant about his own experiences, archeologists open up a space for the peasant to talk about topics that he knows well. Second, having such an educated and presumably well-positioned man as one's student gives the peasant a chance to shine in front of his fellow peasants. The archeologist-student acts as a foil or a good 'excuse' for the peasant to say or do things in front of the audience-that-matters that he might not otherwise have the authority or status to do.[8] The tactic of claiming inferiority, then, often makes up for the fact that the archeologist will eventually leave and never return to the countryside, for the peasant still receives a long-term benefit of increased compatibility among his peers.

The attempt to show respect to peasants by asking questions, seeking guidance, or delivering compliments must change when addressing female peasants. A woman, if she wants to remain a model peasant woman, should not speak too loudly and openly about her expertise in front of men of her class. Moreover, direct compliments about her abilities (in cooking, cleaning, shopping, etc.) are likely to be taken as a compliment to her husband rather than to her. When peasant men are around, then, it is difficult to ask her questions requiring exposition or otherwise show her respect. When no men are around, however, asking questions and giving compliments work with women just as well as they do with men. Compliments might be direct ones about the food or quality of housework, for example, or indirect ones praising the intelligence or health of her children. Since compliments and questions must usually be performed in private, the benefits of showing respect to women are greater for the archeologist than for the woman. Peasant women who believe that the man from the city respects their expertise will be more inclined to help him out and take care of him. Signs that an archeologist has shown respect to the woman of the house include tasty, well-cooked food, cleanliness, and attempts to maintain quiet during midafternoon naps.

A related technique, asking intimate questions, is used as a general tactic in China in any relationship between two strangers. First, to be asked questions about marital status, salary, or *danwei* politics is to be complimented. In asking such questions, the questioner is indicating that he thinks the other interesting and worthwhile enough to deserve an outlay of effort in this way. Second, the questioner is asking questions to determine whether the other is at all compatible or trustworthy enough to enter into a social relationship proper. I have overheard terribly intimate conversations on the train and then watched the two travellers part without so much as a good-bye. What likely occurred was the polite and mutual realization that the two were not compatible – they lived too far apart or did not have access to useful resources. Still, the intimacy of the conversation is a way to show that at least trustworthiness has been perceived. To be thought of as at least potentially trustworthy is a valued compliment on its own, and there may be some benefit in the future. As Teacher Cao put it, 'Be kind to your seat mate; you never know if you'll meet again.'

Evading Entrapment: 'Hosts without Authority'

Claiming the subordinate position is effective yet necessarily difficult to maintain. Archeologists, after all, are forced to take the senior position in anything to do with the excavation: they must explain to the peasants why the excavation is taking place, what archeology is and its goals, and how excavation techniques differ from turning the soil. They also pay salaries and rents and buy supplies. Having money and specialized knowledge helps to position a person as senior. If archeologists allow themselves to be placed in the senior position, then peasants, by acting appropriately as uneducated peasants willing to listen to the advice and wisdom of the intellectuals, can force them into doing more than just paying the peasants wages to work on the excavation. In particular, archeologists can find themselves deeply involved in local politics and can be expected to help with social problems. It is understandable, then, that the archeologist prefers not to incur the requests and responsibilities entailed by the combination of the senior role and the class status of the intellectual.

In an almost absurd attempt to avoid being perceived as too high and mighty, the archeologist tries to separate his authority from his position in the hierarchy and transfer that authority to the peasants. In Chapter 4, we examined how an archeologist can attempt to gain authority (command over the redistribution of resources) far above his station in the hierarchy, attempt to realign his formal hierarchical position with his authority, and attack other people's or *danwei*'s alignments of hierarchy and authority. What we have not seen before is the attempt by an archeologist to disengage his own authority from his hierarchical position and transfer that authority to someone else. The attempt would seem illogical and self-defeating given that both hierarchical position and authority are usually highly desirable objectives that lead to considerable autonomy. When face to face with the peasants, however, archeologists will do almost anything to be seen as 'tigers without claws,' as Teacher Li put it so succinctly.

The strategies involved in removing the tiger's claws tend to be subtle and change radically depending on who is involved. Sometimes it can be a matter of making obvious mistakes or looking confused at the right moment, suggesting that one is somewhat foolish or bumbling; at other times, a note of apology in the voice or an overly relaxed attitude to work might diffuse a situation. It is during the banquet, however, that the complex tactics of divorcing authority from hierarchy come into their own. As we saw in Chapter 4, banquets are important in creating cohort-like cliques among archeologists that realign hierarchy and authority or in attacking the claims to authority made by others. When peasants are involved, however, the banquet changes its meaning. Banquets between archeologists and peasants are required rituals thrown to celebrate a deal, event, holiday, arrival, or departure, indeed almost any occasion at all, and archeologists are necessarily (both because they have money and because their deals, arrivals, and departures initiate the banquets) the hosts of these banquets. Despite the apparent similarity, however, it would be a mistake to imagine that banquets involving archeologists and peasants can be interpreted using the same standards.

When archeologists are at home, it is expected that the host throwing a banquet for his equals or for someone of higher status will reveal how much energy, effort, planning, and expense went into the event. When a higher-status person throws an event for a lower-status person, the event tends to be much more understated. Of course, the situation becomes more interesting when people are near the same hierarchical status. The general rules regulating situations exhibiting large differences in status can be used to wage status wars when the hierarchical positions are close. A person can, for example, be insulting by throwing a banquet deliberately plainer that it 'ought to be' for a colleague. Or perhaps he will throw a more lavish one than expected to show his own access to resources to be much greater than that of his colleagues (with the goal of enticing them into closer relations or, once again, simply to be insulting). The strategies of trustworthiness and compatibility used in banquets among archeologists are, literally, endless and depend entirely on the particular confluence of status and goals in any situation.

In a sharp departure from their normal practice in their home contexts, archeologists attempt to design banquets for peasants such that the former will be perceived as 'hosts without authority.' The banquet is a risky event for archeologists. It must strike a balancing act: lavish enough to be considered respectful and worthwhile yet not so lavish that anyone thinks the archeologists are showing off. The peasant expects it to be that way: a peasant, especially a farmer without any leadership or bureaucratic position, would be offended if subjected to a formal banquet in a grand restaurant. Involving the peasant in such a banquet would be tantamount to asking him to step out of his role – in effect to commit class transgression. If such mistakes in tone and level are made, then the peasants are quick to assume that the archeologist is showing disrespect or being deliberately insulting and begin to question his behaviour in other contexts. Furthermore, as can never be forgotten in the interdependent context that is China, mistakes made in front of the peasants are also made in front of one's students and colleagues.

It is often difficult for the archeologist to figure out how to provide a banquet plain enough yet still lavish by the peasants' standards. He certainly cannot rely on the habits and traditions that he uses at home. Past experience may not be helpful either since different regions in the country have different food and drink preferences. Many archeologists thus use their hosting of a banquet as an opportunity to ask for guidance from the peasants in another attempt to claim the junior position or to give the peasants the opportunity to direct the archeologists to the services of a certain restaurant or cook. The banquet is therefore more than simply a social ritual; it becomes a gift from the archeologists to the peasants: a gift of opportunity for the peasant to enhance his own reputation among his peers.

Unfortunately, the potential problems for archeologists are not removed simply because the peasants have been asked to choose the food or venue. Too many banquets, overly planned banquets, or the appearance of being overly reliant on banquets as gifts (thereby insinuating that the peasants just like to eat and drink) all may be perceived as insults. Archeologists react by attempting to make the banquet seem coincidental, almost an afterthought. They may tell the peasants, for example, that the banquet is being thrown in order to eat up food before it goes bad or simply because it is socially proper to celebrate a holiday. Such excuses allow the situation to be interpreted as if the archeologists were going about their business and suddenly saw a chance to invite the peasants along for a little fun. In fact, the archeologists likely planned the whole thing all along, but the point is to make the banquet seem part of the archeologists' generosity rather than a calculated event. Yet it all depends on context and tradition: if at the end of the excavation the archeologists do not present a more formally planned banquet, as they ought to do by the rules of etiquette, then they risk being seen as unable to understand propriety *(bu dong shi)* and verging on treating the peasants as if they were nothing but hired labourers.

In addition to the pretence that banquets are incidental events, archeologists participate in an elaborate game of deferral. I attended a banquet thrown by the NoDa teachers to commemorate my imminent departure that exemplified the tactics used to transfer as much authority as possible to the peasants. The event of the foreigner's departure was an appropriate and convenient excuse to present the gift of a banquet to the peasants. Members of the peasant family in whose home we lived had cooked the food, as was their usual practice, but when we sat down to eat they sat with us for the first time. We sat outside in the courtyard, so the usual cries of frustration when the electricity failed were not heard that evening. All the workers came, and the food was plain but abundant; the dishes included the peasant leader's favourite fried peanuts dipped in sugar (a Sichuan delicacy) and a startling variety of other local specialties. The alcohol was plentiful: one could not help noticing that, while peasant women may not drink as much as peasant men, they are allowed to enjoy their drinking a great deal more than women of the intellectual class. There was a great deal of fun at my expense – since it had been discovered over the preceding weeks that I could not cook, knit, or carry water – accompanied by many ribald jokes that embarrassed the female students but amused everyone else. Later in the evening, there was a fight between two workers that had the students and teachers rushing to separate them. This event seemed to put everyone in an especially good mood, and the party continued long after the female students had been sent to bed.

The important characteristics of this banquet were matched by nearly every other banquet that I was required to attend. The peasants cook the food themselves but, significantly, sit with the archeologists to eat it. Occasionally, the women of the household would be helped in the cooking by the men of the household, an act considered by the archeologists to be an honour since the men are believed to be better cooks. If we were close enough to the local town, then the banquet would be moved to a restaurant owned by a member or friend of the peasant family. In conversation, the archeologists refrained from discussing archeology, comparing city life to that in the country, or in any way acting as if they had different tastes or expectations from the peasants. Any physical desires, such as wanting to eat a certain kind of food or drink something in particular, were suppressed in favour of the tastes of the peasants. Archeologists obediently suffered through periods of extreme drinking, crude and rude jokes, and physical altercations without once appearing anything other than amused and interested. Their boredom, ulcers, and/or distaste for the peasant lifestyle came out only in conversations among themselves back in the safety of their urban *danwei*.

The attempt to transfer authority from the archeologists to the peasants happens here in a number of ways. Under normal circumstances, a host shows his authority by controlling all aspects of the banquet, including how much people eat and drink, what they talk about, and even when a person may put down his chopsticks to show that he has finished eating. Archeologists eschew the normal duties of the host. Indeed, they take elaborate pains to perform the fact that they are not in control. It is the peasants who take over the usual duties of planning the dishes, choosing the location, apportioning the food, controlling the conversation, and deciding when the banquet starts and ends. Similarly, while normal rules of etiquette suggest that peasants and archeologists should act in a reserved and considered manner with each other, in the context of the banquet peasants are instead encouraged to drink as much and interact as loudly and physically as they like. Archeologists also use a variety of subtle signals, such as emulating peasant slang and accent and wearing certain clothes, in effect deferring to the peasants even in matters of language and fashion, to perform the suspension of normal peasant-archeologist relations during the banquet. By transferring all authority to the peasant in this way, the archeologist maintains as much as possible the junior position in the relationship.

Claims to Seniority: Asserting Knowledge

A claim to seniority is a very different matter from the claim to juniority: it represents an attempt by someone to position himself in the senior spot. *Claiming* the senior position is a very different matter from being *placed* in that position. The person who actively claims to be someone's junior has some reason for wanting to be in that position (and we have seen that there are many benefits to be reaped from that position). In contrast, someone who is placed in the junior position may have no recourse: the person who positions him as junior may have devised a plan that requires instant submission but gives nothing in return for that submission. The placing of someone in a junior position often occurs because the relationship is not expected to last long enough for the junior to realize any benefits of the performance of obedience. Or it may be that the person claiming seniority assumes that the audience will support his claim even if he mistreats the junior.

Moreover, not all junior positions are the same. There is a distinct difference between the junior position taken relative to the father or director and the junior position taken relative to the teacher. The teacher-student relationship, for reasons of positioning and the way that the student's success enhances the teacher's reputation, is more mutually beneficial. Father-child or workplace superior-inferior relations are comparatively more harsh and demand more elaborate performances of obedience. *Claiming* juniority, therefore, usually involves claiming to be a student; being *positioned* as a junior generally involves being positioned as a child or workplace inferior of comparatively low status.

For ordinary archeologists and peasants, claiming the senior position across the urban-rural divide is extremely risky. Since mixed-tie relations require both instrumentality and a quality of emotional affect based on mutual respect, a claim to seniority, with all its implications of superiority, risks being perceived as breaking the code of reciprocity. Once again, it is simply safer to place oneself in the position of submission and obedience and act from that place rather than risk losing the support of both one's co-participant in the relationship and the audience-that-matters. Similarly, if one is going to be positioned as a senior, then it is simply safer not to claim that position from the outset.

Nevertheless, peasants will occasionally claim the senior position, particularly when wanting to frighten the archeologists and increase their feelings of dependency. The strategies used are the opposite of asking questions and seeking advice. Instead of asking questions, one simply tells another person exactly what he thinks about the situation or the person; instead of seeking advice, one simply tells someone what to do whether the person has asked for advice or not. Recall that travellers or strangers often use intimate questions to discover each other's relative trustworthiness and compatibility in a polite and socially acceptable manner. The person claiming seniority does not ask someone where she comes from, what salary she makes, or how many children she has: he *tells* her these details about herself. It may seem unusual, but a man who comes over to explain to you exactly how large a house you must have and that your *danwei* has political problems is not crazy, or some kind of clairvoyant, but merely claiming a position of superiority relative to you for some reason known only to himself – though you may soon discover it.

Asserting knowledge about the lives of others, even going so far as to insist that one knows facts about the family life, salary, and *danwei* politics of a stranger, is an attempt to emulate the normal relations that hold between superiors and inferiors in the *danwei* or between parents and children in the family. The *danwei* director and the father are expected to know everything salient about their juniors. A peasant who begins to list all sorts of random details about an archeologist's life is speaking to that archeologist as if he, the peasant, were the director and the archeologist the inferior. The goal of a peasant who claims seniority is to force the person positioned as junior to obey. Whether or not the claim will be accepted – that is, whether the person positioned as junior will submit to that role – depends not only on which benefits the potential junior sees in taking the role but also on whether the audience-that-matters will support the claim by criticizing the potential junior if he does not submit.

Whether the audience will support the claim of seniority and its implied right to the obedience of the junior depends, of course, on the particulars of the people involved. For an example, let us return briefly to the struggle between Hong and Zhang over the practicum water supply. The peasant Zhang was likely driven to make his claim to seniority because Hong had neglected to pay his respects to Zhang previously. Zhang had stacked the deck against teacher Hong by having so many of his kinswomen in the room. The only audience present therefore clearly upheld Zhang's claim to seniority, and as a result there was no one (other than me) to whom Hong might have been able to appeal to challenge Zhang's claim. Zhang drove his claim to superiority home by not speaking to us upon our arrival and taking no interest in Hong even while sitting beside him watching TV, thereby asserting that he did not have to follow the normal rules of etiquette.

Hong's response was to accept the subordinate role since he had little choice. Once the claim to similarity broke the tension between the two men, Hong did attempt to modify Zhang's behaviour to make the situation more beneficial to Hong. By asking Zhang about rainfall and agricultural yields, and by giving Zhang the opportunity to flaunt his specialized knowledge, Hong attempted to convert his position from that of a workplace inferior or child into that of a student. At no time was Zhang's claim to seniority threatened or resisted; rather, it was subtly modified. As for Zhang, he likely accepted that modification because, now that he had secured Hong's attention, he recognized that a mixed-tie relationship, built on instrumentality and respect, would likely be more productive than one of enmity and tension.

The Authorities of the Three *Xitong*

The claim to *authority* is very different from the claim to *seniority:* the latter is a claim to the right of obedience from the junior; the former is a claim that a man has a certain command over resources such that he can choose how and to whom to redistribute them. Authority is close to the idea of compatibility, which emphasizes the *kind* of resource: an archeologist attempts to modify his choice of topic, site, or teacher in order to position himself closer to resources that other archeologists would consider valuable and worthy of exchange. The concept of authority simply emphasizes *command* over the redistribution of resources: first, it refers to a command that can cross bureaucratic hierarchies and so access resources that, according to the formal rules, ought to be out of reach; second, it refers to whether or not the command is such that the resources can be distributed without regard to the rules; and third, it refers to a quality of performance (authoritarianism) that convinces the audience-that-matters that the claim to authority is legitimate. Claims to authority are thus especially complex because the success of the claim depends not only on the judgments of the audience-that-matters made of a person's performance but also on the eventual appearance of the promised resources.

Claims to authority, like all other claims, are subject to the judgment of the audience and must be seen as appropriate, 'natural,' or commonsensical. While describing the claims to similarity, juniority, and seniority, I downplayed what is actually foundational to the success of any given claim: the audience-that-matters and its perceptions of the right *(zige)*[9] of the actor to make that claim. The archeologist's claim to juniority is successful because it is 'common knowledge' among peasants that the archeologist, as an intellectual, knows nothing about the countryside, farming, or even digging. Of course, it is also common knowledge that the peasants do know about the countryside and digging. The hitch is that 'digging' is not the same thing as 'excavation,' but this fact is ignored in favour of the stereotypical notion that peasants, by virtue of being peasants, know everything there is to know about moving dirt. In addition, the arrival of archeologists as strangers and visitors to the village is generative of such uncertainty that 'everyone agrees' archeologists ought to seek knowledgeable locals to act as guides and protectors. Finally, by showing the audience how the peasant can benefit from accepting the senior position, archeologists are able to perform themselves as people who, despite being strangers, do understand social propriety in the form of reciprocally beneficial relations.

In the struggle to have their claims to authority accepted, archeologists face unfortunate confusions of status that make their efforts far more laborious relative to those of other intellectuals. For archeologists, as a subgroup of the intellectual class, the conditions for claiming authority should already be in place. Unfortunately, when archeologists go to the country, several factors encourage peasants to question the status hierarchy. The most palpable problem, as we have seen, is that coming to the countryside radically changes the context. The traditional respect due to an intellectual is simply lost amid perceptions of the archeologist as a stranger whose spending habits can be controlled by an enterprising local.

Less obvious but far more interesting is another issue particular to archeology. A peasant's image of the intellectual does not usually include excavation or the other physical requirements of archeology. An intellectual 'getting his hands dirty' is perceived to be quite bizarre, and, if he is peculiar in one characteristic, then the audience is quick to question whether he may be unusual in more important characteristics, such as trustworthiness or compatibility. In the 1950s and especially in the 1970s, when traditional class hierarchies were being actively overturned and realigned to the benefit of the peasants and workers, archeologists tended to dig alongside their peasant workers. As the class hierarchy has reasserted itself, however, archeologists have had to reconsider the ways in which they interact with peasants. If they work alongside peasants, then they could conceivably benefit from being perceived as willing to learn from the peasants. On the other hand, by refraining from hard physical labour, or even from looking as if one could do such labour, archeologists guard their reputations as proper (weak, bookish) intellectuals in the eyes of the peasants (as well as, not incidentally, in the eyes of their non-archeological colleagues in the city).

Questions of comportment are thus always important whenever archeologists enter the field. Should an archeologist blend in with the peasants or stand apart? Should he claim juniority or authoritarian seniority? Which claims will be accepted, and which will not? Above all, how will his actions be interpreted by the peasants, and can he prepare for their reactions? The answers to these questions are very dependent on the bureaucratic *xitong* – and the particular level within that *xitong* – in which an archeologist is positioned. Archeologists of the Culture, Education, or Academy *Xitong* use different tactics to claim authority for distinct reasons and with varying rates of success depending on positioning in the bureaucracy, access to resources, and length of their *xitong* ladder (i.e., whether the archeologists have ties to the locals).

The Culture *Xitong:* Blending

The Culture *Xitong* archeologists can be separated into two distinct groups: those at the provincial level or above and those at the lower levels of county, city, or village. Lower-level archeologists, if they have degrees, received them from low-ranked universities or technical colleges; many have never taken formal classes in archeology. A large number were originally dance troupe members and artists forced to become archeologists when the Hall of Culture was called upon to react to the construction boom of 1972-86 and create more archeology *danwei*. From the point of view of claiming authority, the most problematic characteristic of low-level Culture *Xitong* archeologists is that they are often related through kinship networks to their peasant workers or, if not directly related, must live in close contact with the peasants during their working lives. Lower-level archeologists often differ from peasants only in their salaries and by living in the nearest urban setting.

Given their humble backgrounds as well as their local ties, lower-level Culture *Xitong* archeologists clearly cannot style themselves as 'experts' or high-status intellectuals. Instead, they claim a kind of junior status often blended with juniority in the kinship network. Strategies of blending include eating, speaking, acting, and espousing the same views as everyone else. Lower-level archeologists therefore tend to be a motley crew, wearing clothes similar to those of the peasants, appearing weatherbeaten and tired, squatting without so much as a trowel at the edge of a somewhat ragged pit, and rarely having notebooks or other recording instruments in evidence. They use the local accent and enjoy local food and entertainment. Strong kinship ties to the community also change the inferior-superior relations of the workplace. Since many of his *danwei* inferiors may well outrank him in the kinship network, the *danwei* director does not signal his difference in command over resources and looks, lives, and acts indistinguishably from anyone else.

Culture *Xitong* archeologists below the provincial level are restricted by law to salvage archeology and must excavate wherever the construction companies want to build. Those companies are required by law to pay for the excavation and to stay their plans until the archeologists are satisfied. The number of sites to be rescued from construction is always increasing, and the pressure to respond to the building boom is phenomenal. As one low-level archeologist commented, the extent of the willful destruction of antiquities during the Cultural Revolution pales in comparison to the impact of modernization on archeological remains.

Construction companies are less than willing, as might be expected, to cooperate with archeologists and try to bulldoze any archeological remains out of sight as quickly as possible. Lower-level archeologists respond by using their local ties and kinship networks as well as connections to the officials monitoring construction to find out when the bulldozers will be breaking ground and sneak their way onto a construction site. The reactions of the construction companies can be quite unpredictable. Despite the dangers, archeologists persist because the benefits of success are many: in particular, they can make a good amount of money out of the construction companies. Successful archeology *danwei* have elegant offices, cell phones, computers, and excellent living quarters, often of better quality than those of their provincial-level superiors.

One method of ensuring good local connections and a comfortable level of command over the resources represented by construction companies is to indulge in strategies of regional loyalty. Blending is certainly one way to signal local allegiance, but more interesting is the creation of insular cohort-like groups that close ranks against any outsiders. When non-local archeologists arrive, local archeologists use accent, jokes, and other near-hostile performances to maintain the boundary between insider and outsider. The benefits are twofold: on the one hand, they perform their regional allegiance for the locals and guard their reputations as trustworthy people who will protect their own; on the other hand, they minimize the disruptions that outsiders can otherwise cause to their precarious deals and negotiations with local peasants and construction companies. Almost any action by non-locals can threaten previous understandings about salary with the workers or agreements to shorten the time or decrease the expenses of excavation with the companies. For example, non-locals may overpay peasants, but then again they may underpay them. Either way, local archeologists will face significant pressures to respond: a local archeologist whose older brother is being paid a much larger salary than the usual will face significant unwanted pressure to increase the salaries that he pays his other workers. If the older brother is being paid less than usual, then the local archeologist will be required to intervene on his brother's behalf with the non-local archeologists. The local archeologist is constantly placed in the catch-22 of either helping his own people or pursuing relations with non-local archeologists.

Lower-level archeologists may decide that it is more beneficial to cooperate than struggle with non-local archeologists because of the resources that non-locals command (their authority). When cooperating, however, the performative maintenance of the insider-outsider boundary cannot be seen to falter in the eyes of the local peasants. Lower-level archeologists therefore must be careful about their audience: when only non-local archeologists are present, the lower-level archeologists politely use standard Mandarin, discuss subjects of interest to all archeologists, and ask the non-locals many questions about their lives. When peasants or construction companies are present, however, the lower-level archeologist presents himself as being 'forced' against his will to cooperate and uses slang, jokes, and winks and nods to the audience to show them that he is still one of them. Non-local archeologists insist that they do not expect locals to act differently and take no offence.

What does annoy visiting archeologists, however, is the penchant for lower-level archeologists to insist that they are better archeologists than the visitors. Due to the needs of construction, lower-level archeologists maintain complete flexibility in their topics and excavation methods. They have therefore excavated a wide variety of sites and have had access to a broad range of data. Lower-level archeologists will constantly discuss their contempt for higher-level archeologists who do not have a similar breadth of experience. The constant discussion of the importance of experience, in combination with actual control over local data sets, is a not-so-subtle attempt to insult non-local archeologists and remind them that they are dependent on the goodwill of the local archeologists. Since the charge that someone is 'not a very good archeologist' is an extraordinarily efficacious insult among archeologists the world over, this strategy tends to work as intended: non-local archeologists are doubly intent on getting access to data and will barter what they can to get it.

Provincial-level Culture *Xitong* archeologists form an interesting subgroup among the Culture *Xitong* archeologists. In contrast to their lower-level brethren, they are focused on increasing fame and reputation to the extent of being invited to join higher-level *danwei* in Beijing. They have all graduated from university and maintain significant ties to their teachers and cohort mates, and they pursue, maintain, and intensify fictive cohort-type relations with impressive skill and energy. They live in large cities far away from the countryside and are rarely connected by kinship ties to their peasant workers; yet, at the same time, since they grew up in the province and have been restricted to excavation within it, they do know a great deal about the local scene and are not fully outsiders. As a result, they can maintain a certain independence from peasants and, given their high bureaucratic position, have more reason to expect that a claim to seniority will be accepted by the peasants. Focused as they are on climbing the social and bureaucratic hierarchies, provincial-level archeologists do not attempt to blend in to any great extent, although they will use their understanding of local slang or accent to make jokes and otherwise show at least a tenuous connection to the peasants.

The most complex interactions are, of course, between the provincial-level and the lower-level archeologists. Provincial-level archeologists would do well to create long-term and mutually beneficial relations with lower-level archeologists, given that the latter have access to the sites and much of the data needed by the former to offer to their superiors or teachers in Beijing. Provincial-level archeologists thus have a choice: to claim authority alongside seniority, as seems to be logical given their hierarchic position, or to claim juniority. The strategy chosen appears to depend solely on the character of the archeologist and how wedded he is to the idea that his hierarchical position ought to be accompanied by a certain kind of authority and command. If he claims juniority and shows respect to the lower-level archeologists, then he achieves access to data and sites. If he remains authoritarian, however, then he impresses the officials and other archeologists of higher levels. The best strategy, as always, is to be flexible and to change the claim made in response to context and audience.

The Education *Xitong:* Respect
Education *Xitong* archeologists are comprised of the teachers at the eleven universities that have Departments of Archaeology. The role of the Education *Xitong* archeologists is to educate: they cannot organize excavations that do not include students. Their excavations are thus of two types: student practicums and the teaching of special (remedial or retraining) classes for Culture *Xitong* archeologists. From the point of view of archeology, this requirement is no impediment to research. There are always students to teach and, therefore, always a group of willing workers and researchers to exploit.

Education *Xitong* archeologists often appear to use the strategies of blending common among lower-level Culture *Xitong* archeologists to minimize the differences between them and the peasants. They thus make no attempt to wash, eat, dress, or live differently from the locals (with the exception of extra protection for intellectual women). If anything, they eat worse and wash less than both the locals and the Culture *Xitong* archeologists since it is often too inconvenient for them to convince local peasants to get the water and food needed to accommodate the number of people participating in the excavation.

DongDa Teacher Wu, for example, looked significantly worse to my eyes than any local. I knew his work from articles that we had exchanged through the mail and without much thought had expected him to look and act like any other urbanite. I was surprised to be confronted by a thin, scruffy, unwashed man with bad teeth, a worse haircut, and a thick local accent *(fangyan)*. What a shock, then, to visit Wu in his city residence a few months later and be confronted by a well-dressed, urbane, well-appointed young man with fine teeth and good hair, speaking Mandarin as clear as a Beijing bell. Since I was interested enough to mention this transformation, Teacher Wu explained that his discoloured teeth had been the result of some sort of tea that he drinks during the field season. His hair is done by his wife (who takes no small delight in making him look bad), the dirt comes with time, and the accent requires only a small amount of study.

It is unlikely that a local peasant would ever mistake the scruffy, unwashed version of Teacher Wu for anything other than what he is: an urban outsider. Although his strategies appear to be similar to the blending techniques used by lower-level Culture *Xitong* archeologists, they have different implications when used by outsiders rather than insiders. Outsiders use such strategies to show respect and compliment the locals by showing interest rather than to blend in or claim local allegiance. As we have seen, such tactics are also methods of claiming the junior role in archeologist-peasant relations. Education archeologists do overwhelmingly choose to claim the junior position. As outsiders with no local ties or experience, leading a group of uneasy and nervous students who must be protected at all costs, Education archeologists seek to benefit from the junior-senior contract. As Teacher Wu once put it, he would rather banquet 'until his liver failed' than dress himself up fancy, throw his weight around, and otherwise act the 'foolish official.'

Education archeologists can sometimes mix modes of authority to impress and manipulate the peasants. For example, teachers Chen and Huang work as a team to produce a consciously crafted 'good cop/bad cop' performance.[10] Chen affects a relaxed, kind, somewhat bumbling manner and emulates the peasant way of life very well; Huang is relatively impeccably dressed, presents himself as rule oriented, and can be extremely harsh and threatening. Chen, Huang, and the students cause it to be known that Chen can 'barely control' Huang. Thus, when Chen can make no headway with the peasants, he mildly hints that perhaps he should turn to Huang for aid.

Having heard the stories, the peasants certainly prefer to deal with the friendly Chen rather than the unpredictable Huang. Indeed, they even offer Chen sympathy for being 'forced' to work with such a difficult man. Chen usually has much more interaction with the peasants than Huang since the mystery surrounding Huang only increases the less he is seen outside the archeologists' compound; Huang, in return, deals with the students to a much greater extent than Chen. Neither Chen nor Huang is particularly bumbling or harsh while at their home institution. Chen metamorphoses into a cosmopolitan young rising star, well dressed and respectful of his superiors, while Huang becomes a relaxed older man with the confidence and air of authority that arise from many years of having directed the archeology department.

In their relations with lower-level Culture *Xitong* archeologists, Education *Xitong* archeologists face a set of difficulties unique to their *xitong* structure. Universities do not have their own regions or jurisdictions, and therefore any excavation undertaken must be in collaboration with lower-level Culture archeologists. Since such archeologists have rarely attended university, Education archeologists have no direct ties to them. They must rely instead on the teacher-student relations that they do have to the provincial-level archeologists to get access to whatever ties those archeologists have managed to create with the lower-level Culture archeologists. Education *Xitong* archeologists thus have good reason to fear that they will be denied access to sites, data, or workers. Fortunately, Education archeologists do have something that the lower-level Culture archeologists want – that is, the opportunity to go to school or attend special classes that can bestow new forms of status and authority – and they do use these opportunities in barter with the lower-level Culture archeologists.

Education archeologists always insist that they are better archeologists than everyone else. Culture archeologists might have the data, and Academy archeologists all the money, but Education archeologists insist that, as teachers, they know more about more aspects of the Chinese past than anyone else. Culture archeologists are too restricted in scope, and Academy archeologists are too restricted in topic; Education archeologists insist that they, in contrast, are broadly educated and understand the 'big picture' of archeology. It follows, as far as they are concerned, that only they have the right to make grand theoretical statements. Although members of the other *xitong* vehemently disagree with this perspective, from an observer's perspective it appears irrefutable that, of the truly powerful oligarchs in Beijing, most tend to have been teachers in the Education *Xitong*. Nevertheless, their status is more likely to have been a result of the benefits (especially access to data) of their extensive student-teacher and cohort networks than of some essential link between teaching and broadly construed theoretical approaches.

BeiDa archeologists form an important subgroup among the Education archeologists. BeiDa is allowed to excavate anywhere in the country, while the other universities are restricted to their respective regions. BeiDa archeologists therefore have a different mode of interaction with peasants and other archeologists. They have many students, but unfortunately their students tend to be given jobs in extremely high-level *danwei*. While this gives BeiDa teachers unprecedented access to certain resources, they remain separated from the lower-level Culture archeologists and peasants and suffer the consequences of that separation.

BeiDa archeologists are also unusual because they are at the top of both the Education and the Culture hierarchies. Through participation in the policy-making committees that control both *xitong*, BeiDa archeologists control most of the resources that everyone else dearly wants. Given their status, their first priority is to maintain the hierarchical structure of the archeological world, and they tend to claim both hierarchic seniority and authority, often harshly, with peasants and lower-level Culture *Xitong* archeologists. BeiDa archeologists are convinced that, the more one cultivates the peasant workers, the more one cultivates trouble *(duo zhaogu mingong, duo zhaogu mafan)*, and so they lean toward being more demanding and authoritarian. BeiDa can get away with this kind of behaviour because it has so much to offer people in the way of fame, opportunity, and money. JiDa archeologists, at least the older, more famous ones, are the only archeologists who come close to BeiDa's stature and access to resources. Among the rest of the Education archeologists, then, JiDa archeologists are correspondingly the only ones who will combine the senior and authoritarian modes with any regularity.

The authoritarian mode was much in evidence when I visited the BeiDa practicum site. BeiDa archeologists certainly acted as if their workers were nothing more than hired labourers. There were no banquets and no attempts to build reciprocal relations. Indeed, there was little interaction of any kind except to give orders and present wages. If a peasant did not follow the rules, then he was sent away. As a result, I might add, the site had to be monitored at all times by local police, and there were several incidents of attempted looting. At other excavations that I visited, in contrast, there was no need for police and no looting.

In addition to treating peasants as labourers, BeiDa treated lower-level Culture archeologists as people of lesser social status. The students on this practicum were older, local, lower-level Culture archeologists attending the class to upgrade their skills. BeiDa worked hard indeed to make the practicum a liminal space where these local Culture archeologists were forced into a clearly subordinate position. These often forty-five- to fifty-year-old men, who had considerable authority in their own *danwei*, had to follow strict rules, including not being allowed to go home and visit their families, watch

TV, or leave the site to banquet with others. BeiDa archeologists, even the younger ones, acted in a formal manner, calling each other by their titles, and the teachers maintained both a physical and a social distance from their students through different modes of dress, accent, and even eating style. Everyone was friendly, yet it was also clear who was in charge. In this case at least, BeiDa appeared to rely on the overt exercise of authority in the sense of its access to Beijing-based, top-level officials and therefore control over local officials rather than on a simple show of respect or tactical claims to similarity or juniority. Clearly, the more distant (and higher) one is bureaucratically, and the more access to resources everyone wants, the more authoritarian one is allowed to be.

The Academy *Xitong:* Authoritarian Insularity

Academy *Xitong* archeologists are connected to the Chinese Academy of Social Sciences (CASS), a centralized institution that has the right to excavate anywhere in China. Theoretically, it is also the only institution that has the right to cooperate with foreign archeologists, although Education archeologists have found ways around that restriction in the past. CASS has no undergraduate students, only MA or PhD students who, it is assumed, will end up working for CASS itself. They are thus divorced from both the local and, unlike BeiDa, even the provincial-level Culture *danwei*. CASS also does not have to put effort into collaboration with other archeology *danwei*. It has the budget to move into a city or region and set up its own branch institute, hire and train its own workers and technicians, and remain completely separate from all the other archeologists in that region. If it so desires, CASS even has the nominal power to oust any archeology *danwei* from any site. Given its bureaucratic and social positioning, CASS is said to be well known for its arrogance, its preemptory treatment of peasants, workers, local archeologists, and technicians, and its adoption of a more authoritarian manner than even that exhibited by BeiDa.

CASS's tendency to set up separate branch institutes has unfortunate effects. Once the separate institution is established, local archeologists are exasperated by the perceived sense of distrust and become intent on maintaining distance and impeding CASS in every way they can. The effect on archeological research is immediate. We can take, for example, the study of the Xia dynasty. The region in which the archeological culture thought to be the Xia Dynasty is found is divided among six different *danwei*. Each one struggles with the others over data access. When confronted by CASS, however, all six immediately join together to criticize and derail CASS projects.

A second difficulty is that, while the peasants are usually impressed by the authoritarian mode, they unfortunately then assume that CASS is made of money. As one CASS archeologist put it, 'everyone from the farmer to district, county, and provincial officials,' and anyone else with whom a CASS archeologist might come into contact (including his own family), all believe that a CASS man has money. In fact, CASS does have more money than the archeologists of other *xitong*, but it also has more expenses due to its predilection to 'go it alone' rather than cooperate with local archeologists. People also assume that CASS, with its ties to Beijing, should have enormous authority in the form of influence and access to a variety of opportunities. CASS does not educate; its stated goal is to undertake research, and it can only accept students who are clearly prepared for research. Thus, while CASS does have power and influence over policy, it does not have access to the kinds of opportunities held by Education archeologists with their widely flung and varied social networks derived from their students. The constant barrage of requests and the image of them as people with deep pockets encourages CASS archeologists to be self-protective and form insular groups that keep to themselves.

CASS archeologists use topic or research questions to distinguish themselves from each other. They are narrowly focused on the topic assigned to them by the director or, if they are young, by their MA or PhD advisor at CASS. Once they are part of a team assigned to work on a certain time period, region, or topic, CASS archeologists do not change. Zhang and Chen, two younger CASS archeologists who have recently finished their PhDs, were eager to reassure me that the research structure at CASS is not as restrictive as it appears. Especially when they are not out in the field, they can finish what CASS requires of them each month fairly quickly and take the rest of the time for their families. For the most part, Zhang and Chen seemed to think that the worst part about being at CASS is how everyone who is not at CASS treats them.

CASS is highly suspicious and protective of its authority for good reason. CASS and BeiDa have been locked in a struggle over the control of the top committees that direct budgetary and policy issues (especially foreign collaborations) regarding archeology. When the CASS archeologist Xia Nai was alive, CASS's authority was paramount. Xia was without doubt the most powerful and authoritarian archeologist in the central government. He was a member of several foreign academies (e.g., the American Academy of Science), personal advisor to Zhou Enlai and Mao Zedong, and good friends with Guo Moruo (himself a high-ranking historian in the party). After Xia's death in 1986, the BeiDa teacher Su Bingqi became the man in command in archeological circles. When Su passed away in 1997, BeiDa maintained control through BeiDa teacher Su Bai. The change of leadership is not merely a nominal event: when Su Bingqi came to power, there was a corresponding change of leadership in the ranks of the highest officials, a change in the high-ranking committee members, and a complete restructuring of the professorial and research rankings. Many of the people removed or reduced in authority were, of course, CASS archeologists. Since CASS had relied heavily on having its men in high positions and had for many years 'thrown its weight around,' thereby managing to alienate nearly everyone outside its immediate sphere of influence, the number of people sympathetic to CASS's present plight is remarkably small.

Worse, CASS's own students, who took their undergraduate degree at BeiDa or JiDa and do their graduate work at CASS, have conflicting loyalties. When CASS's authority was paramount, it clearly behooved the graduate student to switch allegiance from his undergraduate teachers to his CASS advisor. Since BeiDa's influence has been steadily increasing through its ever-growing group of alumni who permeate all sorts of different circles, including non-archeological ones, CASS students no longer aim to please only their CASS advisors. As long as BeiDa teachers are on the committees and have access to the top authorities while CASS and its affiliates remain on the sidelines, it is far more beneficial to maintain ties with BeiDa (and JiDa) teachers. No tears should be shed for CASS, however, since it remains the *danwei* with the largest and most reliable of budgets, free from reliance on student en-rolment and from the efforts involved in creating cohort-like groups across *xitong* or up and down the *xitong* ladder, and therefore with the most time to concentrate on archeology.

Checks and Balances: Equilibrium

Studies of *guanxi* (however defined) rarely attempt to articulate how differ-ent class groups experience social networking differently. If the term is avoided in preference for issues of trustworthiness, compatibility, hierar-chy, and authority, then the art of social relationships appears to be funda-mentally based on judgments about people's behaviour and their access to resources of interest. Judgment, in turn, is affected not only by credentials and roles that can be applied (or claimed) by the actor but also by the pri-orities of the people who judge. Those audience priorities, of course, can change and be changed depending on the artful combinations of hierarchi-cal position, authority, and status. At every turn, any given attempt to posi-tion or be positioned can be checked and balanced by some other strategy of claiming or other form of audience intervention. Power, however defined, is thus kept flowing back and forth across significant social and bureau-cratic boundaries despite the rigidity that words such as rules, discourses, roles, and credentials appear to imply.

The difficulties of claiming, however, force us to realize that social ex-change is not all that is in effect in the system. There are material checks and balances as well, and they create situations not of an individual's mak-ing but in which, as Marx might say, the individual must nevertheless act. Peasants and archeologists, and archeologists among the three *xitong,* are all startlingly well balanced when it comes to resources: each is limited be-cause no one group has access to all available types of resources, yet each is enabled because each has something to be given as gifts in the creation of mutually beneficial relations. The checks and balances built into the system, material and immaterial, formal and informal, effectively ensure that no one person, no matter his or her hierarchical position or claim to authority, can succeed in gaining complete control over any situation. Exchange is indispensable, of course, in social life; it is merely that under conditions of interdependence it becomes ever more crucial in individual plans and projects.

7
Minority Rights

Whoever, in middle age, attempts to realize the wishes and hopes of his early youth, invariably deceives himself. Each ten years of a man's life has its own fortunes, its own hopes, its own desires.
　　– Goethe, *The Sorrows of Young Werther*

The woman who is known only through a man is known wrong.
　　– Henry Adams, "Silence," *The Education of Henry Adams*

Checks and Balances: Disequilibrium

Systems benefit some more than others. Systems do not differ by being more or less unequal; they 'merely' differ in who benefits, the types of privileges received and redistributed, the habits and strategies of redistribution, and the goals for which redistribution is (or is not) undertaken. In the particular system that applies to archeologists, those who benefit most are Han Chinese, older, and male. At the same time, systems disadvantage some more than others, such that even if they begin by being well positioned they are systematically deprived of what is required for success. In this system, women, by virtue of the norms of prescriptive behaviour ascribed to their sex, are not expected to engage in the many strategies of performance available to men.

We have the background to understand how the strategic combinations and conversions of roles, discourses, and credentials are used in performances of compatibility and trustworthiness as well as in the fruitful attempts to separate or realign authority and hierarchy. Now we are prepared to see how the whole system works over time. That which drives the system is reputation. Success in any one performative event leads to the enhancement of reputation in successive performances. Just as one's reputation of being good at playing roles grows to include more roles under diverse circumstances, so too grows the likelihood that claims – to roles, discourses, credentials, hierarchical position, and authority – will be successful in the eyes of the audience-that-matters. That likelihood of being accepted by the audience increases, in turn, as the actor gains access to those material or immaterial resources that can be used to motivate the audience to participate in the actor's own projects. Under the law of reciprocity, if one can entice the audience by showing its members how they can benefit from acting in certain ways, then one can entice the audience to invest in the particular status claim being made. Under circumstances of interdependency, the success of other people in one's group can lead by association to success for the self. Once the audience is invested, then, it can itself be depended on to cooperate in the actor's project of protecting, grooming, and managing his reputation.

Experiences of 'oligarchs' – older, famed, male archeologists – and women are compared in order to elucidate the rigidities of the system of obedient autonomy. Those rigidities are not due to rules or structures, for those that we have seen merely create more opportunities for fruitful and creative combination. Women will be shown to fail because the audience-that-matters only accepts their deployment of a tiny number of roles-in-relation. When there are fewer rules, fewer models of prescriptive behaviour, and fewer credentials said to apply, there is less room to manoeuvre, and there are fewer opportunities to engage in strategies of motivation, combination, conversion, and reinterpretation. Oligarchs, in contrast, come to deploy the immaterial and material resources that can be used to increase the number of rules and, therefore, the opportunities for them to engage in the strategies of exchange so fundamental to obedient autonomy. Along the way to understanding how the system benefits old men and fails women, we will learn a great deal about behind-the-scenes activities that control the discipline of archeology. To begin, we must understand the doctrine of empiricism and its effects on the value system that archeologists use to judge each other's work (and that of foreigners).

Empiricism and Experience in the Context of Age

As intellectuals, archeologists take great pride in claiming the status entailed by the study of history. The importance of history as a guide for the present was not only emphasized in imperial China but also reemphasized by the introduction of Marxist historical materialism as interpreted by Mao. Historians see themselves as especially beholden to their duties to the nation and the people compared with other intellectuals. The state and often the peasants beg to differ: they prefer the archeologists to historians because they deal with visible, concrete, material (and often valuable) remains of the past and, moreover, do so using the language of objective, value-free science. Concrete material objects take on great power because they seem to be so simply and unarguably real in contrast, say, to historical texts and particularly given the abuse of texts and history over the past fifty years. Traditional respect for the written word has been undermined, and the language of empiricism has come to be seen as a corrective to the abuses of ideology and doctrine. Marxism, of course, exacerbates the valuation of empiricism since it is a theory that opposes the empirically verifiable infrastructure to the false consciousness of the superstructure. The rhetoric of objectivity *(keguan)*, of 'seeking truth from facts' *(shishi qiu shi)* of science *(kexue)*, and of a strong sense of inevitable progress is widespread and constantly reinforced.[1]

The strong form of empiricism has interesting implications for the relationship between theory and data in archeology. Chinese empiricism assumes that data can be gathered and described without being affected by methodological bias. Since methods do not affect the ontological nature of the data collected, archeologists think it perfectly acceptable to take methods from other countries and cultures without trying to understand the cultural or theoretical contexts in which those methods were born. Indeed, trying to understand other cultures' theories is something expressly to be avoided. Theories are understood to be (false) worldviews; thus, learning the theories expressed by people of other nations and races runs the risk of assimilating to their worldviews.[2] Since being an intellectual means maintaining that which is China – its worldview, perspectives, culture, and traditions of research – it is not surprising that nationalism encourages the refusal of Euro-American archeological theory.

Chinese archeologists' doctrine of empiricism also implies distaste for the existence of too many different theories and perspectives in the discipline. Euro-American archeologists may be surprised to learn that, in the Chinese context, a plethora of theoretical perspectives indicates not disciplinary strength but serious weakness. According to empiricism, there can be only one truth; if there are many theories, then people simply have not yet found the truth. As one archeologist, Fan, put it, 'The foreigners, all they talk about is theory. That shows that they know nothing about archeology. As an archeologist, I am interested in how much I can accomplish, not how many theories I can hold at the same time.' In addition to their aversion to diversity in perspective, it is common for archeologists to insist that consistency is the mark of a true scholar. A scholar who changes his ideas over time has failed because change indicates that he has not thought everything through in the first place. The 'doctrine of truth' common to empiricism posits that it is the fault of the scholar if truth is not realized.

The doctrine of empiricism also indicates that if theory is to be discussed at all, it must be presented differently when published. Euro-American theoretical articles are not expected to include a list of practical methodological suggestions entailed by the theory. Indeed, Anglo-North Americans, at least, exhibit a disdain for too many dull, practical suggestions or a plethora of

data and charts. They prefer the elegantly written polemical statement outlining how archeology ought to be written differently, or extolling the importance of some arcane idea such as 'Middle Range Theory,' or applying
Foucauldian insights to archeological thought.[3] Unfortunately, at least for
the purposes of scholarly communication, Chinese archeologists deride such
entirely theoretical articles as armchair archeology *(shafa kaogu xue)*, a term
taken from Anglo-North Americans themselves. The Chinese perspective
insists that truth is in the details. Any article, to be worthwhile, ought to
have immediate, practical implications in excavation and analysis. The foreigners thus appear sloppy. It is considered naïve to assume that a reader
will understand or be able to use a theoretical discussion that does not explain itself through practical methodological examples.

The 'dreaming up' of a multitude of theories without examples of what
they mean in practice indicates for Sun, an Education *Xitong* archeologist,
that 'foreigners have too much free time and too little data.' Data are the
most important resource that an archeologist has but unfortunately are not
fungible or reproducible; a person needs access to particular artifacts and
sites. As we saw in Chapter 4, control over data by teacher or student, junior
or senior, is the main path to archeological success. Relative to all the foreigners who wish to study China, Chinese archeologists clearly have the
ultimate control over data: as a result, they often automatically assume that
foreigners are at a severe disadvantage and that what they have to say is
unimportant unless it is based on a real data set.[4]

To Sun's mind, if the foreigners had access to data, they would stop engaging in theoretical discussions and address the more 'interesting' questions that tackle the data directly. They would ask questions about the origins
of artifact forms, the history of their use, and the documentation of their
disappearance from the archeological record. These questions would address the important issues related to the origins of Chinese civilization and
whether or not its bronze, ceramic, and jade industries are wholly indigenous. Questions commonly asked by foreigners, such as about how people
lived in the past, processes of cultural change, or how symbols have changed
meanings over time, are classified as 'narrow' comparative research and categorized as 'art history' or 'anthropology,' neither of which is the proper
purview of archeology. Archeology is related to the progress of Chinese civilization, or it is nothing.[5]

Empiricism assumes that knowledge can be accumulated over time. That
assumption explains the emphasis on experience in archeology. Archeologists insist that the only way to handle the innumerable puzzles that con-
front them during excavations is through experience. Older archeologists
who have excavated many sites and seen many things are therefore by definition expected to provide advice and guidance to younger men. Archeologists' respect for the knowledge and experience accumulated over time

expresses itself in calling all older archeologists by the title of 'teacher.' In the use of this tradition, archeologists are not unusual. The word for teacher, *laoshi* (literally 'old scholar'), has several possible meanings: it can refer to a person who has the actual job of teacher, but it can also be used as a term of respect by younger people for older people. These older people may never have been the younger people's actual teachers, but, simply because of their age and the experiences that they have accumulated, they are seen as worthy of the title. A younger person may also call an older person 'teacher' in the hope that the older person will respond by providing guidance – that is, by treating him as a 'student.' The term can also, by the way, be *refused*: if a person calls someone teacher and that person refuses the term (an actual refusal as opposed to a polite expression of humility), then the younger person's hope of becoming engaged in a teacher-student relationship is destroyed, and he has been insulted to boot.

The emphasis on experience among archeologists is combined with veneration of the wisdom and experience of aged men that has a long tradition in China. There are highly respected old men at every step along any *xitong* ladder, not just archeological *xitong*. Even at the lowest rungs, in a small village, there are old men to whom people look for guidance, and each rung – county, town, city, and so on – has its set of venerable old men all the way up to the highest levels in Beijing. Whether they be convenient figureheads or people with practical authority depends on many things, but in any case they are respected. Age is so important that even women can eventually become 'lucky older women' and command a great deal of authority, relative to younger women within their ritual and household spheres.[6] As the Chinese saying puts it, *duo nian xifu, ao cheng po*. 'A daughter-in-law *(xifu)* just married into a family will eventually, over many hard years, herself evolve into being the mother-in-law *(po)*.' Simply through the passage of time, anyone (the proverb applies to male and female) who survives long enough will eventually command the authority of age. Believing it makes it so: both young and old agree that the old are essentially wiser than anyone else.

Archeologists use the emphasis on experience and age to 'use' older archeologists. Young archeologists often trot out their elderly 'teachers' to act as advisors *(guwen)* during excavation. In so doing, the young archeologists indicate to their director and colleagues that they are willing to learn from their elders and accept *danwei* hierarchy. More importantly, the old teacher can become a shield: if something goes wrong or there is a mistake identified in the excavation, then the younger archeologist can avoid blame. After all, he asked the teacher for advice. We have seen something similar when officials ask for advice from intellectuals. There is an important difference, however, when the teacher is old and the context is restricted to the discipline of archeology: when something goes wrong, the teacher is not blamed. Blaming the teacher is not only a grave insult but also interrupts the age-experience correlation. Such blaming suggests that perhaps age and archeological ability are not necessarily correlated. Since archeological identity is founded on the belief that experience is accumulated over time, blame is therefore deflected out of the *danwei* completely and comes to rest on the heads of the peasants or perhaps the local officials, who can always be safely accused of interference or willful obstruction.

Age and experience, even in relation to the doctrine of empiricism, are necessary but not sufficient conditions for authority in archeological circles. As always, archeologists are drawn to people who can actually 'produce the goods,' so to speak. Unless an older archeologist has access to the compatible resources that can influence the actions and perceptions of others, he is merely an 'ordinary' older archeologist. Such ordinary older archeologists are, in fact, more likely to be used by younger colleagues for their advice or as a shield, while it is rare that they can turn the tables and use the younger archeologists for their own purposes.

There is a group of archeologists, however, for whom age, experience, and access to material resources combine to create an authority so powerful that it can, if managed correctly, affect the opinions of even *danwei* outsiders such as peasants and officials. It certainly can, to an extent, rouse interest among archeologists, unlike any other form of authority. The 'oligarch' commands this authority because he enjoys the mutually strengthening benefits of hierarchy, authority, trustworthiness, and compatibility.

Oligarchic Positioning

Who are the oligarchs? There are several Chinese terms for the word *oligarch*, ranging from critical (*guatou* – with its implications of elite, sovereign) to a simple description of age (*lao yi dai* – the older generation) to admiring (*yuanlao* – senior statesman, founding member). Nevertheless, it is impossible to understand who they are without understanding the circumstances of their power. Oligarchic 'power' is related directly to the redistributive authority commanded by any one of them. Authority always means both access to resources and the capacity to decide where to distribute those resources. The word compatibility, it must be remembered, refers to the fact that the resources commanded by oligarchs must in themselves be things desired by the archeologists.

Oligarchic authority is also necessarily aligned with high position in the hierarchy. The oligarchs are the men affiliated with BeiDa, the National Palace Museum, the Central Bureau of Cultural Relics, and CASS. These *danwei* are the most important and prestigious institutions at the tops of their respective *xitong*. Men affiliated with the archeological institutes of more prestigious provinces ('prestige' here is related to the perceived quality of their archeological yields) are either already in the group or about to arrive.

The men already in Beijing enjoy the benefits of membership in the National Council on Archaeology and Cultural Relics *(Guojia Kaogu Wenwu Weiyuanhui)*. This council makes all budgetary, professional, and policy decisions for the entire country. All changes in important leadership positions and promotions within and outside Beijing, all collaborative expeditions and publishing decisions, and all foreign collaborations are decided by this council. Its directives are followed by archeologists in all three *xitong,* and, since the Central Bureau of Cultural Relics is required to follow its orders, even the officials and party secretaries of each *xitong* must acquiesce to its directives. Each province has a version of this council, members of which are appointed by the Beijing-based oligarchs, that interprets its directions on behalf of all the archeologists, party secretaries, and officials within the province.

There are, then, gradations within the category of oligarch. Those in Beijing on the National Council are at the top. Those who are provincial-level oligarchs are slightly lesser in stature since their authority is limited to the borders of their province or territory. As an indication of the importance of Beijing for the top-notch oligarch, archeologists who have gained fame in the provinces are always eventually promoted to positions in Beijing.

In addition to being well positioned hierarchically, oligarchs are well positioned *historically*. Archeology has a short history in China. Those who are oligarchs in the present (though this is changing of late due to several recent deaths) are old enough to have been in attendance at the first excavations and, of course, were the directors of all subsequent important excavations. The Chinese term *zhengui jun* (the 'authentic' professionals) calls up the important qualities of having been earliest, of knowing the first scholars, and of having been thoroughly well educated at the best institutions (in contrast to the *yezhan jun* – archeologists who only learned as apprentices or on their own). Additionally, the idea of *kai chuang,* to 'break ground' and start entirely new schools of archeology (a relatively easy feat at the beginning of things), is often applied to the oligarchs. These are the venerable ancestors of archeology itself.

For the archeologists among my readers, these are the men who were there at Anyang; present at Banpo; helped Xia Nai open the Qing tombs; mapped the famed Hougang Stratigraphy; drew the first drawings and helped to build the research complex at Dunhuang; developed the Yangshao chronology; excavated Erlitou; pleaded with Zhou Enlai to allow archeology to begin again in 1972; discovered and reconstructed the Qin Terra Cotta Warriors; and engaged in the first serious archeology ever attempted in Tibet, Xinjiang, Mongolia, Manchuria, Yunnan, and Hainan. For the non-archeologists, suffice it to say that this list is one of great achievement and rich experience. In contrast, oligarchs are somehow not particularly 'present' at the boring sites: even if they were physically in attendance, one can be sure that they do not talk about it much now. Interviewing the oligarchs represents a romp through Chinese political, social, and archeological history: they are truly remarkable people with a wealth of experience that cannot be denied.[7]

Oligarchic positioning is furthermore intimately connected to the history of class struggle in China. Since most oligarchs were educated during the 1930s and 1940s, when only the children of the elite went to school, they suffered terribly beginning with the Anti-Rightist Movement through to the end of the Cultural Revolution. Interestingly, that past suffering is now part of their claim to authority. Their stories of the Cultural Revolution are told and retold given the slightest opportunity, for each insult or blow suffered is (often still visible) proof of their membership in an elite class. Since most of the people who gave them those insults and blows are now their junior colleagues, it can be imagined that oligarchic tales of suffering galvanize their juniors into feats of submission and obedience as great as the guilt that they feel for having persecuted their teachers in the past.

The most important source of oligarchs' authority arises from their relationships with their students. The oligarchs were present either as teachers or as teaching assistants at the first archeology classes held during the 1950s, and most of them continued to teach until 1966. The oligarchs were brought back from the countryside to teach the Worker-Peasant-Soldier (GNB) Schools of the early 1970s. They were also asked to organize the classes that conferred the right to excavate on the *danwei* in the 1980s. As a result of all this teaching, oligarchs have accumulated large numbers of students, who are a resource in themselves to be redistributed as the oligarchs see fit. Since they are so bureaucratically well positioned and already have so many students, their eminently obvious authority attracts more students. Less famous teachers who are not oligarchs themselves will, out of a concern to place their students in better positions, advise a particularly excellent student to switch allegiance and publicly proclaim himself to be the student of a Beijing-based oligarch. The strategy is intended to increase the student's compatibility in the eyes of the *danwei* deciding whether he should be hired or not. The student's 'real' teacher will advise the student to do this not simply because it is good for him but also because it is good for the teacher. In a truly adroit twist of social connections, the less famous teacher will now be able to claim a connection to the famous Beijing oligarch through his connection to his (former) student.

The teacher-student relationship is important to all teachers because they are able to benefit from their efforts on behalf of their students. The relationship between oligarch and student is significantly more tightly controlled than mere teacher-student relations simply because of the worth of the resources commanded by the oligarch. The hope of receiving some portion of these resources commands almost total allegiance from the students.

Teacher Cao exemplifies the kinds of resources that a student can attain when his teacher is also an oligarch. One day I asked Cao what he would do if his PhD advisor, a well-known oligarch indeed, and the two other important oligarchs in Bronze Age archeology were all in the same room together. Just to make it more difficult, I added the stipulation that all three oligarchs were openly arguing over the origins of the Xia Dynasty (a highly contentious topic). Cao replied that it would be highly unlikely that the three great scholars would ask him for an opinion. 'But,' he added with a grin, knowing full well what I was asking, 'if someone as ignorant as you were in the room and asked my opinion, I would reply, "I have no opinion. My teacher has an opinion, ask him." That would be a good way to manage.' I stared at him in disbelief. Cao looked back at me in equal disbelief. He was moved by my expression of surprise to explain that everything I see as his – position, research, comforts of home – is, in fact, the result of his teacher's efforts on his behalf. His PhD research could not have been done had his teacher, despite being over seventy years of age, not accompanied Cao on his excavations. Had his teacher not been present to guide the banquets and help in cohort-building strategies, it would have been impossible for all the *danwei* concerned to have collaborated on the project. Cao's visit to the United States could not have occurred without his teacher's support, and Cao would not have had the experiences, opportunities, or even the computer that he acquired as a direct result of that trip. 'Under no circumstances,' said Cao with force, 'would I throw all that back in my teacher's face by acting incorrectly. The shame – I could not face people.' The mix of morality, instrumental reasoning, and emotional affect involved in teacher-student relations is clearly more intense the more compatible (desirable) are the resources commanded by the oligarch.

While non-archeologists who are not fortunate enough to be teachers can still attain redistributive authority through their positions in the administration, it is simply easier for those who are teachers to expand their influence and access to resources through their students. An oligarch would not consider it strange if some archeologist whom he has never met tried to use his name or claimed to be his student. Why be upset? Not only is his fame increased when people repeat his name, but also, if he finds out that someone has used his name, he will feel quite justified in approaching that person to ask for favours in return. A startling thought perhaps: if an archeologist refers to the name of some luminary in Beijing while engaging in strategies among his own colleagues in his own small and insignificant *danwei*, never imagining that he might actually meet the luminary mentioned, the oligarch may well hear of it and call up to ask to see the data in the storage rooms. Such things have indeed occurred: if someone claims to be an oligarch's student, then he runs the risk of being forced to become that student.

To non-Chinese eyes, using an oligarch's name to enhance one's own reputation appears to be manipulative. But oligarchs are neither unaware nor discomfited by the idea that their students are 'using' them. When they are brought artifacts, asked to perform advisory duties on a site, or invited to write the preface to someone's book, they are pleased with the meaning conveyed by these invitations. The oligarchs are *proud* of being used. The loyalty and devotion of students, as well as their machinations and strategic uses of the oligarch's position, are all taken (by oligarch and his audience-that-matters) as indications that the oligarch has 'arrived.' In fact, the more people who 'use' the oligarch, the more enhanced is his reputation.[8]

The Supreme Oligarch: Kinship

Many are the evenings I have spent watching in fascination as archeologists argue among themselves about who is more 'closely related' to the different oligarchs in Beijing. One might begin by stating that he is of the fifth generation of Oligarch Huang's students, by which he means that he arrived in the fifth year of Huang's teaching career. The closer to the first year one is, the stronger the student-teacher relationship is believed to be. Another archeologist would respond by smugly pointing out that although he himself is only of the sixth generation of Oligarch Chen, since Chen is of the first generation students of the supreme oligarch, that still makes him better than any fifth generation student of oligarch Huang. This is because oligarch Huang is only a third generation student of the supreme oligarch. The 'supreme oligarch' is, like the Emperor, the benchmark from which all distinctions of status can be measured, depending on one's relative 'closeness' to him.

The supreme oligarch changes only slowly over time. At present, it is Su Bingqi, although some are old enough to be able to claim a relationship to Xia Nai. Su is even called teacher by archeologists who spent much of the Cultural Revolution criticizing his ideas on typology as 'unscientific.' Yet now they proclaim themselves as typologists who follow his ideas to the letter.[9] Since Su never wrote any of his ideas down – even his collected essays *(lunwen ji)* lack a clear statement of method[10] – these scholars get away with their claim and, better yet, are able to compete among themselves over who provides the most accurate rendition of what Su 'really' meant. Su is dead, which makes him truly useful. The best supreme oligarch, in other words, is a dead one, since all sorts of claims can be made about relationships with him without the inconvenience of the supreme oligarch asking for favours in return.

By now, it should be obvious that the underlying model here is kinship. In the lineage system, everyone now alive relates himself back to the supreme ancestral originator. When archeologists forget their many actual teachers in favour of a single powerful one (Su) linked to a single powerful one of the generation before (Xia), they shrink ancestral history to a single series of supreme first sons.[11] When the present oligarchs in Beijing pass away without attaining enough authority, their memories will also fade; attention will turn to those new oligarchs with the most authority.

When I ask why there must be only one supreme oligarch at any given time, people just stare in confusion. It seems to be obvious to them: in a system that emphasizes the junior-senior contract and requires the inequality engendered by hierarchy in order to promote mutually beneficial exchange, there must be a way to figure out the relative position of each person in the group. Each oligarch has a distinct kind of authority based on his *xitong* background, archeological experience, age, publications, and/or number of students. Because the standards by which oligarchs may be judged are so various, there is no way to figure out who is senior to whom – much in the same way as it is difficult to judge whether a peasant or an archeologist is hierarchically senior given their different *xitong* and positions across the urban-rural divide. The only way to clarify hierarchical relations is to use a single standard of judgment for all oligarchs. The existence of a supreme oligarch provides a single principle to judge the relative positions of authority. The logic is simple: the closer one claims to be (in age and cohort generation) to the supreme teacher, and the more people who accept that claim, the more authority one has.

The oligarchs in Beijing all vie for the chance to be the supreme oligarch after death. As the saying goes, *yi ri wei shi, zhong shen wei fu*, 'Once someone becomes your teacher, worship him as a father to the end of your life.' The logic is still that of kinship: if the father can create around him a strong and successful family, who will, above all, worship his memory after death, then he not only succeeds in his duty as a father to his sons but also manages to live on after death. There is a subtle but important distinction made between biological death and social death. The former may be inevitable, but the latter can be avoided if a man's sons, grandsons, and so on remember his name.[12]

Oligarchs thus surround themselves with potential heirs who can be trusted to carry on the oligarch's legacy in the form of archeological methods and theories. Once the oligarch has created a recognizable school of archeological thought, potential students can perform their willingness and capacity to be good heirs by promoting his ideas in articles and at conferences. Like a father with his sons, the oligarch works hard to provide the incentives that will entice the students to follow him. To guess who among the oligarchs has a chance at becoming the next supreme oligarch, one need only make a careful accounting of the number of archeologists who self-identify as the students of each oligarch. He with the most 'students' busily studying his topic and espousing his theories wins.

Oligarchic authority is more harsh than that wielded by others in senior positions. Oligarchs rarely engage in face-to-face interactions with the inferiors whose lives they control. The lack of face-to-face contact is no small thing. Remember that the effect of audience means that, when directors are brought into face-to-face contact with their juniors, they can be entrapped by the juniors and forced into acting like good superiors. When there is no audience present, and when the juniors themselves are not present, there is no incentive to act as a good superior willing to submit one's own interests to the needs of the inferior. Oligarchs can act with impunity, moving inferior *danwei* like chess pieces for their own benefit, and remain blissfully unaware of how the people represented by each 'pawn' must scramble to renegotiate authority and hierarchical position in reaction to their new positions on the board.

The willingness to make harsh decisions about other people's lives thus appears to be a direct result of distance. The Beijing oligarchs force the rest of China to follow to the letter the rules, policies, and principles that they themselves, in their lives in Beijing, do not follow. In their own lives, they take care of their own in the way that a director or teacher takes care of his juniors. As the audience-that-matters for each other's interactions, oligarchs are free with their criticism if they believe that one of their number has not taken care of his juniors in an appropriate manner. They may be more harsh than is usual with their juniors, since a father ought to be harsh with his heirs, yet it is a harshness that still takes into account that the junior must be protected and provided with significant resources according to the rules of the junior-senior contract. It is only when oligarchs make decisions that affect people outside Beijing, whom they do not know, that they act like people somehow above or sundered from society who need not worry about what an audience thinks about the quality of their social relationships or reputations.

There is a BeiDa teacher, Dong, whom everyone recognizes is of the age and position to start the process of expanding his network to become an oligarch. Dong has recently been allowed to take PhD students and can now progress mightily in the effort to make a name for himself both in publishing and in teaching his ideas. These ideas are always more than just his theories of archeology and history; they are also ways of training the students to recognize who belongs in the oligarch's cohort and who does not. His students must be able to identify who is friendly, trustworthy, and compatible and who must be rejected as belonging to a different 'tribe' ruled by a different oligarch. In so teaching his students, Dong creates his own clique with its own traditions and ritual invocations of certain teachers, archeological theories, and methods. Since none of this is written down, his students are more reliant on personal interaction to understand their places and those of others in the hierarchy. Note, of course, that no one will ever try to write it down, since after Dong's death the students will benefit from the opportunities to reinvent history that this imprecision bestows on them. Dong, some people say, is too kind and does not have the authoritarianism or the guts to be a good oligarch. Still others laugh and say that 'Absolute power corrupts absolutely': give Dong a few years, and his sweet nature will change of necessity into the harsh paternal authority of the father in relation to his students, and he will become practised in manipulating distant *danwei* with a feeling of impunity.

Oligarchic Cohorts: Topics and Time Periods

How do oligarchs fight among themselves for authority? As nastily and messily as any other academics anywhere in the world. The difference in China is that one has to wait until one is old enough to join the fray. Oligarchs fight with words, through control over opportunities, by getting their official friends to institute budget restrictions, by arguing over fine points of method, or by trying to put an end to any plan that an enemy might support. SoDa Teacher Wu gave me the phrase *wen ren xiang qing*, 'Scholars always feel contempt for each other,' an apt description of the constant bickering and disunity among most archeologists but especially among the oligarchs who, having more to lose, have more incentive to fight.

Most obviously, however, oligarchs compete with each other by creating cohort-like groups. The way of thinking in terms of factions or cliques is called *menfa sixiang* or *menhu zhi guan*, both terms that recall the image of the warlord's home surrounded by his troops and other hangers on. I will call these groups 'oligarch-cohort groups' in order to emphasize the impact on the group of the oligarch or, perhaps more importantly, the resources that he commands. The strategies used within oligarch-cohort groups are not different in kind from those that we have already examined but quite different in intensity.

The process of becoming an oligarch begins with an archeologist. For the archeologist to advance, the support of the *danwei* is tremendously important. That support can be gained through the archeologist's own relationships with his leaders and his strategies of acting appropriately as befitting a junior (entrapment). Unfortunately, the effects of entrapment are long term. It is faster to force change from one's leaders by gaining the support of more powerful people higher up than they in the *xitong*. Theoretically, it should be impossible for lower-level archeologists, that vast group of people who did not graduate from JiDa or BeiDa, to connect to people higher up in the *xitong*. Here, of course, the tactics involved in creating cohort-like groups come into their own. If an archeologist can join a cohort group formed on the basis of shared interests, particularly interests in archeological topics, then people of all bureaucratic levels are brought together, and fresh opportunities for mutually beneficial relations are created.

Topical interests among archeologists are most often categorized by the time period in which they specialize: Physical/Evolutionary/Paleolithic; Neolithic; Three Dynasties (Bronze Age); *Zhan Guo* (Warring States); Qin and Han (Iron Age); Six Dynasties and the Northern and Southern Dynasties; Sui and Tang Dynasties; and, finally, the Song and Yuan Dynasties. Interestingly, beyond excavation of the obvious sites, such as the imperial tombs, there is no Ming and Qing archeology as a topic on its own since the time period is simply considered too modern.[13] Among the different time divisions, archeology of the Three Dynasties (Bronze Age) is considered the most prestigious. This time period is concerned with the rise of Chinese civilization itself, when the attributes that we imagine to be part of Chinese culture today are supposed to have first coalesced into something identifiable. It is notable that historians and archeologists are in competition over this period. Earlier archeology is uninteresting to historians because it is too distant from the historical period, and later periods have enough writing that the historians believe they do not need the help of archeologists. But historians need archeologists to understand the Bronze Age because of the lack of texts. Archeologists, with their understanding of stratigraphy and excavation in general, thus have the rare chance to outdo historians. In addition, since the first sites excavated by Chinese scholars in the 1920s and 1930s were Bronze Age sites, most of the first-generation archeologists were therefore Bronze Age specialists. Unsurprisingly, not only do they continue to help their Bronze Age students get access to more opportunities and become prominent themselves, but the oligarchs also ensure the continued emphasis on Bronze Age archeology through their control over the council that oversees national archeological budgets and policies.

Basing an oligarch-cohort clique on traditional archeological topics is such a common method that these fields have become too crowded to be certain of success. The response has been to create cohort groups based on the newfangled archeologies that sprang up in the 1980s. These new categories include the archeology of agriculture; underwater archeology; environmental archeology; city archeology; as well as regional forms including, for example, the archeologies of the Qijia Culture of Gansu, Western Xia Culture of Ningxia, and Sanxingdui, Ba, and Shu Cultures of the Upper Yangtze. A group was even formed around postprocessual archeology (a postmodern form of archeology that took its inspiration from, of all things, Western theory) but was unfortunately discontinued when the journal that the group produced was taken over by an opposing group of older archeologists who disliked Western theory. Since oligarchs tend to be traditionalists, it is more difficult to get them to support these groups of people interested in new archeologies, but once the group is big and prominent enough even the oligarchs can be enticed into writing a preface for a collective volume of papers or at least contributing a piece of laudatory calligraphy.

Whether such cohort groups are created in relation to chronological or topical divisions, they are all created to cut through bureaucratic barriers both up and across *xitong*. Members of these groups are encouraged to remain in the group because of the potential opportunities provided by knowing so many diverse people. Incentives can also be more immediate since groups based on topics or interests provide acceptable excuses to hold excavations, attend conferences, and offer publishing opportunities.

Group allegiances are subject to processes of segmentary 'fission' and 'fusion.' Many topics crosscut each other: at times, an archeologist might want to position himself as a Bronze Age jade specialist; at other times, he might want to drop the jade part and identify himself solely as a Bronze Age specialist; at still other times, he might want to claim that he is a specialist only of the (famous) site of Anyang. Which credential is claimed depends entirely on context or, more bluntly, which credential the individual feels to be most threatened in any interaction. For example, Bronze Age archeologists, despite fierce internecine struggles, will instantly unite and cooperate as a group to maintain their extremely prestigious position in Chinese archeology when faced with the appearance of artifacts, such as those found at Sanxingdui, that threaten to outshine those of the Central Plains. When not being attacked by their 'enemies,' however, the 'group' disintegrates as each member endeavours to draw distinctions between his own oligarch-cohort clique and that of others. The fission of the group continues if one focuses more narrowly on each oligarch-cohort clique: students of the oligarch, themselves of varying age and experience, are always engaged in competitive strategies to gain the favour of the oligarch.

Oligarch-cohort cliques based on topical or chronological distinctions can subvert the *xitong* structure in productive ways. The proliferation of journals and edited volumes, regional archeologies, and distinctions among kinds of archeology in recent years must be seen as the tip of the iceberg: the concrete manifestations of the innumerable strategies used to create oligarch-cohort structures. Each new topic, after all, requires a budget to support the journals, books, and conferences that it produces; the source of a budget is an oligarch. As we will soon see in detail, the success of strategies used among the archeologists to curry favour from the oligarch is manifested in the number of articles that an individual publishes or the prominence of prefaces or calligraphy pieces written by an oligarch gracing the front pages of his thesis or book.

Symbols of Success: Publications

A striking characteristic of Euro-American archeology is the way in which archeologists raised in that milieu publish their ideas with a sense of both impunity and ownership. Once an idea is published, there are responses both favourable and negative, and the archeological world is (slowly)

changed. Young Euro-American archeologists know that the more they publish, the more apt they are to get better jobs and/or tenure; the more they
are known through their work, the more likely they are to be invited onto
the committees that control the granting agencies and be the editors of the
journals in which everyone wants his work to appear. The best way, then,
for an individual to advance his career, and for archeology as a discipline to
change and grow, is to publish.

The doctrine of 'publish or perish' driving Euro-American archeology simply makes no sense in a context in which everyone has tenure from the
outset, for what it is worth, and cannot leave a job even if he or she wants
to. Publishing, criticism, conferences, participation in professional services,
et cetera are, of course, present in China. In complete contrast to the Euro-
American case, however, these activities are simply not available to the
young. Young archeologists rarely publish their opinions, there are no young
people on the search or grant committees, and there are no young journal
editors or board members. They cannot travel freely or choose to go to a
conference. If a young archeologist does manage to participate in a conference, then he has been given a gift by his teacher or superior for some
reason of positioning or reward, not because he will be presenting his opinions, giving a paper, or even speaking in discussion. Thus, while it is likely
that much of the history of Euro-American archeology, including issues of
interpersonal rivalry, is captured in the pages of journals and books fairly
soon after events unfold, in China it could take literally thirty to forty years
before the results of a young archeologist's ideas, experiences, and career
moves are seen in print.

Then what does it mean if a particular Chinese archeologist is able to
publish often, join several conferences a year, and travel about the country
to visit whomever he wants? Let me make the answer clear: this man must
already be a senior archeologist or even an oligarch. For none of these activities is a path to advancement but a symbol of having *already* arrived at
success. When an archeologist publishes an opinion piece, he is not in the
process of changing the archeological world; rather, that world has already
changed. His publication is the sign of his success. The change may not be
felt at the lower levels of the *xitong* until the paper is published (and the
conference held), but where it matters – at the top in Beijing among the
oligarchs – someone has vanquished someone else, and the publishing of
his article is the indication of that victory.[14]

In the Euro-American context, the type of article published by an academic changes somewhat over time. The older and more established archeologists are freed from the necessity of following strict stylistic practices
and can, simply because of their marketability, float ideas that a younger
archeologist could not get published. Chinese archeologists also change the

type of work that they can publish over time, only in their case the differences are more dramatic and tied more directly to which institution the author graduated from, which teacher he claims as his own, and in which *xitong* and at what level his *danwei* is located.

In general, the beginning of an archeologist's career, between the ages of twenty-one and thirty, is spent almost entirely in the field. Any publishing that occurs is in the form of the archeological report: a dry, exceedingly detailed document in which nothing so overt as an opinion appears. As modernist empiricists, archeologists trust in the ability of scientists to describe facts. There is, moreover, a strong ethical principle in play: since archeological excavation is in effect the destruction of an archeological site, the report ought to be as factual as possible. Any interpretation added to the report is perceived as a return to the 'bad old days' during the Cultural Revolution when the party secretaries forced everyone to produce materials with communist interpretations. The distaste of the Chinese archeologist for the 'impure' report is remarkable yet certainly understandable given past party excesses.

The young archeologist spends most of his time producing these reports. Publication of the report depends not only on the importance of the site but also on the reputation and stature of the young archeologist's *danwei* and the abilities of his *danwei* director to secure publishing opportunities. The report, in other words, has little to do with the abilities or interests of the archeologist himself. Not only are these reports supposed to be written in a standardized order and style, but they are also written by a group of people. One person might write the text, another draw the maps, another organize and label the pictures, and a final person edit and lay out the article for the publishers. To make matters even more difficult, layout has to be done by the authors rather than the publishing company. It is usually a woman who does the editing and layout work since she does not excavate as often as a man. Laying out a book is immensely difficult and requires that she go to Beijing for often up to six months to help the publishers. The first time I heard of this was when a woman in Xining told me how she had lost her health by living for four months in the underground dorm run by the Cultural Relics Press *(Wenwu Chubanshe)*. Other people have since agreed with her description of the press's dank, wet, and extremely cold rooms in which people have to live, eating fast food every night and with nothing to do beyond laying out the book (only enough money to pay for food and travel is provided). The report is not easily prepared and published, and no one individual can relate to it in any sense of ownership over production; indeed, in Marxist terms, all the producers are utterly alienated from the report that carries their names, if at all, only in tiny print hidden within the publishing information.

As archeologists age, they will try to publish in archeological journals. These fall into two main categories: what I call the 'big three' and the 're-gional journals.' The big three refer to the three main journals *Kao Gu* (*Ar-chaeology*, a monthly edited by CASS); *Kaogu Xuebao* (*Archaeological Reports*, a quarterly edited by CASS); and *Wenwu* (*Cultural Relics*, edited by the Cen-tral Bureau of Cultural Relics, the highest-ranking *danwei* in the Culture *Xitong*). The big three are available all over China and have large circula-tions. Before the mid-1980s, they acted as the sole publishing outlets for articles and reports. Such a small number of journals simply could not handle the output, and for many archeologists publishing was simply next to im-possible. In early years, articles had no individual authors listed at all since listing them was considered a capitalist attempt to secure control over the products of intellectual labour. Publishing simply could not be an impor-tant consideration in individual career advancement since it was not a par-ticularly easy, safe, or individual effort.

Regional journals are those edited by certain universities and those pro-duced by provincial institutes and museums. Provincial institutes and mu-seums produce edited volumes made up of articles written by members of their *danwei,* and also journals. There has been a remarkable proliferation of publications by these regional institutions in recent years. Articles can be submitted to regional journals, such as Nanjing Museum's *Dongnan Wenwu* (*Southeastern Cultural Relics*), by anyone writing on a topic of interest to the region, but whose article actually gets published is, of course, a matter of intense competition. The regional journals are limited in circulation to the region or the institution in which they are published, and often they are even restricted from being sent through the post within China (much less outside China's borders). As a result, they reach only a small audience and cannot command the prestige of the big three. Incidentally, limited circula-tion can also be beneficial: they are a way for a *danwei* to publish data, as is ethically mandated, yet still keep the data from falling into the 'wrong' hands.

An archeologist in middle age may begin to publish the occasional opin-ion article in one or another of these journals. Which journal is chosen, and which one accepts his work, depend on the strategies of friendship and cohort networking in which the archeologist has probably been engaging for at least the past ten years. Nevertheless, his work must be placed in a completely different category from opinion articles published by oligarchs. The middle-aged archeologist remains a mouthpiece for his elders, merely repeating or extending their ideas. If a junior, of whatever age, does publish an article that disagrees with his teacher, then the act so flagrantly disrupts ingrained principles of correct behaviour, of reciprocity and trustworthi-ness in particular, that it would be seen by his colleagues and leaders as truly unfathomable.

Let us take Director Sun as an example. Sun is considered to be 'mildly eccentric' because he is known to have opinions different from those of his teacher, a Bronze Age oligarch who commands enormous authority. Sun has spoken out against his teacher's ideas at conferences and excavations. He is aware of his reputation as an eccentric but justifies his actions as a result of being part of the lost generation. As described in Chapter 5, the credentials of this generation give them the right, in the eyes of the audience, to act in a rebellious manner. Nevertheless, despite his rebelliousness, Sun has never published an article that reveals any of his differences of opinion from his teacher. To do so would be a much more serious matter than being mildly eccentric at conferences.

One day, after listening to Sun go on about why his teacher is incorrect, I asked him why he had not published his opinions. He replied,

> If I were to [publish my opinions], people would think that they were my teacher's opinions. They all know I am his student. Students only publish the opinions of their teachers. Therefore, these opinions are my teacher's. They would be very confused because these opinions are different from my teacher's other articles. They would probably approach my teacher [and confront him], asking him why he had changed his opinion without telling them directly. Asking him why he would use his student to do it. Behind his back, they would ridicule him. After all, he has changed his opinion. And if someone knew that actually it was my idea, not my teacher's, then they would ridicule him even more for not being able to control [an insubordinate student]. My teacher may be misguided in his archeology, but I could never do that to him; I could not face myself.

Sun's reply is revealing. An archeologist whose teacher is still alive or very famous writes articles on behalf of that teacher. In fact, a good definition of 'young archeologist' would be 'the archeologist, regardless of physical age, whose teacher is still alive and active in archeology.' The young archeologist is expected to be writing solely in order to show his loyalty to his teacher by developing or using that teacher's ideas.[15] If he writes something different, then it hardly crosses anyone's mind that these could be his ideas. Everything that he writes, even if it seems to be different from what the teacher might write, is assumed to reflect the ideas of the teacher until proven otherwise.

Sun also made the interesting comment that people would ridicule his teacher for having changed his opinion. Once a person publishes, he is supposed to stand by what he has written. The 'Hodderesque' switching of opinions is simply not acceptable. I use the example of Ian Hodder (with apologies) because he is most famously a Euro-American archeologist who made the abrupt switch midcareer from supporting empiricist theory to a rather different kind of contextual, interpretive poststructuralism, even embracing feminism. In China, Hodder would be a laughing-stock: even people who agree with his ideas would ridicule him for having changed them. Only the finding of new data ought to force one to switch positions on a question; it is rare indeed that new data are found that can cause such a conclusive and radical change in theoretical orientation.

Mind you, when Hodder made the switch, he did endure a certain amount of ridicule and criticism from his predominantly empiricist Euro-American colleagues for his 'séance-like' archeology and was even accused of making the switch to advance his career.[16] Neither of these insults would have meaning in the Chinese context. No one would criticize a Chinese Hodder based on the substance of his work; rather, criticism would be based on the fact that he changed his mind. Continuity of ideas is more important than whether someone agrees with the substantive content. Moreover, since publishing in China cannot be used as a method of career advancement, it would make no sense to demean a Chinese Hodder by insisting that he does not really mean what he writes but is merely using it to advance his career. After all, a Chinese Hodder would already have fame and status long before publishing a book on his ideas.

The strong value placed on continuity is an important reason why young archeologists will not publish their own ideas. A 'true scholar' should do the hard work, research, and excavation for however long it takes him until he can organize his thoughts and publish an article or book that will last. The goal is to write something with which many generations will agree. Gai, a newly arrived, extremely young archeologist in Shanghai, explained to me that his greatest fear is to have his work criticized for being unfinished, contradictory, or short of data. He has to wait, he said, until he has the experience to ensure that he knows what he is talking about and is not missing anything. When I mentioned the idealistic view in the United States that one writes in the hope of eliciting audience opinion and debate, he appeared horrified. He does not expect to get around to publishing anything about his own ideas until decades have passed and he believes that he has something important and lasting to contribute.

Sun's final remark, about how his teacher would be treated if people knew that Sun was disobeying him, is familiar to us: the senior – even the oligarchic senior – needs the junior to act appropriately submissive in order to maintain his own reputation. The oligarchs need their immediate juniors who live among them in Beijing to follow this rule in face-to-face interactions with other oligarchs and students. Since the teacher whose student is rebellious loses face, it is unsurprising that teachers base their choices of which students to support on judgments made about their loyalty and moral character and react with alacrity to punish any act that could be seen as rebellious. The demand for overt performances of obedience increases the more resources and fame are at stake.

Overt performances are not necessarily as direct as one might think. Indeed, another teacher in the same department as Sun scoffed at any notion of Sun's 'essential qualities of rebelliousness' that he claimed for himself as part of the lost generation and insisted that Sun was really playing an elaborate game to show his submission to his teacher. She noted that Sun, by talking about his opinions all the time, ensures that everyone knows he has different opinions from his teacher. By being so public with his disagreements, he makes that willingness to play his junior role all the more precious to the teacher. Yet, by not publishing his disagreements, he signifies, both to his teacher and to the audience, that he is an extremely compatible and trustworthy person. Even using the narrative of the essential rebelliousness of the lost generation is a trick, for Sun thereby builds up his teacher's reputation as someone who can control his students, even the really difficult ones. Whether Sun's strategy is intentional or not, whether it is a sign of 'rebellion' or of 'obedience,' it certainly appears to be effective.

Under conditions of interdependence, it is no surprise that criticism takes on a status fraught with danger, emotional risk, and potential misunderstandings. Nevertheless, people will occasionally criticize each other in print. Their criticisms take the form of *shangque* or 'discussion.' I should use the word *critique* here instead of the word *criticism*. I discovered the difference between the two words only after unwittingly disquieting many archeologists by asking them whether they would ever publish a criticism of someone else's work. The word for criticism in Chinese, *piping,* appears to be reserved for ruthless political attacks. Critiques, *shangque,* are in contrast politely and carefully worded attacks against people whom one may never know, someone from another *xitong* perhaps or far away in another province. Critiques can also be launched against people whom one knows well yet who can be counted on not to take it too personally. CASS researchers, in particular, are fond of poking fun at their colleagues in this manner. A little internecine fighting is fondly tolerated by their elders, but if it gets too divisive it will not be allowed to continue.

Critiques often appear in *Zhongguo Wenwu Bao (China's Cultural Relics),* the chatty official newsletter edited by the Central Bureau of Cultural Relics.[17] They take the form of small articles replying to a recently published article pointing out what appears to be a picky, insignificant bit of misinterpretation or a bit of forgotten data. In contrast, they have much more significance when published as full-length articles in one of the big three journals. Since the successful publication of a critique is a manifestation of long-term strategies of loyalty and cohort creation, their mere existence indicates who is a friend of whom. Unfortunately for outsiders hoping to pierce the Chinese archeological veil, critiques are so dangerous that people will publish them under pen names.

Pen names *(biming)* are important strategies in themselves. They can, for example, signal that a person is appropriately humble and in touch with Chinese scholarly traditions, or perhaps that he has decided to publish on a topic not normally his own, or that he is critiquing himself. When a person critiques someone else by using a pen name, he does so not to hide who he is, since everyone who needs to know is aware of which pen name refers to which person, but to give respect to the person whom he critiques. By hiding his name, the author avoids appearing as if he is issuing a direct, face-to-face challenge to a person. Indeed, he performs the following elaborate drama: he is being 'forced by circumstances beyond his control' (he has access to different data) to point out the respected scholar's fault, yet he believes the scholar so worthy of praise and respect in everything else that he must hide his face (his name) when critiquing him.

Using pen names as a strategy to soften the impact of a critique can only go so far, however. Only certain people have the right to critique others, and the rules are clearly related to status and class. A technical worker at the lowest levels of the *xitong* cannot critique a Beijing oligarch even if he has the data to prove the man wrong. His status is so low that to critique someone so high (if he could even get his critique published in the first place) is an enormous affront that no amount of social connections, or the use of a pen name, can obviate. If someone so low can critique someone so high, then the oligarch's mistake must be so obvious and silly that even a technical worker can recognize it – a grave insult indeed. The technical worker can, however, present his information and understanding of the problem (and will expect compensation) to someone higher in status. That higher-level person can then write the critique as his own, and since he is high enough in status it will be taken as respectful correction rather than attack or insult.

Critique, or, to be more precise, the threat of critique, is a powerful motivating tool for the archeologists to obey the authority of their elders. Everyone wants to avoid a critique. The middle-aged archeologist who has finally, through various stratagems, secured the opportunity to write a book can avoid critique by inviting an oligarch to write a preface or contribute calligraphy to the frontispiece. If, for example, this scholar were able to get oligarchs from BeiDa, CASS, and JiDa to write prefaces for his work, then no graduates or teachers of any of those institutions would dare to critique him. He might be critiqued by people from the provincial institute, but their critiques are less worrisome than those of people affiliated with BeiDa, CASS, and JiDa. An oligarch of one of those institutions might dare to critique the rising scholar's work, but in so doing many people would interpret the critique as being really aimed at the rising scholar's teacher (if he is still alive) or at one of the people writing the preface or contributing calligraphy (often the same person). Looking at who is writing prefaces and contributing calligraphy for whom, then, is another surefire indication of who is an oligarch, who is favoured by an oligarch, and who is not.

Given all these limitations on the publication activities of middle-aged archeologists, it is clear that only when an archeologist is nearing retirement can he begin to publish whatever he wants. Why is it only when an archeologist is much older that he can own and control his published work? He has to outlive his teacher, of course. Only when the teacher has passed away or has otherwise left archeology can a person say what he thinks. If one's teacher dies early, then there is much more time to publish. If one's cards are played right, then, by the time retirement arrives, one will be well positioned enough to capitalize on the benefits provided by retirement itself.

Retirement is truly a golden age. CASS archeologists retire at sixty if they are male and at fifty-five if female. BeiDa and other educational institutions do not require retirement for men until sixty-five (still fifty-five for women), and, if a professor is allowed to take on doctoral students, then he can continue until he is seventy. As one might expect, the right to take MA or PhD students is strictly controlled by the oligarchs. Once retired, an archeologist cannot hold any official position. He receives only a pension from the *danwei* and, of course, can no longer take on students. Thus, retirement can be used as a punishment, and people will be forced to retire regardless of their age if they have run into political problems. If an archeologist is already well on the way to becoming an oligarch, however, particularly if he has many students and articles published already, then retirement can be the most liberating event in his career. If famous enough, he can hold certain special hierarchical positions: that of an outstanding scholar *(youxi xuezhe)*, for example, thereby receiving extra money from the government. He can also be elected to the National Council on Archaeology and Cultural Relics – an organization that has no rules regarding retirement – as well as to the many other commissions and committees, provincial or central, that control various aspects of archeology.

Most importantly, however, retirement means that one is no longer forced to ask for permission from the *danwei* to publish, travel, or collaborate with foreigners. Most of the publications in China are therefore edited or written by oligarchs.[18] As long as he has made a name and an extensive social network before retirement, a retired oligarch can be very busy. His many students will ask him to join excavations as an advisor, to comment on artifacts or entire collections, and to copublish articles or contribute prefaces to their published works. Huang, an oligarch in Beijing, has since retirement gone to more countries than he can count, been invited to innumerable conferences, and been asked to write prefaces and contribute ideas to journals in many languages. He pronounces himself satisfied: 'There is no greater happiness than being asked to contribute or seeing other people use one's work.'

For young archeologists, not publishing is, in fact, one of the most important strategies in eventually attaining the authority of the oligarch. Young archeologists are neither stupid nor unobservant: they well know that, as they get older, they will have more data, more ideas, and more opportunities to publish. Not publishing in the present is obviously the best way to ensure that they have something to publish by the time that they are old enough to have the right to publish. Youngsters therefore find that it is best to analyze their data, write up reports, and then sit on those unpublished reports for years in order to come to some conclusions about them. Once old enough, they can publish the reports and, better yet, have a number of articles ready for immediate publication so that they are not 'scooped' by some other scholar. Not insignificantly, as they wait to age, they can also give some of those data as gifts to others in return for opportunities that will position them higher and grant them increased authority.

Non-Chinese archeologists often complain that Chinese reports and articles are not published until years after the original excavations. I hope that the many reasons why are now clear. The lack of publication is not because people fear that they will be accused of misapplying communist ideology, nor is it even crassly related to economics. The act of publishing, or not publishing, is merely one of the more concrete manifestations of strategic successes and failures in the archeological world.

Oligarchs and Change
Such is the extent of the respect and command given to oligarchs by both the system and the people who perpetuate it that oligarchs themselves have every incentive to protect and justify the system against all threats and are fully capable of using their age and position to do whatever is required to maintain their status. It is the oligarchs who stand in the face of change and actively attempt to suppress and oppress other archeologists. I have heard people say that Chinese archeology is run by the party and the government such that it is the totalitarian nature of communism that keeps Chinese archeologists from expressing themselves. They are incorrect. The party and the government have surprisingly little control over China's heritage. Direct control over Chinese archeologists, over excavation, even over the creation of ideological tracts, children's literature, or other forms of publication often labelled 'propaganda' is left in the hands of the oligarchs.

Nevertheless, change still happens even when participants actively resist it, although the process is slow and driven by motivations peculiar to the social contract. For example, given how the relation between oligarch and student depends on the student's obedience, it can be imagined that oligarchs will intervene in any behaviour that verges on rebellion by the young.

Euro-American theory represents an attack on the system exactly because it is something studied and used by the young. When students study things about which the oligarchs know little, the very foundation of the junior-senior contract is threatened. If the student no longer needs the oligarch for his teaching and guidance, then how can the oligarch continue to control him?

Euro-American theory, however, is slowly becoming acceptable. At first, there was only one oligarch-cohort clique created around the topic of foreign theory. The oligarch involved, Chang, was an admitted maverick who took great pleasure in annoying his colleagues by encouraging young people to study foreign theory and reaped the rewards, as a large group of young people chose him as their teacher. Interestingly, a conference was held in 1991 at which this group faced off against the critics of foreign theory. From all reports, it was a lively debate.[19] Indeed, one of the oligarchs, Qi, at the time resolutely against studying foreign theory, gave a brilliant speech that illuminated in excruciating detail the many inconsistencies and lack of practical implementation of Euro-American theories. So brilliant was this speech, said Chang with a certain amount of envy, that several of his students promptly switched allegiance and gave up on the study of Euro-American theory in favour of Qi's more empirical methods.

Yet in recent years, even Qi has relented with regard to Euro-American theory. Qi, along with most other oligarchs, used to complain of the lack of respect shown to him by foreigners but he has been changing his tune in recent years. The foreigners did something very interesting: they invited Qi to the United States and treated him with a great deal of respect. Since that visit, Qi has been much more benevolent toward the foreigners, treating their work with a modicum of respect and allowing that theoretical pursuits can have worth. Once representatives of the group of foreigners claimed juniority, as is appropriate given their ignorance about China and their lack of access to archeological data, Qi accepted the senior position and became interested in the work of these student-foreigners (mainly in the work of the 'new archeology,' a form of empiricist theory imbued with the rhetoric of science so acceptable in Chinese circles). As the foreigners are seen as less of a threat to, or even as participants in, the junior-senior contract, their ideas will become assimilated (much as alien ideas have always been sinified, as Teacher Cao pointed out with a wink).

Yet even if change occurs in the sense that foreign theory or some other newfangled idea or method becomes assimilated into the system, structurally, change is unlikely to occur. The structure of the system is reproduced because it brings significant benefits to both young and old. Younger archeologists provide oligarchs with the important gifts of obedience and submission. In return, oligarchs support and offer younger scholars material and immaterial resources. Oligarchs keep the students in line with the threat of taking away their support and can be both harsh and demanding. Yet, despite the students' experiences of the discomforts and dangers in interacting with oligarchs, when they finally get close to becoming oligarchs themselves they will almost certainly reproduce the same interactions among their own students. The juniors, in other words, maintain the system to reap its benefits when they themselves become the seniors.[20]

Why Women Cannot Be Archeologists

Why are oligarchs men? Sex, from one point of view, is just another form of credential, a rigid model of prescriptive behaviour based on a person's 'essential being' that affects the judgments of the audience-that-matters. Claiming any particular credential is an attempt, on the one hand, to emphasize that credential and, on the other, to elide or curtail any other models of prescriptive behaviour that may entail unwanted judgments in the eyes of the audience. Credentials may share these structural similarities, but they also differ in how easily they can be claimed in any given interaction and in their effects on the roles being inhabited. The credential that applies to the female sex is unusual among credentials in that it both limits the success of a woman's strategies of claiming and reduces the number of roles considered acceptable for a woman to play.

The class system in China encourages people to live up to the role models of their class. Archeologists are expected to act as 'good intellectuals.' Sex intersects class such that acting like 'a good male intellectual' versus acting like 'a good female intellectual' makes all the difference in the world. One reason for this difference is that a woman, from about twenty-one to forty, is expected to be constantly inhabiting her role of 'mother.' A man of the same age can play many roles, one of which is 'father,' but which model of prescriptive behaviour applies to him in the eyes of the audience-that-matters in any given situation depends on his strategies of claiming. Women are in contrast so conflated with their role that they are barred from claiming another role. Or, if they do make the claim to another role, it must be under unusual circumstances (e.g., older women often speak nostalgically of a time when they could claim to be comrades rather than mothers; the role of comrade, however, has been diminished in the aftermath of the Cultural Revolution and the advance of capitalism).

As a woman, having children is behaviour that distinguishes her utterly from men – and, in a world where surfaces and behaviours are more important than inner worlds, that quality of visibility makes childbirth unforgettable. Unsurprisingly, a woman's credentials, by virtue of her sex, assume that the woman will take on the responsibility of motherhood and desire to excel by living up to the widely shared standards of good motherhood. In one sense, a woman is freed from all the behavioural expectations that apply to men; in another sense, she is utterly limited because she is only ever expected to act as a mother. She cannot intervene in the judgment of the audience to change these assumptions because it is the only set of behaviours considered acceptable for her.

The adult woman's sole expected behaviour, of becoming a mother, thus affects all other roles-in-relation. From the perspective of her birth family, getting married is the traditional way by which a daughter becomes engaged in the filial practice of widening the family's social network. She would thus be unfilial to her ancestors if she does not marry. Furthermore, if she does not live up to the standards of good motherhood once married, she threatens her birth family's reputation.

From the perspective of the family that she marries into, the one into which she has been subsumed by rules of patrilineality and patrilocality, her worth comes from her ability to perpetuate the patriline. That is, living up to the standards of good motherhood means that she should have children, hopefully male, and preferably sooner than later; she should also care for and protect these valuable children at all costs. Given that she must have babies and protect and care for them, a good woman must limit herself to the two main relations that will allow her to both have and best care for her children: husband-wife and parent-child. It is acceptable to enter into woman-woman relations (with other women or with her mother and sisters) as long as she can claim that she is doing so for the good of her children and household.[21]

The woman is not only always a mother, but she is also expected to be in the junior position in any relationship with the people around her (who are not her own children). Being always in the subordinate position means that the woman is dependent on the junior-senior contract in order to be successful in any plan. As such, she has two courses of action open to her. First, she can openly act obediently in order to encourage her superior (any man) to act benignly in response. Unfortunately, the gift of obedience must be given in such a way that it is clearly above and beyond the expected submission in junior-senior relations. Since a woman is always supposed to be obedient, it is difficult for her to be obedient *enough* to be perceived as attempting to give a gift. Thus it is that tales of extreme sacrifice or suffering by mothers will excite notice, while their (more difficult because constant) mundane acts of care are expected as natural and unworthy of comment or return gifts of any kind.

Second, a woman can use her capacity to harm the reputations of the men to whom she is related to manipulate the junior-senior contract. A senior's reputation relies on keeping his women in line as much as it relies on maintaining order among any of his other juniors. If the woman acts disobediently, by telling tales or gossiping, for example, then it reflects on his inability to maintain control over her. If she acts foolishly, then it is because he (husband, father, brother) has not taught her well enough. When she acts, then, it is her senior's reputation, not hers, that is more likely to be affected in the eyes of the audience. Concomitantly, if she does something moral or respectable, then it is also thought to be due to her father's or husband's abilities and qualities. Note that, from a man's perspective, tight control over female behaviour is a strategy that the man can use to protect or enhance his own reputation and, by association, that of his family.

For the most part, a woman is restricted to the use of obedience or attack or the adroit combination of the two. Whatever strategy she chooses to use, however, her success depends on her ability to 'inhabit' the junior role with all her energy. Women will thus speak about their roles in the strongest of terms: women, as many will insist, need all the help, guidance, and consideration that a man can give.[22] By speaking in such a way, the woman reminds the audience that men have the responsibility to protect and provide for women, and, at the same time, she implicitly threatens to punish the man through gossip and other interventions in the audience's judgment of him if he fails to live up to the expectations of a senior. By entrapping men through her performance of utter obedience to the expectations of the junior-senior contract, a woman's behaviour may be controlled, but the woman can nevertheless engage in the predicting, planning, and executing of strategies in the pursuit of authority within her own world and in her own context.

Unfortunately, her worlds are also limited by being a mother. Archeology, in particular, is about as far from being an appropriate context for a mother as one can get. The qualities of being a 'good archeologist' and 'intellectual' clash fundamentally with the qualities of being a 'good woman.' To be a good archeologist, one goes into the field for about twenty years; in other words, as if it were not enough that these are the most important childbearing and rearing years of a woman's life, the problem is compounded by the requirement that they be spent in the *countryside*. Bo, an older female worker in an archeology *danwei*, told me how she had to give up archeology. She and her husband both graduated from BeiDa in the early 1960s. Bo wanted to take her children out with her into the field to continue being an archeologist. The result was entirely negative: she was castigated by her birth family and her husband's family for exposing her children to the dangers of the country. Bo's husband said to me that, no matter how often he reassured his parents that the countryside was not unhealthy, particularly dirty, or devoid of food, they would not believe it. They accused him of being a bad son by allowing his wife to endanger the children. Her parents, meanwhile, accused her of being a bad mother and him of being a bad husband by not forcing her to stay at home. Bo managed to take the children out for two seasons before the combined pressures of four parents (and eight grandparents, all of whom were alive and very upset) forced her to give up. She gave up her dream of becoming an archeologist to become the librarian of the archeology *danwei*.

Given the logic that underlies the idea of obedient autonomy, if the rules restricting a woman are more fiercely applied, then there should be more opportunities for her to be creative in setting rules and roles against each other. We have seen how male actors faced with negative credentials can engage in the various arts of combination, reinterpretation, conversion, and motivation that can ameliorate their situation. Why, then, can women not do the same? The reason relates to the issues of compatibility and trustworthiness as represented in the law of reciprocity and is simply stated: women have nothing of importance to give.

Female Incompatibility

The ideal student success story goes something like this. Once there was a promising young student. So promising was he, so willing to do whatever the teacher said, and especially so well behaved at banquets and in other gatherings that the teacher assigned him extra work and offered him the chance to be the teacher's assistant. The student was thereby presented with the keys to the teacher's office and access to all of the teacher's books and materials. The student worked closely with the teacher over the years – eating with him, being introduced to his colleagues and visitors, chatting to him about the different requirements of archeological life, and accepting his advice on many if not most aspects of his life from how to dress to choice of marriage partner. When it came time for the student to graduate, the teacher, of course, wrote the letters and made the phone calls to secure the student a good job in a fairly well-respected urban centre. Both are thus happy: the student acquired a good job, and the teacher, through his student, gained access to materials and information about the archeology done in that region and was therefore able to publish on archeological topics from that region before anyone else. As his prestige thereby rises, so does that of his student, who can always point to this famous man as being his teacher.

From the point of view of the female student, there is an obvious difficulty with this ideal model: no male teacher can allow a female student to live and work in such close proximity to him (female teachers are extraordinarily rare). A female student who spends too much time in a male teacher's office is not only odd but also incites no little scandalized commentary. The resulting gossip would hardly be beneficial to the teacher. A student of either gender who cannot create close ties to the teacher not only escapes the teacher's notice but also does not have the opportunity to learn the techniques of networking, cohort making, banqueting, and all the other subtle strategies that a person must learn to succeed in an interdependent, highly uncertain society.

Escaping the teacher's notice, however, is not the only issue facing women. A female student is also simply not seen as being particularly compatible. Remember that compatibility is the quality of being well placed (or well positionable, from a teacher's point of view) now or in the future such that the junior has access to desirable resources for barter in the teacher-student relationship. For archeologists, a compatible person is someone who has access to data or materials needed for research or who is able to help set up a smooth-running excavation. This means that he has to be able to get a job, somewhere, anywhere, that might be useful. Although half of the archeology undergraduates nowadays are women, they are not wanted by archeology *danwei*. They are too problematic. The *danwei* has to take care of them – and they have more health issues than men, especially during pregnancy – and provide them with housing. A *danwei* cannot force a woman to sleep on a couch in the back of the main *danwei* office for a couple of years as a male archeologist can be made to do. If a director were to force a woman into that situation, one can be sure that the gossip would be terrible indeed. Remember too that, even if the woman herself does not mind physical hardship, the director still cannot put her into that situation because it is the audience's perception of events, not her (or his) personal intentions or desires, that will harm his reputation.

The credentials of women include the assumption that they are better than men at spatial matters, detailed work, and mathematics. A female student can therefore get a job as a technical worker doing artifact drawing, computer analysis, or editing at an archeological *danwei* that can afford to take care of her. Female students can also secure jobs in non-archeological but related *danwei* such as at museums or tourist spots as tour guides, librarians, or secretaries. If they graduate from JiDa or BeiDa, they are sent to more prestigious tourist spots or museums and have better jobs as guides, librarians, or secretaries. The job that a woman is rarely given, however, is the task most important to the career advancement of the Chinese archeologist: excavation. Without excavation opportunities, she has no access to data. She has nothing to offer a teacher in return for his help, so she cannot go to conferences, is not introduced to people whom the teacher knows, and is unable to broaden her social networks among archeologists of different hierarchical levels and from different *xitong*. She is, in other words, utterly incompatible.

Teacher-student relations are strengthened using performances of potential positioning and trustworthiness, and the first real opportunities to engage in such performances come during the student practicum. It is, unfortunately, especially during the practicum that women are set apart and considered more as a nuisance than as potential apprentices. During the practicum, the teacher must ensure the health and safety of the students under his command and, more importantly, must perform that he is caring for them in a way that will be understood as such by the audience. The audience is vast and unknown, so the teacher takes refuge in widely shared gender credentials: girls, being weak and vulnerable, must be protected to a greater extent than boys and must be given clean and comfortable places to live. Boys can be expected to suffer; girls cannot. The teacher must perform his care of the boys as well, by restricting their movements and so forth, but there is so much to be gained by training a boy. He represents a student to add to the teacher's crop, so to speak, and exhibits the potential for a mutually satisfying relationship in the future. Girls, in contrast, are superfluous. Protecting women is a no-win situation: not protecting them can ruin a reputation, but protecting them only maintains a reputation rather than generates further opportunities to increase one's number of students or improve one's reputation.

Female Untrustworthiness

As if a lack of compatibility and a limited authority were not enough, a woman also finds it difficult to perform trustworthiness. This deficiency is not a comment on her personality or character, as it might be under orthodoxy, but a comment on whether or not she is able to use the strategies of maintaining and intensifying social relations. To maintain or intensify her relations, she must be able to perform not only that she has access to valued resources (compatibility) but also that she is a moral person who can be relied on to reciprocate any gifts given (trustworthiness). The mixed-tie relationship ensures that someone perceived not to have access to valuable resources is simply not interesting as a potential partner. Nevertheless, as mentioned in Chapter 3, people without access to resources can still build reputations of trustworthiness that situate them, at the least, as people with potential.

Women cannot engage in strategies of trustworthiness simply because most of these strategies are also the common ways by which masculinity is expressed in Chinese society. These strategies are centred on the comportment of the body during banquets and while in the field. During banquets, a man's ability to drink, smoke, and eat to excess is important. This excess is not in any way considered pleasurable by men and indeed is often cited as a source of considerable hardship by archeologists and their students. Archeologists' tendency to suffer from stomach ulcers and other digestive ailments is the unfortunate result of this practice. While in the field, men stand and speak in ways that indicate both their masculinity, an end in itself, and their authority attendant on that masculinity combined with the other roles-in-relation and credentials said to apply to them. The physical attributes associated with these practices would alone be enough to block women from using them. Women, especially intellectual women, are meant to be refined in manner and comportment.[23] By refraining from male practices and conforming to female practices, women constantly remind the audience-that-matters of their gender. Reminding others of their gender also reminds them of their lack of compatibility and authority associated with that gender. Even men who know a woman well and know that special circumstances have endowed her with valuable resources and the authority to command them might still be impelled by habitual interpretations of her behaviour to forget.

To understand fully the implications of female untrustworthiness, let us return to the important strategy of creating a cohort-like clique to subvert divides of bureaucratic and social position. A male archeologist must constantly reassert and reproduce his trustworthiness in the eyes of his colleagues and teacher-cohort clique by participating in late-night banquets (which, not incidentally, conflict with a woman's role as mother). In this context, having students or juniors present who can drink on the senior's behalf is welcome indeed. A junior's comportment at the banquet and, indeed, in any interaction with other archeologists, peasants, maids, waiters, shoemakers, et cetera is a strong reflection on the senior. Any student, for example, who does well in a drinking contest or can show more generosity than others is valuable to the teacher and highly respected by his cohort mates. Often such students are used by other people to praise the teacher without being too direct. Praise of the student is well understood to be praise of the teacher who taught the student so well. The compliments, moreover, provide the opportunity for the student to show his regard for his teacher by insisting that any ability on his part is a result of the teacher's patience and good teaching. And so it goes, in a mutually enhancing interplay of obedience, respect, and reward.

During banquets among archeologists, male juniors enter into the toasting competitions and drinking games common in the early part of the evening in the name of their senior. If they win, the senior's face is saved; if they lose, the senior bears the brunt of the ridicule. Whatever happens, the important point is that the senior maintain sobriety and control over his body. Thus, at the end of the evening, even if his junior is slumped in the corner highly inebriated (even if he has embarrassed his senior), the senior can still enter into discussions about potential collaborations, copublishing opportunities, and other plans and ideas that only tend to be discussed at that time.

I met a female archeologist named Cui during a special practicum. It was for already well-established archeologists – directors, vice directors, and high-ranking officials – to learn a series of new skills. Cui was the sole representative of her *danwei* among the other 'students.' When invited to drink and stay up late, which these 'students' did every night of the practicum (three months long), she simply could not. She made an appearance, drank a little, and ate some food but did not think she ought to remain when the men really got to drinking, so she left at around 11 p.m. The party would go on until 2 or 3 a.m., at which point the 'students,' all of whom had access to considerable resources, would get around to suggesting collaborative projects with each other; some of these projects were archeological, while others were meant to enrich the several *danwei* involved by creating a tourist site or undertaking a hotel venture. Without Cui present, her *danwei* had no chance to join these ventures. As a result, the twenty or so people whom she represented collectively lost the opportunities that a man would potentially have been able to garner for them. Having observed how much money archeologists are capable of making if they put effort into collaborations with other *danwei*, were I a *danwei* director, under no circumstances would I send a woman (whether or not I respected her) to represent my *danwei* at this kind of practicum. Too many opportunities that affect too many people would be thereby missed.

Is this Cui's personal fault? Is it just that Cui cannot drink as much as other women? A woman is capable of at least some drinking. There is even a traditional saying, *nuzi he ban ping, zou tian xia,* that means, 'If a woman can manage to drink half a bottle [of hard alcohol], she can go anywhere under heaven [move freely in society].' This adage indicates the importance of drinking to being able to 'go anywhere.' At the same time, since she need only drink half a bottle (the standards are lowered for her), this proverb implies that it is so rare for a woman to drink that the normal standards are suspended to give her a chance. Since standards have to be lowered, the further implication is that women are only rarely part of the drinking culture.

Part of the sex-gender confusion that I created was my ability to drink and win at drinking games. Since I was able to drink and was well behaved at banquets (in the sense of being willing to engage in toasting and drinking games), I became a kind of honorary man. Could I not then be trusted to hold up my end of a reciprocal mixed-tie relationship like a man? Indeed, my offer to drink on behalf of a teacher was often accepted, suggesting that the rules can be bent for women if they agree to participate in these rituals. After all, it is not as if the men are doing it because they enjoy it, so requiring women to do it whether they like it or not is no more or less of a burden than that already placed on men. Many women whom I spoke to were also clearly capable of drinking half a bottle of alcohol. Moreover, they were evidently conscious of the importance of banquet behaviour and could describe exactly what they must do to be well received. So, one might well ask, why do they not just do it?

My female colleagues replied, with some asperity, that I was a foreigner and was in China for only a short time. My performance among these men and women did not affect my own future. But for Chinese female archeologists, the opinions of these men – and of other women – do affect their lives. Since a woman's sole route to any kind of authority and autonomy comes from invoking the junior-senior contract through the perpetuation of traditional notions of the weak and needy female, that woman must remain heavily invested in looking and acting like a proper woman. A 're-spectable' woman simply does not smoke, drink, or stay up late with rowdy, drunken men. If a woman were to fail to live up to the stereotype of proper womanhood by trying to engage in these strategies, then so many of her other priorities, especially those of being a good wife, mother, and daughter of her class, would be unattainable.

A female archeologist trying to negotiate a contract by acting like a man is a similar situation to a person trying to act like someone of a different class: she is condemned by colleagues and leaders alike – the very people with whom she needs to maintain good relations – for being so impertinent as to try to step out of her natural role. The woman has authority in certain areas of life by virtue of being a woman; at the same time, her sex precludes her from ever being seen as compatible or trustworthy and, therefore, from gaining the considerable authority that comes from being such a person. There are thus strong incentives for her to be satisfied with her authority in the traditional arenas open to women, the family and children, and dis-incentives to stop her from attempting to extend that authority.

More importantly, however, there are strong disincentives for her superi-ors – workplace director or teacher – to send her into a situation in which the future of the *danwei* depends on her ability to make contacts with other people. It is a self-fulfilling prophecy: since she is clearly perceived to be unable to engage in the strategies of creating, maintaining, or intensifying relations among either a cohort-like group or in a junior-senior contract, she is never positioned in such a way that she can either show herself to be capable or accumulate the experience and training needed to learn how to engage in such strategies. Moreover, since she has not been given these opportunities, it is likely that she does not have access to the resources, material or immaterial, that would make her a valuable and welcomed mem-ber of a group. Even if she does, in fact, have access to those resources, it is difficult indeed for her to perform her access or to have her performance perceived as intended, much less believed. If she herself is not valued or welcomed, then by association any group that she represents cannot be either. It would be a foolish *danwei* director indeed who chose a woman as his representative.

Certain boys, because of their special needs, can be considered as incon-venient and useless as girls. A disabled or otherwise physically impaired male student will be removed from the archeology program faster than any female student. More interesting, however, is that many non-Han minority students are also not particularly welcome. Hui people, for example, are problematic because they do not eat pork and have other special dietary needs. Being a 'good' Hui means that a student cannot be as flexible in his needs as archeologists presumably need to be. The essential nature of many minorities is therefore assumed to conflict with being an archeologist. Nevertheless, minority men have become archeologists by finding jobs in their home regions since it is assumed that they can get their dietary or ritual needs more easily in those regions. If only there were a home region for women, where they could be perceived as being trustworthy, compatible, and having authority such that they could be promoted to high positions in the *danwei* hierarchy that, in an ever-reinforcing spiral, can lead to success in archeology.

Change and Women

Given how much leadership depends on the actions of others, it is to be expected that the leaders of archeological or official *danwei* are rarely women. I have discovered, however, that exceptions may be found in *danwei* at the county-seat level – or even as high as the provincial level, but in the less important (archeologically speaking) provinces. Interestingly, it is at the highest and the lowest bureaucratic levels where the leader is, without exception, male. I suggest that this is because, at the lowest levels, daily interaction with local peasants is absolutely a necessity. At those levels, a female director or official needs to overcome serious problems of kinship ties to the peasant workers. If she is actually related to any male peasant or local official, then she is by definition inferior to him. At the same time, peasant banqueting culture is harsh and heavy on the drinking and eating. A proper peasant woman could not engage in the kinds of activities considered proper for a man of her class and maintain any sense of propriety among her own kin and neighbours. In contrast, in middle-level *danwei*, the *danwei* is somewhat removed from the kin networks of countryside, and the female leader can send male archeologists to the country on her behalf.

As for provincial-level *danwei* and higher, I suspect that women are unwanted as leaders because the *danwei* is important enough to be considered a representative *danwei* of the province to the rest of China or even of China as a whole to the outside world. Unlike middle-level *danwei*, whose social networks extend only up to the provincial-level *danwei* members, higher-level *danwei* leaders must interact with leaders from all over the country. Women's agency, in the sense of how women relate to their reputation and the resources that it represents, does not allow a woman to engage in the mutually beneficial strategies of positioning that would give others incentives to engage with her.

Things have not always been so starkly different for men and women. Older female archeologists wax nostalgic about a past in which women's and men's styles of being in the world were not so markedly different from one another as they are now. There are many more older female archeologists than younger ones in China. These older archeologists all went to school in the 1950s when Mao emphasized female equality a great deal more than during later years. At that time, women made up only about 10 percent of the undergraduate archeology students, yet nearly all of them became full, professional, and excavating archeologists. Nowadays, in contrast, women make up at least 50 percent if not more of the undergraduate class – because most men are entering economics or science departments *(jike)*, leaving the impractical studies of history and other disciplines of the humanities *(wenke)* to women – yet few if any become excavating archeologists.

In the 1950s, older women note, there was an excitement about and desire to sacrifice for the country. For both women and men, sacrifice meant radically breaking with tradition. This was a heady time: people were highly enthusiastic about the future and their roles in that future. Slogans of the time encouraged people to help all of the oppressed – peasants, youth, and women – to break loose from their traditional roles. Students of the time left their hometowns, even their parents. Even women went off to the most poverty-stricken parts of the country and engaged in 'unwomanly' pursuits such as going to school, getting a job, and otherwise sacrificing their responsibilities to family and children. Even the strangest of practices could be justified if it could be claimed as helping the nation.

As for issues of trust and compatibility, at that time being educated carried a great deal more status than it does today simply because it was much more rare. Local people in the countryside are thus said to have been readily overwhelmed by even a woman's intellectual credentials. During the 1950s, women were also given prominent roles in party, educational, and institutional organizations and thereby actually did wield the connections that do lead to authority in Chinese society. At the same time, the role and the importance of the rule of reciprocity were relatively minimized. Reciprocity and mutuality were taken to hold not between actual people in the present but between people and the nation or, more properly, people and their (imagined) descendants. As one older woman put it, 'Everything was free, and everyone gave each other everything; we were one big family.' When the need for reciprocity and mutuality in relations is minimized, worries about whether one should invest in another are relatively minimized too, and women who have hierarchical positions can be imagined to have the authority supposed to accompany those positions.

How 'true' these nostalgic statements are about the past is not really important. My goal here is mainly to mention these tales as an indication that women are both conscious of the barriers that they face and consciously locate the source of their problems in the rule of reciprocity and the need to be perceived as having access to and redistribution rights in resources. A few women of the older generation were able to become heads of institutes or established scholars in their chosen specialties. In contrast, the situation for younger female archeologists is worsening as capitalism increases the economic hardships faced by the *danwei*. Directors are beoming ever more conservative in choosing new recruits and sending out *danwei* representatives to make the deals that will bring in the cash. In such a context of uncertainty, it is rare that the director will take a chance on a woman.

Female and Male Agency

Now we may understand the all-too-common practice of teachers ignoring or undermining female students. The rhetoric of justification and excuse used against women is encapsulated in the phrase *bu fangbian*, meaning, simply, 'inconvenient.' Inconvenience is a convenient excuse under the circumstances of interdependency. Everyone who lives under conditions of interdependency can well imagine the problems of peasants, bureaucracy, and logistics that make of archeology (and particularly the mounting of an archeological expedition) a complex affair. It is a matter of 'common sense' that no one would want to add more problems to the mix. *Bu fangbian* is therefore a powerful intervention in the judgment of the audience. Male students can be inconvenient as well, of course, but there is always a return on an investment in a male student, where there is no return, or very little, on an investment in a female student.

When a woman acts, she is seen as acting not on her own behalf but only to affect men who can then give her the things she needs or desires. Indeed, if a woman is successful in securing a high-level position – and some have been – the audience will simply assume that her teacher installed her in the post to secure a favour from her father or husband. She can thus be seen as an instrument to be used by herself and others to affect (to enhance or attack the reputations of) men, but unfortunately she cannot use herself or her position to enhance her own reputation directly.

When a man acts, in contrast, he both affects the reputations of others joined to him in junior-senior contracts or cohort-like relations and protects, grooms, and enhances his own reputation. His actions are generative of resources for himself, in the form of an enhanced reputation, as well as for others connected to him. As we saw among teachers and students, a teacher positions a student in order to enhance the student's reputation, which, by association, can reflect well on the teacher; the student, for his part, acts to enable the teacher, whose fame, by association, will reflect well on the student. Male agency is thus mutually enhancing, and men have incentives to enable and position each other. They will even cooperate in the arts of conversion: a man will sacrifice something that he has or wants (e.g., an opportunity to publish an article or go back to school for a graduate degree) in the present to place someone else in a senior or materially better-off position in the hope that the other person's success will recursively benefit him in the future. Women break that implicit mutual contract between people: no matter how much a man helps a woman, she will never achieve the kind of reputation from which he can benefit by association.

The comparison of male and female agency reveals how agency inheres in the eyes of the audience and is fundamentally tied to who a person is (or is perceived to be). Agency here means the power to make successful claims about who one is in the eyes of the audience-that-matters. As we saw in Chapter 5, credentials cannot be changed, but they can be manipulated by various arts of conversion and reinterpretation. Unfortunately, such arts require access to the resources that can seduce the audience into complying. Women are prejudged to lack access to resources and therefore thwarted before they even begin to seduce the audience; in contrast, the success of the oligarch is enormously enabled because the audience, in hearing of his history and background, will simply assume – even without tangible proof – that he has access to all the most desirable resources.

8
The Pursuit of Happiness

We ought to have food prepared against their arrival ... Once
they've had a good meal, they'll be in the mood to issue the usual
rebel proclamation stating that they intend the populace no harm.

There's nothing wrong with feasting them, but Yaozong, my esteemed
elder brother, see to it that you don't get your name linked up with
theirs! Let the village headman arrange the matter of the feast.

Just as you say! By the by, Master Yangsheng, could you write the two
characters OBEDIENT SUBJECT on a poster to tack up on my gate?

Don't do anything like that just yet ... While it's true that one can't
risk incurring the anger of such rebels, it is also true that one shouldn't
get too close to them either. Way back when the Long Hair rebels
came, on occasion even OBEDIENT SUBJECT posters didn't save the
homes of the people who put them up. And then when the government armies returned to the area, the families who had put them up
were in serious trouble.

– Lu Xun, Remembrances of the Past

The Achievement – and Appeal – of Orderly Life

Master Yangsheng, an intellectual asked for advice by his illiterate companion, points out a key difficulty with Yaozong's plan to put the characters
OBEDIENT SUBJECT on his gate: one must be judicious in determining whom
to obey in any given situation. Whether of rebel or government, authority
can change suddenly and unpredictably. Rather than being defeated by
uncertainty, however, the master relies on history to support his assumption that the government will, as it always has before, rout the rebels and
return to power. Indeed, history tells us that rebels are as predictable as bad

weather: their acts, and the response by the government, have an orderly progression. As the master intellectual so artfully teaches us, then, we may take refuge from the uncertainties and maddeningly profuse particulars of a given situation by keeping our eyes on the larger, soothingly predictable patterns of social interaction and exchange that can be discerned in past experience. The lessons of history, that the long-haired rebels will be forced to retreat as they always have before, bestows order on any situation. Order endows us with the capacity to distinguish between friend and foe so central to the strategies of reciprocity and the pursuit of mutually beneficial relations.

At the beginning of this book, I asked why unjust systems persist, and the several answers are now available to us. All systems are unjust, and the system of obedient autonomy is no different. What differs are the strategies and structures that make up the system. Let us compare, in exaggerated form for effect, the injustices of the systems of orthopraxy and orthodoxy. We may begin with the pursuit of happiness. As defined in American civics, the pursuit of happiness implies that all citizens have the 'fundamental right to act independently, as long as they do not interfere with the rights of others.'[1] In contrast, the pursuit of happiness as defined among Chinese archeologists in an uncertain world is the right to an orderly set of well-defined role relations, bureaucratic hierarchies, and identity stereotypes that provide the foundations for strategies of obedient autonomy.

Although the right to act independently is protected by the American system of government, achievement of the American Dream of an independent lifestyle is nevertheless difficult for the ordinary citizen. The citizen must struggle against the significant pressures to conform that she faces in all aspects of social life beginning in kindergarten. Fortunately, she is both aided and impelled in her struggle for self-actualization by the common-sense discourses that place a high value on individualism, provide stories of success or failure that can be used as models to emulate or warnings of potential pitfalls, and link individualism to a variety of other highly valued characteristics or social outcomes (success in career and family). She is also assisted by self-help, pop psychology, and other industries aimed at supporting individuals in their quest to align inner belief with outer action. Likewise, her social context tells her what success should look like and provides her with strategies to achieve it. Finally, even if her actions are considered mistaken by friends and family, if she can insist that she 'did it her way,' then, at the very least, she has available a rhetoric of the 'honour' and 'hard choices' of the rugged individual to justify and excuse her choices.

The right to an orderly life is similarly protected by the Chinese system of government, yet the achievement of the Chinese Dream of an orderly life is extremely difficult for the average archeologist. He must struggle with indications that life is not as ordered or as certain as it is said to be, that authority and hierarchy are not necessarily aligned in the way that they ought to be, that the bureaucracies are too multiple to be truly effective as a system of control, and that one's actions are not always understood in the same way by one's interlocutors or the audience-that-matters. A person must intervene in the opinions of others to protect his own reputation and identity. When one depends on the maintenance of order to protect one's reputation, to receive the benefits of the praise of others, and to ward off the attacks of one's enemies, the achievement of order becomes paramount. Fortunately, he is assisted in his pursuit of order by common-sense discourses such as the doctrine of similarity, the intellectual's burden, and the judgment of history. An archeologist's experiences of crossing the urban-rural divide and of the brute complexities of interdependence that by rights should reveal these discourses as being nothing more than wishful thinking instead encourage, further entrench, and, indeed, make them socially true.

A first answer to our question of the persistence of systems, then, is that any given discourse is intertwined with other highly valued discourses in a way that creates the conditions, supplies the goals, and offers the strategies for the successful attainment of those goals. Thus it is that, in the face of the benefits bestowed by order under Chinese conditions of interdependence, the system of US republican democracy, founded on a theory of competitive, rugged independence, seems to be not only entirely alien but also counterproductive. The pursuit of mutually beneficial relations is immeasurably more efficacious, provides a relatively greater and more immediate form of protection, and is relatively more permanent – not least because there exists a will to believe that it will not change, but also because it is underpinned by so many other valued discourses in society – than a judicial system that can be changed by the chairman's fiat or an executive and legislative assembly that changes process and composition whenever the political winds shift.

Given the interdependence among discourses, detaching one part of the system – say the actions of Chinese archeologists – from the rest of the sociocultural context for analysis or evaluation is in effect like removing an artifact from its provenience. An artifact without context can tell us little about past lifeways, though it may take on new meaning (valued art piece, consumer item to show status) as it is bought and sold in the antiquities market. When one part of a cultural system is separated from its context, it, too, takes on different meanings. In the archeological context, those meanings seem to reflect more about the strategies of Euro-American professional careerism, in which careers are made by publishing critical articles of each other as well as 'the other,' than about the desire to understand the Chinese context.

A second answer is that discourses are not only intertwined but also ingeniously structured such that an attack on any one inevitably strikes at what is most important to the participants: autonomy. Whatever form autonomy might take, it is always about being able to predict what others are doing and thinking, plan one's own behaviour, and first define what success would look like and then have a chance at achieving it. It is therefore valuable and must be protected at all costs: why, then, would one be surprised at the emotion engendered by anything that appears to threaten the conditions that make autonomy possible? Just as North Americans can become angry or fearful at perceived erosions of their civil liberties, so too can the Chinese student become alarmed when his teacher does not follow expectations or the Chinese intellectual become anxious when his juniors (peasants, younger colleagues) ignore or criticize him. What is being threatened is not civil liberties or hierarchical junior-senior relations per se, although it begins there, but the autonomy that such conditions entail. Under orthopraxy, the system persists, then, because it is replete with the widely enforced, coercive, conflicting, and hierarchical rules that lead to autonomy.

Systems lead not only to autonomy but also to creativity. They are, through acts of will, habit, and tradition (the process of socialization), the most effective tools to guide one's own behaviour and interpret the actions of others. Yet the mere fact that these tools exist does not necessitate the notion that behaviour (or belief) must therefore be predictable, controllable, or uncreative. 'System' is a misleading word that appears to entail consistency and control, but after learning how truly difficult it is to impose order, even by people trained as well as Chinese archeologists in the imposition of order, it would simply not do to imagine that people live anything but fractured, conflicting, and multiple lives. No system of social behaviour is so strong that it can force all people to inhabit it in the same way; indeed, the more it attempts to create prescriptive rules, the more tools and materials it provides for people to combine in interesting ways for their own purposes.

Systems also produce individuality. The inconsistencies of a cultural system, particularly the disturbing capacity of categories to dissolve and reform depending on point of view, mean that a person is unlikely to have experienced any particular role or status in the same way as anyone else. Social characteristics, roles, scripts, and contexts combine to create new opportunities for action. Individuality – in the sense of a unique bundle of characteristics shared by no other – of any person, in short, is not *prior* to but instead cannot help but *arise* out of these combinations. A system cannot constrain difference; rather, it produces it. In the Chinese system, then, the three most valuable things – autonomy, creativity, and individuality – arise out of the creation of a semblance of systemic order.[2]

A third answer to our question examines the substantive reasons why intellectuals, in particular, have reason to maintain this unjust system. Intellectuals benefit greatly from the combination of orthopraxy, the rule of reciprocity, the junior-senior contract, and class credentialling. They benefit from being given more agency by the audience-that-matters than the members of other classes and thus the authority to command diverse resources. These resources are not limited to money or status but are more often the resources of identity and reputation that are valuable because they generate further material and immaterial benefits under conditions of interdependence.

Yet, by stating that intellectuals benefit from the system, I do not mean to say that they are involved in cruel Machiavellian plots to maintain their positions of privilege to the detriment of others. More often people are unaware, or only half aware, of their participation in oppressive structures. In short, the intertwining of habits, traditions, and discourses and the strong redistributive power of the law of reciprocity creates a situation too complex to sustain the theory that a coven of brilliant masterminds preserves control over Chinese society. I might add that the other theory often advanced (by both Chinese and non-Chinese, though for very different reasons) to explain the persistence of the Chinese system, that there is a failure in the essential Chinese character that leads Chinese to passivity, is also not what is meant here.

Both the 'Machiavellian mastermind' and the 'passive Oriental' theories utterly miss the most important aspect of the system of orderly orthopraxy: its redistributive properties. The system is an ingenious one of checks and balances, where in order to receive, one must give something away. Even those at the top of the heap, so to speak, must scramble to maintain their positions and, more interestingly, doing so more often than not requires raising up others in an attempt to reap the benefits of being associated with a successful person. Given the potential for creativity and autonomy provided by the (seemingly) rigid rules and roles that govern the system, it should come as no suprise that order, with all its generative properties, should be so appealing. Since order is the foundation of all potential strategies to be used in the bartering of resources among and between cohort-like groups, there are strong incentives to maintain, establish, and protect order.

Thinking further about the establishment of order in the face of disorder, I am strangely reminded of Clifford Geertz's discussion of interest theory and strain theory.[3] Geertz separated the two, saying that one was more or less the ideology of what people do (especially as promoted by economists) and that the other was more or less the reality of how people feel as they make choices in everyday life. Interest theory assumes that people have perfect information and make rational decisions based on the principle of self-interest. For Geertz, this model of the world makes unacceptable assumptions about the nature of the individual: first, that a person is an individual, distinct from others and capable of making decisions based only on his own needs and wants, and second, that he is utilitarian and thinks only in terms of profit and loss. A world of people based on such a model can only be manipulative and competitive. The model thus fails to explain why people might cooperate in mutually beneficial relations.

Geertz then posits a 'strain theory' as an opposing worldview. Rather than pursuing rational interests, he suggests, people act so as to flee anxiety. Their actions are reactions to situations perceived as incomplete, disordered, or not in equilibrium such that there is a discontinuity among norms, roles, concepts, and institutions. Structural inconsistencies are experienced as personal insecurity: since the person does not know where she stands in the present, she therefore cannot predict or plan for the future. To remedy the situation, a person acts, in Geertz's metaphor, much like a doctor attempting to cure a disease. After the disease makes the first move, the doctor reacts as best she can to stop its progress or reverse its damage. She has at hand the skills learned in school, but she will do what she must, including combining and even devising new methods, to cure the disease. She will even collaborate with another doctor, even if he is a potential competitor for position and fame, to stop the disease. The doctors' cooperation can create associative benefits for both of them. Thus, anxiety and uncertainty are seen the driving force behind the creation of cooperative relations.

Geertz's goal in presenting these two theories was to denigrate interest theory and promote strain theory as the 'correct way' of understanding social relations. In the case of Chinese archeologists, however, it appears that both theories are perfectly applicable. It is merely that strain (uncertainty) is prior to and creates the ideological foundations necessary for self-interested, individualistic behaviour. In an attempt to escape the uncertainties of social life, the problems of interdependence, and the logical inconsistencies of orthopraxy, members of Chinese society have cooperated in the creation and maintenance of order in the form of hierarchy, role relations, and identity categories. Since identity itself is fractured under orthopraxy, the establishment of order takes on additional importance when it is understood to permit the protection and maintenance of reputation and the interpretation and judgment of the reputations of others. In other words, the establishment of order allows an actor to act *as if* she is able to calculate, predict, and explain everyone else's actions accurately and, most reassuringly, that they can and will do the same for her.[4]

Geertz's strain and interest theories, in other words, are hardly opposed. Uncertainty encourages the establishment of both order and the illusion of knowing enough about a situation to make rational and self-interested choices. Strangely, Geertz imagines in a remarkably one-dimensional fashion that 'self-interest' must necessarily produce cutthroat competition. In this conflation of self-interest and competition, Geertz is mistaken because self-interested calculations can include both cooperation and competition. Surely it is merely a matter of circumstance whether cooperation would provide more benefit than competition. In the context of orthopraxy and in light of the rule of reciprocity, at least, a person's best bet is to combine strategies of cooperation and competition by promoting relations of mutual benefit among one's own cohort-like groups and using the combined resources of that group to attack the bureaucratic position or authority of others. Fei Xiaotong puts it succinctly: 'A man who sees the world only through human relations is inclined to be conservative, because in human relations the end is always mutual adjustment.'[5]

Interestingly, and despite the best hopes of the orthodox, the arrival of capitalism – that extreme example of interest theory – will both extend and heighten the strategies of obedient autonomy and likely make the achievement of order that much easier.[6] Capitalism is an economic worldview that thrives on inequality, hierarchy, and the existence of both rules and concerted attempts to evade those rules. An effective method for the reduction of uncertainty and the circumvention of rules is the creation of transnational corporations with cohort-like networks that extend through a variety of diverse national contexts and economic sectors and are based on close mixed-tie relations of both instrument and affect. Capitalists, in other words, are already well practised in combining the performance of submission with the strategic execution of creative plans and projects. Far from requiring the structures of democracy, orthodoxy, or even a Weberian 'Protestant work ethic,' capitalism is thus both conducive to and enabled by strategies of obedient autonomy.

In sum, while an outside observer may not have the background needed to understand how a pile of broken potsherds can bestow influence, how the intricacies of toasting practices at banquets can make or break friendships, or even how those friendships must always be simultaneously emotionally and instrumentally satisfying, that lack of experience should not prevent the outsider from understanding that if there are strategies that make life easier and bring material and immaterial satisfaction, then of course people will continue to engage in such practices. Nor should it be difficult to understand that, in acting in this manner, in which short-term and traditionally recognizable benefits are gained, people may not recognize how in the long term they not only perpetuate the privileges that they might have but also inadvertently reinscribe the conditions of oppression inflicted on both themselves and others. Nor, really, should it be too difficult to understand that the response to the trade-offs is weighted toward short-term benefit rather than some imagined social change that may or may not alleviate oppressions as intended.

The achievement of orderly life requires strategies to maintain order in the face of disorder; the appeal of orderly life arises out of the benefits – particularly in the form of autonomy – that it bestows. If change in this complex system is desired – and there are certainly many aspects that Chinese archeologists, women, and peasants alike would like to see changed –

then what might constitute that change, and how it might be accomplished, cannot be understood without reference to both the incentives that guide action and the discourses that interweave to make the foundation for action. There is something woefully insular about the contention commonly espoused by those under orthodoxy that 'other people' are morally obligated to pursue actions despite the fact that they are very likely to increase life's difficulties. What if those 'other people' are so interdependent that one person's actions affect innumerable others? How is it moral, exactly, to act to increase harm to other people? Change under any system will occur only if people are motivated to seek old benefits in new ways, or new benefits in old ways, in order to redefine the meaning of life, liberty, and the pursuit of happiness.

Notes

Chapter 1: Autonomy and Autonomies

1 The word *foreigner* translates the term *waiguo ren* used by Chinese to describe any non-Chinese person.

2 The word *peasant* is, for better or for worse, the traditional English translation of *nongmin* (farmer). It is not intended as insulting but appears to have been chosen to indicate the similarities between the feudal social structure and the lives of Chinese farmers.

3 See Chen Xingcan 1997 or the *Encyclopedia of Chinese Archeology* for the history of the discipline.

4 My citizenship is Canadian, and I position myself as Canadian if asked; nevertheless, in China people preferred to characterize me as American. For race and nationality in China, see Blum 2001 and Dikötter 1992, 1997.

5 Including, as will be discussed below, the rule of reciprocity, the doctrine of similarity, and the tenacious maintenance of class boundaries.

6 Austin 1975. See Lakoff 1987; Lakoff and Johnson 1980; and Shohat and Stam 1994 for more detailed examinations of the baggage that words may carry. See Pred 1990; Blu 1980; and Schneider and Bloch 1971 for excellent and telling studies of the creative and productive properties of words.

7 In the present era of identity politics in Europe and America, the ideal of the 'autonomous individual' is being discarded in favour of the feminist, psychoanalytic, and/or ethnic studies concept of the relational or collective theory of individual subjectivity (among others, Lacan 1968; Irigaray 1985; Strathern 1988; Trinh 1989; Collins 1990; Haraway 1991; Schor 1994; Harding 2000). It has been argued that the vision of the 'rugged individual' pervading Western thought is inherently male, educated, upper middle class, and most often white. The requirements of financial independence and a moral certitude based on claims of universal and objective principles do not adequately encompass the social experiences or goals of many social actors even in Euro-American contexts. In the quest, then, to supply different visions of autonomous social interaction, one would expect that the trope of the individual, as well as the philosophies of democracy, capitalism, and the social contract that it underpins, would need to be dissolved or decentred. Unfortunately, the high value placed on the themes of resistance and an identity based on distinction remains remarkably common as both goal and metaphor in the struggle of historically underrepresented groups for increased sociopolitical and economic power. As a result, their struggle to become part of the dominant discourse of rugged individualism is one of assimilation rather than creation of a different vision of identity and autonomy. See Shohat and Stam 1994 for an excellent review of these issues.

8 And assumes, moreover, that the individual has an unchanging essence stable over time and unaffected by social context.

9 Definition taken from the *Merriam-Webster Online Dictionary* 2002.

10 See Schneider 1984 for an excellent critique of these four tired categories. See Ruskola 2000 and Christiansen and Zhang 1998 for discussions of the differences in Chinese categorizations.

11 See de Certeau 1984; Althusser 1984, 1969 (interpellation); and Gramsci 1994 (hegemony) as further examples. See also Wittfogel 1957. The work of Tönnies, Durkheim, and Maine presents similar visions. Lucian Pye (1985; 1988) offers an excellent example of an orthodox critique of China, filled with orthodox vitriol against Chinese bureaucracy.

12 Herzfeld 1992.

13 Foucault 1976, 1977. The pronoun *he* fits this worldview alarmingly well.

14 That a single form of obedience, one requiring the alignment of inner belief and outer action, is upheld as one of the highest values in religious and military groups does not help its reputation among Euro-American intellectuals in general, who pride themselves on their critical stance toward the military and who have, since at least Voltaire, maintained a deep suspicion of the opiate of religion. It is also not popular among female feminist scholars, who have engaged in considerable struggle to dispel the idea that women ought, as a natural law, to be 'obedient' to men, husbands, and sons. See Butler 1990 and Strathern 1988 for attempts to replace the distinct individual with the relational 'individual' that still display the agonistic and iconoclastic suspicion of state projects and praise resistant persons over those who collude.

15 Weber 1983; Wittfogel 1957. See Said 1979.

16 Hastrup 1985; Douglas 1986; Said 1979.

17 Anthropology is an eager student of boundary crossing as well as of the relationship between political power and identity. Topics include ethnic boundary maintenance (the legacy of Barth 1969); boundary maintenance within as well as between groups (Douglas 1986, 1992; Bourdieu 1984); and studies of consumption (Douglas 1996; Miller 1998) or apprenticeship studies (Willis 1977; Coy 1989); power and ethnic and identity boundaries (Althusser 1984, 1969; Gramsci 1994; Strathern 1988; Jackson 1998); self-other boundary maintenance and its effects on ethnography (Clifford and Marcus 1986; Stocking 1991; Rosaldo 1993; di Leonardo 1998). One could go on indefinitely, for at some level all anthropology is about the negotiation of social relations across boundaries.

18 Compare Kohl 1998; Kohl and Fawcett 1995; Trigger 1984, 1986; Shaw 1986; Fotiadis 1995; Schmidt and Patterson 1995; El-Haj 1998; Pluciennik 1998; and Pai 1999. See also *World Archeology* 13, 2 (1981) and *Antiquity* 73, 281 (1999) for symposia on perceptions of 'foreign archeologies.' As for Anglo-American perspectives on Anglo-American archeology, there are extensive discussions on topics related to cultural resource management (CRM), archeological ethics, site protection, and government policy (e.g., Turnbull 1976; Fowler 1987; Potter and Leone 1987; Tainter 1987; Miller et al. 1989; Neumann 1991; Pinsky 1992; Elia 1993; Blakey 1997). Many more articles are devoted to how Euro-American culture – ideas of rugged individualism, freedom, legalism, racism, capitalism, nationalism, or progress and efficiency, to name just a few – have affected archeological explanation, writing, and practice (e.g., Lowenthal 1985; Patterson 1986; Blakey 1987, 1994; Dennell 1990; Trigger 1989; Paynter 1989; McGuire and Paynter 1991; Pinsky and Wylie 1989; Shanks and Tilley 1989; Baker and Thomas 1990; Hodder 1991, 1998, 1999; Claassen 1992; McGuire 1992; Shanks 1993; Shanks and McGuire 1996; Leone et al. 1987; Kohl 1998; Kehoe 1998; Boswell and Evans 1999). When discussing themselves among themselves, anglophone archeologists appear eager to point out how their society and government affect archeology. When speaking about 'other' archeology, the tone is remarkably different. See Borneman 1995 for a parallel discussion of American sociocultural anthropology and its relation to American foreign policy; Herzfeld 1987 for a discussion of the complicity of sociocultural anthropologists in the perpetuation of stereotypes; and Dominguez 1994 for a discussion of the complicity of American academics in race and class hierarchies internal to American society. Finally, see Wu 1996 for a Chinese archeologist's very different take on the issue of culture and archeology and Chen and Lin 1996 more generally for Chinese anthropologists' understanding of the role of their discipline.

19 These tendencies are not limited to archeologists. Nevertheless, some non-archeologists are beginning to recognize that Chinese academics 'do things differently.' For example,

Weatherley 1999 makes an offhand remark while discussing human rights discourse and notes that some Chinese academics stay within the system yet still manage to push at the restrictions with some success. See also Farquhar and Hevia 1993 for a critique of the relations between American culture, politics, and the historiography that they produce about China. See also Wang and Li 1991 for a Taiwanese critique of international Sinology. See Herzfeld 1987 about the complicity of anthropologists in the perpetuation of stereotypes.

20 Hodder 1989; Tilley 1990, 1999; Shanks and Tilley 1989; Dilley 1999.

21 Appadurai 1986. See also Wittgenstein 1979; Dilley 1999; Shohat and Stam 1994; Bloor 1987; Stocking 1991; and Royce 1982.

22 Latour and Woolgar 1979. See also the ethnographic studies produced by Traweek 1988; Gusterson 1996; and Reid and Traweek 2000; the more theoretical approach to similar issues by Latour 1993; Tambiah 1990; and Douglas 1986; Franklin 1995; and Cussins 2000 for overviews. For archeological versions of the sociology of archeology, see Hodder 1999 and Preucel and Hodder 1996 for excellent reviews.

23 See Argyrou 1999 for a discussion of similar issues.

24 'For now we see through a glass, darkly; but then face to face: now I know in part; but then shall I know even as also I am known' (1 Corinthians 13: 12).

25 I.e., Binford 1962. See Chinese archeologists tackling similar issues in Wang Changhua 1997 and Wu Chunmin 1996. See Wylie 2002 for an excellent overview of the theoretical and philosophical issues involved.

26 For more on the importance of history to Chinese intellectuals, see Qian Liqun 1999; Xu Ming 1994; Tu Wei-ming 1993; and particularly Huang Minlan 1995 and Li Renkai 1992. The importance of history in the present is not limited to communist China. See, for example, the controversy over history textbooks in Taiwan and the proper role of history in the education of young people on culture and nationalism. A representative sample of articles can be found in volume 120 of the journal *Tang-tai* (1997).

27 Much has been written about intellectuals in China, mostly from a historical standpoint that describes either their changing relationship with Chinese politics (e.g., Goldman 1981; Buckley 1991; Goldman et al. 1987; Franklin 1989; Barlow 1991; Rai 1991; Cherrington 1997; Mok 1998; Ben 1999; Tang 1999; Shi 1988) or the changes in particular ideas or schools of thought over time (Shapiro and Liang 1986; Liu James 1988; Bol 1992; Fu Keng 1993; Yu Taifa 1994; Lin Chunmin 1993; He Xiaoming 1997; Huang Ping 1994; Liu James 1988; Tsao 1984; Zheng Hailin 1990; Zhang Zhizhong 1994). Very little has been done, however, from an ethnographic standpoint that looks at how the widely shared notions of behaviours and characteristics appropriate to the stereotypes associated with the class label of 'intellectual' affects social interactions both among archeologists and between archeologists and non-intellectuals (but see interesting ethnographic studies by Yeh 1984; Kitching 1993a, 1993b; Shapiro 1986; Link 1992; Gu 1997, 1999; Zhou 1988; Zheng Yefu 1994; Zhong Yan 1996; a combined Taiwanese, Hong Kongese, and Overseas Chinese take on Chinese [PRC] intellectuals in Tang and Yang 1994; Yang Kuanghan 1994; Zheng Wan 1993; and a critique of the disunification and tension among intellectuals in Jia and Sun 1997).

28 See Wang Ban 1997; Goldman 1981; and Goldman et al. 1987.

29 One of the more famous being the story of Hai Rui, a tale of official virtue in the face of incorrect rule that purportedly began the Cultural Revolution when it was retold at a sensitive political moment by Wu Han. See Fisher 1982 and Sullivan 1990. See Wang Changhua 1997 for an analysis of spring and autumn period intellectuals and politics; see also Yan Buke 1996 and Yu Yingshi 1996 for more historical takes on the same subject.

30 See Liu Xiuming 1997 for historical and modern takes on Confucian scholars, the state, and history. See, especially, Wang Ban 1997; Wang Changhua 1997; and Edward Wang 2001.

31 For more on the responsibilities of those in the present to those who have gone before, see Edward Wang 2001; Wang Shounan 1981; Xu Jilin 1994; and especially Long 1996.

32 The assumption of Chinese intellectuals that their goal is to strengthen the Chinese state is well represented by the changes in attitudes of major thinkers beginning at least by the time of the late-Qing 'Self-Strengthening Movement.' Liang Qichao and Yan Fu were representative in their desire to use whatever notions they could, including Western ideas, to

strengthen China against Western imperialism. Ideas such as human rights and democracy were imported not because of any primary interest in the visions of the individual funda- mental to such ideas but because they were believed to give Westerners the edge. After the Republican experiment began to go wrong, and 'the people' *(renmin)* had become selfish rather than properly seeing that their individual rights are bound up with collective rights, the same thinkers dropped such ideas in preference for authoritarianism. Stricter laws and duties are now heralded as the salvation of the Chinese state and a corrective to the ex- cesses of freedom that had led the people astray. See Weatherley 1999, 72. See also Edward Wang 2001 and Zhang Mengyang 1997 for more detail on Lu Xun's vision of the appropri- ate relationship between the intellectual and the state and Jia Chunzeng 1996 and Zheng Hailin 1990 for a series of investigations into the involvement of intellectuals and mod- ernization. See also Wang Shounan 1981; Tang Tsou 1983; Wu Bingyuan 1991; Huang Ping 1999; Hook 1996; Cherrington 1997; Cai 1992; Xu Jilin 1994; Cheng 1994; Fewsmith 2001; and Liu Meiru 2001 for more discussions on the mutual (and changing) influences between intellectuals and the state. See Laodong Renshi Bu 1985 for CCP policies on intellectuals.

33 English-Lueck 1997; Tsao 1984.

34 Tu Wei-ming 1994; English-Lueck 1997; Goldman et al. 1987; Ben Xu 1999; Bo Yand 1991; Fu Keng 1993; Gu Edward 1999; Liu James 1988; Mok 1998; Shapiro 1986.

35 See more discussion in Wang Shounan 1981; Lin Chunmin 1993; Huang Ping 1999; Cai 1992; and Jin Dakai 1971. For a Chinese mainland take on whether or not the Taiwanese still shoulder the burdens appropriate to intellectuals, at least in literary circles, see Yang Kuanghan 1994. See also the differences in responsibilities ascribed to and undertaken by female intellectuals in Taiwan in the March 1987 edition of *Chungkuo Lun-t'an*. For a re- minder that just because a group of people may formally espouse the same political theory does not mean that they cannot find ways to argue, see Sullivan 1990 (about communist intellectuals) or Ma Shu-yun 1993 (about dissidents). See also Halpern 1988 and Kitching 1993a, 1993b, for discussions of the role of scientists in politics.

36 Euro-American intellectuals share, or at least used to, a similarly high opinion of them- selves. See Jacoby 1987.

37 See Zheng Hailin 1990 and Yeh Ch'i-cheng 1984 for more on the high expectations of intellectuals' moral qualities.

38 For more on Chinese scholars' take on the proper relationship between intellectuals and the state, see Zhou Yushan 1988; Huang Ping 1994; Ye Sixun 1984; Xu Jilin 1994; Su Bingqi 1994; Wu Chunmin 1996; and Jiang Zukang 1988. See Zhang Chun 1977 for a Taiwanese- produced, highly exaggerated take on the orthodox CCP vision of the appropriate relation- ship between history and the state. Zhang makes it clear that, in his opinion, the most orthodox mainland scholars still maintain their integrity in the face of pressure by the CCP and even as they follow the directives of the party (67, speaking of the *mei'e* [a kind of plum] flower that hides undiscovered in the snowdrifts of January yet flourishes and puts forth a lovely smell).

39 Chen Xingcan 1997 provides a description of pre-1949-era archeologists and their back- grounds and relationships with the Republican and Communist parties, while Tong Enzheng 1994 examines archeology and archeologists from 1949 to 1979. See also Von Falkenhausen 1995.

40 In their willingness to become involved in social and political affairs, archeologists fall squarely into the category of intellectuals often called 'public intellectuals.' The voices of these intellectuals have had an impact in both China and Taiwan as well as in Singapore. For more information on the 'intellectuals' burden,' see Yang Wenhu 1994; Yang Xianbang 1991; Yang Guoqiang 1997; Wei Fuming 1996; Hung 1988; Tu Cheng-Sheng 2000; Tu Wei- ming 1994; Yu Yingshi 1997; and Halpern 1988. See Guangming Ribao 1989 and Jin Tong 1994 for collections of articles and papers by Chinese intellectuals and Yu Yingshi 1991 for a pessimistic view that Chinese intellectuals are losing their power in society and politics. See Jacoby 1987 for a discussion of the American version of the public intellectual. See Wright 2001 on student activism in China and Taiwan. See, finally, O'Brien 1996 for an- other take on the interaction between intellectuals and the state.

41 It cannot be emphasized enough that what looks like resistance may not have the motivations or goals of what looks like resistance in some other context. Once again, the analogy is to an artifact: found in one context, a cup is a bit of daily crockery and nothing more; find the same cup on a pedestal in a temple and one's interpretation must change. See Barme 2000 for a refreshing, culturally sensitive, and critical take on Chinese dissidents; see Farquhar and Hevia 1993 for a history of the American search for identity through the study of Chinese culture.

42 Ma Shu-yun 1993; Gu Edward 1999; English-Lueck 1997; Rubie Watson 1994.

43 My position includes the fundamental premise that all scholars, in every country, are affected both consciously and unconsciously by the historical, social, religious, and political contexts in which they work. Their beliefs and agendas are reflected in their work whether they hold positions in the academy or hold government and party jobs: the opposition between 'pure' academia and 'dirty' politics is, in short, spurious.

44 Goffman 1959, 1974; Leach 1954; James 1984.

45 James Watson 1994, 1996; Rubie Watson 1994; Johnson 1989. Note that Leach's 1954 *as if* models and examples of his thought in Leach 1989-90 are similar to orthopraxy, and performance or practice theory more generally is also similar in orientation. See also Goffman 1959, 1974; Bailey 1981, 1983; Bourdieu 1977; Turner 1974, 1988; Pred 1990a; and Butler 1990. For Chinese takes on performance theory, see Wang and Zheng 2000 and Sponsler and Chen 2000.

46 The writings of scholars in political science, law, and business all have their 'social constructivists,' but the greater majority of writings assume the universality of the cherished definitions of the individual, life, liberty, and happiness and the categorization of human activity on which they rest. See also Weatherley 1999.

47 Leach 1954; Goodman 1978; Gadamer 1989. See also Wittgenstein 1979 and Austin 1979. For an excellent discussion, see Karp and Maynard 1983 and Dorfman 1996.

48 Ho 1975; Hu 1944; Hwang 1987; King 1991; Kipnis 1995. Note that the concept of face itself is predicated on the notion that reputation is visible: what is important is the surface of the person's head, how a person is seen, the face he shows to others, not what goes on inside his head. See, especially, Wang Ming-ke 1996.

49 Schneider 1984.

50 Warner 2000; Christiansen and Zhang 1998; Greenhalgh 1994; Solinger 1992; Yang Mayfair Mei-hui 1989; Rubie Watson 1994.

51 Walder 1986; Ruan 1993.

52 Hanks 1996; Briggs 1986; Bourdieu 1977.

53 For performance theory, see Goffman 1959, 1974; Austin 1975, 1979; Leach 1989; Bailey 1981, 1983; Pred 1990a, 1990b; Bourdieu 1977; an ethnographic example in Herzfeld 1985; and Chinese versions in Sponsler and Chen 2000.

54 The friend-friend relation touted by Confucius as one of equality is here seen more as one in which one man is senior to the other in one context but junior to him in another. Rather than being a relation of equality, it is a relation of multiple inequality that, by restraining any one person from having too much power over the other, leads to equality in practice.

55 Foucault 1977.

56 The terminology is classic Mauss 1990. See Raheja 1988 and Strathern 1988.

57 Whenever social relations are discussed in regard to China, the concept of *guanxi* must be mentioned. Social solidarity in China is said to be achieved through the particularistic relations between and among people that are termed *guanxi* networks (Kipnis 1997; Yang Kuanghan 1994; King 1991; Hwang 1987). *Guanxi* has been studied in the tradition of Mauss as a gift-giving economy or as an expression of the universal principle of reciprocity *(bao)* (Kipnis 1997; Yan Yunxiang 1996; Yang Mayfair Mei-hui 1994; Yang Liensheng 1957). It has also been analyzed through the relationship between affect and instrumentality as understood in the concept of *renqing* (King 1991; Yan Yunxiang 1996). Concepts of face and reputation, known in Chinese as *lian* and *mianzi*, have also been addressed (classic texts include Ho 1975; Hu 1944; Kipnis 1995). Mayfair Yang, in the most exhaustive account of *guanxi* yet produced, discusses it as a discipline to be mastered like

any other, a '*guanxi*-ology,' so to speak. For her, it is a tradition of interaction that has built up over the years a set of strategies, ethical orientations, and etiquettes to be followed (Yang Mayfair Mei-hui 1994). Kipnis 1997, on the other hand, disagrees in his theory that it is a modern phenomenon related to the difficult transition from Marxist socialism to capitalism with Chinese characteristics.

58 Needham 1972.
59 See Leach 1954; James 1984 for 'Western' ideas of social truth; and the writings of Confucius and his many commentators for more on the importance of right ritual (orthopraxy) rather than right thought (orthodoxy) (e.g., Tu Wei-ming 1992, 1994).

Chapter 2: The Social Contract

1 Wittgenstein 1979; Douglas 1996; Bourdieu 1984; Appadurai 1986.
2 King 1991; Jun Jing 1996; Yang Mayfair Mei-hui 1994; Yan Yunxiang 1996. See Pye 1985, 1988, for the 'oppression' view.
3 For orthopraxy, see Watson 1993, 1994, 1988 and Johnson 1989.
4 Herzfeld 1985.
5 See Skinner 1992; Sussman 1972; Tanner and Feder 1993; Wang and Zhang 2000; James Watson 1975 for the role of kinship terminology in politics. See Dorfman 1996 for another take on the doctrine of similarity as well as Leach 1954; Barth 1969; and Evans-Pritchard 1969 for ethnographic accounts of various other forms of social truth that affect relations.
6 The *ming'e* are dreaded and dreadful because they are so strict. If there are only fifteen spaces for students from Sichuan province, then the sixteenth student is out of luck, even if his grades are as good as the lucky fifteen.
7 For changes in parent-child relations, see Jun 2000 and Davis and Harrell 1993. For other takes on the socialization process, see Ames et al. 1994, 1998; Hook 1996.
8 The children of the Cultural Revolution generation ranged in age from fifteen to twenty-five at the time of my fieldwork. Many of the archeologist-parents to whom I spoke, then, were in the middle of preparing their children for the university entrance exam or had recent memories of doing so.
9 China has a 6-3-3 educational system (six years primary, three years junior secondary, and three years senior secondary). See Gao 1993. For further discussion of Chinese education, see Lin Jing 1999; Thorgersen 1989; and Tanner and Feder 1993. See also Peterson et al. 2001; Rai 1991
10 See Barlow and Lowe 1987 for similar experiences.
11 As of the last census, published in November 2000, 3.6 percent of the population received a university education; 11.1 percent a senior high school education; 23 percent a junior high school education; and 35 percent elementary education. See Gao 1993.
12 See Shirk 1982 for more on student strategies. See Qian Ning 1997 for Chinese student strategies as foreign students in the United States.
13 As will be discussed in Chapter 3, students must also learn to compete with classmates for the teacher's attention. Suffice it to say here that grades are probably the first and most obvious way to be noticed favourably by the teacher, but of course gender and other social attributes likely come into play. For more on teacher-student relations, see Yang Wenhu 1994.
14 For changes in education in China, see Unger 1982; Petersen et al. 2001.
15 Turner 1974.
16 University 'professor' is the more common term in English, but in Chinese the word that means professor (*jiaoshou*) is rarely used except in times of extreme formality or when foreigners are present. The generic term for teacher, *laoshi*, has the perfect combination of respect and breadth of meaning (it can refer to an actual teacher or simply to someone to whom one wishes to show respect) that allows it to be used in all arenas of daily life. See Yeh 1992 for a Taiwanese take on the roles appropriate to professors.
17 For one thing, these practicum teachers, though still young, are likely to be more important within the discipline of archeology than the cohort teacher. In Chapter 3, I examine the implications of the fact that these teachers, once they have observed students during the practicum, will guide the careers and lives of the students whom they choose as deserving of such assistance.

18 There are good reasons to be worried about 'what can happen' on the excavation, not least of which is that peasant workers attempt to terrorize both teachers and students in order to control them. The intricacies of the archeologist-peasant relationship are examined in detail in Chapter 6.

19 See the discussion of the import of grass versus leather shoes above. For more on class in China, see Rubie Watson 1994.

20 Herzfeld 1985.

21 Rubie Watson 1994.

22 Chapter 3 will raise the issue of moral domestications, while Chapter 4 will examine the use of stereotypes and ideals in the domestication of difference.

23 For more on cohorts in China, see Broaded 1990; Yahuda 1979; Shirk 1982; and Unger 1987. See Jankowiak 1993 and Dutton 1995 for discussions of other forms of community policing.

24 See Lave and Wenger 1991 for an interesting review.

25 Teachers and students would maintain that all students were the same age, despite the often obvious differences in age among the people sitting right in front of me. When this was pointed out, they explained that they meant, in general, all students of the cohort should be the same age; their own cohort was always an exception to the general rule. I never met a cohort in which all students were of the same age.

26 As I mentioned above, only one group, the SoDa students, ever visited any other group, and they had teacher trouble and were therefore an exception.

27 Leach 1954.

Chapter 3: The Rule of Law

1 See Wilson et al. 1981; Sun Ling-kee 1991; Yan Yunxiang 1996; and Yang Mayfair Mei-hui 1994. Compare Holland and Kipnis 1994 and Jackson 1998 on American versions of worrying about exposure to the audience.

2 My reading of discourses relies in the main on Goodman's concept of worlds and the strategies and use of discourse on consumer studies that, in their turn, rely on a Wittgensteinian emphasis on meaning from use and context of use. See also Weatherley 1999 for an interesting comparison of the rhetoric of human rights in Euro-American and Chinese contexts. See also Sponsler and Chen 2000; Tang Xiaobing 1993; Wang Jing 1993; Lydia Liu 1993; Barlow 1993; and a useful overview of anthropological approaches to discourse and language in Parkin 1984.

3 These two discourses are related to those commonly called the 'rule of law' *(fazhi)* and the 'rule of men' *(renzhi)*. That terminology has unfortunately been overused. See Ruskola 2000; Merry 1992; and Mertz 1994. The phrase 'rule of law' has been co-opted to refer only to one perspective on law found only among common law countries and is an ideal vision of an orderly world untainted by interpersonal relations and bias. The ideal persists despite the efforts beginning with Oliver Wendell Holmes through to present-day legal realists to point out how laws are written and cases decided by men, men of a certain race and class, and therefore deserves the term 'rule of men' as much as any other legal system. Rather than wasting time arguing whether some legal system is 'better' than another, as those who use the term 'rule of law' so often want to do, this study simply begins with the assumption that all systems have rules and structures and that the rules and their interpretations benefit some people more than others. If someone tries to use the tools given to him by his own system in the context of some other system, then he should not be surprised to find that those tools do not bring him the same benefits that they do in his own context. Much of the distress of those who promote an idealized 'rule of law,' as if it were somehow different in kind from all other systems, is likely due to their not having figured out how to use those other systems to benefit themselves.

4 Like any analytical tool, the single word *guanxi* makes whatever it is appear much greater yet much simpler than it is. Yet the analytical disintegration of the term into face *(mian or lian)*, affect *(ganqing)*, and reciprocity *(bao)* makes it difficult to imagine how it all works together and still leaves out too many important issues. The only way to deal with this problem, so far as I can tell, is just to cut things up differently and see if anything new shows up. Such is my approach here.

5 Kipnis 1997; Yan Yunxiang 1996; Yang Mayfair Mei-hui 1994.
6 Marxist theory of value in Tucker 1978 and Mauss 1990; see Godelier 1999.
7 Austin 1979.
8 Fei Xiaotong 1994.
9 Hwang 1987; Yang Lien-sheng 1957.
10 Hwang 1987; King and Myers 1977; Ho 1976; Kipnis 1995.
11 See Kipnis 1997; Jing Jun 1996; Yan Yunxiang 1996; and Yang Mayfair Mei-hui 1994.
12 Walder 1986, 1996.
13 Hwang 1987.
14 See King 1980.
15 Mauss 1990.
16 Kipnis 1997; Jing Jun 1996; Hwang 1987.
17 'Being positioned' is not merely an abstract anthropological concept in China. The process of getting the students jobs requires ever-greater effort by the teacher because the old *fenpei* system has largely disappeared. In that system, students were automatically assigned jobs in *danwei* at graduation. The teacher's efforts were limited to distributing these jobs among the students as the teacher saw fit. Unfortunately, that system has now been dismantled. Student, teacher, and *danwei* must now find each other on their own, a process that gravely complicates things.
18 Herzfeld 1985.
19 Kipnis 1995.
20 Appadurai 1986.
21 Yan Yunxiang 1992, 1996; Yang Mayfair Mei-hui 1994.
22 Douglas 1996; Appadurai 1986.
23 For class, and occasionally caste, in China, see Zang Xiaowei 2000 and Esherick and Rankin 1990. For the terminology and rhetoric of class, see Godelier 1978.
24 In this way, class is a credential, as will be discussed in Chapter 5.
25 See Rubie Watson 1985, 1991, for an interesting take on class and inequality within the family.
26 Lévi-Strauss 1966, 278.
27 Yan Yunxiang 1996.
28 Ibid.
29 That 'tendency to behave' in one way or another is merely another way of speaking about the *habitus* (Bourdieu 1977, 1984).
30 Gadamer 1989; Goodman 1978.

Chapter 4: The Separation of Powers

1 Binford 1962.
2 Binford and Ho 1985; see also Kohl and Fawcett 1995 for examples.
3 Trigger 1984; Lowenthal 1985; Blakey 1987, 1994; Dennell 1990; Trigger 1989; Paynter 1989; Pinsky and Wylie 1989; Shanks and Tilley 1989; Turnbull 1976; Baker and Thomas 1990; Hodder 1991b, 1998, 1999; Claassen 1992; McGuire 1992; Shanks 1993; Shanks and McGuire 1996; Craig 1997; Kohl 1998; Kehoe 1998; and, especially, Neumann 1991.
4 Herzfeld 1985, 1992; Douglas 1984, 1986, 1992.
5 See Wittfogel 1957, especially Chapter 3.
6 For a helpful review of the anthropological perspective on social stratification and its complexity, see Cancian 1976. Both Herzfeld 1992 and Douglas 1986 present insights into the relationship between the person and the bureaucracy under orthodoxy. Wolf 1974; Manson 1987; Harding 1981; James Watson 1975, 1988, 1996; Rubie Watson 1981, 1985, 1991; Johnson 1989; Lieberthal and Lampton 1992; Unger 1987; Yang Mayfair Mei-hui 1989; Pieke 1995; Anderson 1972; Hymes 1996; Solinger 1992; Walder 1986; Jankowiak 1993; Fewsmith 2001; Huang Shumin 1998; Li Wei 1994; and Whyte 1980 present pertinent discussions of the present-day Chinese context. Keightley 1978 and Chang 1986 discuss similar issues in the Chinese past.
7 See Lü and Perry 1997.
8 Evans-Pritchard 1979.

9 Peasants and other uneducated people can be party members without becoming cadres, but this is rare and usually a function of exceptional military service; most people with any sort of government or party position ought to be able to pass the cadre test to ensure that they are literate and know basic political theory.

10 Note that the peasant workers and local officials themselves are within an entirely different *xitong*, the Agriculture *Xitong*, with their own complex of leaders.

11 Bourdieu 1977.

12 See Douglas 1972 and James Watson 1987 on commensality.

13 See the orthodox (and negative) impression of bureaucracy in Sarangi and Slembrouck 1996; Heyman 1995; or Wittfogel 1957.

Chapter 5: Majority Rule

1 *Merriam-Webster Dictionary* 2002.

2 For a review of literature on stereotypes, see Young-Breuhl 1996. For anthropological perspectives, see Barth 1969 and Cohen 2000. For the intersection between stereotypes and naturalness, see Lee 1996; Anderson 1991; Dikötter 1992, 1997. For stereotypes and socialization, see Giddens 1971, 1984, 1991; Godelier 1978; and, of course, Goffman 1959 and Goodenough 1973. For a linguistic perspective, see Pred 1990a, 1990b; Lakoff and Johnson 1980; Lakoff 1987; Lacan 1968. For specifically China-related perspectives, see Jiang and Ashley 2000; Oakes 2000; and Eberhard 1965.

3 Warnke 1987.

4 Foucault 1976; Douglas 1986. See also Turner 1974, 1988; Sahlins 1976; and, of course, Kuhn 1962.

5 de Certeau 1984; Althusser 1969, 1984; Gramsci 1994; Bourdieu 1977, 1984.

6 de Certeau 1984; Foucault 1977; and consumption studies (see Douglas 1996 for a review, also Appadurai 1986; Gilette 2000; Miller et al. 1989; Daniel Miller 1998; Oakes 1999).

7 de Certeau 1984; Wolf 1982.

8 Austin 1979.

9 Ibid.

10 Hanks 1996.

11 The ten universities are Beijing University (BeiDa) in Beijing; JiDa in Jilin City, Jilin; ChuanDa, in Chengdu, Sichuan; WuDa in Wuhan, Hubei; XiaDa in Xiamen, Fujian; XibeiDa in Xian, Shaanxi; ShanDa in Jinan, Shandong; NanDa in Nanjing, Jianxi; ZhongshanDa in Guangzhou, Guangdong; ZhengDa in Zhengzhou, Henan. The institute is the Chinese Academy of Social Sciences (CASS).

12 The exceptions, of course, are the two schools in Beijing. An entire book could be written about the struggles over which person will have sole authority to lead the discipline as a whole.

13 On the reinterpretation of identity through social boundaries, see Barth 1969 and Douglas 1984.

14 See early editions of K.C. Chang's 1986 textbook: 1963, 1968, and 1977; Li Renkai 1992; Keightley 1983; and Chen Xingcan 1997.

15 Yue and Yang 1996. Note that this was the English translation of the book and that I was not able to find it in the original Chinese version. That this book was chosen to be translated into English is interesting in itself since the topic is not that interesting to non-archeologists.

16 Yue and Yang 1996, 18-21.

17 In one of the ironies common to tales of Chinese intellectuals in their relations with the state, Wu Han is the same intellectual whose covert resistance to the Maoist state, in the form of a play about loyal officials, written to correct party excesses, is said to have begun the Cultural Revolution and to have precipitated his own death.

18 Yue and Yang 1996, 276.

19 See Margery Wolf 1972 for the use of reputation as social constraint.

20 Such discourse has been used to blame Chai Ling for Tiananmen; Mao's wife, Jiang Qing, for the Cultural Revolution; Empress Ci Xi of the Qing Dynasty for imperialism; and Empress Wu of the Han Dynasty for the decline of the Han empire.

21   See Jiang and Ashley 2000; Yahuda 1979; Yang Fan 1991; Zang 2000; and Munro 1980 on the concept of 'generation' in general and the lost generation in particular.

Chapter 6: Interest Groups

1   The urban-rural discourse has been reinscribed through scholarly discourse. Knight and Song 1999 exemplifies studies premised on the usual belief in the great divide between urban and rural lifeways. However, see the differing and often contradictory views in Xin 2000; Oakes 1999; Oi 1999; Christiansen and Zhang 1998; Kelliher 1992; Shumin Huang 1998; Yan Yunxiang 1992; and Skinner 1985.
2   Since the dismantling of the communes, directors are farmers who have been elevated to a position of authority over issues of planting, irrigating, and harvesting – the *yewu* or work directly related to farming as a profession.
3   Officials undertake the *zhiwu* work directly related to the management of farming and farmers.
4   Party secretaries translate central directives into changes in the way that farming is done.
5   Bourdieu 1984.
6   Yang Mayfair Mei-hui 1994.
7   Given the common assumptions that archeologists are male, that people who travel alone are male, and that people with short hair and dark clothes are male, my conformity to male behaviours caused my gender to be questioned.
8   Austin 1979.
9   *Zige* is an interesting word in itself: it means qualifications or credentials but also *seniority*. Older people everywhere, and especially oligarchs, clearly benefit from this conflation of credibility with age.
10 Known in Chinese as *hong lian, bai lian*, a phrase taken from Chinese opera, in which the red face *(hong lian)* is the good cop and the white face *(bai lian)* is the bad cop.

Chapter 7: Minority Rights

1   See Wang Hui 1995; Miller 1996; Duara 1991; and Kitching 1993a, 1993b, for more on the role of science and empiricism in China. See also Reid and Traweek 2000 and Latour and Woolgar 1979.
2   For interesting commentaries on what happens to theories when they are removed from context, see Wang Jing 1993 and Tang Xiaobing 1993.
3   See examples in Hodder 1989; Shanks and Tilley 1989; Tilley 1990; and Preucel 1991.
4   Although who is excavating where is often a closely guarded secret, the official version of what is going on may be found in the *Zhongguo Kaogu Xue Nian Jian* – an almanac listing what happened in archeology the previous year. Insiders, of course, can compare what is actually written in the almanac with what they know is going on (or suspect – paranoia and conspiracy theories abound in academic circles the world over). Since official records are not reliable, teachers can use insider knowledge to bind the students more closely to them: the student requires the teacher to find out the truth of events.
5   See Tu Cheng-Sheng 2000 and Wu Chunmin 1996 for explicit discussions of the sinification of archeology.
6   Margery Wolf 1972. See also Rubie Watson 1986, 1991.
7   See Chen Xincan 1997 for more details; also see Tu and Wang 1998. For examples of the memoirs and exploits of the *zhengui jun*, see any of the collected essays produced by the various universities, each of which begins with a series of memoirs of the department's great men. Or see the trade paper *Zhongguo Wenwu Bao*, in which hardly an issue goes by without the publication of a memoir.
8   See Yang Wenhu 1994 for more on the 'supreme oligarch.' See Cheng Li 1994 and Tanner and Feder 1993 for more examples of the positioning and strategies of becoming an oligarch in other professions. For an example of the effect of the Cultural Revolution on the teacher-student relation, see Munro 1980; Rai 1991.
9   One archeologist mentioned that one of the most important causes of Su Bingqi's elevation to the exalted position of being 'everyone's teacher' was that Bingqi refused to remember or take personally any of the criticisms levied at him during the Cultural Revolution.

He understood the motives of fear and self-preservation that caused people to make such dreadful accusations about him and his work and, therefore, 'completely forgot' the entire period.

10 Su Bingqi 1994.
11 Margery Wolf 1972; Rubie Watson 1985, 1986.
12 See Yang Wenhu 1994 for a more in-depth discussion of the relationship between kinship and academia. See James Watson 1975; Skinner 1972; Wang and Zheng 2000 for more on kinship terminology.
13 When I describe historical archeology in the United States – a subdiscipline that often excavates sites dated only to a hundred or so years ago – my Chinese colleagues are incredulous. My protest that archeology can deepen our understanding of even the consumption and waste management practices of 1970s America and can change our understanding of the written record falls on uninterested ears. See Rathje 1992 and Deetz 1977.
14 Note that here I only examine work published by archeologists for other archeologists. More general work aimed at the public presents a different set of issues entirely. See an analysis of historians coming to similar conclusions in Wiegelin-Schwiedrzik 1987.
15 See Alford 1995 for the implications of the different concepts of publishing in the sphere of intellectual property.
16 See Binford 1989.
17 For examples of *shangque*, see page 3 of the *Zhongguo Wenwu Bao*. For more overt styles of disagreement, see the journal *Dongnan Wenhua* between the years 1987 and 1994 (after 1994, it reverted to the traditional, careful, *shangque* style).
18 See Su Bingqi 1994 or Zhang Zhongpei 1994 for examples of oligarchic writing style. Or see any of the collected essays produced by the archeology departments.
19 The official report is published by the Zhongguo Shehuikexueyuan Kaogu Yanjiusuo 1996.
20 See Wang and Zheng 2000 for similar issues in the political realm.
21 Rubie Watson 1981, 1985, 1986, 1991; Margery Wolf 1972; West et al. 1999.
22 See Judd 1990 and Li Chenyang 2000 for more examples of why women acquiesce to the credentials applied to their sex. See Xu Xiaoqun 1996 for the impact of nationalism and capitalism on women; for general overviews of these issues, see Ong 1991 and Silverblatt 1988.
23 West et al. 1999.

Chapter 8: The Pursuit of Happiness
1 Civics Online: (Re) Envisioning the Democratic Community, <http://www.civics-online.org> (accessed 14 September 2003).
2 Bourdieu 1984 gives us an understanding of how we are embedded; Douglas 1986 outlines strategies of combination and juxtaposition across 'institutional' boundaries that create difference; and Giddens 1984 provides both the notion of resources so helpful in understanding motivations and goals of behaviour.
3 Geertz 1973.
4 Leach 1954.
5 Esherick and Rankin 1990, 3.
6 See Fu Keng 1993 and Dirlik 1989, 1994.

Glossary of Chinese Terms

The official *pinyin* system of the People's Republic of China (PRC) is used in the transliteration of Mandarin Chinese terms unless a tradition of use suggests an alternative spelling of a name, place, or thing (e.g., 'Yellow River' instead of 'Huanghe'). Although complex characters are increasingly common in the PRC – particularly when a person's or institution's ties to traditional culture and history are being accentuated – the official simplified characters are given here. All translations are the author's own.

Chinese Journals and Trade Papers

Pinyin	*Characters (PRC)*	*English Equivalent*
Dongnan Wenhua	东南文化	*Southeast Culture*
Kaogu	考古	*Archaeology*
Kaogu Nianjian	考古年鉴	*Archaeological Almanac*
Kaogu yu Wenwu	考古与文物	*Archaeology and Cultural Relics*
Wenwu	文物	*Cultural Relics*
Zhongguo Kaogu Nian Jian	中国考古学年鉴	*Chinese Archaeology Almanac*
Zhongguo Wenwu Bao	中国文物报	*Chinese Cultural Relics Newspaper*

Institutions and Administrative Terms

Pinyin	*Characters (PRC)*	*English Equivalent*
bowuguan	博物馆	museum
bu	部	ministry
bumen	部门	department, branch of government
fu	副	deputy; vice
fu yanjiu yuan	副研究员	deputy researcher
ganbu	干部	cadre
Gongchan Dang	共产党	Chinese Communist Party
Gongnongbing Xuexiao	工农兵学校	Worker-Farmer-Soldier Schools
Guojia Kaogu Wenwu Weiyuanhui	国家考古文物委员会	Natural Council on Archaeological and Cultural Relics
Guojia Wenwu Ju	国家文物部	Central Bureau of Cultural Relics

ju	局	department, bureau
kaogu suo	考古所	institute of archeology
sheng	省	province
sheng wenhua ting	省文化厅	provincial hall of culture
shuji	书记	party secretary
ting	厅	hall
wenhua ting	文化厅	Hall of Culture
wenwu bu	文物部	department of cultural relics
Wenwu Chubanshe	文物出版社	Cultural Relics Press
wenwu ju	文物局	bureau of cultural relics
yanjiu yuan	研究员	researcher
yanjiu zhuli	研究助理	research assistant
yewu	业务	work related to the profession
zhengfu	政府	government
zhiwu	职务	work related to administration
zhuli	助理	assistant
Zhongguo	中国	China
Zhonghua	中华	Chinese

Other Terms and Expressions

Pinyin	*Characters (PRC)*	*English Equivalent*
baiwu jinji	百无禁忌	nothing is forbidden
bao	报	reciprocity
baohu wei zhu, qiangjiu di yi	保护为主，抢救第一	protect and salvage
biming	笔名	pen name
bu dong shi	不懂事	naïve, cannot understand society
caichan	财产	resources
cha dui	插队	to enter a team, workforce
chi he la niao shui	吃喝拉尿睡	eat, drink, defecate, urinate, and sleep
chi ku	吃苦	hardship; to 'eat bitterness'
(qiang da) chutou niao	(强打)出头鸟	(hit hard) the bird with its head stuck out
danwei	单位	work unit
datong xiaoyi	大同小异	(a situation of) great similarity, little difference
de gao wang zhong	德高望重	to have high expectations for a person's moral quality
dong naozi	动脑子	think, cogitate
du daxue, chuan pixie; bu du, chuan caoxie	读大学穿皮鞋，不读穿草鞋	go to university, you can wear leather shoes; don't go, you'll have to wear grass shoes.
duo nian xifu, ao cheng po	多年媳妇熬成破	to finally become a mother-in-law, after many years a new bride
duo zhaogu mingong, duo zhaogu mafan	多照顾民工，多照顾麻烦	if you cultivate the peasant workers, you cultivate trouble

fangyan	方言	local accent, local language
fajue	发掘	to excavate
fajue zige	发掘资格	the right to excavate
fazhi	法制	rule of law
fen gong	分工	the division of labour
fenpei	分配	to distribute (resources)
gan yi hang, ai yi hang	干一行，爱一行	enjoy whatever job you do
gaokao	高考	university entrance exam
geti hu	个体户	entrepreneur
gongzuo xuyao	工作需要	the requirements of the job
guanxi	关系	social network
guatou	寡头	oligarch (negative term)
guobao	国宝	national treasure
guwen	顾问	advisor
hao diulian	好丢脸	terribly embarrassing
hong lian, bai lian	红脸白脸	red face, white face ('good cop, bad cop')
houqin	后勤	preparatory and administrative work
Huaren	华人	Chinese people (ethnic Chinese)
Huanghe zhongxin shuo	黄河中心说	the theory of China's origins along the Yellow River
jian ku	艰苦	physical deprivation
jiaohua	狡猾	sly
jiaoshou	教授	professor
jigong	技工	technical worker
jihua bu ru bianhua	计划不如变化	a plan is never as good as [being prepared to] change
jike	技科	technical studies
kai chuang	开创	to be the first to establish (a new field or topic)
kai wei	开胃	appetizers, enticements
kan zhong	看中	choose, settle on
kaogu	考古	archeology
ke yu bu ke zhi	可遇不可制	you can encounter it, but you cannot control it
keguan	客观	objective
kexue	科学	science
laoshi	老师	teacher
lao yi dai	老一代	the older generation
lengmen	冷门	cold door (unpopular subject)
lian	脸	face, image
lishi	历史	history
li suo dangran	理所当然	a fortiori, due to inescapable logic
lingdao	领导	leader
lunwen ji	论文集	collected essays
meiyu	美语	American English
menfa sixiang	门阀思想	school of thought

mian	面	face, reputation
mingong	民工	peasant worker
ming'e	名额	quota
nongmin	农民	farmer
nuzi he ban ping, zou tian xia	女子喝半瓶，走天下	a woman who drinks but half a bottle can go anywhere
pai mapi	拍马屁	pat the horse's ass (suck up to)
pushi	朴实	honest, straightforward
qifu	欺负	to bully
qing chu yu lan	青出于蓝	turquoise comes out of blue (the student outdoes the teacher)
remen	热门	hot door (popular subject)
renao	热闹	bustling with noise and excitement
ren dao zhongnian, xia yao guan xiao, shang yao guan lao	人到中年，下要官小，上要管老	when one comes to middle age, one must manage the young and take care of the old
renlei xue	人类学	anthropology
renqing	人情	emotion arising out of instrumental relationship; human feeling, sympathy
renzhi	人制	rule of 'men' (i.e., not rule of law)
ru jing, bu ru ting jing	入景，不如听景	going to a place is never as good as hearing about a place
ru xiang sui su	入乡随俗	follow customs when you enter a region ('when in Rome, do as the Romans do')
san	散	scattered; loose
san nian zai hai	三年灾害	three years of natural disasters
shafa kaogu xuezhe	沙发考古学者	'armchair' archeologist
shangque	商榷	scholarly disagreement
shang you zhengce, xia you duice	上有政策，下有对策	from above come policies; from below come countermeasures
shenjing bing	神经病	crazy
shi	士	scholar
shidaifu	士大夫	literati; scholar-official
shishi qiu shi	实事求是	seek truth from facts
shitu guanxi	师徒关系	relations between master and disciple
shixi	实习	practicum
suzhi	素质	quality
ting hua	听话	'listen' (to orders); be obedient
tong	同	the same
tongbao	同胞	compatriot
tongxue	同学	fellow student
tuanjie	团结	cohere, unite

waiguo ren	外国人	foreigner
wei wei nuo nuo	唯唯诺诺	never say no directly
wending	稳定	stable, controllable, fixed
wenhua	文化	culture
wenhua dian	文化点	cultural (tourist) spot
wenhua qinru	文化侵入	cultural imperialism
wenke	文科	the humanities
wenping	文凭	academic degree
wen ren xiang qing	文人相轻	the literati hold each other in contempt
wenwu	文物	artifacts; cultural relics
xia xiang	下乡	sent down to the countryside
xilai shuo	西来说	the theory of Western origins
xinli you shu	心里有数	calculation (hidden agenda)
xitong	系统	vertically organized government bureaucracy
xuedi	学弟	school little brother
xuejie	学界	academic circles
xuejie	学姐	school older sister
xuemei	学妹	school younger sister
xuesheng	学生	student
xueshu dai tou	学术带头	academic research should take the lead
xuezhang	学长	school older brother
yezhan jun	野战军	'field soldiers' (learning archeology through apprenticeship)
yichan	遗产	inheritance
yi guo liang zhi? yi shu liang wen!	一国两制？一书两文！	one country, two systems? one book, two languages!
yingyu	英语	English language
yin yi fei shi	因一废十	because of one, ten are lost
yi ri wei shi, zhong shen wei fu	一日为士，终审为夫	once someone is your teacher, worship him as a father for the rest of your life
yizhi	遗址	archeological site
yong ren	用人	to use people
you wenhua	有文化	cultured, educated
youxi xuezhe	游戏学者	outstanding scholar
yuanfen	缘分	fate, coincidence, predestination
yuanlao	元老	oligarch (connotation neither negative nor positive)
ze lai zhe, ze ai zhe	则来者，则爱者	enjoy whatever comes along
zhaodai suo	招待所	'flophouse,' dormitory
zhengui jun	珍贵军	the 'real' professional archeologist
zhishifenzi	知识分子	intellectual

zhiyuan	志愿	wish, choice
zhongdian	重点	key site, key school
Zhongguo Ren	中国人	Chinese national, citizen
Zhongguo tong	中国通	one who understands China
zige	资格	the right to (do something)
zuo guan	做官	to become an official

References

Alford, William. 1995. *To Steal a Book Is an Elegant Offense: Intellectual Property Law in Chinese Civilization*. Stanford: Stanford University Press.

Althusser, Louis. 1969. *For Marx*. London: Allen Lane. Reprint, New York: Pantheon.

–. 1984. *Essays on Ideology*. London: Verso.

Ames, Roger T., Thomas P. Kasulis, and Wimal Dissanayake, eds. 1994. *Self as Person in Asian Theory and Practice*. New York: State University of New York Press.

–. 1998. *Self as Image in Asian Theory and Practice*. New York: State University of New York Press.

Anderson, Benedict. 1991. *Imagined Communities: Reflections on the Origin and Spread of Nationalism*. New York: Verso.

Anderson, Eugene, Jr. 1972. 'Happy Heavenly Bureaucracy: Supernaturals and the Hong Kong Boat People.' In *Essays on South China's Boat People*, 10-19. Taipei: Orient Cultural Service.

Apel, Karl-Otto. 1984. *Understanding and Explanation: A Transcendental-Pragmatic Perspective*. Cambridge, MA: MIT Press.

Appadurai, Arjun. 1986. *The Social Life of Things: Commodities in Cultural Perspective*. Cambridge, UK: Cambridge University Press.

Argyrou, Vasso. 1999. 'Sameness and the Ethnological Will to Meaning.' *Current Anthropology* 40 (supplement): s29-s41.

Austin, J.L. 1975. *How to Do Things with Words*. 2nd ed. Oxford: Clarendon Press.

–. 1979. *Philosophical Papers*. Edited by J.O. Urmson and G.J. Warnock. Oxford: Oxford University Press.

Bailey, F.G. 1981. 'Dimensions of Rhetoric in Conditions of Uncertainty.' In *Politically Speaking: Cross Cultural Studies of Rhetoric*. Edited by Robert Paine, 27-38. Philadelphia: Institute for Studies of Human Issues.

–. 1983. *The Tactical Uses of Passion: An Essay on Power, Reason, and Reality*. Ithaca: Cornell University Press.

Baker, Frederick, and Julian Thomas, eds. 1990. *Writing the Past in the Present*. Lampeter: St. David's University Press.

Barlow, Tani. 1991. 'Zhishifenzi [Chinese Intellectuals] and Power.' *Dialectical Anthropology* 16, 3-4: 209-32.

–. 1993. 'Colonialism's Career in Postwar China Studies.' *Positions* 1, 1: 224-68.

Barlow, Tani, and Donald Lowe. 1987. *Teaching China's Lost Generation*. San Francisco: China Books.

Barme, Geremie. 2000. *In the Red: On Contemporary Chinese Culture*. New York: Columbia University Press.

Barth, Fredrik. 1969. *Ethnic Groups and Boundaries: The Social Organization of Culture Difference*. Boston: Little, Brown.

Bauman, Richard, and Charles Briggs. 1990. 'Poetics and Performance as Critical Perspectives on Social Life.' *Annual Review of Anthropology* 19: 59-88.

Beetham, David. 1996. *Bureaucracy*. 2nd ed. Buckingham: Open University Press.

Beijing Daxue Kaoguxue Xi, ed. 1992. *Beijing Daxue kaoguxue xi sishi nian 1952-1992* [Forty years of the Department of Archaeology at Beijing University]. Beijing: Beijing University Press.

Ben Xu. 1999. *Disenchanted Democracy: Chinese Criticism after 1989*. Ann Arbor: University of Michigan Press.

Bender, Barbara, Sue Hamilton, and Christopher Tilley. 1995. 'Leskernick: The Biography of an Excavation.' *Cornish Archaeology* 34: 58-73.

Binford, Lewis. 1962. 'Archaeology as Anthropology.' *American Antiquity* 28, 2: 217-25.

–. 1989. *Debating Archaeology*. San Diego: Academic Press.

Binford, Lewis, and Chuan-kun Ho. 1985. 'Taphonomy at a Distance: Zhoukoudian, "The Cave Home of Beijing Man"?' *Current Anthropology* 26, 4: 413-42.

Blakey, Michael L. 1987. 'Skull Doctors: Intrinsic Social and Political Bias in the History of American Physical Anthropology (with Special Reference to the Work of Ales Hrdlicka).' *Critique of Anthropology* 7, 2: 7-35.

–. 1994. 'Passing the Buck: Naturalism and Individualism as Anthropological Expressions of Euro-American Denial.' In *Race*. Edited by Steven Gregory and Roger Sanjek, 270-84. New Brunswick, NJ: Rutgers University Press.

–. 1997. 'Past Is Present: Comments on "In the Realm of Politics: Prospects for Public Participation in African-American Plantation Archaeology."' *Historical Archaeology* 31, 3: 140-45.

Bloor, David. 1987. 'Durkheim and Mauss Revisited: Classification and the Sociology of Knowledge.' *Studies in Philosophy of Science* 13, 4: 267-97.

Blu, Karen. 1980. *The Lumbee Problem: The Making of an American Indian People*. Cambridge, UK: Cambridge University Press.

Blum, Susan. 2001. *Portraits of 'Primitives:' Ordering Human Kinds in the Chinese Nation*. Lanham: Rowman and Littlefield.

Bo Yang. 1991. *The Ugly Chinaman and the Crisis of Chinese Culture*. Trans. Don Cohn and Jing Qing. Sydney: Allen and Unwin.

Bol, Peter. 1992. *'This Culture of Ours': Intellectual Transitions in T'ang and Sung China*. Stanford: Stanford University Press.

Borneman, John. 1995. 'American Anthropology as Foreign Policy.' *American Anthropologist* 97: 663-72.

Borofsky, Robert. 1997. 'Cook, Lono, Obeysekere, and Sahlins.' *Current Anthropology* 38, 2: 255-82.

Boswell, David, and Jessica Evans, eds. 1999. *Representing the Nation: A Reader*. Cambridge, UK: Routledge.

Bourdieu, Pierre. 1977. *Outline of a Theory of Practice*. Trans. Richard Nice. Cambridge, UK: Cambridge University Press.

–. 1984. *Distinction: A Social Critique of the Judgment of Taste*. Trans. Richard Nice. Cambridge, MA: Harvard University Press.

Boyle, James. 1991. 'Is Subjectivity Possible? The Postmodern Subject in Legal Theory.' *University of Colorado Law Review* 62: 489-517.

Bray, Warwick, and Ian Glover. 1987. 'Scientific Investigation or Cultural Imperialism: British Archaeology in the Third World.' *Institute of Archaeology Bulletin* 24: 109-25.

Briggs, Charles. 1986. *Learning How to Ask: A Sociolinguistic Appraisal of the Role of the Interview in Social Science Research*. Cambridge, UK: Cambridge University Press.

Britan, Gerald M., and Ronald Cohen. 1980. 'Toward an Anthropology of Formal Organizations.' In *Hierarchy and Society: Anthropological Perspectives on Bureaucracy*. Edited by Britan and Cohen, 9-30. Philadelphia: Institute for the Study of Human Issues.

Broaded, C. Montgomery. 1990. 'The Lost and Found Generation: Cohort Succession in Chinese Higher Education.' *Australian Journal of Chinese Affairs* 23: 77-95.

Buckley, Christopher. 1991. 'Science as Politics and Politics as Science: Fang Lizhi and Chinese Intellectuals' Uncertain Road to Dissent.' *Australian Journal of Chinese Affairs* 25: 1-36.

Butler, Judith. 1990. *Gender Trouble: Feminism and the Subversion of Identity*. New York: Routledge.

Cai Mingde. 1992. 'Dalu zhishifenzi zhi zhengzhi canyu [The political participation of Chinese mainland intellectuals].' *Chin-tai Chung-kuo* December: 129-49.

Calhoun, Craig, Edward LiPuma, and Moishe Postone. 1993. *Bourdieu: Critical Perspectives*. Chicago: University of Chicago Press.

Cancian, Frank. 1978. 'Social Stratification.' *Annual Review of Anthropology* 5: 227-48.

Chang Kwang-chih. 1983. *Art, Myth, and Ritual*. Cambridge, MA: Harvard University Press.

–. 1986. *The Archaeology of Ancient China*. New Haven: Yale University Press.

Chen Guoqiang and Lin Jiahui, eds. 1996. *Zhongguo renleixue de fazhan* [The development of Chinese anthropology]. Shanghai: Sanlian Chubanshe.

Chen Xingcan. 1997. *Zhongguo shiqian kaoguxueshi yanjiu 1895-1949* [A history of Chinese archeology from 1895 to 1949]. Harvard University Yenching Library Scholarly Series. Beijing: Sanlian Chubanshe.

Chen Yongsheng. 1991. 'Zhongguo dalu zhishifenzi de wuzhi daiyu [The material compensation of Chinese mainland intellectuals]. *Chung-kuo ta-lu yen-chiu* 34, 11: 1-9.

Chen Zufen. 1988. *Zhongguo pai zhishifenzi* [Intellectuals in support of the Chinese state]. Nanjing: Jiangsu Wenyi Chubanshe.

Cheng Li. 1994. 'University Networks and the Rise of Qinghua's Graduates in China's Leadership.' *Australian Journal of Chinese Affairs* 32: 1-30.

Cheng Weili. 1994. 'Zhongguo zhishifenzi wenren jingshen de xiandai yanyi [An elaboration on the contemporary humanist spirit of Chinese intellectuals].' In *Zhongguo zhishifenzi de renwen jingshen* [Essays on the humanist spirit of Chinese intellectuals]. Edited by Xu Ming. Zhongguo zhishifenzi congshu [Series on Chinese intellectuals]. Zhengzhou: Henan Renmin Chubanshe.

Cherrington, Ruth. 1997. *Deng's Generation: Young Intellectuals in 1980s China*. New York: St. Martin's Press.

Christiansen, Flemming, and Zhang Junzuo, eds. 1998. *Village Inc.: Chinese Rural Society in the 1990s*. Honolulu: University of Hawaii Press.

Chung-kuo Lun-t'an, ed. 1987. *Nuxing zhishifenzi yu Taiwan fazhan* [A symposium on female intellectuals and the development of Taiwan]. *Chung-kuo Lun-t'an* 10.

Claassen, Cheryl, ed. 1992. *Exploring Gender through Archaeology: Selected Papers from the 1991 Boone Conference*. Monographs in World Archaeology, no. 11. Madison: Prehistory Press.

Clifford, James, and George E. Marcus, eds. 1986. *Writing Culture: The Poetics and Politics of Ethnography*. Berkeley: University of California Press.

Cohen, Abner. 1981. *The Politics of Elite Culture: Explorations in the Dramaturgy of Power in a Modern African Society*. Berkeley: University of California Press.

Cohen, Anthony. 2000. *Signifying Identities: Anthropological Perspectives on Boundaries and Contested Values*. New York: Routledge.

Collins, Patricia Hill. 1990. *Black Feminist Thought: Knowledge, Consciousness, and the Politics of Empowerment*. New York: Routledge.

Cote, James. 1994. *Adolescent Storm and Stress: An Evaluation of the Mead-Freeman Controversy*. Hillsdale, NJ: Erlbaum.

Coy, Michael, ed. 1989. *Apprenticeship: From Theory to Method and Back Again*. Albany: State University of New York Press.

Croll, Elisabeth. 1995. *Changing Identities of Chinese Women: Rhetoric, Experience, and Self-Perception in Twentieth-Century China*. London: Zed Books; Hong Kong: Hong Kong University Press.

Cullen, Sandra, and Leo Howe. 1991. 'People, Cases, and Stereotypes: A Study of Staff Practice in a DSS Benefit Office.' *Cambridge Anthropology* 15, 1: 1-26.

Cussins, Charris M. Thompson. 2000. 'Primate Suspect: Some Variations of Science Studies.' In *Primate Encounters: Models of Science, Gender, and Society*. Edited by Shirley Strum and Linda Fedigan, 347-68. Chicago: University of Chicago Press.

Czarniawska, Barbara. 1997. *Narrating the Organization: Dramas of Institutional Identity*. Chicago: University of Chicago Press.

Davis, Deborah, and Steven Harrell, eds. 1993. *Chinese Families in the Post-Mao Era*. Berkeley: University of California Press.

de Beauvoir, Simone. 1993. *The Second Sex*. Trans. H.M. Parshley. New York: Knopf.

de Certeau, Michel. 1984. *The Practice of Everyday Life*. Berkeley: University of California Press.

Deetz, James. 1977. *In Small Things Forgotten: The Archaeology of Early American Life*. Garden City, NY: Anchor Press/Doubleday.

Dennell, Robin. 1990. 'Progressive Gradualism, Imperialism, and Academic Fashion: Lower Paleolithic Archaeology in the 20th Century.' *Antiquity* 64, 244: 549-58.

Dikötter, Frank. 1992. *The Discourse of Race in Modern China*. London: Hurst.

–. 1997. *The Construction of Racial Identities in China and Japan*. St. Leonards: Allen and Unwin.

di Leonardo, Micaela. 1998. *Exotics at Home: Anthropologies, Others, American Modernity*. Chicago: University of Chicago Press.

Dilley, Roy. 1999. *The Problem of Context*. New York: Berghahn Books.

Dirlik, Arif. 1978. *Revolution and History: The Origins of Marxist Historiography in China, 1919-1937*. Berkeley: University of California Press.

–. 1989. *Marxism and Capitalism in the People's Republic of China*. Lanham: University Press of America.

–. 1994. *After the Revolution: Waking to Global Capitalism*. Hanover: University Press of New England.

–. 1997. *The Postcolonial Aura: Third World Criticism in the Age of Global Capitalism*. Boulder: Westview Press.

Dissanayake, Wimal. 1996. 'Introduction: Agency and Cultural Understanding: Some Preliminary Remarks.' In *Narratives of Agency: Self-Making in China, India, and Japan*. Edited by Dissanayake, ix-xxi. Minneapolis: University of Minnesota Press.

Dominguez, Virginia R. 1994. 'A Taste for the Other: Intellectual Complicity in Racializing Practices.' *Current Anthropology* 35, 4: 333-48.

Dong Naibin. 1994. 'Xia yu Zhongguo zhishifenzi de renge lixiang [Chivalry and the ideal personality of the Chinese intellectual].' In *Zhongguo zhishifenzi de renwen jingshen* [Essays on the humanist spirit of Chinese intellectuals]. Edited by Xu Ming. Zhongguo zhishifenzi congshu [Series on Chinese intellectuals], 407-28. Zhengzhou: Henan Renmin Chubanshe.

Dorfman, Diane. 1996. 'The Spirit of Reform: The Power of Belief in Northern China.' *Positions* 4, 2: 253-89.

Douglas, Mary. 1972. 'Deciphering a Meal.' *Daedelus* 101: 61-81.

–. 1984. *Purity and Danger: An Analysis of the Concepts of Pollution and Taboo*. London: Ark.

–. 1986. *How Institutions Think*. Syracuse: Syracuse University Press.

–. 1992. *Risk and Blame: Essays in Cultural Theory*. London: Routledge.

–. 1996. *The World of Goods: Towards an Anthropology of Consumption*. Rev. ed. London: Routledge.

Duara, Prasenjit. 1991. 'Knowledge and Power in the Discourse of Modernity.' *Journal of Asian Studies* 50, 1: 67-83.

du Gay, Paul. 2000. *In Praise of Bureaucracy: Weber, Organization, Ethics*. London: Sage.

Dutton, Michael. 1995. 'Dreaming of Better Times: "Repetition with a Difference" and Community Policing in China.' *Positions* 3, 2: 415-17.

Eberhard, Wolfram. 1965. 'Chinese Regional Stereotypes.' *Asian Survey* 5: 596-608.

Eddy, Elizabeth M. 1979. 'Initiation into Bureaucracy.' In *Anthropology and Educational Administration*. Edited by Ray Barnhardt, John H. Chilcott, and Harry F. Wolcott, 115-46. Tucson: Impresora Sahuaro.

Einhorn, Barbara, and Eileen Jane Yeo, eds. 1995. *Women and Market Society: Crisis and Opportunity*. Brookfield: Edward Elgar.

El-Haj, Nadia Abu. 1998. 'Translating Truths: Nationalism, the Practice of Archaeology, and the Remaking of Past and Present in Contemporary Jerusalem.' *American Ethnologist* 25, 2: 166-88.

Elia, Ricardo. 1993. 'US Cultural Resource Management and the ICAHM Charter.' *Antiquity* 67, 255: 426-38.

English-Lueck, J.A. 1997. *Chinese Intellectuals on the World Frontier: Blazing the Black Path*. London: Bergen and Garvey.

Esherick, Joseph, and Mary Backus Rankin. 1990. *Chinese Local Elites and Patterns of Dominance*. Berkeley: University of California Press.

Evans-Pritchard, E.E. 1969. *The Nuer: A Description of the Modes of Livelihood and Political Institutions of a Nilotic People*. New York: Oxford University Press.

Faludi, Susan. 1999. *Stiffed: The Betrayal of the American Man*. New York: W. Morrow.

Fanon, Frantz. 1968. *The Wretched of the Earth*. Trans. Constance Farrington. New York: Grove.

–. 1991. *Black Skin, White Masks*. Trans. Charles Lam Markmann. New York: Grove.

Farmer, David John. 1995. *The Language of Public Administration: Bureaucracy, Modernity, and Postmodernity*. Tuscaloosa: University of Alabama Press.

Farquhar, Judith, and James L. Hevia. 1993. 'Culture and Postwar American Historiography of China.' *Positions* 1, 2: 486-525.

Fawcett, Clare. 1986. 'Politics of Assimilation in Japanese Archaeology.' *Archaeological Review from Cambridge* 5, 1: 43-57.

Fei Xiaotong. 1994. *From the Soil: The Foundations of Chinese Society*. Trans. Gary Hamilton and Wang Zheng. Berkeley: University of California Press.

Feinberg, Richard. 1994. 'Contested Worlds: The Politics of Culture and the Politics of Anthropology.' *Anthropology and Humanism* 19, 1: 20-35.

Ferguson, Kathy. 1984. *The Feminist Case Against Bureaucracy*. Philadelphia: Temple University Press.

Ferns, H.S. 1978. *The Disease of Government*. London: M. Temple Smith.

Fewsmith, Joseph. 2001. *Elite Politics in Contemporary China*. Armonk: M.E. Sharpe.

Firth, Raymond. 1977. 'Foreword.' In *Political Systems of Highland Burma*. By Edmund Leach, v-viii. Monographs on Social Anthropology 44. London: Athlone Press.

Fisher, Tom. 1982. 'The Play's the Thing: Wu Han and Hai Rui Revisited.' *Australian Journal of Chinese Affairs* 7: 1-35.

Fotiadis, Michael. 1995. 'Modernity and the Past-Still-Present: Politics of Time in the Birth of Regional Archaeological Projects in Greece.' *American Journal of Archaeology* 99, 1: 59-78.

Foucault, Michel. 1976. *The Archaeology of Knowledge*. New York: Harper and Row.

–. 1977. *Discipline and Punish: The Birth of the Prison*. London: A. Lane.

–. 1980. *Herculine Barbin: Being the Recently Discovered Memoirs of a Nineteenth Century French Hermaphrodite*. Trans. Richard McDougall. New York: Pantheon Books.

Fowler, Don D. 1987. 'Uses of the Past: Archaeology in the Service of the State.' *American Antiquity* 52, 2: 229-48.

Fox, Richard. 1996. 'Self-Made.' In *Narratives of Agency: Self-Making in China, India, and Japan*. Edited by Wimal Dissanayake. Minneapolis: University of Minnesota Press.

Franklin, Richard. 1989. 'Intellectuals and the CCP in the Post-Mao Period: A Study in Perceptual Role Conflict.' *Journal of Developing Societies* 5, 2: 203-17.

Franklin, Sarah. 1995. 'Science as Culture, Cultures of Science.' *Annual Review of Anthropology* 24: 163-86.

Freedman, Maurice. 1970. *Family and Kinship in Chinese Society*. Stanford: Stanford University Press.

Fu Keng. 1993. 'Chinese Intellectuals and the Drive Towards Capitalism.' *Anthropology of Work Review* 14, 2-3: 31-34.

Gadamer, Hans Georg. 1989. *Truth and Method*. 2nd rev. ed. Trans. Joel Weinsheimer and Donald G. Marshall. New York: Crossroad.

Gao Liandi. 1993. 'Dalu xuexiao jiaoyu zhidu chulun [A preliminary discussion of the educational system of Mainland China].' *Shehui Kexue: Zhongguo Wenhua* 1: 9-16.

Geertz, Clifford. 1973. *The Interpretation of Cultures: Selected Essays*. New York: Basic Books.

Giddens, Anthony. 1971. *Capitalism and Modern Social Theory: An Analysis of the Writings of Marx, Durkheim, and Weber*. Cambridge, UK: Cambridge University Press.

–. 1984. *The Constitution of Society: Outline of the Theory of Structuration*. Cambridge, UK: Polity Press.

–. 1991. *Modernity and Self-Identity: Self and Society in the Late Modern Age*. Stanford: Stanford University Press.

Gilette, Maris. 2000. *Between Mecca and Beijing: Modernization and Consumption among Urban Chinese Muslims*. Stanford: Stanford University Press.

Gilmartin, Christina, Gail Hershatter, Linda Rofel, and T. White, eds. 1994. *Engendering China: Women, Culture, and the State*. Cambridge, MA: Harvard University Press.

Glenn, Evelyn Nakano. 1992. 'From Servitude to Service Work: Historical Continuities in the Racial Division of Paid Reproductive Labor.' *Signs* 18, 1: 1-43.

Goffman, Erving. 1959. *The Presentation of Self in Everyday Life*. Garden City, NY: Doubleday.

–. 1974. *Frame Analysis: An Essay on the Organization of Experience*. New York: Harper and Row.

Godelier, Maurice. 1978. 'Infrastructures, Societies, and History.' *Current Anthropology* 19, 4: 763-71.

Goldman, Merle. 1981. *China's Intellectuals: Advise and Dissent*. Cambridge, MA: Harvard University Press.

Goldman, Merle, Timothy Cheek, and Carol Lee. 1987. *China's Intellectuals and the State: In Search of a New Relationship*. Cambridge, MA: Council on East Asian Studies, Harvard University; Harvard University Press.

Goodenough, Ward Hunt. 1973. *Culture, Language, and Society*. Reading: Addison-Wesley.

Goodman, Nelson. 1978. *Ways of Worldmaking*. Indianapolis: Hackett.

Graham, Mark. 1996. 'Bureaucrats and Barflies: Subject Positions in the Field.' *Antropologiska Studier* 54-55: 37-51.

Gramsci, Antonio. 1994. *Letters from Prison*. Trans. Ray Rosenthal. Edited by Frank Rosengarten. New York: Columbia University Press.

Greenhalgh, Susan. 1994. 'De-Orientalizing the Chinese Firm.' *American Ethnologist* 21, 4: 746-75.

Gu, Edward X. 1997. *The Structural Transformation of the Intellectual Public Sphere in Communist China (1979-1989): A New Institutionalist Perspective*. Leiden: Sinological Institute.

–. 1999. 'Cultural Intellectuals and the Politics of the Cultural Public Space in Communist China (1979-1989): A Case Study of Three Intellectual Groups.' *Journal of Asian Studies* 58, 2: 389-431.

Guangming Ribao Qunzhongbu, ed. 1989. *Zhishijie remen huati* [Burning questions among intellectuals: A compilation from China's *Guangming Daily*]. Beijing: Guangming Ribao Chubanshe.

Gulden, Greg, and Aidan Southall, eds. 1993. *Urban Anthropology in China*. Leiden: E.J. Brill.

Gusterson, Hugh. 1996. *Nuclear Rites: A Weapons Laboratory at the End of the Cold War*. Berkeley: University of California Press.

Halpern, Nina. 1988. 'Social Scientists as Policy Advisors in Post-Mao China: Explaining the Pattern of Advice.' *Australian Journal of Chinese Affairs* 19-20: 215-40.

Hamilton, Gary, and Zheng Wang. 1992. 'Introduction: Fei Xiaotong and the Beginnings of Chinese Sociology.' In *From the Soil: The Foundations of Chinese Society*. By Fei Xiaotong, 1-34. Berkeley: University of California.

Handler, Richard. 1988. *Nationalism and the Politics of Culture in Quebec*. Madison: University of Wisconsin Press.

Hanks, William F. 1996. *Language and Communicative Practices*. Boulder: Westview Press.

Haraway, Donna. 1991. *Simians, Cyborgs, and Women: The Re-Invention of Nature*. London: Free Association.

Harding, Harry. 1981. *Organizing China: The Problem of Bureaucracy, 1949-1976*. Stanford: Stanford University Press.

Harding, Sandra. 2000. *Decentering the Center: Philosophy for a Multicultural, Postcolonial, and Feminist World*. Bloomington: Indiana University Press.

Hastrup, Kristin. 1985. 'Anthropology and the Exaggeration of Culture.' *Ethnos* 50, 3-4: 313-24.

He Xiaoming. 1997. *Bainian youhuan: Zhishifenzi mingyun yu Zhongguo xiandaihua jincheng* [100 years of misery: Intellectuals and the process of Chinese modernization]. Shanghai: Dongfang Chuban Zhongshe.

Heper, Metin. 1985. 'State and Public Bureaucracies: A Comparative and Historical Perspective.' *Comparative Studies in Society and History* 27, 1: 86-110.

Herzfeld, Michael. 1985. *The Poetics of Manhood: Contest and Identity in a Cretan Mountain Village*. Princeton: Princeton University Press.

–. 1987. '"As in Your Own House": Hospitality, Ethnography, and the Stereotype of Mediterranean Society.' In *Honor and Shame and the Unity of the Mediterranean*. Special Publication 22: 75-89. Washington, DC: American Anthropological Association.

–. 1992. *The Social Production of Indifference: Exploring the Symbolic Roots of Western Bureaucracy*. New York: St. Martin's.

–. 2000. *Anthropology: Theoretical Practice in Culture and Society*. Boston: Blackwell Publishers.

Heyman, Josiah. 1995. 'Putting Power in the Anthropology of Bureaucracy: The Immigration and Naturalization Service at the Mexico-United States Border.' *Current Anthropology* 36, 2: 261-87.

Ho, D.Y.F. 1975. 'On the Concept of "Face."' *American Journal of Sociology* 81: 867-84.

Hodder, Ian. 1989. 'Writing Archaeology: Site Reports in Context.' *Antiquity* 63, 239: 268-74.

–. 1991a. *Reading the Past: Current Approaches to Interpretation in Archaeology*. 2nd ed. Cambridge, UK: Cambridge University Press.

–. 1991b. 'Archaeological Theory in Contemporary European Societies: The Emergence of Competing Traditions.' In *Archaeological Theory in Europe: The Last Three Decades*. Edited by Hodder, 1-24. New York: Routledge.

–. 1993. 'Narrative and Rhetoric of Material Culture Sequences.' *World Archaeology* 25, 2: 268-82.

–. 1996. *On the Surface: Catalhöyük 1993-95*. Cambridge, UK: McDonald Institute for Archaeological Research; London: British Institute of Archaeology at Ankara; Oakville: David Brown.

–. 1998. 'Whose Rationality? A Response to Fekri Hassan.' *Antiquity* 72, 275: 213-17.

–. 1999. *The Archaeological Process: An Introduction*. Malden: Blackwell.

Hoebel, Edward Adamson. 1958. 'The University as Bureaucracy.' In *Systems of Political Control and Bureaucracy in Human Societies*. Proceedings of the 1958 Annual Spring Meeting of the American Ethnological Society, 58-63. Seattle: AES Press.

Hoffer, Eric. 1951. *The True Believer: Thoughts on the Nature of Mass Movements*. New York: Harper.

Holland, Dorothy, and Andrew Kipnis. 1994. 'Metaphors for Embarrassment and Stories of Exposure: Not-So-Egocentric Self in American Culture.' *Ethos* 22, 3: 316-42.

Hook, Brian. 1996. 'Introduction: Reshaping the Relationship between the Individual and the State in China.' In *The Individual and the State in China*. Edited by Hook, 1-15. Oxford: Oxford University Press.

Hu, Hsien-chin. 1944. 'The Chinese Concept of Face.' *American Anthropologist* 46: 45-64.

Huang Minlan. 1995. *Xueshu jiuguo: Zhishifenzi lishi guan yu Zhongguo zhengzhi* [Scholarship to save the county: Intellectuals' sense of history and Chinese politics]. Zhengzhou: Henan Renmin Chubanshe.

Huang Ping. 1994. 'You mudi zhi xingdong yu wei yuqi zhi houguo: Zhongguo zhishefenzi yu wushi niandai de jingli tansuo [Goal-oriented actions and unexpected consequences: A discussion of the experience of Chinese intellectuals in the 1950s].' *China Social Sciences Quarterly* 9: 30-38.

–. 1999. *Zai piaobo zhong xunqiu guisu* [Looking for home in floating (sic)]. Jinan: Shandong Renmin Chubanshe.

Huang, Shumin. 1998. *The Spiral Road: Change in a Chinese Village through the Eyes of a Communist Party Leader*. Boulder: Westview.

Hung Lien-te. 1988. 'The Changing Perspectives of Contemporary Chinese Marxism: A Sociological Study of National Ideology [in Chinese, with English abstract].' *National Taiwan University Journal of Sociology* 19: 179-94.

Hwang, Kuang-kuo. 1987. 'Face and Favor: The Chinese Power Game.' *American Journal of Sociology* 92, 4: 944-74.

Hymes, Robert. 1996. 'Personal Relations and Bureaucratic Hierarchy in Chinese Religion: Evidence from the Song Dynasty.' *Unruly Gods: Divinity and Society in China*. Edited by Meir Shahar and Robert P. Weller, 37-69. Honolulu: University of Hawaii Press.

Irigaray, Luce. 1985. *This Sex Which Is Not One*. Ithaca: Cornell University Press.

Jackson, Michael. 1998. *Minima Ethnographica: Intersubjectivity and the Anthropological Project*. Chicago: University of Chicago Press.

Jacoby, Russell. 1987. *The Last Intellectuals: American Culture in the Age of Academe*. New York: Basic Books.

James, William. 1984. *William James: The Essential Writings*. Albany: State University of New York Press.

Jankowiak, William. 1993. *Sex, Death, and Hierarchy in a Chinese City: An Anthropological Account*. New York: Columbia University Press.

Jia Chunzeng. 1996. *Zhishifenzi yu Zhongguo shehui bianqe* [Chinese intellectuals and the evolution of Chinese society]. Beijing: Huawen Chubanshe.

Jia Pingan, and Sun Xin, eds. 1997. *Zhongguo zhishifenzi da liebian* [The disunification of Chinese intellectuals]. Beijing: Minzhu yu Jianshe Chubanshe.

Jiang Yaorong, and David Ashley. 2000. *Mao's Children in the New China: Voices from the Red Guard Generation*. New York: Routledge.

Jiang Zukang. 1988. 'Zhongguo dangdai kaoguxuejie dui Zhongguo zhi wenming qiyuan wenti de butong kanfa [The differences of opinion about the rise of Chinese civilizations within present-day archeological circles].' *Chiu-chou hsüeh-k'an* 2, 3: 139-42.

Jin Dakai. 1971. 'Lun Zhonggong wenhua zhengce texing [A discussion of the cultural policies of the CCP].' *Chin-rih T'ai-wan* 349-50: 17-25.

Jin Tong, ed. 1994. *Pipan Zhongguo* [To criticize China]. Taipei: Ke-ning.

Johnson, David. 1989. 'Actions Speak Louder than Words: The Cultural Significance of Chinese Ritual Opera.' In *Ritual Opera, Operatic Ritual*. Edited by Johnson, 1-45. Berkeley: University of California Press.

Jun Jing. 1996. *The Temple of Memories: History, Power, and Morality in a Chinese Village*. Stanford: Stanford University Press.

–, ed. 2000. *Feeding China's Little Emperors: Food, Children, and Social Change*. Stanford: Stanford University Press.

Judd, Ellen. 1990. '"Men Are More Able": Rural Chinese Women's Conceptions of Gender and Agency.' *Pacific Affairs* 63, 1: 40-61.

Karp, Ivan, and Kent Maynard. 1983. 'Reading the Nuer.' *Current Anthropology* 24, 4: 481-503.

Kehoe, Alice. 1998. *The Land of Prehistory: A Critical History of American Archaeology*. New York: Routledge.

Keightley, David. 1978. 'The Religious Commitment: Shang Theology and the Genesis of Chinese Political Culture.' *History of Religion* 17: 211-25.

Kelliher, Daniel. 1992. *Peasant Power in China: The Era of Rural Reform 1979-1989*. New Haven: Yale University Press.

King, Ambrose. 1991. 'Kuan-hsi and Network Building: A Sociological Interpretation.' *Daedalus* 120, 2: 63-84.

Kipnis, Andrew. 1995. '"Face": An Adaptable Discourse of Social Surfaces.' *Positions* 1, 3: 119-47.

–. 1997. *Producing Guanxi: Sentiment, Self, and Subculture in a North China Village*. Durham: Duke University Press.

Kitching, B.M. 1993a. 'Scientism as Ideology: Science, Philosophy, and Politics in the People's Republic of China.' Discussion Papers in Economics and Public Policy. Discussion Paper 6. School of Economics and Public Policy, Queensland University of Technology.

–. 1993b. 'Science Policy and the Role of the Scientist in the People's Republic of China.' Discussion Papers in Economics and Public Policy. Discussion Paper 10. School of Economics and Public Policy, Queensland University of Technology.

Knight, John, and Lina Song. 1999. *The Rural-Urban Divide: Economic Disparities and Interactions in China*. Oxford: Oxford University Press.

Kohl, Philip. 1998. 'Nationalism and Archaeology: On the Constructions of Nations and the Reconstructions of the Remote Past.' *Annual Review of Anthropology* 27: 223-46.

Kohl, Philip, and Clare Fawcett, eds. 1995. *Nationalism, Politics, and the Practice of Archaeology*. Cambridge: Cambridge University Press.

Kuhn, Thomas. 1962. *Structure of Scientific Revolutions*. Chicago: University of Chicago Press.

Lacan, Jacques. 1968. *The Language of the Self: The Function of Language in Psychoanalysis*. Baltimore: Johns Hopkins University Press.

Lakoff, George. 1987. *Women, Fire, and Dangerous Things: What Categories Reveal about the Mind*. Chicago: University of Chicago Press.

Lakoff, George, and Mark Johnson. 1980. *Metaphors We Live By*. Chicago: University of Chicago Press.

Laodong Renshi Bu. 1985. *Zhishifenzi zhengce wenjian huibian* [Policies on intellectuals (microfilm)]. Beijing: Laodong Renshi Chubanshe.

Latour, Bruno. 1993. *We Have Never Been Modern*. Trans. Catherine Porter. Cambridge, MA: Harvard University Press.

Latour, Bruno, and Steve Woolgar. 1979. *Laboratory Life: The Social Construction of Scientific Facts*. Beverly Hills: Sage.

Lave, Jean, and Etienne Wenger. 1991. *Situated Learning: Legitimate Peripheral Participation*. New York: Cambridge University Press.

Leach, Edmund. 1954. *Political Systems of Highland Burma: A Study of Kachin Social Structure*. Cambridge, MA: Harvard University Press.

–. 1989. 'Masquerade: The Presentation of the Self in Holiday Life.' *Cambridge Anthropology* 13, 3: 47-69.

Lee, Gregory. 1996. *Troubadours, Trumpeters, Troubled Makers: Lyricism, Nationalism, and Hybridity in China and Its Others*. London: Hurst.

Leone, Mark, Parker Potter, and Paul Shackel. 1987. 'Toward a Critical Archaeology.' *Current Anthropology* 28, 3: 283-302.

Lévi-Strauss, Claude. 1966. *The Savage Mind*. Chicago: University of Chicago Press.

Li Chenyang. 2000. *The Sage and the Second Sex: Confucianism, Ethics, and Gender*. Chicago: Open Court.

Li Jinshan. 1998. *Bureaucratic Restructuring in Reforming China: A Redistribution of Political Power*. Singapore: Singapore University Press.

Li Renkai. 1992. *Dongdang zhong de lishi jueze: Jindai zhishifenzi de zhuiqiu* [Choices in the midst of turbulence: The motivations of present-day intellectuals]. Zhengzhou: Henan Renmin Chubanshe.

Li Wei. 1994. *The Chinese Staff System: A Mechanism for Bureaucratic Control and Integration*. Berkeley: University of California Press.

Lieberthal, Kennith, and David Lampton. 1992. *Bureaucracy, Politics, and Decision Making in Post-Mao China*. Berkeley: University of California Press.

Lin Chunmin. 1993. 'Lun zhishifenzi de shehui diwei [A discussion of the social position of intellectuals].' *Shehuikexue: Zhongguo Wenhua* 2: 65-71.

Lin Jing. 1999. *Social Transformation and Private Education in China*. New York: Greenwood.

Link, Perry. 1992. *Evening Chats in Beijing: Probing China's Predicament*. New York: Norton.

Liu, James T.C. 1988. *China Turning Inward: Intellectual-Political Changes in the Early Twelfth Century*. Cambridge, MA: Council on East Asian Studies, Harvard University; Harvard University Press.

Liu, Lydia. 1993. 'Translingual Practice: The Discourse of Individualism between China and the West.' *Positions* 1, 1: 160-93.

Liu Meiru. 2001. *Intellectual Dissidents in China*. Lewiston: Edwin Mellon.

Liu Xiuming. 1997. *Rusheng yu guoyun* [The Confucians and the fate of the nation]. Hangzhou: Zhejiang Renmin Chubanshe.

Liu Zeming. 1993. *Zouxia shengtan de Zhongguo zhishifenzi* [Leaving the altar: The fall of Chinese intellectuals from their former high social position]. Beijing: Junshi Yiwen Chubanshe.

Long Xilin. 1996. *Chanshi bing shouhu shijie yiyi de ren: Renwen zhishifenzi de qiyuan yu shiming* [To explain matters and protect worldly significance: The origins and mission of the literary intellectuals]. Zhengzhou: Henan Renmin Chubanshe.

Lowenthal, David. 1985. *The Past Is a Foreign Country*. Cambridge, UK: Cambridge University Press.

Lü, Hsiao-po, and Elizabeth J. Perry. 1997. *Danwei: The Changing Chinese Workplace in Historical and Comparative Perspectives*. Armonk: M.E. Sharpe.

Lu, Xun. 1990. *Diary of a Madman and Other Stories*. Trans. William Lyell. Honolulu: University of Hawaii Press.

Lynott, Mark, and Alison Wylie, eds. 1995. *Ethics in American Archaeology: Challenges for the 1990s*. Washington, DC: Society for American Archaeology.

Ma Shu-yun. 1993. 'The Exit, Voice, and Struggle to Return of Chinese Political Exiles.' *Pacific Affairs* 66, 3: 368-85.

Ma, Stephen. 1996. *Administrative Reform in Post-Mao China: Efficiency or Ethics*. Lanham: University Press of America.

Macdonald, Sharon, and Gordon Fyfe, eds. 1996. *Theorizing Museums: Representing Identity and Diversity in a Changing World*. Cambridge, UK: Blackwell.

Maine, Henry Summer. 1972 [1861]. *Ancient Law*. London: Dent.

Manson, William. 1987. 'Incipient Chinese bureaucracy and Its Ideological Rationale: The Confucianism of Hsün Tzu.' *Dialectical Anthropology* 12, 3: 271-84.

Mao, Tse-Tung (Zedong). 1966. *Quotations from Chairman Mao*. Beijing: Foreign Languages Press.

Mauss, Marcel. 1990 [1925]. *The Gift: The Form and Reason for Exchange in Archaic Societies*. Trans. W.D. Halls. New York: W.W. Norton.

McGuire, Randall. 1992. 'Archeology and the First Americans.' *American Anthropologist* 94, 4: 816-36.

McGuire, Randall, and Robert Paynter, eds. 1991. *The Archaeology of Inequality*. Cambridge, UK: Blackwell.

Merry, Sally Engle. 1992. 'Anthropology, Law, and Transnational Processes.' *Annual Review of Anthropology* 21: 357-79.

Mertz, Elizabeth. 1994. 'Legal Language: Pragmatics, Poetics, and Social Power.' *Annual Review of Anthropology* 23: 435-55.

Miller, Daniel. 1998. *Material Cultures: Why Some Things Matter*. London: University College of London Press.

Miller, Daniel, M.J. Rowlands, and Christopher Tilley, eds. 1989. *Domination and Resistance*. London: Unwin Hyman.

Miller, H. Lyman. 1996. *Science and Dissent in Post-Mao China: The Politics of Knowledge*. Seattle: University of Washington Press.

Mok, Ka-Ho. 1998. *Intellectuals and the State in Post-Mao China*. New York: St. Martin's Press.

Moore, Sally Falk. 1972. 'Legal Liability and Evolutionary Interpretation.' In *The Allocation of Responsibility*. Edited by Max Gluckman, 51-107. Manchester: Manchester University Press.

Muller, Jon. 1991. 'The New Holy Family: A Polemic on Bourgeois Idealism in Archaeology.' In *Processual and Post-Processual Archaeologies*. Edited by Robert Preucel, 251-64. Occasional Paper 10. Carbondale: University of Southern Illinois.

Munro, Robin. 1980. 'Settling Accounts with the Cultural Revolution at Beijing University, 1977-79.' *China Quarterly* 82: 308-33.

Needham, Rodney. 1972. *Belief, Language, and Experience*. Chicago: University of Chicago Press.

Neumann, Loretta. 1991. 'Politics of Archaeology and Historic Preservation: How Our Laws Really Are Made.' In *Protecting the Past*. Edited by George S. Smith and John E. Ehrenhard, 41-46. Boca Raton: CRC Press.

Oakes, Tim. 1999. 'Bathing in the Far Village: Globalization, Transnational Capital, and the Cultural Politics of Modernity in China.' *Positions* 7, 2: 307-42.

–. 2000. 'China's Provincial Identities: Reviving Regionalism and Reinventing "Chineseness."' *Journal of Asian Studies* 59, 3: 667-93.

O'Brien, Kevin. 1996. 'Rightful Resistance.' *World Politics* 49, 1: 31-55.

Oi, Jean C. 1999. *Rural China Takes Off: Institutional Foundations of Economic Reform*. Berkeley: University of California Press.

Ong, Aihwa. 1991. 'The Gender and Labor Politics of Postmodernity.' *Annual Review of Anthropology* 20: 279-309.

Pai, Hyung Il. 1999. 'Nationalism and Preserving Korea's Buried Past: The Office of Cultural Properties and Archaeological Heritage Management in South Korea.' *Antiquity* 73, 281: 619-25.

Parkin, David. 1984. 'Political Language.' *Annual Review of Anthropology* 13: 345-65.

Parkin, David, Lionel Caplan, and Humphrey Fisher, eds. 1996. *The Politics of Cultural Performance*. Providence: Berghahn Books.

Patterson, Thomas. 1986. 'The Last Sixty Years: Toward a Social History of Americanist Archaeology in the United States.' *American Anthropologist* 88: 7-26.

Paynter, Robert. 1989. 'Archaeology of Equality and Inequality.' *Annual Review of Anthropology* 18: 369-99.

Peterson, Glen, Ruth Hayhoe, and Yongling Lu, eds. 2001. *Education, Culture, and Identity in Twentieth Century China*. Ann Arbor: University of Michigan Press.

Pieke, Frank. 1995. 'Bureaucracy, Friends, and Money: The Growth of Capital Socialism in China.' *Comparative Studies in Society and History* 37, 3: 494-518.

Pinsky, Valerie. 1992. 'Archaeology, Politics, and Boundary-Formation: The Boas Censure (1919) and the Development of American Archaeology during the Inter-War Years.' In *Rediscovering Our Past: Essays on the History of American Archaeology*. Edited by Jonathan Rayman, 161-89. Aldershot: Avebury.

Pinsky, Valerie, and Alison Wyle, eds. 1989. *Critical Traditions in Contemporary Archaeology: Essays in the Philosophy, History, and Socio-Politics of Archaeology*. Cambridge, UK: Cambridge University Press.

Pluciennik, Mark. 1998. 'Archaeology, Archaeologists, and "Europe."' *Antiquity* 72, 278: 816-24.

Potter, Parker B., and Mark Leone. 1987. 'Archeology in Public in Annapolis: Four Seasons, Six Sites, Seven Tours, and 32,000 Visitors.' In *American Archeology* 6, 1: 51-61.

Pred, Allen. 1990a. 'In Other Wor[l]ds: Fragmented and Integrated Observations on Gendered Languages, Gendered Spaces, and Local Transformation.' *Antipode* 22, 1: 33-52.

–. 1990b. *Making Histories and Constructing Human Geographies: The Local Transformation of Practice, Power Relations, and Consciousness*. Boulder: Westview Press.

Preucel, Robert. 1991. 'Introduction.' In *Processual and Post-Processual Archaeologies*. Edited by Preucel, 1-14. Occasional Paper 10. Carbondale: University of Southern Illinois.

Preucel, Robert, and Ian Hodder. 1996. *Contemporary Archaeology in Theory*. Oxford: Blackwell.

Pye, Lucian. 1985. *Asian Power and Politics: The Cultural Dimensions of Authority*. Cambridge: Belknap.

–. 1988. *The Mandarin and the Cadre: China's Political Cultures*. Ann Arbor: University of Michigan Press.

Qian Liqun. 1999. *Huashuo Zhoushi xiongdi: Beida yanjiang ji* [The words of the colleagues of Zhou: A compilation of lectures given at Beijing University]. Jinan: Shandong Huabao Chubanshe.

Qian Ning. 1997. *Liuxue Meiguo: Yige shidai de gushi* [Studying in the US: The story of an era]. Taipei: Mai-tien.

Raheja, Gloria Goodwin. 1988. *The Poison in the Gift*. Chicago: University of Chicago Press.

Rai, Shirin. 1991. *Resistance and Reaction: University Politics in Post-Mao China*. New York: St. Martin's Press.

Rathje, William. 1992. *Rubbish! The Archaeology of Garbage*. New York: HarperCollins.

Reid, Roddy, and Sharon Traweek. 2000. *Doing Science + Culture*. Cambridge, UK: Routledge.

Rosaldo, Renato. 1993. *Culture and Truth: The Remaking of Social Analysis*. With a new Introduction. Boston: Beacon Press.

Royce, Anna Peterson. 1982. 'Neither Christian nor Jewish ...' In *Ethnic Identity: Strategies of Diversity*. Bloomington: Indiana University Press. 17-33.

Ruan, Danching. 1993. 'Interpersonal Networks and Workplace Controls in Urban China.' *Australian Journal of Chinese Affairs* 29: 89-105.

Ruskola, Teemu. 2000. 'Conceptualizing Corporations and Kinship: Comparative Law and Development Theory in a Chinese Perspective.' *Stanford Law Review* 52: 1599-1732.

Sahlins, Marshall. 1976. *Culture and Practical Reason*. Chicago: University of Chicago Press.
–. 1985. *Islands of History*. Chicago: University of Chicago Press.
Said, Edward. 1979. *Orientalism*. New York: Vintage Books.
Sarangi, Srikant, and Stefaan Slembrouck. 1996. *Language, Bureaucracy, and Social Control*. New York: Longman.
Schmidt, Peter R., and Thomas Patterson, eds. 1995. *Making Alternative Histories: The Practice of Archaeology and History in Non-Western Settings*. Santa Fe: School of American Research Press; Seattle: University of Washington Press.
Schneider, Axel, and Suzanne Weigelin-Schweidrzik, eds. 1996. *Chinese Historiography in Comparative Perspective. History and Theory* 35,4.
Schneider, David. 1984. *A Critique of the Study of Kinship*. Ann Arbor: University of Michigan Press.
Schneider, David, and Maurice Bloch. 1971. 'The Moral and Tactical Meaning of Kinship Terms.' *Man* 6, 1: 49-87.
Schor, Naomi, and Elizabeth Weed. 1994. *The Essential Difference*. Bloomington: Indiana University Press.
Serber, David. 1981. 'The Masking of Social Reality: Ethnographic Field-Work in the Bureaucracy.' In *Anthropologists at Home in North America*. Edited by Donald Messerschmidt, 77-87. Cambridge, UK: Cambridge University Press.
Shanks, Michael. 1993. *Re-Constructing Archaeology: Theory and Practice*. 2nd ed. London: Routledge.
Shanks, Michael, and Randall McGuire. 1996. 'Craft of Archaeology.' *American Antiquity* 61, 1: 75-88.
Shanks, Michael, and Christopher Tilley. 1989. 'Archaeology into the 1990s.' *Norwegian Archaeological Review* 22, 1: 1-12.
Shapiro, Judith, and Liang Heng. 1986. *Cold Winds, Warm Winds: Intellectual Life in China Today*. Middletown: Wesleyan University Press.
Shaw, Thurstan. 1986. 'Archaeology and the Politics of Academic Freedom.' *Archaeological Review from Cambridge* 5, 1: 5-24.
Shen Zhanyun, Liang Yichi, and Li Yingyuan, eds. 1993. *Zhongguo zhishifenzi beihuanlu* [The sorrows of China's intellectuals]. Guangzhou: Huacheng Chubanshe.
Shi Ping. 1988. *Zhishifenzi de lishi yundong he zuoyong* [The participation in historical movements and utility of intellectuals]. Shanghai: Shanghai Shehui Kexue Yuan Chubanshe.
Shirk, Susan. 1982. *Competitive Comrades: Career Incentives and Student Strategies in China*. Berkeley: University of California Press.
Shohat, Ellen, and Robert Stam. 1994. *Unthinking Eurocentrism: Multiculturalism and the Media*. New York: Routledge.
Silverblatt, Irene. 1988. 'Women in States.' *Annual Review of Anthropology* 17: 427-60.
Skinner, William. 1985. 'Rural Marketing in China: Repression and Revival.' *China Quarterly* 103: 393-413.
–. 1992. 'Seek a Loyal Subject in a Filial Son: Family Roots of Political Orientation in Chinese Society.' Paper presented at the Conference of Family Process and Political Process in Modern Chinese History, sponsored by the Institute of Modern History, Academia Sinica, Taipei.
Solinger, Dorothy. 1992. 'Urban Entrepreneurs and the State: The Merger of State and Society.' In *State and Society in China: The Consequences of Reform*. Edited by Arthur Rosenbaum, 121-41. Boulder: Westview Press.
Spinoza, Benedictus de. 1951. *Philosophy of Benedict de Spinoza*. Trans. R.H.M. Elwes. New York: Dover Publishing.
Spivak, Gayatri. 1994. 'In a Word.' Interview. In *The Essential Difference*. Edited by Naomi Schor, 151-84. Bloomington: Indiana University Press.
Sponsler, Claire, and Xiaomei Chen, eds. 2000. *East of West: Cross-Cultural Performance and the Staging of Difference*. New York: Palgrave.
Stocking, George. 1991. *Colonial Situations: Essays on the Contextualization of Ethnographic Knowledge*. Madison: University of Wisconsin Press.

Strathern, Marilyn. 1988. *The Gender of the Gift: Problems with Women and Problems with Society in Melanesia*. Berkeley: University of California Press.

Su Bingqi. 1994. *Huaren, Long de chuanren, Zhongguoren: Kaogu xungen lun* [The ethnically Chinese people, descendants of the Dragon, people of the Chinese nation: Looking for the origins of the Chinese through archeology]. Shenyang: Liaoning University Press.

Sullivan, Lawrence. 1990. 'The Controversy over 'Feudal Despotism': Politics and Historiography in China 1978-82.' *Australian Journal of Chinese Affairs* 23: 1-31.

Sun Ling-kee. 1991. 'Contemporary Chinese Culture: Structure and Emotionality.' *Australian Journal of Chinese Affairs* 26: 1-41.

Sung Kuang-yu. 1992. *Dalu kaogu gongzuo gaikuang* [The working conditions of archeology in Mainland China]. Commissioned by the Department of History, China Culture University. Taipei: China Culture University.

Sussman, Marvin. 1972. 'Family, Kinship, and Bureaucracy.' In *Human Meaning of Social Change*. Edited by Angus Campbell and Philip Converse, 127-58. New York: Sage.

Tainter, Joseph. 1987. 'Politics of Regional Research in Conservation Archeology.' *American Archeology* 6, 3: 217-27.

Tambiah, Stanley J. 1990. *Magic, Science, Religion, and the Scope of Rationality*. Cambridge, UK: Cambridge University Press.

Tang Tsou. 1983. 'Back from the Brink of Revolutionary-Feudal Totalitarianism.' In *State and Society in Contemporary China*. Edited by Victor Nee and David Mozingo, 16-31. Ithaca: Cornell University Press.

Tang Wenfang. 1999. *Party Intellectuals' Demands for Reform in Contemporary China*. Stanford: Hoover Institution on War, Revolution and Peace.

Tang Xiaobing. 1993. 'Orientalism and the Question of Universality: The Language of Contemporary Chinese Literary Theory.' *Positions* 1, 2: 409-31.

Tang Xuezhi, and Yang Kuanghan, eds. 1994. *Tai Gang ji haiwai xuejie lun Zhongguo zhishifenzi* [Taiwanese, Hong Kongese, and Overseas Chinese discuss Chinese intellectuals]. Zhengzhou: Henan Renmin Chubanshe.

Tanner, Murray Scott, and Michael Feder. 1993. 'Family Politics, Elite Recruitment, and Succession in Post-Mao China.' *Australian Journal of Chinese Affairs* 20 : 89-119.

Thorgersen, Stig. 1989. 'Through the Sheep's Intestines: Selection and Elitism in Chinese Schools.' *Australian Journal of Chinese Affairs* 21: 29-56.

Tilley, Christopher. 1990. *Reading Material Culture: Structuralism, Hermeneutics, and Post-Structuralism*. Oxford: Blackwell.

–. 1999. *Metaphor and Material Culture*. Malden: Blackwell Publishers.

Tong Enzheng. 1994. 'Zhongguo kaoguxue sanshi nian 1949-1979 [Thirty years of Chinese archeology 1949-1979].' *Han-hsueh yen-chiu* 12, 1: 349-63.

Traweek, Sharon. 1988. *Beamtimes and Lifetimes: The World of High Energy Physicists*. Cambridge, MA: Harvard University Press.

Trigger, Bruce. 1984. 'Alternative Archaeologies: Nationalist, Colonialist, Imperialist.' *Man* 19, 3: 355-70.

–. 1986. 'Prospects for a World Archaeology.' *World Archaeology* 17, 4: 1-20.

–. 1989. *A History of Archaeological Thought*. Cambridge, UK: Cambridge University Press.

Trinh, Minh-Ha. 1989. *Woman, Native, Other: Writing Postcoloniality and Feminism*. Bloomington: Indiana University Press.

Tsao, Kai-fu. 1984. *The Relationship between Scholars and Rulers in Imperial China: A Comparison between China and the West*. Lanham: University Press of America.

Tu Wei-ming. 1992. *The Confucian World Observed: A Contemporary Discussion of Confucian Humanism in East Asia*. Honolulu: Institute of Culture and Communication, the East-West Center.

–. 1993. *Way, Learning, and Politics: Essays on the Confucian Intellectual*. Albany: State University of New York Press,

–. 1994. *The Living Tree: The Changing Meaning of Being Chinese Today*. Stanford: Stanford University Press.

Tu Cheng-Sheng.1997. 'Xin shixue yu Zhongguo kaoguxue de fazhan [The new historiography and the evolution of Chinese archeology].' In *Zhongyang Yanjiuyuan Lishi Yuyan*

Yanjiusuo Fu Sinian Xiansheng Jinianhui [Symposium in Remembrance of Fu Ssu-nien of the Department of History and Linguistics, Academia Sinica]. Nan-kang: Academia Sinica.

–. 2000. *Zouguo guanjian shinian 1990-2000* [Experiences during the ten key years, 1990-2000]. Taipei: Mai-tian.

Tu Cheng-Sheng, and Wang Fan-sen, eds. 1998. *Xinxue zhi lu* [Along new pathways of research: Essays in honour of the seventieth anniversary of the Institute of History and Philology]. Nan-kang: Academia Sinica.

Tucker, Robert. 1978. *The Marx-Engels Reader*. New York: W.W. Norton.

Turnbull, Christopher. 1976. 'Of Backdirt and Bureaucracy: The Role of Government in Canadian Archaeology.' In *Symposium on New Perspectives in Canadian Archaeology*. Ottawa: Royal Society of Canada. 119-36.

Turner, Victor. 1974. *Drama, Fields, and Metaphors: Symbolic Action in Human Society*. Ithaca: Cornell University Press.

–. 1988. *The Anthropology of Performance*. New York: PAJ Publications.

Ulrich, Laurel Thatcher. 1990. *A Midwife's Tale: The Life of Martha Ballard, Based on Her Diary, 1785-1812*. New York: Knopf.

–. 1991. *Goodwives: Image and Reality in the Lives of Women in Northern New England, 1650-1750*. New York: Vintage.

Unger, Jonathan. 1982. *Education under Mao*. New York: Columbia University Press.

–. 1987. 'The Struggle to Dictate China's Administration: The Conflicts of Branches vs. Areas vs. Reform.' *Australian Journal of Chinese Affairs* 18: 14-45.

–. 1993. *Using the Past to Serve the Present: Historiography and Politics in Contemporary China*. Armonk: M.E. Sharpe.

van Dommelen, Peter. 1997. 'Colonial Constructs: Colonialism and Archaeology in the Mediterranean.' *World Archaeology* 28, 3: 305-23.

Von Falkenhausen, Lothar. 1995. 'The Regionalist Paradigm in Chinese Archaeology.' In *Nationalism, Politics, and the Practice of Archaeology*. Edited by Philip L. Kohl and Clare Fawcett, 198-217. Cambridge, UK: Cambridge University Press.

Walder, Andrew G. 1986. *Communist Neo-Traditionalism: Work and Authority in Chinese Society*. Berkeley: University of California Press.

–. 1996. 'Workers, Managers, and the State: The Reform Era and the Political Crisis of 1989.' In *The Individual and the State in China*. Edited by Brian Hook, 43-69. Oxford: Oxford University Press.

Walker, Alice. 1983. *In Search of Our Mothers' Gardens*. New York: Harcourt Brace.

Wang Ban. 1997. *The Sublime Figure of History: Aesthetics and Politics in Twentieth-Century China*. Stanford: Stanford University Press.

Wang Changhua. 1997. *Chunqiu zhanguo shiren yu zhengzhi* [The relationship between politics and the scholars of the Spring and Autumn and Warring States Periods]. Shanghai: Shanghai Renmin Chubanshe.

Wang Changlin. 1987. 'Haixi liangan de wenhua jiaoliu: Guanyu yiwen, keji yu jiaoyu jiaoliu [Cultural exchange across the Taiwan Strait: Comments on exchanges in the literary and artistic, technical, and educational fields]. *Kung-tang wen-t'i yen-chiu* 20, 7: 3-19.

Wang Chia-feng, and Li Kuang-chen. 1991. *When East Meets West: International Sinology and Sinologists* [in both Chinese and English]. *Sinorama Magazine* 17.

Wang, Edward. 2001. *Inventing China through History: The May Fourth Approach to Historiography*. Albany: State University of New York Press.

Wang Gungwu, and Zheng Yongnian, eds. 2000. *Reform, Legitimacy, and Dilemmas: China's Politics and Society*. Singapore: Singapore University Press; London: World Scientific Publishing Company.

Wang Hui. 1995. 'The Fate of "Mr. Science" in China: The Conception of "Science" and Its Application in Modern Chinese Thought.' *Positions* 3, 1: 1-68.

–. 1997. 'Guanyu Zhongguo kaoguxue shijian he lilun de tansuo yu sikao: Zhang Zhongpei jiaoshou fangtanlun [Thoughts about Chinese archeological practice and theory: An interview with Professor Zhang Zhongpei].' *Shixue Yanjiu* 3: 11-16.

Wang Jing. 1993. 'The Mirage of "Chinese Postmodernism": G.E. Fei, Self-Positioning, and the Avant-Garde Showcase.' *Positions* 1, 2: 349-88.

Wang Ming-ke. 1996. 'Shei de lishi: Zizhuan, zhuanji yu koushu lishi de shehui jiyi benzhi [Whose history: The value of the social memory in autobiography, biography, and oral history].' *Ssu yu Yen* 34, 3: 147-84.

Wang Shounan. 1981. 'Zhongguo chuantong zhishifenzi de lishi zeren gan [The sense of historical responsibility of China's traditional intellectuals].' *Zhongguo Wenhua Yuekan* 21: 93-111.

Wang Zengru. 1999. *Shangshan xiaxiang: Zhongguo 1968* [Climb the mountains, enter the fields: China in 1968]. Beijing: Jiefangjun Chubanshe.

Warner, Martin, ed. 2000. *Changing Workplace Relations in the Chinese Economy*. New York: St. Martin's Press.

Warnke, Georgia. 1987. *Gadamer: Hermeneutics, Tradition, and Reason*. Cambridge, UK: Polity Press.

Watson, James L. 1975. *Emigration and the Chinese Lineage: The Mans in Hong Kong and London*. Berkeley: University of California Press.

–. 1984. 'Introduction: Class and Class Formation in Chinese Society.' In *Class and Social Stratification in Post-Revolution China*. Edited by Watson, 1-15. Cambridge, UK: Cambridge University Press.

–. 1987. 'From the Common Pot: Feasting with Equals in Chinese Society.' *Anthropos* 82, 4-6: 389-401.

–. 1988. 'The Structure of Chinese Funerary Rites: Elementary Forms, Ritual Sequence, and the Primacy of Performance.' In *Death Ritual in Late Imperial and Modern China*. Edited by James Watson and Evelyn Rawski, 3-19. Berkeley: University of California Press.

–. 1993. 'Rites or Beliefs? The Construction of a Unified Culture in late Imperial China.' In *China's National Identity*. Edited by Samuel Kim and Lowell Dittmar, 80-103. Ithaca: Cornell University Press.

–. 1994. 'Past, Present, and Future.' In *Cradles of Civilization: China*. Edited by Robert Murowchick, 176-85. Norman: University of Oklahoma Press.

–. 1996. 'Fighting with Operas: Processionals, Politics, and the Spectre of Violence in Rural Hong Kong.' In *The Politics of Cultural Performance*. Edited by David Parkin, Lionel Caplan, and Humphrey Fisher, 144-59. Providence: Berghahn Books.

–. 1997. 'Introduction: Transnationalism, Localization, and Fast Foods in East Asia.' In *Golden Arches East: McDonald's in East Asia*. Edited by Watson, 1-38. Stanford: Stanford University Press.

–. 2000. 'Food as a Lens: The Past, Present, and Future of Family Life in China.' In *Feeding China's Little Emperors: Food, Children, and Social Change*. Edited by Jing Jun, 199-212. Stanford: Stanford University Press.

Watson, Patty Jo. 1995. 'Federal U.S. Funding: First Americans Research.' In *Public Trust and the First Americans*. Edited by Ruthann Knudson and Bennie C. Keel, 160-66. Corvallis: Oregon State University Press.

Watson, Rubie. 1981. 'Class Differences and Affinal Relations in China.' *Man* 16: 593-615.

–. 1985. *Inequality among Brothers: Class and Kinship in South China*. Cambridge, UK: Cambridge University Press.

–. 1986. 'Named and the Nameless: Gender and Person in Chinese Society.' *American Ethnologist* 13, 4: 619-31.

–. 1991. *Marriage and Inequality in Chinese Society*. Berkeley: University of California Press.

–. 1994. *Memory, History, and Opposition under State Socialism*. Santa Fe: School of American Research Press.

–. 1997a. 'From Hall of Worship to Tourist Center: An Ancestral Hall in Hong Kong's New Territories.' *Cultural Survival Quarterly* 21, 1: 33-35.

–. 1997b. 'Museums and Indigenous Cultures: The Power of Local Knowledge.' *Cultural Survival Quarterly* 21, 1: 24-25.

Weatherley, Robert. 1999. *The Discourse of Human Rights in China: Historical and Ideological Perspectives*. New York: St. Martin's Press.

Weber, Max. 1983. *Max Weber on Capitalism, Bureaucracy, and Religion: A Selection of Texts*. Edited by and in part newly trans. Stanislav Andreski. Boston: Allen and Unwin.

Wei Fuming. 1996. 'Rujia de minzu wenhua yishi ji xiandai jiazhi [Modern values and the ethnic and cultural consciousness of Confucian scholars].' *Dongnan Wenhua* 1: 9-15.

Wei Jingsheng. 1997. *The Courage to Stand Alone: Letters from Prison and Other Writings.* Trans. Kristina Torgeson. New York: Viking.

West, Jackie, Zhao Minghua, Chang Xiangchun, and Cheng Yuan, eds. 1999. *Women of China.* New York: St Martin's Press.

Whyte, Martin King. 1980. 'Bureaucracy and Antibureaucracy in the People's Republic of China.' In *Hierarchy and Society: Anthropological Perspectives on Bureaucracy.* Edited by Gerald M. Britan and Ronald Cohen, 123-41. Philadelphia: Institute for the Study of Human Issues.

Wiegelin-Schweidrzik, Suzanne. 1987. 'Party Historiography in the People's Republic of China.' *Australian Journal of Chinese Affairs* 17: 77-94.

Willey, Gordon, and Jeremy Sabloff. 1993. *A History of American Archaeology.* New York: W.H. Freeman.

Williams, Kimberlé Crenshaw. 1994. 'Mapping the Margins: Intersectionality, Identity Politics, and Violence against Women of Color.' In *The Public Nature of Private Violence.* Edited by Martha Albertson Fineman and Roxanne Mykitiuk, 93-118. New York: Routledge.

Willis, Paul. 1977. *Learning to Labour: How Working Class Kids Get Working Class Jobs.* Farnborough: Saxon House.

Wilson, Richard, Sidney L. Greenblatt, and Amy Auerbacher Wilson, eds. 1981. *Moral Behavior in Chinese Society.* New York: Praeger.

Wittfogel, Karl. 1957. *Oriental Despotism: A Comparative Study of Total Power.* New Haven: Yale University Press.

Wittgenstein, Ludwig. 1979. *The Central Texts of Ludwig Wittgenstein.* Trans. Gerd Brand. Oxford: Blackwell.

Wobst, Martin. 1989. 'Commentary: A Socio-Politics of Socio-Politics in Archaeology.' In *Critical Traditions in Contemporary Archaeology.* Edited by Valerie Pinsky and Allison Wylie, 136-40. Cambridge, UK: Cambridge University Press.

Wolf, Arthur. 1974. *Religion and Ritual in Chinese Society.* Stanford: Stanford University Press.

Wolf, Eric. 1982. *Europe and the People without History.* Berkeley: University of California Press.

Wolf, Margery. 1972. *Women and the Family in Rural Taiwan.* Stanford: Stanford University Press.

Wright, Teresa. 2001. *The Perils of Protest: State Repression and Student Activism in China and Taiwan.* Honolulu: University of Hawaii Press.

Wu Bingyuan. 1991. *Zhongguo gongchandang yu shehuizhuyi jingshen wenming jianshe* [The Chinese Communist Party and the establishment of spiritual values of socialism]. Chongqing: Chongqing Chubanshe.

Wu Chunmin. 1996. 'Kaoguxue Zhongguohua de tansuo: Huigu yu sikao [Exploring the sinification of archeology: A retrospective].' In *Zhongguo renleixue de fazhan* [The development of Chinese anthropology]. Edited by Chen Guoqiang and Lin Jiahui, 174-83. Shanghai: Sanlian Chubanshe.

Wylie, Alison. 2002. *Thinking from Things: Essays in the Philosophy of Archaeology.* Berkeley: University of California Press.

Xin, Liu. 2000. *In One's Own Shadow: An Ethnographic Account of the Condition of Post-Reform Rural China.* Berkeley: University of California Press.

Xu Jilin. 1994. 'Zai xueshu yu zhengzhi jian paihuai de jindai Zhongguo zhishifenzi [Modern Chinese intellectuals hesitating between research and politics].' In *Zhongguo zhishifenzi de renwen jingshen* [Essays on the humanist spirit of Chinese intellectuals]. Edited by Xu Ming. Zhongguo zhishifenzi congshu [Series on Chinese intellectuals]. Zhengzhou: Henan Renmin Chubanshe.

Xu Ming, ed. 1994. *Zhongguo zhishifenzi de renwen jingshen* [Essays on the humanist spirit of Chinese intellectuals]. Zhongguo zhishifenzi congshu [Series on Chinese intellectuals]. Zhengzhou: Henan Renmin Chubanshe.

Xu Xiaoqun. 1996. 'The Discourse of Love, Marriage, and Sexuality in Post-Mao China: Or, a Reading of the New Journalistic Literature on Women.' *Positions* 4, 2: 382-401

Yahuda, Michael. 1979. 'Political Generations in China.' *China Quarterly* 80: 793-805.

Yan Buke. 1996. *Shidaifu zhengzhi yansheng shigao* [A history of the political transformation of the literati]. Beijing: Beijing Daxue Chubanshe.

Yan Yunxiang. 1992. 'The Impact of Rural Reform on Economic and Social Stratification in a Chinese Village.' *Australian Journal of Chinese Affairs* 27: 1-23.

—. 1996. *The Flow of Gifts: Reciprocity and Social Networks in a Chinese Village*. Stanford: Stanford University Press.

Yang Fan. 1991. *Gongheguo de di sandai* [The third generation of the People's Republic of China]. Chengdu: Sichuan Renmin Chubanshe.

Yang Guoqiang. 1997. *Bainian shantui: Zhongguo jindai shi yu shehui* [100 years of change: The relationship between society and contemporary Chinese intellectuals]. Shanghai: Sanlian Chubanshe.

Yang Kuanghan. 1994. 'Lun Taiwan dangdai wenxue zhong de Zhongguo renwen jingshen [The Chinese literati humanist spirit in present-day Taiwanese literary circles].' In *Zhongguo zhishifenzi de renwen jingshen* [Essays on the humanist spirit of Chinese intellectuals]. Edited by Xu Ming. Zhongguo zhishifenzi congshu [Series on Chinese intellectuals]. Zhengzhou: Henan Renmin Chubanshe.

Yang Lien-sheng. 1957. 'The Concept of "Pao" as the Basis for Social Relations in China.' In *Chinese Thought and Institutions*. Edited by John Fairbanks, 291-309. Chicago: Chicago University Press.

Yang, Mayfair Mei-hui. 1989. 'Between State and Factory: The Construction of Corporateness in a Chinese Socialist Factory.' *Australian Journal of Chinese Affairs* 22: 31-60.

—. 1994. *Gifts, Favors, and Banquets: The Art of Social Relationships in China*. Ithaca: Cornell University Press.

Yang Wenhu. 1994. 'Guanyu "erzi" de shenhua yu Zhongguo zhishifenzi de xingge [The myth of 'the son' and the personality of the Chinese intellectual].' In *Zhongguo zhishifenzi de renwen jingshen* [Essays on the humanist spirit of Chinese intellectuals]. Edited by Xu Ming. Zhongguo zhishifenzi congshu [Series on Chinese intellectuals]. Zhengzhou: Henan Renmin Chubanshe.

Yang Xianbang. 1992. 'Wenhuaren zai xiandai shehuizhong de shiming yu zeren [The mission and responsibility of the literati in present-day society].' *Dongnan Wenhua* 4: 5-7.

Yang Zhao. 1992. 'Shangzai miwu zhong de kaogushi: Shi-san Hang shijian yu Taiwan kaoguxue [Archeology still lost in the fog: The Shi-san Hang incident and Taiwanese archeology].' *Chung-kuo lun-t'an* 32, 5: 88-92.

Ye Sixun. 1984. 'Dalu zhishifenzi dui Zhonggong de yuewang yu fankang [Chinese mainland intellectuals' hopes for and resistances to the CCP].' *Kuang-fu ta-lu* 209: 24-28.

Yeh Ch'i-cheng. 1984. *Shehui, wenhua, he zhishifenzi* [Society, culture, and intellectuals]. Taipei: Dongda.

—. 1992. 'Daxue jiaoshou de jiaose he shiming [The roles and moral mission of university professors].' *Dang-dai* 73: 16-35.

Yin Chang-yi, and Yang Tsu-chun, comp. 1994. *Dalu wenhua zichan (wenwu) weihu zhi xingzheng tizhi ji xiangguan faming zhi diaocha yanjiu* [Report on the investigation into Mainland China's legislative system of cultural resource (cultural relics) management and related laws]. Commissioned by the Department of Culture, Legislative Yuan, Taiwan. Taipei: Department of Culture.

Young-Bruehl, Elisabeth. 1996. *The Anatomy of Prejudices*. Cambridge, MA: Harvard University Press.

Yu Mingxia. 1992. 'Yibu juyou tese de yanjiu jindai zhishifenzi de xinshu: Ping Li Liangyu zhu "Dongdang shidai de zhishifenzi" [A new and rather unique book about modern intellectuals: A critique of *Intellectuals in a turbulent world* by Li Liangyu].' *Dongnan Wenhua* 4: 248-50.

Yu Taifa. 1994. 'Intellectuals' Role in China's Four Modernizations: Conflicts between Ideas and Ideology.' *Journal of Developing Societies* 10, 1: 101-15.

Yu Yingshi. 1991. 'Zhongguo zhishifenzi de bianyuanhua [The marginalization of China's intellectuals].' Paper presented at Ershi shiji Zhongguo de lishi fansi [Critiques of the history of twentieth-century China]. In *Compilation of Papers from the February 1991 Conference*, 15-25. Honolulu, Hawaii: East-West Center.

–. 1996. *Xian dai ru xue lun* [Discussions of modern studies of Confucianism]. River Edge, NJ: [Bafang wenhua qiye gongsi].

–. 1997. *Zhongguo zhishifenzi zhi lun* [A Theory of Chinese intellectuals]. Zhengzhou: Henan Renmin Chubanshe.

Yue Nan, and Shi Yang. 1996. *The Dead Suffered Too: The Excavation of a Ming Tomb*. Trans. Zhang Ting Quan. Beijing: Panda Books; Chinese Literature Press.

Zang Xiaowei. 2000. *Children of the Cultural Revolution: Family Life and Political Behavior in Mao's China*. Boulder: Westview Press.

Zhang Chun. 1977. 'Zhuanmen zhi xue he kaogu gongzuo: Zhonggong de lishi yanjiu gongzuo [Specialized study and archeological work: The work of historical studies as directed by the CCP].' *Chung-k'uo Hsüeh-jen* 6: 67-83.

Zhang Mengyang. 1997. *Wuxing yu nuxing: Lu Xun yu Zhongguo zhishifenzi de 'guominxing.'* [Comprehension and servility: Lu Xun and the coming to a 'national consciousness' by Chinese intellectuals]. Zhengzhou: Henan Renmin Chubanshe.

Zhang Zhizhong. 1994. *Mimang de bashe zhe: Zhongguo xiandai zhishifenzi xintai lu* [Confused travellers: A report on the state of Chinese intellectuals]. Zhengzhou: Henan Renmin Chubanshe.

Zhang Zhongpei. 1994. *Zhongguo kaogu: Shijian, lilun, fangfa* [Chinese archeology: Methodology, theory, and method]. Zhengzhou: Zhongzhou Fangji Chubanshe.

Zheng Hailin. 1990. *Zhishifenzi yu Zhongguo xiandaihua yundong* [Intellectuals and China's modernization movement]. Changsha: Hunan Renmin Chubanshe.

Zheng Wan. 1993. 'Liangan wenhua chayi yu xueshu jiaoliu: Fang Xiamen Daxue Taiwan yanjiusuo suozhang Chen Kongli jiaoshou [The impact of cultural differences on academic contacts across the Taiwan Strait: An interview with Professor Chen Kongli, director of the Department of Taiwan Studies, Xiamen University].' *Dongnan Wenhua* 95: 18-21.

Zheng Yefu. 1994. 'Shichang yu Zhongguo zhishifenzi [The market and Chinese intellectuals].' *Zhongguo Shehui Kexue Jikan* 9: 39-43.

Zhong Yan. 1996. *Zhongguo xinsanji xueren* [China's new intellectuals]. Hangzhou: Zhejiang Renmin Chubanshe.

Zhongguo Shehuikexueyuan Kaogu Yanjiusuo, ed. 1996. *Kaogu Yanjiusuo zhong qingnian xueshu taolunhui wenji* [Seeking truth in the field of archeology: The symposium of promising youngs in the Institute of Archaeology (sic)]. Beijing: China Social Sciences Publishing House.

Zhongnan Yanjiuyuan Lishi Yuyan Yanjiusuo, ed. 1996. *Taiwan kaogu bainian jinian yantaohui: Huiyi lunwen ji baogao* [Reports and papers of the symposium on 100 years of Taiwanese archeology]. Nan-kang: Academia Sinica.

Zhou Yushan. 1988. 'Bashi niandai Zhonggong de zhishifenzi zhengce [The policies of the CCP relating to intellectuals in the 1980s].' *T'ung-fang Tsa-chi* 22, 1: 55-61.

Index

Academy *Xitong,* 111, 112, 200, 205, 207-9
access to resources, 25, 26; authority and, 112, 113; compatibility and, 27; inequality and, 31; reputation and, 71; in superior-inferior relations, 69; in teacher-student relations, 72; trustworthiness and, 27, 80; by women, 244
action(s): audience and, 14, 160; beliefs and, 27-28, 59; conformity and, 14; describing vs justifying, 170; independent, 250; intent and, 7, 14, 15, 48, 59
actors: audience and, 24-25; autonomy of, 23; role-playing of, 23-24
age: authority and, 216; cohort, 171; veneration for, 215; women and, 215
agency, 6, 15; in gift giving, 92; male vs female, 247-48; under orthodoxy, 25-26; under orthopraxy, 26
Agriculture *Xitong,* 177, 188
Anglo-Europeans. *See* Euro-Americans
Anglo-North Americans: independence of, 251; role of government and, 100; view of Chinese archeology, 8, 100-1
anthropology: archeology and, 9, 99, 141; as study of dispossessed, 27
Anti-Rightist Movement, 158, 218
Anyang, 2
Appadurai, Arjun, 83
Archaeological Council, 117, 118-20
archeologist-director relations, 93-95
archeologist-peasant relations, 88, 161-62, 173, 176; of Academy *Xitong* archeologists, 207-9; authority vs hierarchy in, 193; balanced resources in, 209-10; banquets in, 193-96; of BeiDa archeologists, 206-7; CASS archeologists and, 207-8; claiming of juniority in, 188-89; claiming

of juniority in, 197, 203; claim to similarity in, 184-87; as cohort, 182; compatibility and, 178; competition over resources in, 179; controlling spending in, 179; of Culture *Xitong* archeologists, 200-3; of Education *Xitong* archeologists, 203-7; entrapment within, 182; hierarchy within, 187-89; of JiDa archeologists, 206; kinship ties in, 200-1; lower-level archeologists in, 201; peasants as teachers to archeologists, 191; power in, 183; provincial-level archeologists and, 202-3; reputation and, 182-83; respect in, 191-92; short-term nature of, 179; trustworthiness and, 178; withholding in, 179. *See also* urban-rural divide
archeologists: attention to personal relations, 5; BeiDa (*see* Beijing University); CASS (*see* Chinese Academy of Social Sciences); CCP's view of, 12; characteristics, 3; children of, 107, 110; and charges of collusion, 100; comparative breadth of experience in field, 202; comportment of, 200, 241; connections of, 4; county-level, 115, 135; credentials of, 161; entering the field, 177; gift giving of, 85; of Han ethnicity, 5, 9, 14, 27, 211, 244; higher-level, 114, 115, 116, 117, 135; ideal, 154, 159; knowledge of life of peasants, 191; levels within *danwei,* 107, 110; lines of control, 107; lower-level, 115, 116, 117, 135, 200, 201, 203, 206; marriages of, 110; as martyrs, 100-1; middle-aged (*see* middle-aged archeologists); museologists, split from, 128-34; networks of, 75; older, 215-16; peasants' perception of, 161-62; promotion of, 107, 110; provincial-level, 114, 115, 116, 200, 202-3; qualities of,

182-83; attacks upon, 95; audience memory and, 20; authority and, 112; concept of, 19; and control over women, 238; credentials and, 160; and entrapment, 92; exemplary life and, 10; and fracturing of identity, 19, 20, 169; hardship narratives and, 175; interactions with others and, 21; and interdependence, 94-95; in mixed-tie relations, 71; performance of compatibility and, 77; reciprocity and, 68-72; reification of, 20; as rhetorical construct, 20; roles-in-relation and, 68; social interaction and, 96; of students, 119; of teachers, 231; teacher-student relations and, 247; of women, 247; women upholding men's, 237-38. *See also* identity
researchers, 107
resistance, 6, 11, 13-14, 159
resources, 26; access to (*see* access to resources); in archeologist-peasant relations, 209-10; authority and, 25; distribution of, 98-99; redistribution of, xi, 27, 198-99, 216. *See also* artifacts; data
respect, 207; in archeologist-peasant relations, 191-92; at banquets, 121-26; and class, 87; in mixed-tie relations, 190, 198; in students, 45, 74; and use of pen names, 232
rewards, 25
role conflicts, 162-63
role models, 36, 87, 236
roles, 23-24; achievement of, 168; actions appropriate to, 59; audience judgment of, 137; combination, 163; identity and, 19, 58-59, 67, 68; inhabiting of, 58, 59, 68, 160, 161; motherhood, 236; multiplicity of, 24, 25, 68; playing, 23-24, 47; stepping out of, 89-90
roles-in-relation, 25, 26, 58, 59, 168; class membership and, 86-87; deployment of women in, 212; motherhood and, 237; reputation and, 68
rule of reciprocity, 66-67, 138; audience and, 212; claim to seniority and, 197; continuity and, 178; guide for interpretation of action and, 76; interdependence and, 69-70; manipulation and, 95, 97; during 1950s, 246; and self-sacrificing discourse, 171; strategies, 67; values, 67
rules, xi, 6; number of, 212; obedience to, 101-2; and separation between authority and hierarchy, 134

san nian zai hai, 2
Sanxingdui, 140, 151, 225
School of Workers, Peasants, and Soldiers *(Gong Nong Bing Xuexiao),* 43
schools, first- vs second-level, 33
scripts, 21-22, 23, 24, 26
self-actualization, 6, 17, 250
self-esteem, 7
self-interest, ix, x, 13, 50, 170, 171
seniority, 25-26; authority vs, 198, 203, 206; claims to, 196-98
senior-junior relationship. *See* junior-senior relations
sex, as credential, 236
Shaanxi, 127
shafa kaogu xue, 214
shangque, 231
shenjing bing, 177
shishi qiu shi, 213
shitu guanxi, 39
Sichuan University (ChuanDa), 140
Sima Qian, 9-10, 55
similarity, doctrine of, 16, 20, 22, 26, 31, 48, 56, 169; claim to, 184, 187
site(s), 4; archeologists leaving for another, 189-90; categorization of, 116-17, 120; examination of, 113; excavation as destruction of, 227; first arrivals at, 189-90; looting of, 206; managers, 89; naming of, 113
social contract: defined, 29; education as, 36; within student relationships/groups, 31; uncertainty and, 70
social distance, 104
social events coordinator, of student cohort, 53, 61
social interaction(s), 12, 26-27, 56-57; checks and balances on, 96; and doctrine of similarity, 57; as investments, 68; orthopraxy in, 46; reputation and, 96; visible indicators in, 71
socialization, 30, 84, 252; gift exchanges and, 84; of students, 47, 51
social networking, 4-5, 26-27, 69, 134, 209, 210; marriage and, 237; merit-based approach vs, 62; success and, 62; of teachers, 78. *See also guanxi*
social relations, xi; autonomy in, 67; moral behaviour and, 80; personal space within, 143; of students, 31
social ties, instrumental vs affective, 70-1
society, categories of, 17
southerners vs northerners, 150-53
state, the, 6-7; archeologists and, 12-13; and archeology, 99-102, 234; Chinese

archeologists and, 9; compromise with, 159; historians and, 10-11; party vs, 106-7; relations with peasants, 188; visibility vs invisibility, 100
stereotypes, 6, 49, 138, 139
strain theory, 253, 254
strangers, relationships with, 192, 197
student cohort leaders, 52-53, 54, 61, 73
students, 29; as apprentices of teachers, 44-46; attitude, 51; choices of, 50; compatibility of, 73; demands of, 43; differences among, 49, 53; doctoral, 233; as entrepreneurs, 73-74; experience of, 51; female, 180-1, 183, 239-40, 247; first-year, 50; as 'good archeologists,' 73, 75; individualized teaching of, 51; intensity, 76-77; interactions with peasants, 176; interpersonal relations, 45, 53; and liking for archeology, 74-75; minority, 244-45; of oligarchs, 218-20, 221, 225; power of, 40, 43; reputations of, 119; social interaction of, 51; socialization of, 51; social networking, 39; teacher choice of, 75-76; teacher judgment of compatibility (*see also* teacher-student relations); temperament, 51. *See also* cohort(s): student; oligarch-student relations; teacher-student relations
student-university teacher contracts, 38-44, 44
Su Bai, 123, 208
Su Bingqi, 123, 208, 220
submission: as gift, 189; of juniors, 85, 189
success, 211, 250; conversion of failures into, 156; defined, 32; education and, 32, 33; merit approach, 62, 63, 66; parent-child relations and, 36; publication and, 226; social networking and, 62; teacher-student relations and, 38, 96
superior-inferior relations, 25, 197; access to resources in, 69; compatibility in, 79-80; gift giving and, 85; parent-child relations and, 102-3; role conflict and, 162, 164
Suzhou, 115

teachers: as advisors during excavation, 215-16; appropriate behaviour of, 78; on Archaeological Council, 119; choice of students, 75-76; differences of opinion with, 228-30; evaluation by students, 78; in the field, 182-83; interactions with peasants, 176; judging compatibility of students, 73; meanings of word,

215; older archeologists named as, 215; relationship with peasants, 181; reputation of, 231; social networks of, 78; students as apprentices of, 44-46; urban-rural divide and, 174
teacher-student relations, 4, 44, 197, 215; access to resources in, 72; and choice of archeological topic, 77; compatibility in, 73, 76-77, 78; competition in, 96; gift giving and, 85; individual student teaching, 51; mutuality of compatibility in, 75-76; oligarch-student relations cf., 218-19, 221; reputation and, 247; and teachers' appointment to Archaeological Council, 119, 120; women and, 239-40, 247. *See also* high school teacher-student contracts; student-university teacher contracts
technicians (excavations), 89, 90
theories, in archeology, 213-15
Three Dynasties (Bronze Age), 224
toasting, 123; competitions, 242; rules of, 125
trustworthiness, 67; archeologist-peasant relations and, 177-78; banquets and, 121, 194; and cohorts, 120-1; compatibility vs, 80; credentials and, 142, 144; defined, 27, 72; dependence on future actions, 82; and disagreements with teachers, 231; gift giving and, 83; reciprocity and, 80, 177-78; regional credentials and, 153; and relationships with strangers, 192; uncertainties over, 82-83; women and, 241-45, 246
truth, reputation and, 10
Turner, Victor, 38

uncertainty, 15-17; in childhood, 38; credentials and, 141, 142; freedom from, 48; of gift giving, 83-84; in interactions, 58; interdependence and, 72; over trustworthiness, 82-83; reciprocity and, 82; social contract and, 70; of university students, 30-1
uncompromising autonomy, ix; obedient autonomy vs, xi-xii
United States: archeology and government in, 99-100; publication in, 16; racial thinking in, 16
universities: credentials of, 140-1; with Departments of Archeology, 203; prestige of, 37. *See also names of individual universities*
university entrance examination, 32, 33-34, 35, 37, 43, 49

Printed and bound in Canada by Friesens

Set in Stone by Artegraphica Design Co. Ltd.

Copy editor: Dallas Harrison

Proofreader: Susan Safyan

Indexer: Noeline Bridge

Cartographer: Eric Leinberger